THE ILLUSTRATED
HOME
ELECTRONICS
FIX-IT BOOK
SECOND EDITION

I dedicate this book to my latest grandchildren: Justin, Lesley, and Katherine.

THE ILLUSTRATED
HOME ELECTRONICS FIX-IT BOOK
SECOND EDITION

HOMER L. DAVIDSON

TAB BOOKS

Blue Ridge Summit, PA

SECOND EDITION
SEVENTH PRINTING

Library of Congress Cataloging-in-Publication Data

Davidson, Homer L.
    The illustrated home electronics fix-it book.

    Includes index.
    1. Electronic apparatus and appliances—Maintenance
and repair.   I. Title.
TK7870.2.D38   1988   621.381′028′8   87-33519
ISBN 0-8306-7883-2
ISBN 0-8306-2883-5 (pbk.)

TAB Books offers software for sale. For information and a catalog, please contact TAB Software Department, Blue Ridge Summit, PA 17294-0850.

Contents

Sound • Loud Hum • High-Pitched Whistle • Distorted Music • No AM but Normal FM • Motorboating • Noisy Reception • Radio Works Out of the Car but Not When Installed • Front Speaker Dead—Rear Okay • Keeps Blowing Fuses

Acknowledgments

Many manufacturers have contributed circuits and data for use in this volume and to them—many thanks. Without their help this book would have been most difficult. A great deal of thanks goes to friends and fellow technicians who throughout the years have contributed greatly.

Introduction

This is a how-to electronics servicing book for the handyman or handywoman, novice, experimenter, hobbyist, technician, and/or homeowner. It shows you how to repair everything from small pocket radios to large color television receivers.

To use this book, simply turn to the chapter that deals with your defective unit. Within each chapter, you can find the most common problems listed. Select the most closely related problem and make the needed repairs. If you make even one electronic repair in these chapters, it will be well worth the price of this book. Besides saving money, repairing your own equipment is a lot of fun and provides great satisfaction.

For example, this book shows you how to fix that old broken radio or tape player. Chapter 17 deals entirely with how to obtain replacement parts. Chapter 11 discusses 37 of the most common question and answers about TV. Almost every electronic unit in the home is listed.

Much new material has been added in updating *The Illustrated Home Electronics Fix-It Book.* In addition to updates on each chapter, three new chapters have been added: Chapter 14, VCR Repairs; Chapter 15, Telephone Answering Machines and Cordless Telephones; and Chapter 10, Compact Disc Players.

Chapter 7, Portable Cassette Players, has an added section on boom box repair. Another new section, Battery Charger Repair, was added to Chapter 16. Additionally, throughout each chapter, new schematics and photographs have been added to help better illustrate this second edition.

The text is divided into four sections: Part 1 describes tools and tips, Part 2 deals with audio, Part 3 discusses video, and Part 4 covers the miscellaneous category.

Part 1

Tools and Tips

1

A Few Tools Will Do

This chapter covers all the small tools and test equipment needed to make the various repairs listed in each chapter. You'll probably discover that in most cases all of the hand tools are already on the work bench. This chapter shows you how to use the volt-ohmmeter for making various voltage and resistance tests. You will find the VOM is the most helpful test instrument.

There is no heavy electronics theory in this book. It is a practical, hands-on book for those who are interested in electronics. Besides showing you how to use the test equipment, you will be shown how to locate defective parts and how to replace them. Simple instructions are given on how to test each component. Repairing your own electronic equipment can be fun, so let's get started.

HAND TOOLS

Before you can make soldered connections, you must have a soldering iron or soldering gun. A 100- to 150-watt soldering gun is okay for some electronic soldering, but for printed circuit boards and transistor soldering use a 25- or 30-watt pencil-type or cordless rechargeable soldering iron. The rechargeable soldering iron isn't absolutely necessary, but it does a great job in tight places (Fig. 1-1).

A couple of different sized screwdrivers are handy and may already be in your tool rack. Small hobby-type screwdriver sets are very handy to get into those small tight places. You should have a

Fig. 1-1. Small pencil iron, cordless rechargeable iron, and soldering gun can make all the required soldered joints.

small nut driver set from ⅛-inch to ⅜-inch for those small nuts found in most electronic chassis. If you don't have a pair of needle nose pliers, choose one with a very sharp tip for curling the wire ends of components. A 6-inch diagonal wire cutter should be small enough to get between parts to snip off their leads. Practically everyone has a pair of slip-joint pliers to remove and tighten large nuts and bolts (Fig. 1-2).

Choose a combination drive socket set to go with the nut drivers. A set of Allen hex key wrenches will help remove those stubborn knobs and various setscrews. For electronic adjustment, use a TV alignment tool kit with hex and screwdriver ends.

TEST INSTRUMENTS

Two of the most useful test instruments are the VOM and the DMM. If you don't already have one, choose a 20,000 ohm/volt type. The ac and dc voltage range should extend from 0 to 1200 volts (V). Most VOM meters have a 0 to 2 megohm resistance scale. Although a 0- to 300-milliamp (mA) current scale is handy, you won't use this scale very often in the tests in the following chapters.

You should be able to purchase a 20,000 ohm/volt VOM at your local electronics store for under $20. The VOM should be placed flat and on a non-metallic surface when taking measurements. Keep magnetized screwdrivers away from the meter area. Before starting to use the instrument, make sure the small pointer rests exactly over zero. With this particular type meter, zero is on the left side (Fig. 1-3). If the pointer is not centered on zero, adjust the plastic screw in the lower center of the meter face. When not in use, always leave the range switch in the OFF position.

There are a few do's and don'ts to remember when using the small VOM meter. Do make sure of what type of voltage you are going to measure before picking up the meter leads. When measuring ac voltage and the voltage is unknown, always use the highest ac voltage range. Do be careful when measuring voltages of 150 V or over. Don't take voltage readings when the switch is on resistance range. You will ruin the meter in seconds. Observe correct polarity when taking voltage measurements. The following describes how to adjust the meter for typical voltage and resistance measurements.

VOM Dc Voltage Measurements

■ Plug the test leads into the correct jacks—black into the negative and red into the positive.

■ Set the range function switch to one of the dc positions. It's

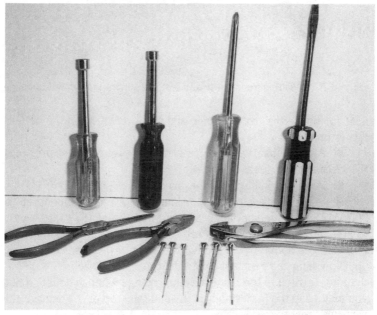

Fig. 1-2. You might find these hand tools are already be on your bench.

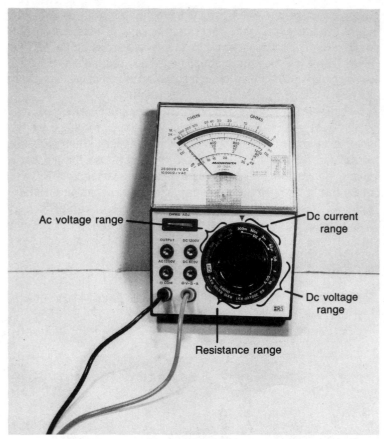

Fig. 1-3. This VOM is the most useful test instrument around the house.

best to choose the highest scale and work down when the dc voltage is unknown.

■ Always observe correct polarity. Touch the test probes to the circuit under test.

■ Read the voltage on the black dc scales.

■ Use extreme care when making voltage measurements above 300 V. For voltages between 300 and 600 V, set the range switch to 300 and up. Then plug the red test lead into the dc 600 V jack. For voltages above 600 V, leave the range switch set at 300 and up. Now plug the red test lead into the 1200 V jack. Always set the range switch to the highest voltage range when in doubt. If not, you may wrap the meter pointer around the stop pin or damage this particular meter range.

Ac Voltage Measurements

■ Plug the test leads into the correct jack.

■ Set the range switch to one of the ac positions. Always choose the highest ac voltage range when not certain and work down.

■ Touch the test probe tips to the circuit under test.

■ Read the voltages on the red ac scales.

■ For voltages between 600 and 1200, set the range to 600 V and up. Now plug the red test lead into the ac 1200 V jack. Be careful when taking high ac voltage measurements, especially from the 115 Vac power line.

Resistance Measurements

■ Before taking any resistance measurements, disconnect the power cord from the ac socket. Discharge all large electrolytic capacitors with a screwdriver and test lead. When working on components with batteries, remove the batteries before taking resistance measurements. Don't leave the meter in the resistance range as you may quickly run down the small internal batteries or accidentally touch the test leads to a voltage circuit. Always turn the range switch back to the off position.

■ Plug the test leads into the negative and positive jacks.

■ Set the range switch to one of the OHM positions. Touch the test probes together and adjust the OHM ADJ control to bring the pointer to the zero on the ohm scale.

■ Now touch the probe tips across the circuit or component under test. Read the resistance on the ohms scale. Use the proper multiplier to obtain the correct value ($R \times 1$, 10, 100, or 1000, depending on the position of the range switch. For instance, if you wanted to measure a 100-ohm resistance you can use $R \times 1$, $R \times 10$, or $R \times 100$ scale. A 1000-ohm resistor may be measured on the $R \times 10$ and $R \times 100$ scale. If at any time the small pointer will not zero in the ohms scale with the leads touched together, replace the small internal battery.

Dc Current Measurements

The only way current measurements can be made are in the circuit. Insert the test leads in series with the component to ensure correct current measurement. For instance, if you suspected your small radio of pulling too much current because the batteries only last a few days, insert the ammeter in series with the positive battery terminal. Remove the wire going to the radio from the positive terminal. Insert the meter terminals between the removed wire lead and battery terminal. Remember to place the red meter lead to the battery terminal. (If the meter reads backwards, reverse the test leads.)

Because most transistor portable radios pull less than 20 mA of current, lower the range switch to 30 mA on the dcA scale. If the meter hand goes above 20 mA, place it on the next highest current range. Look for a leaky transistor or leaky electrolytic capacitor when the current is more than 20 mA.

■ Plug the test leads into the correct jacks (the black lead to negative and the red lead to positive).

■ Set the range switch to the 300 m dcA position (300 milliamp). Always start at the top and work down.

■ Open the circuit where you want to measure the current and connect the black lead to the negative side and the red lead to the positive side.

■ Apply power to the circuit under test and read the current on the black dc scales. If the meter hand moves backward, shut off the unit and reverse the test leads.

These particular meter settings may be a little different from the settings on your VOM. Read the instructions with your VOM carefully before using it. The better you know how to use any test instrument, the easier it is to locate a defective component. However, you must remember the voltage or resistance readings of a 20,000 ohms-per-volt multitester (VOM) is not as accurate as a digital voltmeter or VTVM.

Voltage Measurements within the Circuit

Most VOMs have a voltage accuracy of 3 percent or less. The voltages shown on the schematic of any electronic unit are usually taken with a VTVM or digital voltmeter. When measuring voltages within the circuit with a pocket VOM, don't be alarmed if the voltage measurements are off one volt or so. Although the voltage readings taken with the VOM on transistor terminals are quite critical, at least the VOM reading is accurate enough to tell whether, voltage is present or not.

Let's take the voltage readings of the output circuit of a transistorized auto radio (Fig. 1-4). You know that the car battery is never over 14 Vdc, so the VOM is set at the 15 Vdc scale. With

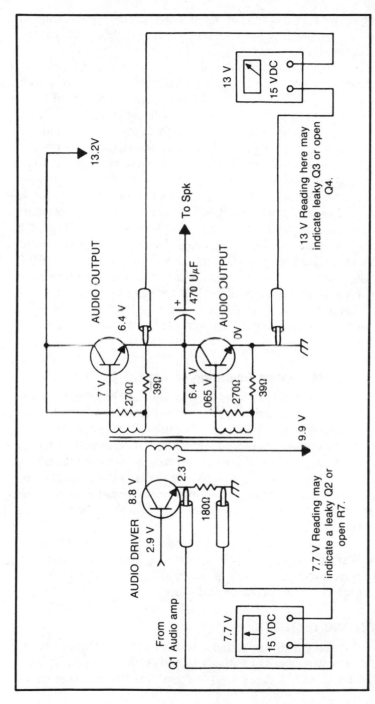

Fig. 1-4. Circuit diagram of the output stages in an AM-FM-MPX compact tape player.

9

the black lead plugged into the negative jack and the red lead plugged into the positive jack, you are ready to take the voltage measurements.

Don't be alarmed if the voltage measured at the collector terminal is 12 volts or less; the measurement may be normal with this type of VOM reading. But if the voltage had increased to 14 volts (the battery source) you may assume the transistor is open. You can prove this with a voltage measurement of the emitter terminal. When the voltage is zero, this indicates that the transistor is open. In case the voltage is about the same on all three terminals (5.5 V or so) you can assume the transistor is leaky. Now remove the suspected transistor from the circuit for outside transistor tests.

Voltage reading with the VOM from base and emitter to common chassis ground may be the same. The forward bias voltage of a transistor is the difference in voltage between base and emitter terminals. Of course, the VOM may not show the difference of 0.6 V, like a more expensive meter. What I am trying to prove here is that the voltage readings of the VOM will almost never be exactly the same as those found on the schematic or in the service literature. However, low voltage readings compared with those found on the schematic may indicate defective components.

Resistance Readings within the Circuit

When checking suspected components within the circuit, it is best to remove one end of the component to ensure correct resistance measurements. With one end removed, measure the resistance across the component terminals. In transistor circuits, especially, you might find inaccurate readings because transistors, diodes, and small bias resistors have a tendency to throw off resistance readings. In making resistance measurements around the transistor, the resistance will always be less than the measured component.

You might be able to read the resistance of a motor, coil, or transformer winding correctly within the circuit, but transistors, diodes, resistors, and capacitors should have one terminal unsoldered from the circuit for accurate resistance readings.

CONTINUITY TESTS

Continuity tests can be made with a battery and light bulb taken from a flashlight, but with a small VOM you can take all kinds of continuity and resistance measurements with the ohmmeter range.

A continuity or ohmmeter test can be taken on coils, transformers, diodes, motors, etc. Normal continuity or ohmmeter tests indicate if the component is open or has the required resistance.

Antennas

The only continuity check you can make on a dipole antenna with a portable radio is on the connecting wire from antenna to the radio circuits. Most dipole antennas get broken when accidentally raised or dropped before being extended. Portable TVs with a dipole antenna may have a broken wire or clip at the terminal. Sometimes these dipole antenna leads are not connected inside the plastic cover when the plastic TV backs are installed.

An outside TV antenna with a folded dipole can be checked with the ohmmeter from the antenna lead-in (Fig. 1-5). Here you can determine if the lead-in is defective or if the dipole has been broken. You should have a reading of less than 30 ohms. TV antennas without the folded dipole cannot be checked for continuity. Short or shunt a clip lead across the antenna leads at the antenna. Now with the ohmmeter, check the lead-in for continuity. Remove the leads from the TV receiver to make these tests.

Antenna Coils

Radio antenna coils can be checked with an ohmmeter. All coil winding resistances should be very low, usually under 10 ohms (Fig.

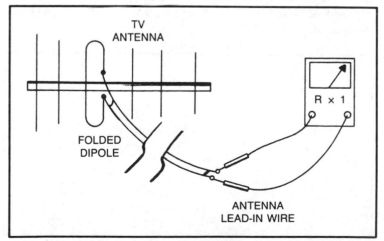

Fig. 1-5. If your TV antenna has a folded dipole, you can check the antenna and lead-in for an open circuit with the ohmmeter.

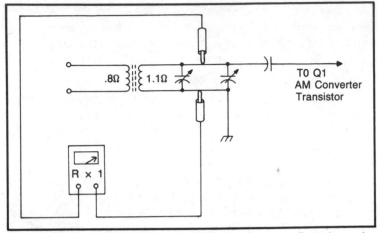

Fig. 1-6. Check antenna or rf coils in the radio chassis with the R×1 ohm scale.

1-6). Some windings may be less than one ohm. (Don't worry about the antenna coil shorting out.) It's best to remove one end of each separate coil to correctly measure continuity in antenna coils.

Cables

The ohmmeter is very handy in making continuity tests on cables or any type of wiring. A broken or intermittent speaker lead can be found with the VOM. Simply short out one end with a clip lead, and flex the cable for a break in the wiring. If intermittent, the meter hand will flash up and down, or no reading will be obtained with an open cable (Fig. 1-7).

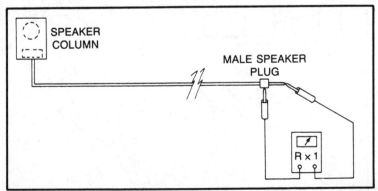

Fig. 1-7. Use the R×1 ohm scale when checking for cable continuity. An erratic reading indicates a broken wire.

Capacitors

You should never have a fixed ohmmeter reading across the terminals of a capacitor—the capacitor is shorted or leaky. In-circuit ohmmeter tests of an electrolytic capacitor are very inaccurate in transistor circuits. Remove the suspected capacitor for leakage tests. Set the meter to R × 1000 (1 K) scale. Clip one lead to the capacitor terminal. Now touch the other lead to the other terminal. The ohmmeter hand should go high in the ohmmeter scale (Fig. 1-8). The capacitor is charging at this point. The hand will slowly return to zero after the capacitor is charged. You will find the larger the capacity, the higher the hand will rise on the scale. A defective electrolytic capacitor will not charge and you may have a leaky reading across the capacitor terminals. Check for correct polarity of the electrolytic coupling capacitor.

Small bypass and fixed coupling capacitors will not charge on the ohmmeter scale because they have a very small capacity. Only electrolytic capacitors will respond to a charge-up test. Remove the suspected capacitor from the circuit. Check on the high (R × 1 K) scale for leakage. Discard the bypass capacitor (for leakage) when any type of ohmmeter reading is found across the terminals with a small VOM.

You must remove the coil lead from the variable tuning capacitor when making ohmmeter tests. If the tuning capacitor has two

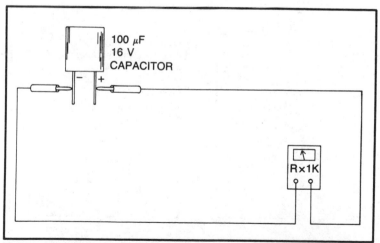

Fig. 1-8. Use the R × 1 K ohm range to check small electrolytic capacitors. The greater the capacitance, the larger the swing of the meter hand. Charging and discharging the capacitor with reversed test leads indicates if the capacitor is defective or not.

separate sections, each section has a coil winding across it. Remove one end of each coil. When the variable capacitor creates noise or a station is shorted out at any part of the dial, you may assume the plates of the capacitor are touching for that instant. The ohmmeter can show this temporary short between rotor and stator plates. Alignment of rotor plates may solve the noisy or shorting condition. A drop of oil in each end bearing may help cure the noisy tuning capacitor.

Cartridges

Basically there are two different types of phono cartridges found in phonographs. A crystal cartridge is used in most phono turntables. In larger, more expensive models, a dynamic or moving-coil cartridge is found. The dynamic cartridge must have an added stage of amplification, because very little voltage is developed within the cartridge. You should have a very low ohmmeter reading across the phono leads from a dynamic cartridge (Fig. 1-9).

When any type of ohmmeter reading is found across the crystal cartridge cables, suspect a shorted cable or wires at the cartridge. Sometimes the small wire clips will touch and short out where they plug into the cartridge. A normal crystal cartridge will never have an ohmmeter reading even on the lowest ohmmeter scale.

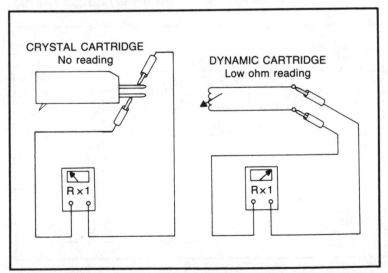

Fig. 1-9. You should have a very low ohmmeter reading across dynamic cartridge terminals, and an infinite reading across the terminals of a crystal cartridge.

14

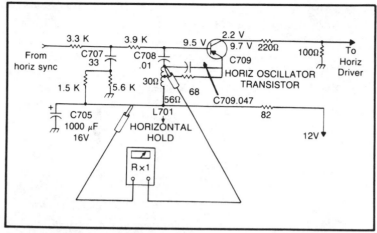

Fig. 1-10. Check the resistance of the horizontal oscillator coil and compare the reading against the schematic.

Coils

All coils found within a radio or TV should show continuity or very low ohmmeter readings unless in some tuned circuits a blocking capacitor is in series with the coil winding. Most tuned coils have very low ohmmeter readings. For instance, the primary of an oscillator coil in a small radio might be 0.3 ohms and the secondary, 2.6 ohms.

A horizontal oscillator coil within a TV chassis might have a resistance of about 94 ohms (Fig. 1-10). It's best to check the measured resistance against those readings on the schematic. You might find the horizontal oscillator coil open because this coil can easily be bumped from the rear of the TV. Very seldom do these coils increase in resistance. If the ohmmeter reading is within a few ohms of the original, you can assume the coil is good.

Diodes

The silicon diodes (Fig. 1-11) found in most low-voltage power supplies can be tested with the ohmmeter. With the positive lead connected to the negative or anode terminal of the diode and the negative or black lead attached to the positive or cathode terminal of the diode, you should have a reading of around 10 ohms. Now reverse the test leads. Place the ohmmeter in the highest ohmmeter range. No reading (infinite) should be obtained with a normal diode. A leaky diode will measure a resistance value in both directions.

15

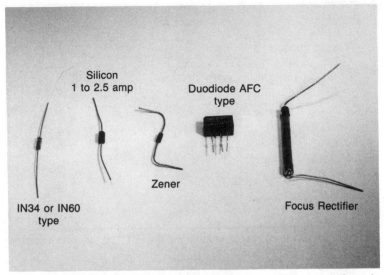

Fig. 1-11. Use the R×1 scale to determine if a silicon diode is open or shorted. A reading in both directions indicates a leaky diode.

Always remove one end of the diode for correct tests. An open diode will have infinite reading.

Selenium rectifiers, found in the early TV or radio chassis, will read in both directions. You should have a very high reading in one direction and a low reading (somewhere under 100 ohms) in the other direction with a normal selenium rectifier. A defective selenium rectifier will have burned spots on the plate area and have a sweet smell (when running excessively warm).

A duodiode found in the afc oscilloscope circuits of the TV chassis will measure around 150 to 300 ohms in one direction. With reversed test leads the resistance may run somewhere between 100 KΩ and 200 KΩ. Measure the resistance from cathode or common terminal to each anode. Check each diode section against the other. If both readings are fairly close in both directions of each section, you can assume the duodiode is okay. A high resistance in one or both sections might produce poor horizontal sync.

Focus or boost rectifiers are made up of many different rectifier coils connected in series. These diodes cannot be checked with the ohmmeter. If you get a reading on the highest ohmmeter range of a pocket VOM, replace the rectifier. The hv rectifiers found in many B&W transistor TVs are of this same variety. You might find a

16

burned or overheated mark on the hv rectifier body. Do not touch any rectifiers when the set is operating.

Dial Lights

A normal dial light will have a low ohmmeter reading. Infinite reading may indicate an open dial light. Either remove the dial bulb for tests or unsolder one lead for proper tests. You can measure the resistance of the filament winding of the power transformer or other bulbs in series.

In some TVs you might find a neon channel light bulb in place of an incandescent type. These bulbs operate from the dc power supply. You might find a small voltage-dropping resistor in series with the neon dial light. When these bulbs go bad, only one side of the bulb glows or the glass might appear dark and burned. You cannot measure any continuity across these neon bulbs.

The LED-type bulbs will measure continuity like a regular silicon diode. If unlit, measure voltage across the lamp terminals. Then remove it and take ohmmeter readings. Be sure to observe correct polarity in replacement. These bulbs will not light when installed backward and may produce heavy current drain.

Headphones

The old-style headphones may have a resistance between 150 to 1 K ohms while the new stereo headphones have a 4- to 16-ohm impedance (resistance). The resistance may be about 7.5 ohms. Actually, the stereo headphones can consist of two small permanent magnet speakers enclosed in plastic. In some transistor radios, you might find a mono-crystal headphone. In this case, no resistance will be found across the headphone terminals (Fig. 1-12).

If one headphone becomes intermittent or dead, recheck the leads for continuity with the R×1 ohmmeter range. Clip the ohmmeter leads to the headphone male plug sections. In stereo units, you will have three different sections of the male plug. The resistance from common ground to the other two sections should be the same. Now flex the cord and note if the meter hand becomes erratic. Generally, the headphone cable will be broken close to where it enters the headphone case. The simplest way to repair the broken or poor connecting wire is to cut the cable about three inches down from the headphone. Slit the cable two inches and remove the outside rubber cover. Scrape back each wire lead and tin the wire. Use

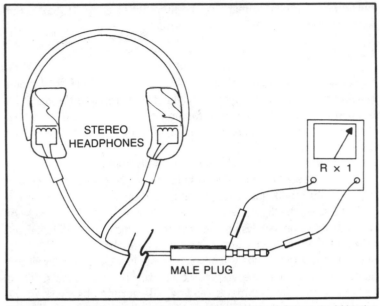

Fig. 1-12. The resistance across the dynamic stereo headphones could be the same as a small speaker. Crystal headphones will not show continuity, but a possibly broken cable lead can be checked on the low-ohms scale.

soldering paste on each wire end. Then locate and solder each color coded wire inside the headphone assembly.

Checking ICs

A suspected IC component cannot be measured for continuity with the ohmmeter. Voltage readings and signal tests might locate a defective IC. If the IC plugs into a socket, check the socket terminals for open or broken connections with the ohmmeter. After a new power output IC has been installed within the transistorized amplifier, use the ohmmeter to check the resistance from common ground to each terminal. Then compare these readings with the good IC. This may indicate the IC is installed properly and that no other components tied to the IC terminals are leaky.

Meters

VU or signal meters can be checked with the ohmmeter. Remove one lead from the meter and set to R×1 scale. These meters should have a resistance of under 300 ohms. If the meter is functioning with correct polarity, the meter hand will rise when checked with the VOM. If the winding is open, check for broken leads on the meter terminal bolts.

When the meter hand sticks at a certain place on the dial, remove the plastic front piece and bend the meter hand upwards with a pocket knife. Be careful because it takes a steady hand to straighten a meter pointer. If the meter hand sticks any place on the dial, check for a small adjustment screw at the bottom of the meter hand, and turn the screw until the hand is at zero.

Microphones

The microphone can have an impedance from 200 to 50,000 ohms. You might find a few crystal mikes, but most are dynamic types. The crystal microphone cannot be checked with the VOM. The dynamic mike is constructed like a small permanent magnet speaker. You can make continuity tests with a dynamic microphone. Clip the VOM leads across the mike plug, set on the R×1 range. You might hear a click in the microphone when the meter leads are attached to the male plug. The small cassette microphone can vary between 200 and 500 ohms. You can check the cable and ON/OFF switch on both types of microphones with the ohmmeter.

Motors

All motors can be checked for correct continuity with the VOM. Set the meter to the R×1 scale. Measure the resistance across the motor terminal leads. It's best to remove one lead for accurate tests. The defective motor winding may be open or have an erratic reading with poor brushes (Fig. 1-13).

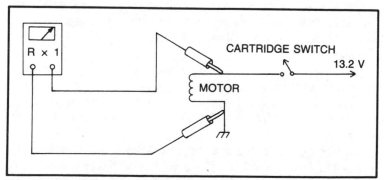

Fig. 1-13. Remove one of the motor leads and check the resistance with the R×1 range. You might find another wire from the motor for fast-forward operation.

The resistance of a phonograph motor should be in the neighborhood of 40 to 200 ohms. The resistance of the dc motor found in cassette, eight-track, and auto cassette players varies from 10 to 25 ohms. The motor found in a clock radio might be 750 ohms.

Picture Tube Heaters

When the TV picture tube will not light up, check for an open heater across the socket. Remove the picture tube socket and harness. Set the VOM on the R×1 scale. Usually the filament terminals are on each side of the small guide pin. The guide is a raised area of plastic. Infinite reading indicates open heaters or filaments. The picture tube should be normal if it has a continuity reading.

Relays

The field winding and contact points of a relay can be checked with the ohmmeter. Remove one end of the solenoid winding from the circuit. The resistance of these small relays can have a wide range. The winding is normal if it has a continuity reading.

To check the contact points, set the VOM to the R×1 scale. Clip the meter leads across the terminal going to each set of contacts, then close the relay points. Each contact should have a low ohm reading. Some contacts might be closed when the solenoid is not energized; these will show a shorted condition.

Resistors

Each fixed resistor should read within ten percent of the color code. You may find 5- and 10-watt resistors have a better resistance tolerance. Fixed resistors have a tendency of either increasing in resistance or opening. Resistors in the megohm range have a tendency to increase in resistance. However, a burned resistor may decrease in resistance.

Remove one end of a variable resistor for correct resistance measurements. Volume controls for the small radio or amplifier can vary from 5 KΩ to 10 KΩ. Large volume controls in the tube chassis can vary from 500 KΩ to 2.5 MΩ. Check the schematic for correct resistance.

Low-ohm controls such as speaker or power rheostats may have a resistance from 5 to 50 ohms. Disconnect one outside lead from the circuit to see if the control is open. Measure the total resistance across the two outside terminals on the R×1 scale. Many of the low ohm controls are wirewound types.

If the schematic is not handy, rotate the meter to the highest ohmmeter scale. Now connect the meter to the outside terminals for the maximum reading. You will find this reading on high-resistance controls will always be less than the original value. For instance, if a volume control measurement is around 400 KΩ resistance, the original value was probably that of 500 KΩ. Now connect one meter lead to the center and one to the outside terminal. Rotate the control and note if the meter hand follows the rotation of the control. Most controls are replaced when open or erratic.

Speakers

The ohmmeter is very handy in checking the continuity of speaker cables and the voice coil. If the speaker circuit is normal, you should hear a click in the speaker with the ohmmeter connected to the speaker plug, on the R×1 scale. Simply flex the speaker cable for possible breaks in the cable. The meter hand will fluctuate when a break exists.

Don't be misled by speaker ohm impedance. Your speaker will never measure the same in resistance as the impedance. Table 1-1 shows the various speaker resistance measurements with a small multitester. The speaker can still be good if the reading is off only a few ohms.

Where more than one speaker is enclosed within a cabinet, remove one lead from the speaker for correct resistance measurement. Similarly, remove one lead from the speaker inside a table model radio for correct measurements. In some radio and TV tube models, the audio output transformer has a low-ohm winding and if not disconnected, the speaker voice coil may be open while

Table 1-1. Actual Speaker Resistances of Various Speakers.

Impedance	Resistance	
Speaker size ohms	Actual measurement	
	VOM	DMM
3.2 Ω	3.0 Ω	3.1 Ω
4.0 Ω	3.5 Ω	3.9 Ω
8.0 Ω	7.5 Ω	7.8 Ω
16.0 Ω	14.5 Ω	15.9 Ω
25.0 Ω	22.0 Ω	24.9 Ω
40.0 Ω	29.5 Ω	38.0 Ω

showing a continuity reading of the transformer winding. Always disconnect one side of the speaker voice coil terminal from the circuit.

Solenoids

Solenoid coils, like those found in stereo eight-track tape players, can be checked for continuity with the VOM. Most channel-changing solenoids have a resistance of fifty ohms or less, so set the ohmmeter on the R×1 range. The defective solenoid may be open or have burned windings. A visual inspection of the solenoid cover will show signs of it being too warm or overheating.

Soldering Iron

When a soldering iron will not heat up, suspect an open heating element. You might also locate a defective switch or open coil in the soldering gun. In guns with two different areas of heat, suspect a defective switch. Broken coil or transformer windings on the switch terminals are likely suspects.

To determine if the heater or winding is open, clip the ohmmeter leads across the ac plug. You should be able to check the continuity on the R×1 range. A 60-watt iron may have a resistance of less than 500 ohms. The resistance of a soldering gun may be somewhere around 15 ohms. Don't overlook a defective ac cord. Usually the cord breaks right where it goes into the soldering iron or at the ac plug.

Switches

All switch contacts can be checked with the ohmmeter. Clip the meter leads across the switch terminals, and set the meter to the R×1 range. Flip the switch on, and the meter hand should go to zero. Now turn it off for a reading of infinity. If the reading is erratic, suspect burned or dirty switch contacts. Replace the switch when erratic or open.

Tape Heads

Remove one terminal of the connecting cable to the suspected tape head. Measure the continuity or resistance across the tape head terminals. In a stereo-8 tape head, you will find two windings; in a quad-8 tape head, four different windings or a total of 8 terminals. Both windings should have the same resistance or be within a few ohms of each other. The stereo-8 tape head resistance can vary from 430 to 830 ohms.

Mono or stereo cassette tape heads may be checked by the same method. It's possible to find one terminal as common ground with a total of three connections. In some tape cassette heads, one terminal may be grounded inside the metal mounting bracket. The resistance of a mono cassette head can vary from 200 to 370 ohms.

You might find the resistance of a cassette erase head to be only a few ohms. Some of these erase heads are excited by the dc power supply, while others are excited by an oscillator voltage. Remove one end of the cable for correct measurements. It's possible to have a grounded cable going to the erase head, preventing the tape head from erasing the previous recording.

Transformers

Always check the primary winding of a small power transformer for an open winding. Overloaded conditions in the secondary circuit often open up the primary winding. Remove one end of the primary winding for correct measurement. The two black wires going to the transformer are generally the primary or ac winding.

In large power TV transformers, check both primary and secondary windings with the R×1 scale of the VOM. The resistance of a center-tapped winding should be quite close on both sides of the center-tap. It's possible to find an open or an increase in the higher ac voltage winding going to the full-wave rectifiers. Sometimes the center-tapped heater windings may heat one of the internal hook-up wire connections. This is caused by a poor soldered or clamped connection. Typical transformer resistances are shown in Fig. 1-14.

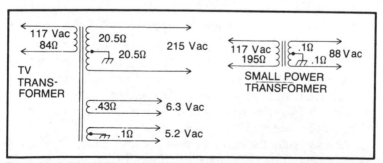

Fig. 1-14. A typical TV transformer with the various voltage and resistance measurements. These resistance readings are without any leads connected in the circuit.

A defective transformer found in radios can either appear open, increase in resistance, or have a burned winding. Measure the resistance across both primary and secondary windings. It's possible to incorrectly measure a certain audio frequency winding when a dc blocking capacitor is wired in series with this particular winding. Check the schematic before tearing out the suspected transformer. Also, watch for separate FM (10.7 MHz) i-f windings which may be tied to the regular 455 kHz or 262 kHz windings. The 262 kHz i-f transformer is found in automotive receivers. The primary winding can vary between 0.3 and 1.6 ohms, while the resistance of the secondary can be 4.0 to 7.8 ohms.

You might find two different types of choke or coil transformers in a TV chassis. Small peaking coils usually open. The resistance of these coils will have a wide variance determined by the working circuit. A defective choke transformer may cause 60-cycle hum in the raster or a no raster condition. Check these choke transformers on the R × 1 scale. Visually inspect the insulated cover for overheated or burned motors. These power choke transformers may get so hot that the windings short out, producing less resistance and poor ac filtering in the power supply.

Transistors

Determine if a transistor is leaky or open with an ohmmeter test. A leaky or shorted transistor will have a reading in both directions across the same two terminals. An open transistor may not have a reading even on the high R × 1 K range between emitter and base terminals. Figure 1-15 shows three typical transistor resistance readings of different transistors.

Tube Heaters

The tube heaters or filaments should have a low-ohm continuity if normal. However, this resistance check of the tube heater does not determine whether the tube is good or not; it is simply a test to determine if the heaters are open. An open heater is very common in radio and TV series string tubes. None of the tubes will light up with an open heater circuit.

Always pull the power plug before taking resistance measurements. Set the ohmmeter on the R × 1 range. Check for continuity between the two heater pins. These pins are different on various size tubes. Look which tube is open in the heater string. Figure 1-21 shows the most common heater connections.

24

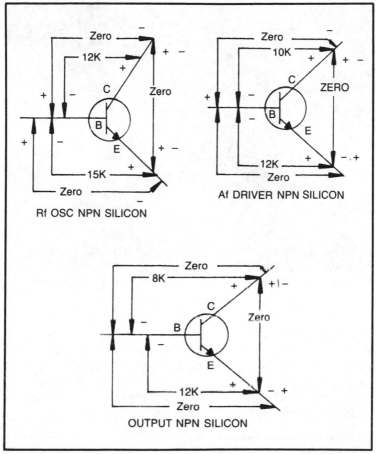

Fig. 1-15. Three different transistors with various ohmmeter readings using the 20,000 ohms/volt meter.

DIGITAL MULTIMETER (DMM) TRANSISTOR TESTS

The pocket DMM is a handy test instrument to quickly locate a defective transistor in or out of the circuit (Fig. 1-16). Switch the DMM to diode or diode-transistor function tests. Place the positive probe (red) to the base terminal of the suspected transistor. If the transistor is an npn type, place the negative probe (black) to the collector terminal. Note the measurement on the LCD meter scale. Remove the black probe and touch the emitter terminal. Most silicon transistors have a normal measurement between 550 to 950 ohms; when both emitter and collector measurements are within a few ohms of each other, you can assume the transistor is normal.

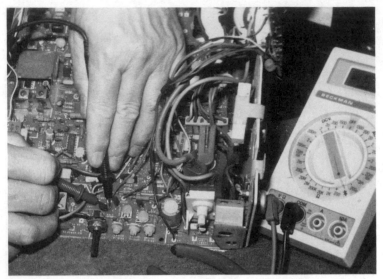

Fig. 1-16. Check transistors in or out of the circuit with a digital multimeter (DMM).

Place the negative probe (black) to the base terminal in testing a pnp-type transistor, then place the positive probe (red) to the collector terminal. Note the resistance measurement. Likewise, place the red probe on the emitter terminal and compare the two measurements (Fig. 1-17). The normal pnp transistor will have similar resistance measurements in other directions.

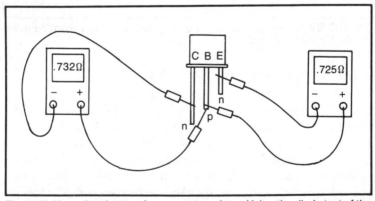

Fig. 1-17. Normal resistance for an npn transistor. Using the diode test of the meter, place the positive probe (red) on the base terminal with the negative (black) probe at the collector and then at the emitter terminal of the transistor to be tested. Both measurements should be quite close in resistance.

A leaky transistor may have a low resistance measurement between any two elements. Most transistors show a leakage between the emitter and collector terminals. It's possible to have an audio output transistor with high leakage between all terminals. Reverse the test probes in making leakage tests to determine if there is leakage in both directions. For instance, a normal measurement might result between base and collector terminals with a leakage test between collector and emitter (Fig. 1-18). Remove the suspected leaky transistor from the circuit and repeat the leakage test.

The normal silicon transistor will have a higher measurement than the germanium transistor. A germanium pnp audio output transistor may have a normal resistance measurement from 150 to 350 ohms. If a transistor has a poor or high-resistance junction, it will be noted by two very different measurements (Fig. 1-19). Remember, the two measurements of a normal transistor should be within a few ohms. If not, replace it.

CHECKING ICs WITH THE DMM

Accurate voltage and resistance measurements on the terminals of an IC can determine if the component is open or leaky. The oscilloscope can help to locate the defective IC in a TV chassis. Signal-in and signal-out tests might determine if the IC component is defective.

First take a voltage measurement of each terminal and compare them with those in the schematic. If the supply voltage terminal is

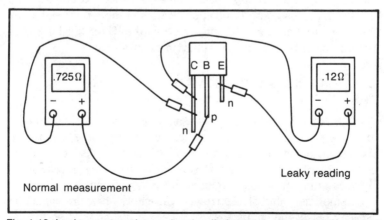

Fig. 1-18. Leaky npn transistor using the diode test on the meter. The leaky transistor has a very low resistance measurement compared to a good transistor. The low measurement will remain the same with reversed test leads.

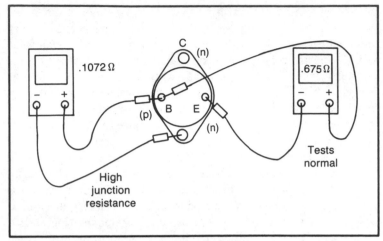

Fig. 1-19. Power transistor, bottom view. Those with a higher measurement might indicate a high junction resistance. Always replace a defective transistor in this case.

very low, suspect a leaky IC (Fig. 1-20). The IC might be open if the supply voltage is too high. Feel the body of the IC and note if the component is very warm or red hot. A leaky IC will run very warm. Inspect the IC body and terminals for overheated marks.

Before removing the IC, check all possibly defective components that are tied to the IC terminals. A leaky bypass capacitor can lower the supply voltage. Double-check all resistance measurements with the schematic diagram. If a coil or diode is in the circuit and a low resistance measurement is found, remove the IC terminal from the circuit, and take another resistance measurement.

CHECKING CAPACITORS WITH
THE DIGITAL CAPACITY METER

The portable digital capacitance meter is a handy test instrument to check electrolytic and bypass capacitors (Fig. 1-22). Turn the instrument on and zero the meter. Hook up the capacitor, noting proper polarity, and push in the selector button. Capacitors can be checked in or out of the circuit with the digital meter.

Sometimes normal electrolytic capacitors measure higher in capacity out of the circuit than the actual value marked on the capacitor. In Fig. 1-22, a 470 μF filter capacitor measures 507 μF. The capacity of in-circuit tests always measure lower in value. You can

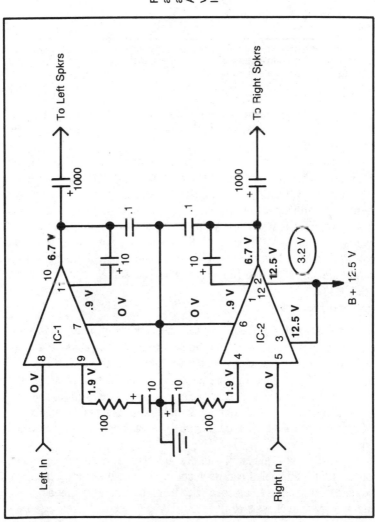

Fig. 1-20. Take accurate voltage and resistance measurements on all terminals of the IC component. A very low voltage at the supply voltage terminal often indicates a leaky IC.

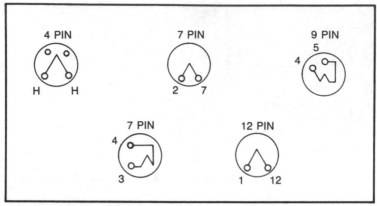

Fig. 1-21. The most common tube pins are shown with correct heater terminals. All tube filaments should show a very low resistance reading. Infinite reading indicates the tube heater is open.

have a very low measurement if diodes or resistors are in parallel with the capacitor to be checked. Remove the capacitor from the circuit if in doubt.

Replace a defective electrolytic capacitor when the capacity is 5 μF lower than the original. If the measurement has a high leakage or a very low reading, suspect a shorted or leaky capacitor. Always remove the capacitor from the circuit and take another measurement. If the capacitor tests normal after being removed, suspect another leaky component in the circuit. Recheck for a low-value resistor, coil, or diode in the circuit. All bypass and electrolytic capacitors can be quickly tested in the circuit with the digital capacity meter.

OTHER TEST INSTRUMENTS

The transistor and tube tester are handy test instruments for determining if a transistor or tube is defective. You may be able to pick up a dynamic transistor checker for under $15. Let the TV shop test your tubes unless you already have a tube tester. Although the scope, VTVM, audio signal generator, rf signal generator, and video amplifier are great test instruments for servicing electronic equipment, practically all the tests made in this book are accomplished with the VOM.

You can invest in handy gadgets such as test lead jumper cables. These test lead cables can be made up of small alligator clips and flexible wire. Make an ac cord with alligator clips to apply ac inside the TV or radio chassis (Fig. 1-23). Have an extra "cheater cord"

Fig. 1-22. The pocket digital capacity meter checks filter or bypass capacitors. Here a 470 µF filter capacitor is acceptable with a 50 µF measurement, but you should replace any capacitors with a lower-than-normal reading or a shorted measurement.

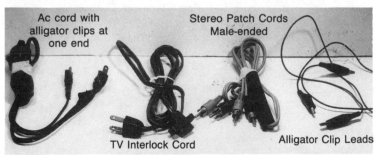

Fig. 1-23. Clips and test leads you can make to ensure quicker servicing. A test-lead jumper connects various circuits and test instruments. The ac cord with alligator clips at right enables direct hook-up to the transformer or ac circuitry.

around, so you can leave the one on the back cover of the TV receiver attached. Construct or purchase a set of shielded cables that can be connected from a phono changer to an amplifier chassis. You might find that as you go along repairing various electronic components in the house, you might want to rig up a few of your own cables for easy servicing.

2

Twenty-Eight Important Tips

Here are 28 important tips that might save you money or some embarrassing moments.

■ **Soldering Irons.** *Don't* use a large one for a small job. *Do* employ a 65-watt or less soldering iron when making transistor and wiring connections on a printed circuit (pc) board. In fact, a hand-held pencil soldering iron works best on these connections. Use a 100 watt or larger iron on large soldering connections. A 300 watt iron may be used when trying to remove a component or wiring soldered to the metal chassis. Be careful with the soldering iron when working around plastic components.

■ **Solder.** *Don't* use acid core solder. *Do* plan to use rosin core solder on all electronic components and connections. If a better connection should be made, place rosin flux on the soldered area. Apply the soldering iron tip to the joint or material to be soldered. Now apply rosin core solder to the material and joint. Make a good clean solder joint. Rosin core 60-40 solder is suggested for electronic work.

■ **Pc Boards.** *Don't* rip out the defective component when removing it from the pc board. *Do* be careful. Mark down all color-coded leads. Make a rough drawing of how the component is mounted. Not only will this save you valuable time, but the unit will be easier to install and wire correctly.

■ **Cabinets.** *Don't* lay the plastic or wooden cabinet of a radio or TV directly upon the workbench. *Do* use an old rug or towel underneath the unit to prevent scratches. Keep other objects away from the working area so you have plenty of working room.

■ **Power.** *Don't* leave the unit power on when soldering replacement components or taking resistance measurements. *Do* make sure the power switch is off. Better yet, pull the ac cord from the outlet when making these tests.

■ **Insulating.** *Don't* operate a hot (power on) chassis on a metal workbench or near grounded pipes. *Do* lay the chassis on a rug or towel away from any grounded objects. It's best to work on a wooden or plastic table than to take chances. Remember, one side of the power line may be grounded to the TV or radio chassis and when you or the chassis touch a grounded pipe or metal object, you might get shocked.

■ **Isolation Transformer.** *Don't* work on a hot chassis without added protection. *Do* use an isolation transformer when repairing or taking voltage measurements on a hot TV or radio chassis. Repairing your own unit can be fun, but *don't* take chances of being hurt in the process.

■ **Worn Power Cords.** *Don't* use frayed or cracked ac cords with your radio or TV receiver. *Do* replace any power cords that are old and cracked. A lot of fires are caused by defective ac power cords.

■ **Power Drills.** *Don't* use an electric power drill without proper grounds. *Do* make sure your power drill has a center grounded lug for proper grounding.

■ **Charged Capacitors.** *Don't* pick up a charged electrolytic capacitor with your bare hands. *Do* discharge all electrolytic capacitors with a shorting clip or discharge on a metal chassis before touching the bare leads. You can get a terrible shock and burn from a highly charged filter capacitor. Remember, electrolytic capacitors can hold a charge for a long time.

■ **Plastic Knobs.** *Don't* let alcohol or cleaning fluid drip or run on plastic dials or the front of a stereo player. *Do* be careful as these cleaning liquids may tarnish the plastic front dial or knobs. If cleaning fluid is spilled on a plastic area, wipe off or soak up with a paper towel at once.

■ **Cleaning Fluids.** *Don't* leave cleaning fluid where children might play with it. *Do* place all cleaning fluid out of children's reach. It's best to lock it inside a cabinet.

■ **Speakers.** *Don't* turn on your tape player or amplifier without the speakers connected. *Do* keep the volume turned down and keep the speakers connected at all times to prevent damage to the output transistors. It's possible to blow the output transistor or IC without a lead attached to the speaker jacks.

■ **Speaker Connections.** *Don't* haphazardly add extra speakers or cables without correct solder joints. *Do* solder all speaker cable connections. When adding extra speaker wire, stagger the two wires so the wired joints are not side by side. Make a good soldered connection and tape each joint separately. Then you can add tape over both connections for a better appearance.

■ **Study the Problem.** *Don't* just jump into a repair job and tear it apart without thinking first. *Do* study the problem and line up the possible trouble points. Look the chassis over for burned or overheated components. Take correct resistance and voltage measurements before removing the suspected component.

■ **Check Plug.** *Don't* forget to check the ac power plug before calling a TV technician. *Do* make sure the ac cord is plugged into the power line. Push in the interlock plug where the ac cord enters the TV set. The interlock plug may be damaged if you forget to pull the plug out of the outlet before moving the TV cabinet.

■ **Unplug Cord.** *Don't* forget to unplug the ac cord from the wall outlet when going on vacation or during a storm. *Do* unplug the ac cord and remove the antenna connections from the TV set before going on vacation.

■ **TV Lead-in.** *Don't* coil up the antenna wire behind the TV set. *Do* cut the TV cable or lead-in to the correct length. Extra wire coiled up may weaken the TV signal. If you must have extra wire for moving the set about, lay the lead-in flat and over a larger area.

■ **TV Controls.** *Don't* forget to turn up the brightness control when the picture tube appears dead. *Do* adjust the TV controls after children have been operating it. Sometimes the brightness control is just turned down. Before calling the TV technician make sure all of the controls on the front of the TV are adjusted properly.

■ **TV Overload Button.** *Don't* forget to push in the overload button at the rear of the TV when the set will not function. *Do* push the red overload button in and quickly release. Sometimes an internal or power-line overload may cause the circuit breaker to kick out. If the TV set comes on and goes right out, try it once more. *Don't* hold the button in if the TV set will not stay on. You may damage the circuit breaker or other components.

■ **Selector Knobs.** *Don't* use a pair of pliers to turn the TV channel selector after the tuning knob is broken. *Do* purchase a new replacement knob. If a new selector knob is not available, try to get a used one. Generally, when a pair of pliers is used to turn the tuner, the shaft becomes worn and might not allow the new knob to seat properly. Extensive damage may require a new tuner shaft or tuner, resulting in an expensive repair job.

■ **TV Service Controls.** *Don't* turn every control in the back of the TV set when it fails to operate. *Do* try to learn what each service control is for on the back of the TV set. If the set will not function after checking the TV cord, interlock button, and ON/OFF switch, the trouble is inside the TV chassis. Most TV receivers have screen and grid bias or drive controls for correct black and white adjustment. Also, you might find a service normal switch can be found for service set-up procedures. You might find vertical controls protruding through the rear cover, or a horizontal hold control on the rear of the chassis.

■ **Coils.** *Don't* turn every coil slug in a radio or TV chassis unless you are performing alignment procedures. *Do* leave these small coil slug adjustments where they are unless you have the proper test equipment.

■ **Color TV Top Controls.** *Don't* attempt to adjust every small control located on top of the color chassis without knowing why they should be adjusted. *Do* leave all top controls alone. Most of these control settings are color adjustments. If turned only a fraction of a turn, you can throw off or destroy the color from the picture. This means the color chassis must go to the shop for critical color alignment.

■ **Spills.** *Don't* spill any type of liquid inside the TV cabinet. *Do* keep flower pots from on top of the TV set. *Do* keep glasses and pop cans off the TV set. When liquid is spilled inside a TV set, you might short out components and start a fire. If the components become burned too badly, a whole pc board may need replacement. This can run into a lot of money.

■ **IC Voltage Measurements.** *Do* be careful when taking voltage measurements on the terminals of an IC. If two terminals are accidentally touched together, the IC component might be damaged. Always take critical voltage and resistance measurements before removing the suspected IC. You may uncover a leaky diode or bypass capacitor tied to the IC and find the IC component normal. Do not replace the old IC if another component is causing the low-voltage problem.

■ **Solder Joints.** *Don't* forget to check each terminal for a good soldered connection before firing up the unit. Clean off excess solder with iron and solder-wick when two terminals are soldered together that should not be connected. Use a low-wattage iron while making soldered connections on the IC terminals. The battery-operated iron is ideal for IC pin terminals.

■ **Insulators.** *Don't* forget to replace all insulators between a transistor and heat sink. Before removing the transistor, note if there is a piece of insulation between the heat sink and transistor. Replace the old insulator with a new one when possible. Coat both sides of the insulator with silicon grease. The clear silicon grease will not mess up your hands or clothes when applying it to the transistor.

Part 2

Audio

3

Common AM/FM Radio Repair

Servicing FM problems within the AM/FM chassis is no more difficult than repairing the AM radio. Most AM/FM radio tube receivers can be fixed with simple tube testing and replacement. However, this is not true of the transistorized chassis. The transistorized AM/FM/MPX chassis may be found in the portable, table model, compact, or combination tape decks. Here are some of the most common problems found in the AM/FM transistorized radio chassis (Fig. 3-1).

NO OUTPUT AND NO DIAL LIGHTS

A completely dead transistorized radio chassis may be caused by a defective ac cord or ON/OFF switch, or open fuses, transistors, or power transformers. Look for lighted dial lights; this will indicate power is getting to the receiver. When the dial lights are out and there is no sound from the speaker, suspect a broken ac cord, defective ON/OFF switch, or open power transformer or fuse.

In large receivers you may find an ac line fuse. Check the back panel or chassis for a fuse holder. If a fuse is found, remove it and check it on the R×1 scale of the ohmmeter. An open fuse with have infinite reading. When open, replace the defective fuse with one having the very same current rating.

With just one test you can check the power transformer, power switch, and ac cord. Set the ohmmeter to R×1 scale. Unplug from

Fig. 3-1. A typical AM/FM/MPX radio. This same chassis could appear with an eight-track, cassette, and/or phonograph. (Courtesy Radio Shack.)

the outlet but turn the receiver switch on. Connect the meter to the ac plug terminals. If normal, you should have an ohmmeter reading under 20 ohms. Infinite reading indicates that one or more of the components is open. See Fig. 3-2.

When the receiver starts to come on with blinking dim dial lights, suspect a poor ac connection to the power transformer. Wiggle each lead going into the power transformer. Sometimes the connecting wire may not be soldered to the actual winding. Check all taped ac wires that are connected to the power cord. A dirty ac power switch may have the same symptoms.

Check for continuity across the two ac leads going to the power transformer. An open primary winding could be caused by a shorted rectifier or output power transistor, so before changing the power transformer, check these two components. The power transformer should be replaced with one having the very same part number. Order it from the manufacturer or through your local radio/TV dealer.

Remove one end of each silicon diode in the rectifier circuit for ohmmeter tests. Set the ohmmeter to the $R \times 1$ scale. With the black lead connected to the positive terminal of the diode, you should have a reading under 10 ohms. Now reverse the test leads and you should have an infinite reading, even if the ohmmeter is turned to the $R \times 1$ K scale (Fig. 3-3). When a reading is found in both directions, replace the diode. Most silicon diodes found in the power supply may be replaced with a 1- or 2.5-amp type.

KEEPS BLOWING FUSES

When the ac line fuse keeps blowing or the dial lights go dim, check the silicon diodes in the power supply. If they test okay, cut off the lead from the power supply to the output power transistor.

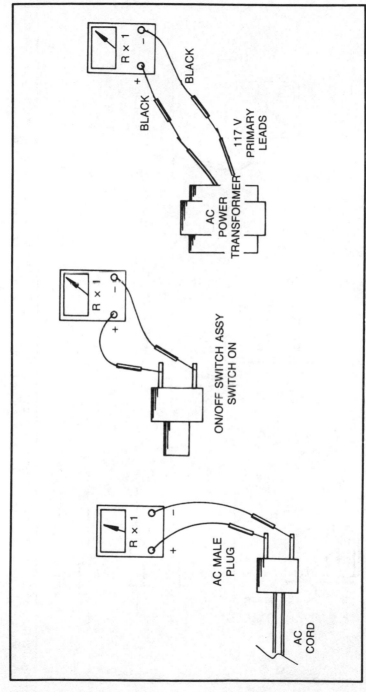

Fig. 3-2. The ac cord, power switch, and power transformer are checked for continuity.

43

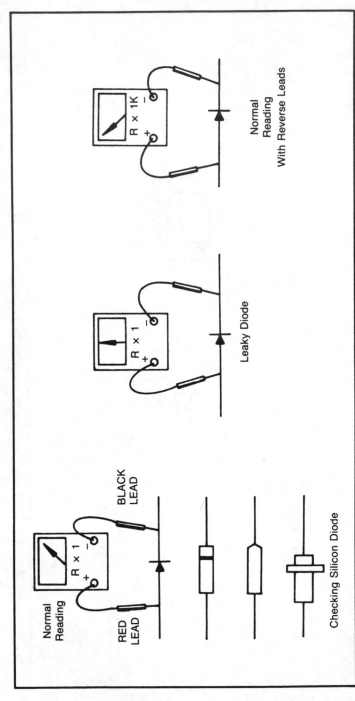

Fig. 3-3. Set the VOM at R×1 scale. Remove one end of the silicon diode. With the black lead connected to the positive terminal of the diode you should have a reading under 10 ohms. A reading in both directions indicates a leaky or shorted diode.

44

With some pc boards you may have to cut out a piece of wiring foil too cut off voltage supplied to the output transistors. If this is too difficult, simply remove the output transistors. Now plug in the power cord and note if the fuse is okay and the dial lights are bright. You might not have sound in the speaker, but you have located the overloading transistors. Also look for burned bias resistors around the output transistors.

If the fuse holds but the power transformer runs hot, suspect a shorted winding. Remove all the secondary leads from the power transformer. In a simple, low-voltage power supply, usually two red wires go to the silicon diodes, while two green wires go to the dial light circuits. Always mark where all leads were connected. Now plug the ac cord into the outlet. If the transformer overheats without a load on the secondary, the primary of the transformer has shorted and must be replaced.

In larger amplifier units, you might find a fuse protecting each amplifier channel. After replacing the blown fuse with one with the exact current rating, note if the fuse opens each time the switch is turned on. Sometimes these fuses open when the volume is turned too high. Simply replacing a fuse is all that's needed. If the fuse still blows, do not insert a larger one. Check the audio output transistors for leaky conditions. Fuses inserted in series with the speakers usually open up when too much volume is applied to the speakers.

REPLACING DIAL LIGHTS

At least two dial lights are normally found in the AM/FM tuning dial assembly, but in some units there could be a total of fourteen. Replace only the bulbs that do not light up. Sometimes two bulbs are wired in series, but only one bulb is defective. Remove the suspected bulb and check continuity with the ohmmeter (Fig. 3-4).

You might find a large resistor in series with a string of lights. Most dial bulbs operate in a parallel circuit. A separate winding on the power transformer can provide voltage for the ac dial lights. Some dial lights operate directly from the dc power source. Dial bulbs found in the AM/FM chassis come in all sizes and may vary from 6 to 30 volts. Some screw into a socket while others have long flexible wire leads. The bayonet or screw-type dial bulbs are easy to replace. Simply remove and take to your local radio/TV dealer for replacement. The voltage or lamp number is usually found on the base of the bulb. If there are no numbers on the dial bulb, look in the receiver's literature. In case there is no identification, measure

Fig. 3-4. Six bayonet-type pilot lights illuminating sections of the radio dial. Measure the voltage across the bulb for correct voltage rating replacement. These are plug-ins for easy replacement.

the voltage across the dial bulb. If the voltage measured is 5.5 volts or so, use a 6-volt type. Select a 12-volt bulb when the measured voltage is between 7 and 12 volts.

Small bulbs with long leads are used mostly in tape players. These bulbs may be 6- or 12-volt types. Some operate from a separate ac power transformer winding and others work from the same dc voltage source as the drive motor. After replacement, apply a coat of silicon cement to hold them in place. Solder the respective leads where the defective bulb was connected.

STRINGING THE DIAL CORD

You might find the dial/cord arrangement in the AM/FM/MPX compact receiver a little more difficult than the ordinary radio. Usually, the front dial covers half the front area, with several more small pulleys creating an elaborate dial assembly. A dial/cord stringing guide should be used. Look for one in your service literature (Fig. 3-5). Sometimes it's difficult to restring the dial cord without a guide.

Select the same size of dial cord as the original. If the dial cord is broken into a couple of pieces, lay them together and measure the required length. Add six inches extra for tying the various knots. The dial/cord pointer is fastened into position after the stringing is completed.

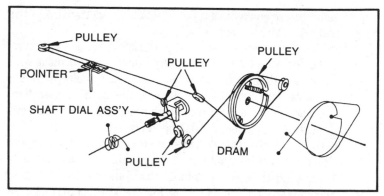

Fig. 3-5. Check the service literature for a dial cord-stringing guide.

Always start the cord from the solid end of the dial drum. The dial cord should be taut at all times. Wind the cord around the various pulleys and at least 3½ times around the dial shaft assembly. Check the direction the dial cord goes around the dial shaft. This will determine in which direction the pointer moves. Remember, the dial pointer goes in the same direction as the dial knob. Tie the dial cord to one end of the small spring with several knots. After the entire dial assembly has been checked out, apply silicon cement or glue at both dial/cord connections.

NO AM

The AM/FM/MPX receiver might have no AM, FM, or neither. To isolate the possible component, check both the AM and FM functions. If the FM is normal with no AM, go directly to the AM section. When the AM section is dead with very weak FM, suspect a defective i-f section. Both AM and FM front ends use the same i-f section.

Measure the voltage on the oscillator or converter transistor within the AM section. Locate this transistor with a parts layout schematic. When touching the probe to the base terminal, you should be able to tune in a weak local AM station at any point on the dial if the AM transistor is normal. If not, compare the voltage readings with those of the schematic.

Improper voltage readings on the AM oscillator transistor may indicate a defective transistor. Mark down the various transistor terminals. Remove the transistor with solder wick. Now test the transistor out of the circuit. Sometimes these small transistors will test okay but will not work in the circuit. Look up the exact replacement or use a universal type. Most universal transistors will function in the AM/FM chassis.

If an IC component is used as the oscillator, i-f, and detector, measure the voltage on all terminals. Write down each terminal voltage and compare them with the schematic. These voltages might be off only a fraction of a volt and still make the circuit inoperative. All voltages are generally incorrect within a leaky IC component, and the entire IC component must be replaced.

When only a couple of weak AM stations can be tuned in, suspect a defective rf transistor or antenna coil assembly. Sometimes only one AM converter transistor combines the rf and oscillator stages. Check the antenna coil connections for weak reception. These connection wires are very fragile and could be broken off the variable capacitor or at the antenna coil (Fig. 3-6). Check continuity with the R×1 scale of the VOM.

If the wire is broken off the variable capacitor and no leads are left on the capacitor terminals, solder the broken lead to the capacitor terminal with the most moving plates. Usually, an rf trimmer capacitor is close to this connection. Most antenna coils are wound with Litz wire that is difficult to solder. This smaller flexible wire must be tinned before it will make a good connection. Scrape back the cloth insulation with a pocket knife. Clean off the wire until you can see some copper. Now dip the wire end into rosin solder paste. Apply solder and tin the wire end. Now the connecting coil lead can be soldered to the broken connection.

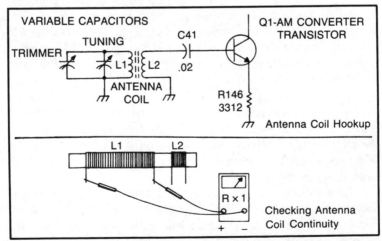

Fig. 3-6. For weak or local station reception only, check for broken leads to the antenna coil.

A weak FM and no AM problem might be caused by a defective first AM and second FM i-f amp transistor. This transistor amplifies both the FM and AM signals. Sometimes when this transistor is intermittent, you might find an i-f squeal or howl on the AM band. Measure the voltages of the transistor terminals and compare them with the schematic. The i-f transistor can be replaced with a universal type. Don't overlook a dirty or broken function switch when there is no AM or FM reception.

NO FM

When the AM/FM receiver has no output on FM but is normal on the AM band, suspect a defective FM oscillator transistor. Before removing the transistor, take a voltage measurement and compare it to the schematic. Check the voltage on each transistor in the FM section before any transistors are removed. Try to tune in a local FM station with the voltage test probe on the base terminal. If the station is weak but can be tuned in, the oscillator transistor is okay. Improper voltages and no signal might indicate the oscillator transistor is defective. High voltages might indicate a defective voltage-regulator circuit in the power source.

Note where and at what angle the oscillator transistor is mounted. Choose the original or a universal transistor. Use solder wick to remove the transistor from the pc board. Cut the leads of the new transistor the same length as the original, and mount the transistor back in the very same spot. If the terminal leads are too long or out of place, the transistor may not oscillate or the FM station will not be at the right frequency on the dial assembly.

FM fading or shifting frequency can be caused by a defective oscillator transistor or varicap diode. You might find the local station has shifted up or down the dial a quarter of an inch or so. First replace the oscillator transistor. If the stations still fade or shift in frequency, replace the varicap diode in the tuning circuit. You might have to retune the oscillator coil or trimmer after the varicap diode is replaced. Also, FM fading with microphonic noises might be caused by a defective padder capacitor mounted on top of the large tuning capacitor.

Intermittent FM reception can result from any faulty FM transistor, poor connections, or poorly soldered joints on the pc board. Press against various areas of the pc board and note when the FM reception cuts in and out. Move various components with an insulated tool. Soldering several pc board component connections might cure the intermittent problem. Spray each transistor with cold spray and watch for a reaction.

Check the rf FM transistor for weak FM reception. Measure the voltages on each terminal and compare them to the schematic. A leaky or open rf transistor may cause weak FM reception on local stations. The rf FM transistor may be replaced with the original or a universal replacement.

Very weak and noisy FM reception might be caused by the multiplex section. Check the circuit for an IC component. When the FM is weak and the FM stereo light stays on all the time, suspect a leaky MPX IC component. Replace the IC if it feels very warm. IC components do not ordinarily run warm unless they are in the audio output circuit.

When weak reception is noted in both AM and FM, check the first and second i-f stages. Because both AM and FM utilize the same i-f section, weak reception would be at the input side of the i-f stages. Check and compare the voltages of the two transistors. Remove the transistor and check for an open or leaky condition. All i-f transistors can be replaced with universal replacements.

ERRATIC FM

Clean the AM/FM switch or selector if the FM cuts out or appears erratic. Spray cleaning fluid down into the switch assembly and work the switch back and forth to clean the contacts. The FM station now should stay put. Likewise, clean all switch terminals on the selector assembly. Rotate the selector switch over and back to help clean the contacts.

Erratic FM reception can be caused by intermittent transistors or IC components. Spray each component with coolant and note if the stations appear normal. Loose or broken variable capacitor ground and bottom-board connections can produce erratic FM. Solder all contacts around the variable capacitor. Recheck the FM antenna connections.

FM ANTENNA PROBLEMS

When FM stations cut down in volume, suspect poor antenna FM connection at the receiver or a broken lead-in wire. FM hissing noise will appear with a weak FM station. Check the local FM stations for normal reception. If the local FM stations are normal and the distant stations are weak, check the FM antenna and cable connections.

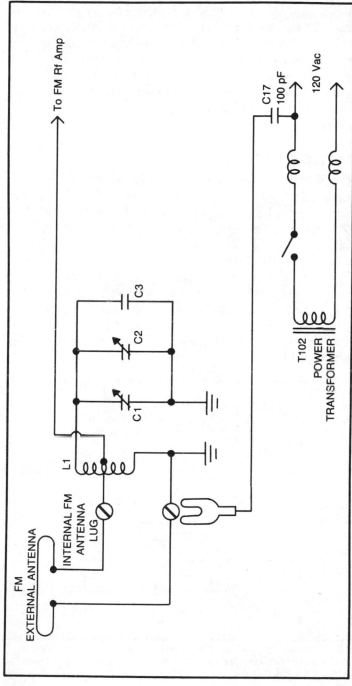

Fig. 3-7. Make sure the small wire lug is fastened to one of the antenna screws for good local FM reception. A good directional outdoor FM antenna will pull in distant stations.

Make sure the small lug wire is tight and snug at the FM terminals. Change the lug to the other screw terminal and note if the FM reception is improved (Fig. 3-7). Actually, the lug wire connects to a small capacitor on one side of the power line. If the receiver is connected to the outside antenna, check the cable wire for breaks. Check all 76-ohm cable connections if round cable is used. Note if the antenna is turned in the right direction with a yagi-type FM antenna (Fig. 3-8).

DEFECTIVE STEREO INDICATOR

The FM stereo light will come on when you tune through the FM band, indicating a stereo broadcast station. You might find that a defective stereo light never comes on, stays on for only a few seconds, or stays on all the time. The FM stereo indicator may or may not have a small rheostat to adjust the threshold lighting of the stereo light bulb (Fig. 3-9).

These stereo bulbs are very small in size. Some come with long leads, like those found in the eight-track tape player track indicator lights. Remove one lead of the bulb and measure for continuity. Set the VOM to R×1 scale. An open bulb will read infinite. Check the literature for correct bulb replacement. It's best to obtain one from the manufacturer.

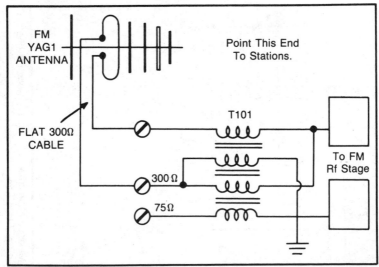

Fig. 3-8. Erratic or noisy FM reception can be caused by a broken antenna lead-in or poor connection. Make sure the directional antenna is pointing toward the distant FM stations.

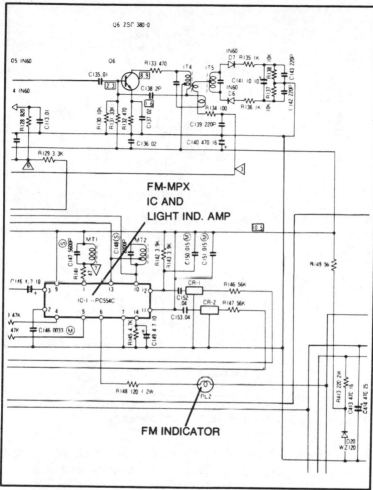

Fig. 3-9. The FM indicator light comes on when the dial tunes in a stereo station. The indicator light can operate from an IC or transistor amplifier.

The FM indicator light may not come on if the reception is weak or if there is a defective indicator light circuit. A transistor or IC component usually precedes the indicator light. Clip the voltmeter across the FM indicator light bulb terminals. Now tune through a known FM stereo station. The voltage should sharply peak or dip when the FM station is tuned in (Fig. 3-10).

Check the voltages on the transistor or IC indicator terminals. A leaky IC or transistor might cause the light to stay on at all times. An open indicator component will not allow the light to come on.

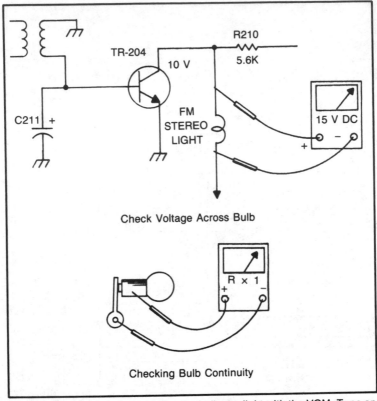

Fig. 3-10. Check the voltage across the indicator light with the VOM. Tune an FM station in and note the dip of the meter pointer.

If the lightbulb continuity is normal with the same voltage, it's best to replace the suspected IC or transistor indicator amplifier.

Do not attempt to adjust any of the i-f or multiplex coils and transformers without proper test equipment. You might make things worse by diddling with the core of the transformer. Take the unit to a qualified audio receiver technician if i-f and multiplex alignment is needed. Very seldom do these receivers get out of alignment unless someone fools with these adjustments.

NOISY VOLUME CONTROL

Spray a noisy volume control with cleaning fluid while rotating the control back and forth. Place the small tube of the spray can inside the control terminals of a round volume control. Flat, sliding-type controls can be sprayed from the front; then slide the control up and down to clean it. When the control is very noisy and the sound cuts out at a certain point on the control, replace the control. All round controls can be replaced with the original or universal types, but most sliding controls should be obtained from the manufacturer. The resistance of the volume controls within the receiver runs from 5 K to 50 K ohms. Volume controls are easy to acquire and replace.

If the volume can't be turned up or down, suspect a broken control. This usually occurs in shipment or when the unit is dropped. Replace the entire control when the wiper blade or the control resistance is broken. If you encounter a balance control acting like a volume control, check for a broken ground connection at the speaker terminal (Fig. 3-11).

LOCATING VARIOUS CHANNEL NOISES

Excessive hum, crackling, "frying" noise, or motorboating sounds might be heard in an amplifier channel. First isolate the amplifier section by turning down the volume control. If the hum or noise is present with the volume control turned down, the noisy component is in the output section. On the other hand, if the noise can be controlled with the volume control, the defective part is in the input section.

When excessive hum is heard in both the speaker and in an amplifier channel, suspect a defective filter capacitor. These capacitors are very large types, ranging from 1000 to 4700 μF. Sometimes only one large filter capacitor is used with several decoupling capacitors in the lower voltage stages. Simply shunt a 2200 μF capacitor across the suspected filter capacitor with the

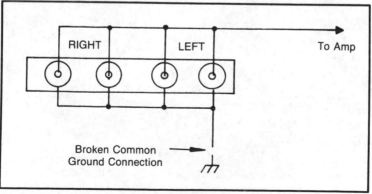

Fig. 3-11. When the balance control acts like a volume control, check for a broken ground connection at the speaker terminal.

power cord disconnected. Remove the old capacitor and install a new one if the hum disappears. Also, check for a broken lead or poorly soldered connection on the filter capacitor.

A low hum might be heard in only one channel, caused by a defective decoupling filter capacitor. If the hum is present at all times and rotating the volume control does not isolate the trouble (Fig. 3-12), start by shunting a 500 μF capacitor across each decoupling capacitor in the defective channel disconnecting the power before each. Tack the shunting capacitor across the suspected one with a soldering iron. Check the capacitor by restoring the power. When the hum disappears, remove the old capacitor and install a new one.

Look for a defective transistor when a popping or frying noise is heard. Locate and isolate the correct channel. Apply several coats of coolant to the suspected transistors, one at a time. When the frying noise ceases, replace the defective transistor.

Most frying noises are caused by a transistor or IC in the audio output stages. The noisy transistor may be located by using a sepa-

Fig. 3-12. A defective decoupling capacitor might cause low hum in one channel. With the power plug pulled, shunt each one, one at a time, with a known electrolytic capacitor. Temporarily tack on each capacitor with a soldering gun.

56

rate amplifier and speaker. Simply signal-trace each audio stage until you can hear the noisy one, then remove and replace the suspected transistor. Noisy transistors cannot be located with a transistor tester.

A frying noise with a low hum could be caused by a leaky output transistor and burned bias resistor. Check near the audio output transistor for overheated resistors. Replace both audio output transistors if you have noisy conditions. Don't overlook a small leaky bias diode in the input circuit of one of the output transistors.

If only one IC is found in the audio output circuits, replace the IC. Sometimes spraying coolant on the IC will make it act up. A defective IC audio output component can cause motorboating sounds. Tighten all pc board screws and check for broken ground straps or metal shields found in the audio circuit for possible sources of motorboating conditions.

DEFECTIVE CHANNELS

Either sound channel can develop a weak, dead, or intermittent condition. When both channels are dead, suspect problems in the power supply. Measure the voltage source to the output transistors. Suspect a defective voltage regulator circuit or burned voltage-dropping resistors. It's possible to find one or two separate IC output components defective when both channels are weak or dead.

If either channel is dead, measure and compare the voltage on the output transistors. Check around the output transistor for burned bias resistors (Fig. 3-13). When one or both output transistors become leaky, the emitter bias resistor will usually become overheated and burn. Sometimes the shorted condition may overload the power supply and burn out the primary winding of the power transformer. Also, check for burned pc wiring around the output transistor terminals.

Dead conditions might be caused by open or leaky af or driver transistors. If handy, use a separate amplifier to signal-trace the dead channel. Go from base to collector of each transistor and note the gain of each stage. You might want to compare the signal at any given point with the other good channel. The signal can be traced right to the speaker terminals. Don't overlook the large electrolytic speaker coupling capacitor for possibly creating a dead channel (Fig. 3-14).

Suspect the output IC for a no-sound condition. Check the sound at the input terminal. If it's good and there's no signal at the output,

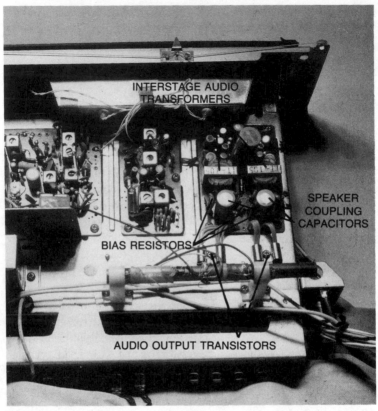

Fig. 3-13. Check around the output transistors for burned bias resistors. Both output transistors should be replaced when one is found to be defective.

suspect a defective IC. Measure and compare the voltages on the IC terminals. If the IC is leaky, all voltages will be lower. Replace the IC with the original or a universal replacement.

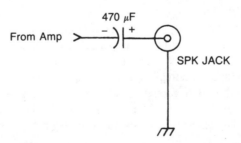

Fig. 3-14. A no-output condition might be caused by open speaker coupling capacitors. Either shunt the capacitor with another or signal-trace with a separate amplifier to locate the defective one.

When one of the channels is a lot lower in volume than the other and will not balance, check for a weak stage. Weak conditions are caused by open or leaky transistors, coupling capacitors, and by resistors changing their value. A weak stage may be located with an outside amplifier or scope. After the weak stage is found, take voltage and resistance measurements to locate the defective component.

A weak stage may be caused by a leaky or open transistor. A transistor itself never becomes weak; it is either good, open, or leaky. Higher-than-normal collector voltage may indicate the transistor is open. No emitter voltage indicates the transistor is open. Practically the same voltage measurement on all terminals might point to a leaky transistor. Incorrect bias voltage between emitter and base terminals can indicate a leaky or open transistor.

Repeated weak conditions might be caused by an open or dried-up coupling capacitor. These capacitors are electrolytic types located in the transistorized circuits. They are usually found in the pre-amp and af sections of the amplifier (Fig. 3-15). Sometimes the internal connecting terminals open or the dielectric material loses capacitance.

Use a separate amplifier to locate the defective capacitor. Check the signal on both terminals of the capacitor. Replace the capacitor when the signal is weak on one side. The same signal should be heard on both sides of the capacitor. Shunting a known capacitor across the suspected one can locate the defective one.

Intermittent conditions within the amplifier circuits can be caused by transistors, coupling capacitors, variable resistors, or poorly soldered board connections. The intermittent transistor might act

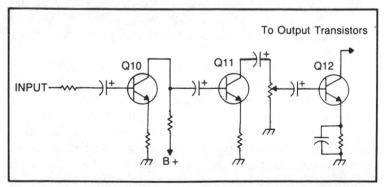

Fig. 3-15. Weak signal can be caused by an open or shorted electrolytic coupling capacitor found in the front end of most amplifiers. Locate the defective capacitor with a separate amplifier or shunt a known capacitor across the suspected one.

up when coolant is sprayed on it or just by moving the transistor on the pc board. Checking the transistor in a tester will not show an intermittent problem unless the transistor acts up when tested. The intermittent transistor usually snaps on when checked in an outside transistor tester. Locate the defective transistor by signal-tracing and voltage measurements, then replace the suspected transistor with a new one.

Check the signal on both sides of a suspected intermittent coupling capacitor with a separate amplifier. Sometimes, moving the capacitor around will make it cut in and out. If the suspected capacitor comes out of the intermittent state when the test leads are applied to the terminals, replace it. The same thing may occur with another capacitor shunted across it. Replacement of a suspected capacitor usually solves many intermittent signal problems. Always observe correct polarity when replacing an electrolytic capacitor.

DISTORTED CHANNELS

Excessive distortion found in any channel can be caused by a defective transistor, burned bias resistor, leaky or open bias diode, or a leaky coupling capacitor (Fig. 3-16). The distorted stage can be located with an external amplifier. Switch the radio on and signal trace the music from the base to the collector terminal of each transistor. When the signal can no longer be heard, replace the suspected transistor.

Most distortion problems are caused by the driver and audio output transistors or both. The driver transistor can go open or become leaky. On local radio stations, the signal can usually still be heard with an open driver transistor. Check the volume of the collector load and emitter bias resistor while the driver transistor is out of the circuit. You might find defective output transistors and a leaky driver transistor.

Excessive distortion is generally caused by leaky audio output transistors. Check around the output transistors for burned bias resistors. These resistors may be under 1 ohm. Remove each audio output transistor and test it out of the circuit for leakage or open tests. You might find one output transistor leaky while the other is open (Fig. 3-17). Sometimes only one transistor will be found open, but it's best to replace both transistors when one is found defective. Also check the driver transistor and bias resistors with the two output transistors out of the circuit.

Distortion may be produced by a leaky bias diode. These diodes are found in the base and emitter circuits of the audio output

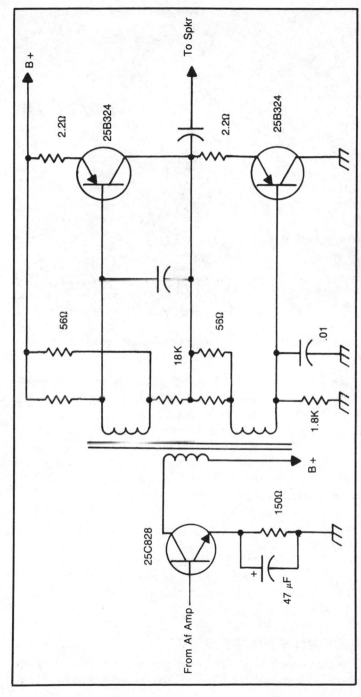

Fig. 3-16. Excessive distortion can be caused by defective transistors, burned bias resistors, leaky or open bias diodes, or coupling capacitors in the audio output stages.

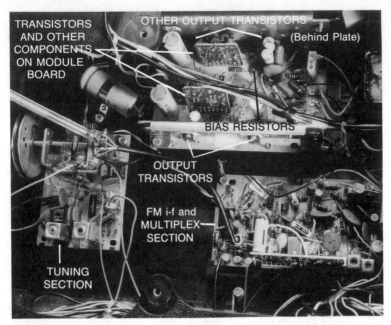

Fig. 3-17. Replace both audio output transistors when one is found leaky or open. Check the resistance of all bias resistors with the output transistors out of the circuit.

transistor. Be careful to install them with correct polarity. If the diode is installed backwards, you might still have distortion. Remove one end of the diode for correct ohmmeter tests.

When an IC is found in an audio output stage having distortion, replace the IC. In some larger amplifiers, you may find one large power IC for both channels. Check the signal at the input terminal of the IC with an external amplifier. If the signal is normal but there is distortion on the output terminal, replace the leaky IC.

Excessive distortion might occur with a low hum in IC or transistor circuits. Don't overload a floating electrolytic capacitor to cure excessive hum and distortion. One of the filter capacitor leads may be off, reducing the B+ voltage source. In turn, low voltage applied to the output transistor may produce distortion and hum conditions. A shorted speaker cable may also cause distortion and weak volume.

CHECKING THE SPEAKERS

You might find one or two permanent magnet (PM) speakers in each stereo channel of the FM-MPX stereo receiver. Suspect one of the speakers is open when less volume is noted in either channel. A vibrating or erratic speaker can result from a loose speaker cone. Check each speaker with the low-ohm range of the DMM or VOM. An open speaker will read infinity. The speaker impedance should be quite close to the resistance measurement with an accurate DMM (Fig. 3-18).

If only one large speaker is found in each stereo channel, clip another speaker across the dead one. Disconnect the speaker wire if the sound is distorted or mushy before clipping another speaker into the circuit. Try to replace the defective speaker with the same impedance, size of magnet, and diameter. If possible, replace it with the manufacturer's replacement speaker.

DEFECTIVE HEADPHONE JACKS

The sound may be dead in either or both channels with a defective headphone (earphone) jack. If only one channel is dead, signal-trace with an external amplifier or speaker. Clip a speaker with a small 5 μF capacitor (50 V) in series to chassis ground (Fig. 3-19). Start at the audio output transistor in the dead channel. Signal-trace to the speaker coupling capacitor. From the speaker coupling capacitor, the amplifier leads usually go to the self-shorting headphone jack. Then signal-trace the signal in and out of the headphone jack.

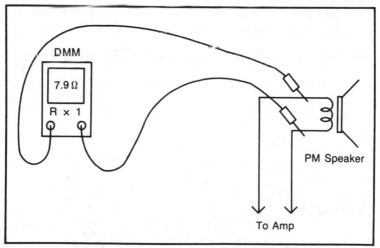

Fig. 3-18. Check the suspected speaker with the ohmmeter. When checking the voice coil resistance with the DMM, the measured resistance should match the speaker impedance.

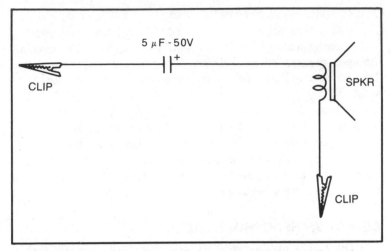

Fig. 3-19. Use clip leads with a 5-μF, 50-volt electrolytic capacitor to locate the defective channel or headphone jack. Check the signal into and out of the suspected headphone jack.

You should have a signal from both the right and left channels of the headphone jack. If the signal goes in but doesn't come out, suspect a defective self-shorting contact (Fig. 3-20). Spray tuner lube down into the headphone plug area. Push the headphone plug in and out to help clean the contact points. Replace the stereo headphone jack if the music still cannot be heard after cleanup. You might also find a separate switch on the front panel that switches out the speakers before the headphone jack is active.

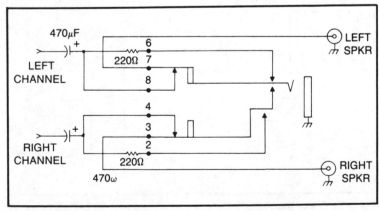

Fig. 3-20. A typical headphone jack circuit showing how the signal is coupled to the input terminals 8 and 4.

HOW TO CHECK HEADPHONES

Defective headphones might have erratic reception, with one dead headphone or they cut in and out when the cable is moved. The music may become erratic when the male plug is moved. Only one of the headphones may have mushy or distorted sound. The same headphone problems can occur in both low priced and expensive headphones (Fig. 3-21).

The headphone impedance can vary from 8 to 2000 ohms. The headphone impedance in small radios or cassette players can vary from 8 to 39 ohms. The old-style crystal sets and radios have headphones having about 2000 ohm impedance. The frequency varies from 20 to 20,000 Hz.

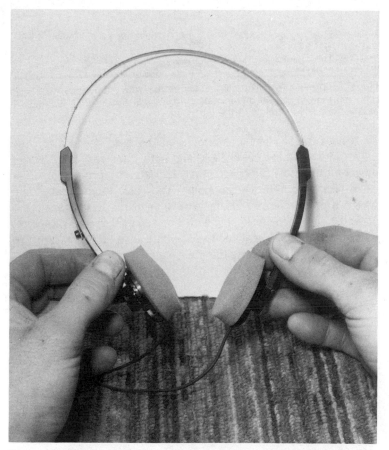

Fig. 3-21. Check the continuity of headphones with the low-ohm scale of the DMM. Flex the headphone cord when reception is broken or erratic.

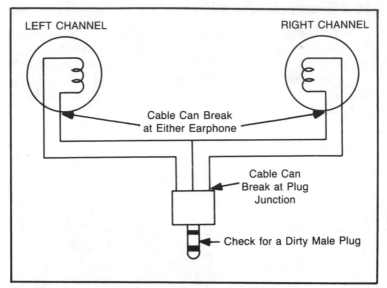

Fig. 3-22. The headphone cable usually breaks where it enters the case or right at the male plug. Cut off the male plug and install a universal headphone plug if the cable is broken at the plug end.

Check the headphone continuity at the male stereo plug (Fig. 3-22). Flex the headphone cable and note if the resistance varies or goes to infinity; the latter might indicate an open voice coil or cable wire with a dead headphone. The cable often breaks right where it enters the molded male plug or at the headphones. Replace the headphone male plug with a stereo universal replacement. Finally, a dirty male headphone plug can cause erratic sound; this can be detected by rotating the male plug in the headphone socket.

4

Car Radio Repairs

Making repairs on your own car radio is not only fun, but it can also save you money. You might have to stand on your head to make a few tests or remove the defective radio, but it's not all that bad. Usually car radio repair is not too difficult.

CHECKING THE FUSE

Before removing the car radio, check the fuse, antenna, and speaker. These three things should be checked thoroughly before going any further. You can save yourself a lot of time and trouble by checking these three items. The radio might be dead because of an open fuse (Fig. 4-1). The fuse can be located in a fuse holder close to the radio or on the firewall, or it might be on a block with other fuses. The radio fuse should be marked. Also check for a fuse holder in series with the hot lead going to the radio. Remove the fuse and test it. Set the VOM on the R×1 ohm scale. A good fuse will show a shorted condition or about zero ohms. No reading will indicate the fuse is open and should be replaced.

If bad, replace the fuse with a new one with the same value. This amp value will be marked on one end of the fuse or holder. Keep the radio switch off when inserting a new fuse. Install the fuse and turn the radio on. If the fuse blows out at once, the radio must be pulled for repair.

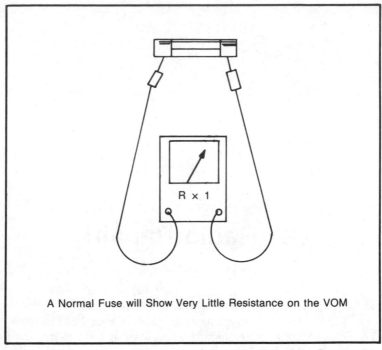

A Normal Fuse will Show Very Little Resistance on the VOM

Fig. 4-1. Before removing the radio from the car, check the fuse. Remove the fuse and check continuity with the VOM on the R×1 scale.

CHECKING THE ANTENNA

If the radio sounds noisy, intermittent, or very weak, suspect a defective antenna. Remove the antenna lead from the radio. Be very careful not to pull the antenna cable from the plug—sometimes these shielded antenna plugs are just crimped to the mesh part of the cable. Also, if the antenna is molded right in the windshield, you might accidentally pull the wires out of the windshield. Carefully remove the antenna plug.

When only local stations can be heard, suspect a broken antenna lead. Also, water inside the antenna cable can cause weak or dead conditions. Excessive noise can be caused by a poor ground connection at the base of the antenna. You might hear excessive motor noise if you have a loose male antenna plug. Motor noise can be reflected to the antenna from the hood area. A poor bond at the base of the antenna can pick up motor noise when the auto is running. If the antenna is loose at the mounting area, tighten it with a wrench. Do not use a pair of pliers or you will scratch and mar the antenna assembly.

When the auto antenna is mounted properly outside on the top cowl or fender, you can quickly check the condition of the antenna with the VOM (Fig. 4-2), set at the R×1 scale. Now connect the meter lead to the center terminal of the antenna plug. Place the other lead on the outside antenna dipole. If the antenna is normal, you should have a resistance of under 10 ohms. Infinite reading indicates the antenna lead is open. An erratic reading indicates a poor or broken lead.

If the VOM readings are normal but the radio is weak in volume, suspect water inside the antenna cable. Set the VOM to the R×1 scale. Connect one lead to the shielded cable and the other lead to the center terminal of the antenna plug. If the meter shows any reading at all, install a new antenna.

The internal wire of the antenna cable usually breaks right at the male plug or where it connects to the base of the dipole assembly. If the wire is open, cut off the male plug at the cable end. Now measure for continuity between antenna dipole and cut wire. If normal, install a new antenna plug. With an infinite reading, pull on the end of the small wire. If broken, the small copper wire will pull right out of the cable. Either replace the antenna cable or install a new antenna.

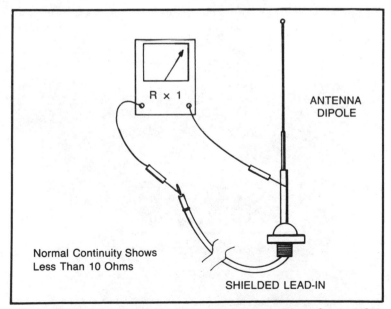

Fig. 4-2. Check the auto antenna for open or leaky conditions. Set the VOM on the R×1 scale. Check from center antenna plug terminal to antenna dipole.

If you find that the antenna cable is broken and the antenna is located inside the windshield, you can install a dipole antenna outside. Use a fender or top cowl mounting antenna. It's a lot cheaper than putting a new windshield in an automobile, which is a rather expensive proposition!

After the new antenna is installed, adjust the antenna trimmer. This trimmer capacitor is usually located at the front of the radio, behind the tuning-shaft knobs (Fig. 4-3). In some models, the antenna trimmer might be located quite close to where the antenna plug enters the radio. Pull the antenna dipole to the correct extended length, then adjust the antenna trimmer capacitor. Select a station, above 1400 kHz, and adjust the trimmer for maximum volume.

CHECKING THE SPEAKERS

Most auto radios have a speaker under the dash or in the back seat area. With the addition of a tape player, there might be several speakers located around the sides, back, or front of the auto. When only one speaker sounds mushy and distorted, remove the defective speaker. If all speakers are dead or distorted, suspect problems within the radio.

Before removing the car radio, check for an open or distorted speaker. The speaker voice coil can open, producing intermittent

Fig. 4-3. After repairing the antenna, tune the antenna trimmer to match the radio input. Adjust the antenna to the correct height; now turn the trimmer screw for maximum volume with a weak station tuned in (above 1400 kHz).

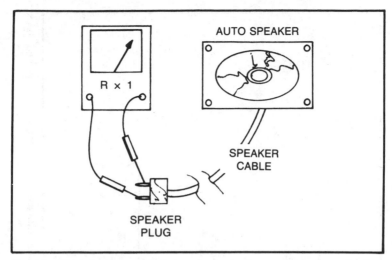

Fig. 4-4. Check the voice coil of the speaker before removing the radio. Set the VOM to R×1 and check to the speaker cable.

or no reception. For an intermittent condition, turn the volume up halfway and push against the cone of the speaker. Note if the volume cuts up and down. If the reception is mushy or tinny, suspect that the speaker cone has been dropped. Since a car is out in all kinds of weather, the speaker cone can become warped. It's possible that water has leaked down from the windshield area onto the speaker.

Check the speaker continuity with the VOM set on the R×1 scale (Fig. 4-4). Connect the VOM leads to the speaker cable. Some of the early speakers have a 3.2-ohm impedance. Today the speaker impedance is from 8 to 40 ohms. Any continuity reading usually indicates the speaker voice coil is normal. To be sure, clip an extra speaker to the speaker cable connections and turn the radio on. If the substitute speaker is normal, replace the old speaker.

After removing the defective speaker, check for the correct voice coil impedance. The new speaker should have the same impedance. Sometimes the impedance value is stamped on the frame of the speaker. If not, check the radio service literature. Most car radio service books list the correct impedance. Take the speaker to your local radio, TV or radio parts dealer for replacement. Most speaker types are readily available; only a few special speakers are difficult to locate.

Some auto radios have a fader control (Fig. 4-5). The fade control is found when speakers are mounted in both the front and rear or

71

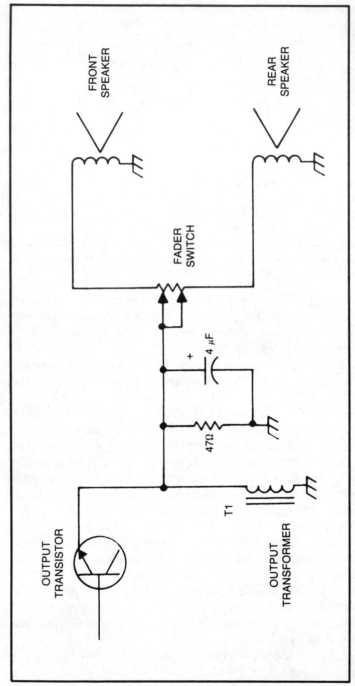

Fig. 4-5. In some car radios, a fader control is used to balance the front and rear speakers. Turn the fader control to midrange and check the sound of each speaker.

in stereo operation. Make sure the fade control is in the center of rotation when checking sound at either speaker location. An open or damaged fade control can be checked with the VOM, set to the R×1 scale. These fade controls are wire-wound controls, mounted behind the tuning shaft on most auto radios.

DIAL POINTER WON'T MOVE

The radio must be pulled from the auto to make dial cord or other similar repairs. You might find the radio is held in place with two mounting nuts at the front and one bolted strap at the rear. Remove all of the knobs. Use a long pair of pliers or sockets to remove the shaft mounting nuts. Then remove the one mounting bolt at the rear of the radio. In some autos, you find one or two rear mounting bolts to the rear side of the radio.

The dial cord might be broken or the dial pointer could be loose or slipping on the dial knob shaft. Some of these dial cord assemblies are very simple and others very complex (Fig. 4-6). Try to figure out how the broken cord goes around the various shafts and pulleys. If you can't figure it out, then check the service literature for correct dial cord replacement (Fig. 4-7). Use the same size cord for replacement. Note if the dial pointer moves in the same direction as the dial knob. Check for local radio stations at the correct frequency on the dial. Cement the pointer knob and cord ends with glue or silicone cement.

Before leaving the dial assembly, check the dial light. Most dial bulbs are located just behind or at the ends of the dial assembly.

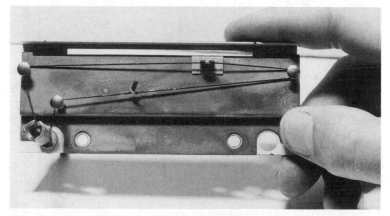

Fig. 4-6. A simple dial-cord assembly. Note that no springs are used to keep the dial cord taut.

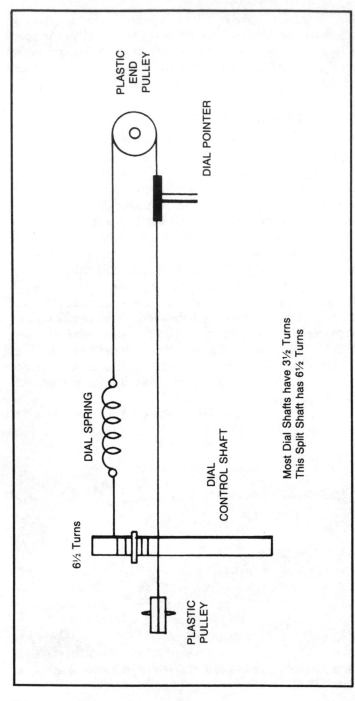

PLASTIC
END
PULLEY

DIAL POINTER

DIAL SPRING

DIAL
CONTROL SHAFT

Most Dial Shafts have 3½ Turns
This Split Shaft has 6½ Turns

6½ Turns

PLASTIC
PULLEY

Fig. 4-7. A typical dial-cord arrangement in a car radio. Be sure to move the dial pointer for correct position on the dial scale. Tune in a known local station and set the dial pointer.

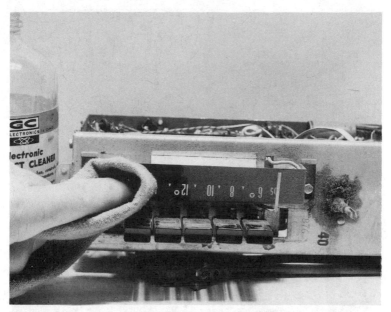

Fig. 4-8. Clean the front dial and push-button assembly with window spray. Use a cloth or small brush to get to the most difficult places. Also check the dial light while the dial assembly is apart.

If the dial light will not light or the glass appears dark, replace it. Also, clean the dial and glass enclosure with cleaning fluid or window cleaner (Fig. 4-8). A small paint brush with window cleaner does a nice job of cleaning the dial and push-button assembly.

If the dial-cord assembly is normal but the dial does not function, suspect a defective push-button assembly. In some car radios, the push-button assembly might not spring back into dialing position. Check for slippage at the cam assembly. Apply rosin or non-slipping compound between the rubber and cork drive areas. Sometimes bending the shaft lever outward provides more tension (Fig. 4-9).

DEAD RADIO

A dead radio can be caused by a defective fuse, bad on-off switch, defective output transistors, or improper voltage applied to the various circuits (Fig. 4-10). While in the car, turn the radio on and off and listen for a clicking noise in the speaker. You know the speaker and audio circuits are functioning if a thump or click is heard each time the radio is turned on. Quickly rotate the volume control up and down. A scratchy sound indicates normal audio signal. If the audio

CLUTCH AREA
Coat with Liquid Rosin
to Avoid Slippage

Pry out Bar
With
Screwdriver
for More
Tension

Fig. 4-9. Check the push-button assembly when the dial pointer doesn't move. A jammed or damaged push-button assembly can keep the dial drum from turning.

circuits do not pass the on/off clicking test, suspect a defective audio output transistor. Also check the speaker and audio circuits.

After the radio is removed from the car, it must be connected to a 12-volt dc power supply or battery. Be very careful to apply the correct polarity. Most American made cars are negative ground. Clip the speaker leads to another speaker for sound tests.

Turn the volume control wide open and place a screwdriver blade against the center terminal of the volume control. You should hear a loud hum. A weak hum might indicate weak audio circuits. No hum at all indicates that the audio section is dead.

If it is dead, remove the audio output transistor. Some are located on the rear apron or on the front mounting plate. Here you might find one or two mounting screws (Fig. 4-11). Check closely for a piece of insulation between the power transistor and chassis heat sink. This piece of insulation isolates the metal part of the transistor from the chassis. Usually the metal mounting area of the power-output transistor is the collector terminal.

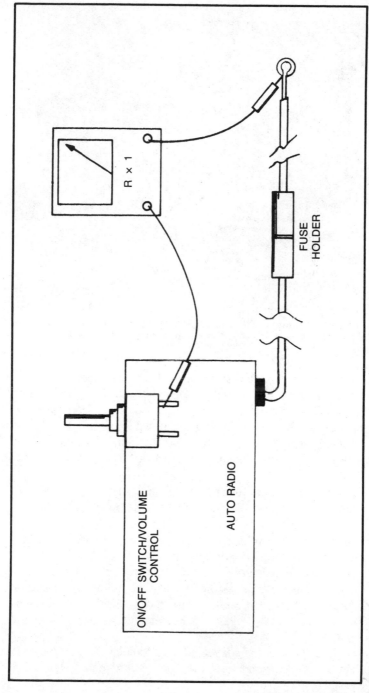

Fig. 4-10. In a dead radio, check continuity from the fuse holder to the ON/OFF switch. Set the VOM to the R×1 scale.

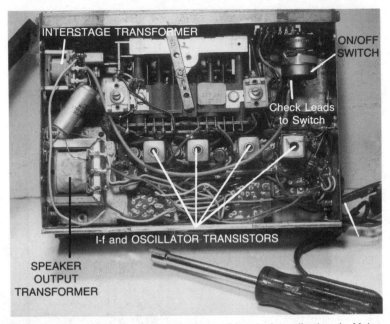

Fig. 4-11. Various areas to check for dead conditions in the radio chassis. Make sure the fuse, antenna, and speakers are checked in the auto before removing radio.

After taking the transistor out of the circuit, check it with a transistor tester. If a tester is not handy, accurate ohmmeter readings of the various terminals might indicate a leaky or open condition. A low ohmmeter reading between the collector and emitter terminals indicates that the transistor is leaky. Compare the ohmmeter readings of the suspected transistor with those in Fig. 4-12.

If the output transistor appears normal, suspect one of the af or driver transistors in the audio section. Remove one transistor at a time and test it with a transistor tester. Check for an open or leaky condition. Take voltage measurements and compare them with those found on the schematic diagram.

If a loud hum is heard during the screwdriver test at the volume control, suspect a dead front-end section. A defective oscillator or i-f transistor can also cause a dead radio condition. Again, test each transistor. Take voltage measurements at each transistor terminal.

When a transistor is suspected to be defective and a tester is not handy, take it to a radio/TV shop for accurate tests. When exact

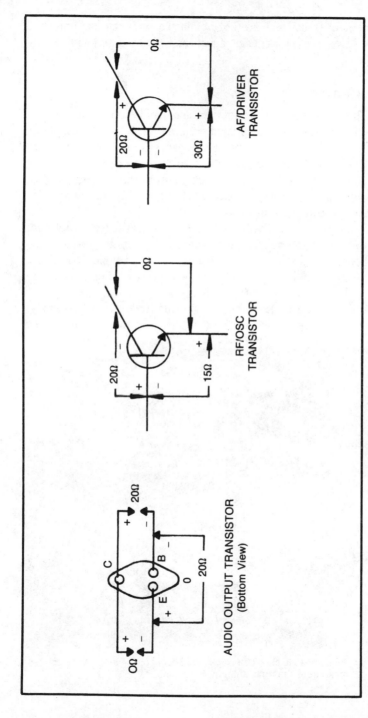

Fig. 4-12. A suspected transistor can be checked with the VOM. The power output transistor will usually show a leakage between collector and emitter if it is defective.

replacement transistors are not obtainable, you can use universal types. Most transistors in car radios can be substituted without any trouble.

WEAK RADIO

When only a few local radio stations can be received, suspect a defective rf transistor or antenna system (Fig. 4-13). If the antenna was checked while the radio was in the car, suspect a defective front end. Check for an open rf transistor. First measure the voltage on the transistor terminals and compare them to the schematic. High collector voltage indicates the transistor might be open. Remove the transistor and test it out of the circuit.

If the radio signal is still weak after the rf transistor is replaced, check for poor antenna jack connections. Sometimes the antenna coil (tied to the antenna jack) is broken off at one end. You might find the small coil is loose inside the chassis area. Simply re-tin the ends and solder it back into position.

Also check for broken wiring connections on the rf coil assembly. This coil assembly is a permability type located in the oscillator tuning

Fig. 4-13. Some areas to check for weak radio reception. Besides those pointed out here, make sure the auto antenna is normal.

assembly. Measure the coil windings for open conditions with the R×1 scale of the VOM. The coil wires usually break where they attach to the terminal strips. A broken iron core inside the tuning assembly can produce weak reception.

INTERMITTENT SOUND

Intermittent sound from a car radio can be caused by defective transistors, poor connections, a bad i-f transformer, a leaky coupling capacitor, or a cracked pc board. The intermittent condition of any electronic unit is obviously the most difficult to locate. Servicing the intermittent radio takes a lot of time and patience, but with several service aids and the proper know-how, the intermittent problems can be cured.

Try to isolate the intermittent problem to the front end or audio section of the auto radio. Spray each transistor with three coats of cold spray to determine if the transistor is intermittent. The defective transistor might have a poor internal connection causing intermittent reception. Cold spray should be applied when the radio is dead or with weak reception. If the radio "pops" on, suspect a defective transistor. Double check and apply heat from the soldering iron on the body of the transistor, but leave the iron on the transistor for only a second or two. The radio might cut out or drop in volume. Now spray the suspected transistor with cold spray. If the sound returns to normal, replace the intermittent transistor. The flat-type audio output transistors are noted for having internal intermittent conditions (Fig. 4-14).

The intermittent condition can also be caused by poorly soldered connections on the pc board. Gently flex or bend the board and note if the sound comes and goes. Solder all of the small connections in this section. (Always turn the radio off before soldering any pc connections.) Now check by twisting and pushing against the same section. A poorly soldered connection frequently occurs under a large blob of solder. Be very careful not to run solder between different areas of pc wiring.

Check for broken components or leads mounted on the pc board. Cracked or broken resistors cause a lot of intermittent problems. Move or twist the electrolytic coupling capacitor to check for internal breaks. Sometimes pulling on a certain component causes the radio to act up. You might have to, in very difficult situations, solder each and every soldered connection on the pc board to solve the intermittent condition.

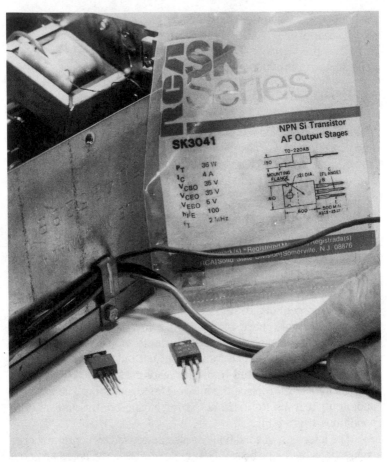

Fig. 4-14. If the output transistors are the flat, power-output types, check them for intermittent conditions. Take a pencil eraser and move each terminal. The sound will cut up and down if there is a bad internal connection.

LOUD HUM

A loud hum can be caused by a dried-up filter capacitor, leaky output transistor, or shorted output transformer. Shunt a 1000 μF 16-V capacitor across each filter capacitor until the hum disappears (Fig. 4-15). When the hum diminishes, replace the defective capacitor. In a car radio, you might find three or more capacitors in one can. Replace the entire filter can when one of the capacitors is defective.

If the hum is still present after shunting all filter capacitors, go directly to the audio output transistors. Note if the hum still exists

Fig. 4-15. Shunt a 1000 μF, 16-volt electrolytic capacitor across each filter until the hum disappears. Turn the power off first, then clip the capacitor in place, observing correct polarity.

with the volume turned down. If so, the hum is in the audio-output stages. Here you may find one or two power output transistors. Replace each one until the hum disappears. Usually the defective transistor is leaky, but it might not necessarily register on the transistor tests. If a faulty power IC output is found in the final stages, replace it.

After replacing the power output transistor and the hum is still present, suspect a burned or charred audio output transformer. You might find an audio output transformer with one or two transistors in push-pull operation. In some auto receivers you may also find transformerless transistors and IC output stages.

If a power output transformer is used, peel back the cover and note if the winding shows signs of running too warm. Generally, a leaky or shorted output transistor causes the transformer to overheat, resulting in shorted turns within the transformer winding. The VOM or VTVM might not accurately diagnose the suspected transformer if the winding is less than one ohm. The defective transformer should be replaced with the exact replacement.

HIGH-PITCHED WHISTLE

When a high-pitched whistle is heard with some hum, suspect the main filter capacitor. Note if the noise can be controlled with the volume. If not, the whistle is caused by the filter or output stages. Clip and shunt each filter capacitor with a 1000 μF capacitor until the whistle disappears. Turn the radio off while connecting the capacitor. Then replace the suspected capacitor. Also check for a broken tiewire at the filter capacitor terminals. A broken capacitor lead will act the same way.

If the whistling noise is still present after shunting all of the filter capacitors, then shunt each decoupling capacitor. Usually there are two or three of these 50-to 100-μF capacitors located on the pc board. Shunt each decoupling capacitor with one of the same value. Each capacitor should be clipped into the circuit with the power turned off. Then turn on the radio to see if the noise disappears.

A howling noise can be caused by a defective audio IC. Suspect the input audio IC when two different IC components are found in the audio circuit. You might find only one IC in the audio stages. Replace the suspected IC with an exact replacement.

DISTORTED MUSIC

Before working on the audio stages, check the speakers by clipping another speaker to the car radio. If all speakers are distorted, suspect problems in the audio output stages. You will find two separate audio stages in a radio with an eight-track stereo tape player. Distortion with weak conditions can be caused by a leaky or open power output transistor. It's possible to find both output transistors defective in a push-pull audio output stage. You might find one of the transistors running very hot. Replace both transistors (Fig. 4-16).

In audio stages with power IC components, suspect a leaky IC. Note if the IC is warm. If it is, replace it with an exact replacement.

Always check for burned bias resistors in the audio stages. Sometimes when a transistor becomes leaky or shorted, several bias resistors become overheated. These resistors have a very low resistance, sometimes below one ohm. Check the schematic and parts layout for the correct resistor value. Always replace these burned resistors with the exact value. For instance, if you have a burned resistor with a .47-ohm resistance, you can replace it with a .47-or .5-ohm resistor. Never replace the defective resistor with a 1-or 5-ohm value. If you do, you might still have distortion in the audio stage. Double check the bias resistor values with the schematic diagram.

NO AM BUT NORMAL FM

With no AM and normal FM reception, you know all of the stages

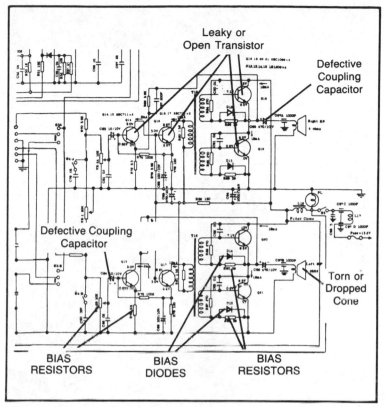

Fig. 4-16. Components causing possible distortion are found in this audio output circuit. A leaky or open power output transistor can cause excessive distortion. However, before replacing the transistor, check for correct resistance of the bias resistors

are functioning in the receiver except the AM section. First check for a dirty or defective AM/FM switch (Fig. 4-17). Then go directly to the AM stages. Usually a separate AM rf and AM oscillator stage is found in a car radio. Now locate the oscillator transistor from the chassis layout chart. Place the VOM test probe on the base terminal of the oscillator transistor. Tune the radio to a local station on the dial. You should be able to hear the local broadcast in the speaker. If you can't hear a local station, suspect a defective oscillator transistor (Fig. 4-18). Take voltage measurements on the transistor terminals and compare them with the schematic. Voltage tests with a VTVM or digital voltmeter should give accurate readings if the transistor is normal. You will find the voltages a little lower with the VOM. A higher-than-normal collector voltage indicates the transistor

Fig. 4-17. A dirty or worn AM/FM switch can cause dead or erratic AM reception. Spray the switch with tuner spray. Double-check the switch continuity with the VOM, set at the R×1 scale.

is open. The collector voltage usually equals the supply voltage if the transistor is open. Fairly equal voltages on all transistor terminals can indicate a leaky transistor. Replace the oscillator transistor if in doubt.

If you hear a local station with the test prod on the base terminal of the oscillator transistor, suspect a defective AM rf transistor. The same signal should be heard when you touch the test probe to the collector terminal of the rf transistor. Now touch it to the base terminal. If the signal remains the same or is lower, replace the rf-AM transistor. Remember to have the volume control wide open with these touch tests.

See also Chapter 6 "Common Portable Tape Player Tips," under the heading "NO AM BUT NORMAL FM."

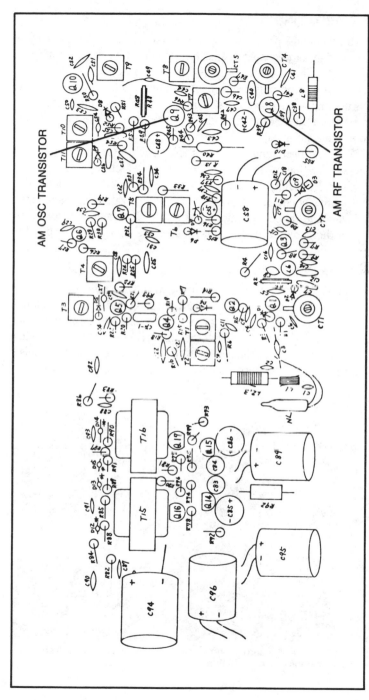

Fig. 4-18. No AM with normal FM reception can be caused by the AM oscillator transistor. Check the AM rf transistor for weak AM reception.

MOTORBOATING

Motorboating or a "putt-putt" noise might be caused by a defective filter or decoupling capacitor, power IC, or output transistor (Fig. 4-19). Check each suspected filter and decoupling capacitor by clipping or shunting a new capacitor across each one until the motorboating noise disappears. Clip the capacitor in place and then turn on the radio. Most car radio motorboating noises are caused by defective filter capacitors.

If the motorboating still exists after each filter and decoupling capacitor has been shunted, suspect a defective audio output transistor. Each output transistor must be replaced to eliminate the motorboating conditions. However, voltage or transistor tests might not reveal the defective output transistor. If a faulty power IC is found in the audio output circuits, the entire IC must be replaced.

NOISY RECEPTION

Determine if the noise is occurring in the car radio or is caused by the motor. Simply disconnect the antenna and turn the volume up (Fig. 4-20). Noisy ignition or pick-up noise by the antenna can often be eliminated by removing the antenna connection. If a frying noise is still heard, pull the car radio. Excessive car or ignition noise should be left to the auto mechanic or electronics specialist.

Fig. 4-19. Shunt the filter and decoupling capacitor for motorboating. A defective power-output transistor or IC may also cause motorboating.

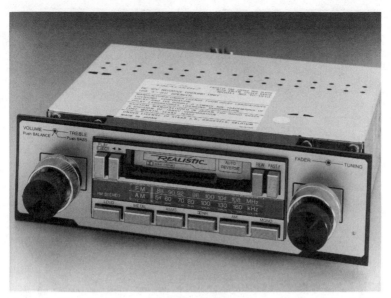

Fig. 4-20. Disconnect the antenna turn up the volume, and note if the frying noise is still present. If it is, pull the car radio.

A constant frying noise might be caused by a defective transistor or IC circuit. Determine if the noise is in the front end of the radio or in the audio circuits by lowering the volume control (Fig. 4-21). If the noise quits, it is in the front end. On the other hand, if the noise is still present with the volume control down, the noise is generated in the audio circuits. Signal-trace the noise with the external amp to locate the noisy stage, then replace the transistor or IC component in the noisy circuit. The intermittent frying noise might be caused by IC driver or power-output components.

Suspect a noisy i-f transformer, transistor, IC, or trimmer capacitor when noise occurs ahead of the volume control. Push and prod around on the i-f transformer and trimmer capacitors for noisy components with an insulated rod or pencil (Fig. 4-22). Check the body of the trimmer capacitors for water or white lines. Water inside the trimmer capacitors can cause them to arc when dc voltage is applied. Pushing down against the capacitor plates can cause the noise to stop or become intermittent. Solder all ground connections. Replace the entire IC component of the rf, oscillator, mixer, and i-f stages if the noise is still present after checking the other components.

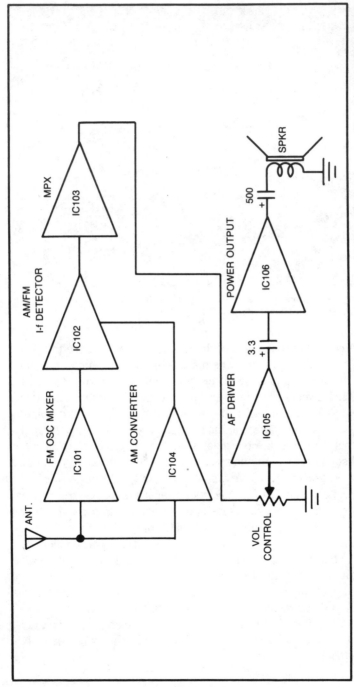

Fig. 4-21. Turn the volume control all the way down to see if the frying noise disappears. Suspect a noisy power IC or transistor if the noise is still audible.

RADIO WORKS OUT OF THE
CAR BUT NOT WHEN INSTALLED

Sometimes the car radio acts intermittently in the auto but plays perfectly on the repair bench. While the radio is on the bench, check for loose wires and broken ground terminals. Sometimes just twisting the radio cabinet can cause it to act up. Try spraying each transistor or IC with several coats of coolant to make it act up. Spray cleaning fluid inside the volume control and switches to clean possibly dirty contacts. Lower the "A" lead voltage to 9 volts and note if the radio cuts out, indicating a defective oscillator transistor or IC.

Inspect the fuse-connecting wire for loose or poor contacts inside the auto. Measure the dc car battery voltage at the radio terminal. Check the speaker plug for proper seating. Sometimes external speaker switches get broken and make poor contact. If one set of stereo speakers cuts in and out, check the speakers and cable for poor connections. After making repairs, give the radio a tryout over a bumpy road or street.

FRONT SPEAKER DEAD—REAR OKAY

Clip another PM speaker across the front speaker to determine if the speaker is open. Sometimes pushing up and down of the speaker cone will make an intermittent speaker act up. Recheck the

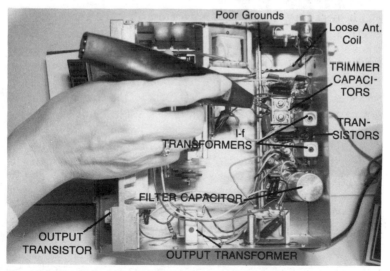

Fig. 4-22. Check the indicated parts for noise problems in the car radio. Solder all loose wires and ground connections.

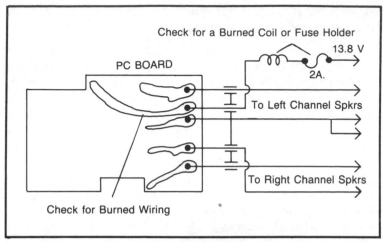

Fig. 4-23. Inspect the pc wiring after finding a shorted output IC or transistor. Carefully check the fuse holder and switch connections for burned wires.

speaker for an open voice coil with the ohmmeter. Inspect the speaker terminals for broken or poorly soldered connections. Suspect a defective audio channel or poor speaker wire connections when one complete stereo side is dead.

KEEPS BLOWING FUSES

Inspect the audio output transistors or IC components for overheating if there is a blown-fuse symptom. A leaky power IC or transistor can keep blowing the fuse. Test each output transistor in-circuit with the diode/transistor test of the DMM, or use a transistor tester, for leakage conditions. Take a resistance measurement at the voltage supply terminal of the power IC. A very low resistance measurement might indicate a leaky or shorted IC component.

After locating and replacing the leaky output transistor or IC, inspect the pc writing (Fig. 4-23). Sometimes a shorted component will burn the pc wiring in two or damage it. Repair burned pc wiring with short lengths of regular hook-up wire. Check the fuse holder for burned contacts or wiring. Inspect the switch terminals for burned or poorly soldered connections. Sometimes, if a higher amperage fuse or tin foil is placed around the fuse, you see a charred "A" lead and fuse assembly. In this case, replace the fuse assembly and burned pc-board wiring.

5

Car Cassette Player Repair

Many service problems of a car cassette player are identical to those of any other tape player. Tape head cleaning, typical lubricating areas, and speed functions are all similar.

In this chapter, you'll learn how to repair loading and ejecting problems and how to service the switching mechanism and solve abnormal speed conditions, for example. Here are some of the most common problems found in these units (Fig. 5-1).

RUNS TOO SLOW

Most speed problems can be solved with a good cleanup of the belt, pulleys, and all drive surfaces. Replacing a worn or stretched belt can solve a lot of speed problems (Fig. 5-2). Correct lubrication of the capstan, motor, and various pulley bearings can help, but when the tape barely moves, look for unusual conditions.

Over-lubricating the pulleys can result in very slow speeds. Do *not* spray oil on the rubber drive areas or capstan. Each bearing of any rotating component requires only a drop of light oil. Either remove the pulley or apply a drop of oil right on top of the bearing surfaces.

When excessive oil is found on the various pulleys and drive surfaces, clean each one carefully. Use alcohol and a cleaning stick. Clean off each drive area several times. Always remember that excessive oil might drip down on the other drive areas. You might

Fig. 5-1. The various components that are located on the top side of the car cassette player. Radio components are also found in this model.

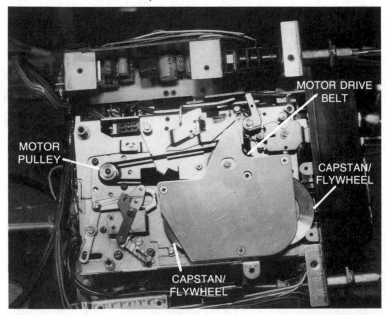

Fig. 5-2. Replacing a worn or stretched belt can solve a range of speed problems.

have to replace the rubber motor belt if it is saturated with oil. Cleaning up excessive lubrication can take a lot of time, but it is very necessary.

One of the least expected slow speed problems is caused by low battery voltage. Remove and repair the cassette player if it runs slow, however, if it still runs slow after being repaired, suspect a weak car battery. In most cases, the car can start and run when the battery is at 10 volts or less. Then again the car can also run with the battery installed backwards. But the cassette player or radio will not. Set the VOM at 15 Vdc and check the battery supply voltage (Fig. 5-3). The speed of any tape player might slow down with a 10- or 11-volt source. (Normally, the voltage of the car battery measures from 12 to 14 volts.)

RUNS TOO FAST

Most cassette speed problems are either slow or erratic speeds. If the player runs too fast, suspect (1) a defective motor, (2) excessive tape wrapped around the capstan, or (3) the speed control circuits. Although very few car cassette players have a separate speed control circuit, check the manufacturer's literature to see if your player has one.

To determine if the motor is running too fast, measure the voltage at the motor terminals. Set the VOM at the 15 Vdc scale. If

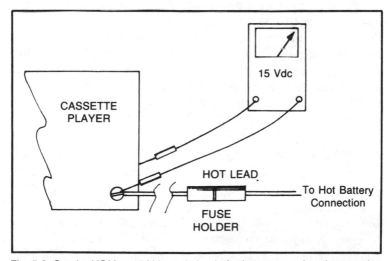

Fig. 5-3. Set the VOM at 15 Vdc and check the battery supply voltage at the cassette player terminals. Slow speed can occur if the car battery voltage falls to 10 volts or less.

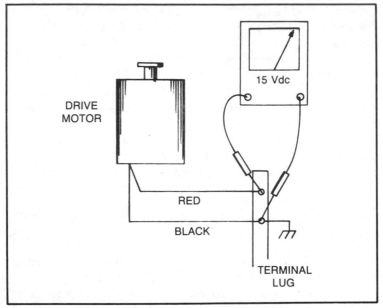

Fig. 5-4. Check the voltage at the drive-motor terminals.

the voltage is between 12 and 14 volts and the motor is running fast, replace it. These small motors will turn at 2400 rpm with 13.9 volts (Fig. 5-4).

Before removing the motor, check for excessive tape wrapped around the capstan or pinch roller. Excessive tape can pull out of the cassette and wrap tightly around the capstan drive area. The cassette is then usually discarded without any thought that it might have caused additional problems. Then, after a good cassette is inserted the recorder seems to be turning too fast. To remove all of the tape from around the capstan and pinch roller, you may have to remove both the top and bottom covers or the capstan/flywheel.

NORMAL SPEED FORWARD BUT TOO FAST IN REVERSE

Today a lot of cassette players can play both sides of the cassette without you having to turn the cassette over and insert again. The player automatically reverses direction at the end of the cassette, and plays the other side of the recording. Also, the tape can be reversed at any time by just pushing a reverse button.

Usually this whole process is accomplished with two different capstan/flywheels, a reversible motor, and switches. When the motor polarity is switched, the motor reverses direction, driving a different capstan/flywheel assembly. The other pinch roller and flywheel is disengaged from the tape area. Hence, there might be only one motor and stereo tape head in this system.

There are many mechanical problems that can occur with this system. The player might keep reversing directions after playing a small portion of the tape, and the speed might be different in the other direction. If the speed is normal in one direction and fast in reverse, suspect problems around the capstan/flywheel area.

Check for oil on the capstan/flywheel and drive pulley. Clean off with alcohol and a cleaning stick. Visually check if the drive pulley is slipping or has a worn rubber tire. The flywheel area might be shiny with a trace of silver on the drive pulley, indicating slippage at this point.

Because the same motor is unlikely to change speeds when the polarity is reversed, most inconsistent speed problems are caused by the capstan drive assembly. Check the capstan drive area for excessive tape wrapped around it. Only a few turns are needed to change the speed of the tape. The tape may be difficult to remove since it is wrapped tightly around the small capstan drive shaft. Always check for tape wrapped around the capstan when the speed changes in a reverse direction.

KEEPS REVERSING DIRECTIONS

There are several things that can be wrong when a cassette player keeps changing directions before one side is fully played. Suspect a defective cassette if the speed slows down and after a few minutes the player reverses direction. Excessive tape drag (jammed tape) can cause the reverse mechanism to switch automatically. If the same cassette is the only one that plays slow and reverses direction, discard it. Undoubtedly the tape is wound too tight.

If the player switches erratically without playing any portion of the tape, suspect a dirty commutator switch. The switch is made up of several metal rings around a plastic dowel with spring-wire contacts (Fig. 5-5). When the commutator stops rotating or poor switch contact is made, the dc polarity to the small motor is reversed. Look closely and you will find this slip-ring type switch on the end of a rotating pulley.

Clean the commutator rings with alcohol and a cleaning stick. Also, wipe off the three spring-like tongs on the commutator area. If the tong assembly is held into position with a small mounting screw,

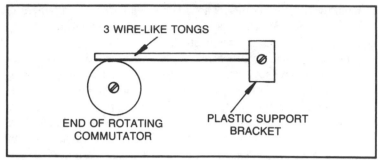

Fig. 5-5. A dirty commutator can cause the player to change directions rapidly. Check for a loose or broken belt if the commutator is belt driven.

loosen it so the switch assembly can be turned up away from the commutator area. Clean it thoroughly and reseat the assembly, making sure that the contact assembly is tight and will not shift out of position.

In some players, the mechanism might reverse automatically when the small belt driving the commutator is off. You may find the broken belt in the bottom pan area. With the belt off, the stopped commutator can cause the solenoid to keep energizing, resulting in erratic direction reversal. In some models, a reversing light will indicate which direction the tape is traveling. These two lights keep flashing on and off as the player changes direction. Replace the small belt with one having the same part number.

CASSETTE WON'T LOAD

When inserting a cassette to be played, the loading mechanism either snaps up into the cassette or it pulls the cassette down into the loading assembly. Power is applied to the motor and the tape begins to move. If the loading mechanism will not spring into position, the cassette will not play (Fig. 5-6); even the motor won't come on.

Because most types of cassette loading are mechanical in the car cassette player, check for bent cams, dry sliding areas, and loose springs. First clean all the sliding areas and bearings with alcohol. Apply light oil to the small bearings and light grease to the sliding areas. Visually inspect the different cams and levers to see if they are bent out of line.

Now insert another cassette to see if it will load. If the mechanism seems to pull or drag on one side before snapping into place, suspect a bent lever or loose spring. To tighten a loose spring, cut off a couple of winds.

Fig. 5-6. A cassette is loaded inside the cassette player. Notice the large loading spring to one side of the loading assembly.

You might find the loading mechanism snaps into place but will allow the tape to turn. Look for bent spindles or cassette alignment levers. See if the spindle or turntable is inside the spider area of the cassette. If the spindle is bent too far out of line or downward, the cassette will not load properly. Sometimes the spindles are bent out of line when the mechanism is sluggish and extra force is applied in loading the cassette (Fig. 5-7). If the spindle is pushed downward, it might turn but not touch or engage the spider of the cassette.

When the loading mechanism is bent too far out of line the whole loading unit must be replaced. It's best to try to repair the loading mechanism, because they are very difficult to obtain. Most loading mechanisms can be repaired by realigning the small levers and cams. A good job of cleaning and lubrication usually solves most loading problems.

WON'T EJECT

Cassette ejection can be either mechanical, electrical, or both. Generally, one or two large springs are used in either system to

TURNTABLE

CASSETTE
KEEPER

Fig. 5-7. In this model the cassette is loaded lengthwise. Check for a bent turntable or bent cassette keeper if the cassette will not load properly.

apply pressure against the loading mechanism (Fig. 5-8). When the eject button is pushed, the lever releases the loading assembly and out pops the cassette. The cassette switch is disengaged and the motor shuts off.

In an electrical system, a solenoid is used to pull the lever away, unlocking the loading mechanism. With this type of system, only a pushbutton or switch is found on the front panel. This type of system works rather smoothly and quietly, whereas the mechanical ejection button must be pushed rather hard to get the lever to release the loading assembly.

When the cassette or loading mechanism will not release for ejection, suspect a bent or frozen lever. Look for one or both of the large springs to be loose or unhooked. Locate the trip lever and pull it to one side. The loading mechanism should eject the cassette. Clean the binding levers and cam area with alcohol and a cleaning stick. Apply light grease to all sliding areas.

If the solenoid will not release the trip lever, suspect a dry or frozen plunger (Fig. 5-9). Try tripping the lever by hand. Remove the solenoid assembly if the plunger will not move freely inside the solenoid. Two screws usually hold the solenoid to the metal chassis.

Clean the dirt and grease from around the plunger. A coat of graphite can be applied to the metal plunger. Cleaning the plunger and the inside of the solenoid area cures most dry-plunger problems.

In case the lever trips by hand but not electrically, suspect a dirty switch or defective solenoid. Check the switch and solenoid with a continuity reading. Set the VOM to the R × 1 scale and check for a shorted reading across the winding. These solenoids are somewhat similar to those found in the eight-track type car player and have only a few ohms of resistance. The solenoid should be replaced when found to have a burned winding. Sometimes when the eject button is pushed, the fuse opens—this indicates a shorted or burned solenoid.

KEEPS EJECTING CASSETTE

Suspect a worn trip lever or defective electronic ejection assembly when the cassette keeps ejecting. Visually inspect the edge

Fig. 5-8. Bottom view showing loading springs and pulley drive assembly.

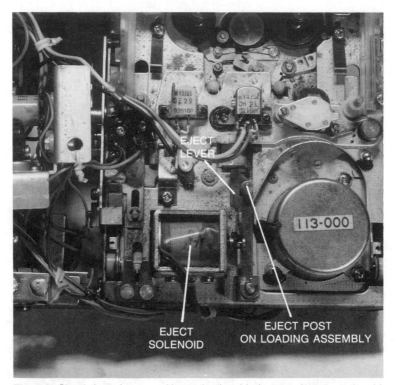

Fig. 5-9. Check for a frozen or jammed solenoid plunger when the solenoid will not trip to eject the cassette. The solenoid should be removed and cleaned if erratic.

of the trip lever. If the edge of the lever is worn, the loading mechanism will release. Try to file off the rounded edge, or order a new lever.

If the cassette plays for a few seconds and then kicks out, suspect a defective electric system. First clean all levers and cams with alcohol. Apply a light grease to all sliding surfaces. Now recheck the ejecting assembly.

In some loading and ejection systems, a small revolving switch is found with little wire contacts. The contacts can become dirty and cause poor switching. In some tension-loaded assemblies the ejection system can trigger when the cassette is wound too tight and drags.

SQUEAKING NOISE

A squeaking noise in a cassette player is generally a sign of worn or dry bearings. Check for dry pulleys or turntables (Fig. 5-10). Try

Fig. 5-10. Check all rotating pulleys for a squeaky noise. Determine in what function the noise occurs. Then double check each pulley, motor and the capstan/flywheel assembly.

to locate the noisy bearing by touch or listening. Stop or move the pulley or drive wheel away from a drive surface to determine which component is causing the noise. A drop of light oil on each pulley might help, but do not apply too much lubricant to a suspected pulley. Excess oil might run down on the drive surfaces, causing slow or erratic speed.

A dry motor bearing can produce a squeaky noise. Place a drop of oil on the motor bearing. Usually this is only a temporary repair. If the motor bearings are worn, the small motor should be replaced. Most motor bearings do not require extra lubricant during their lifetime.

GRINDING NOISE

Slow or erratic speeds can be accompanied by a grinding noise. Sometimes the grinding noise only exists in the reverse direction. Try to locate which idler pulley or capstan/flywheel is making the scraping sound. Usually one of the flywheels is rubbing against the bottom support plate (Fig. 5-11).

If the flywheel is making the noise, note if the support bracket

103

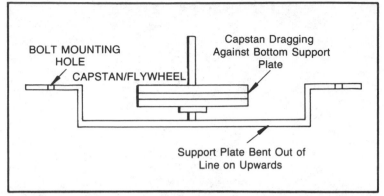

Fig. 5-11. For scraping or grinding noises, check the metal bottom support of the capstan/flywheel assembly. If the support is bent out of line, the flywheel might scrape against the support or chassis.

is bent out of line. You might have to remove the entire cassette assembly from the chassis. Check for three or more mounting bolts on the bottom side of the chassis (Fig. 5-12). Loosen all connecting wires. Remove tie twists and connecting wires to the other components. Always mark down where each wire connects before removal. Now remove the support bracket. Because these brackets are made of very light, stamped metal, they have a tendency to bend out of shape. Straighten and replace the bracket. Rotate the capstan/flywheel by hand to see if it scrapes against the metal bracket. If the bracket support is badly bent, replace it. Also check for turntable or reels rubbing against the top panel.

NO SOUND

The car cassette sound system is practically the same as that of the eight-track player. Usually four to six transistors are found in each channel. In a modern auto cassette player, you might find a couple of transistors and one IC output circuit. A few of the latest layers have only two IC circuits in each channel or a total of two input and two output IC components.

Before bothering to remove the player from the car, make sure it has power and that the speakers are normal. You can assume voltage is getting to the player if the program light is on or you can hear the motor turning. When one channel is dead and the other is normal, temporarily connect another speaker to the dead channel or switch speaker terminals to determine if the speaker is defective. If that doesn't work, remove it for service.

You might find one channel dead, intermittent, or both channels inoperative (Fig. 5-13). If only one channel is dead turn the balance control to that channel. Turn the volume wide open. Flick a screwdriver blade across the tape head. A fluttering noise should be heard in the speaker. If not, place the screwdriver blade at the center terminal of the volume control. You should hear a fairly loud hum. If a hum is heard, the output stages are normal and the defective component is somewhere before the volume control. If not, the output stages are defective. Dead, weak, or distorted conditions are generally caused by the final audio output stages.

Check for correct voltage measurements on the audio output transistors or IC circuits. Compare these readings with the schematic. If a diagram is not handy, compare the same readings

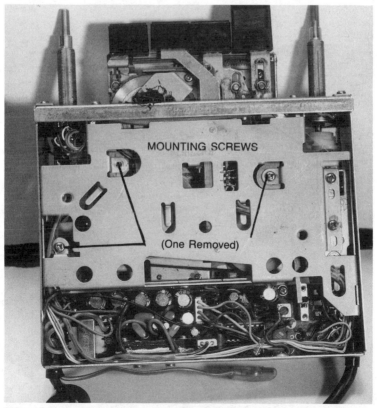

Fig. 5-12. You might have to remove three or four small bolts to free the cassette assembly from the chassis. Sometimes to remove the capstan/flywheel assembly or loading mechanism, the whole assembly must be removed from the player.

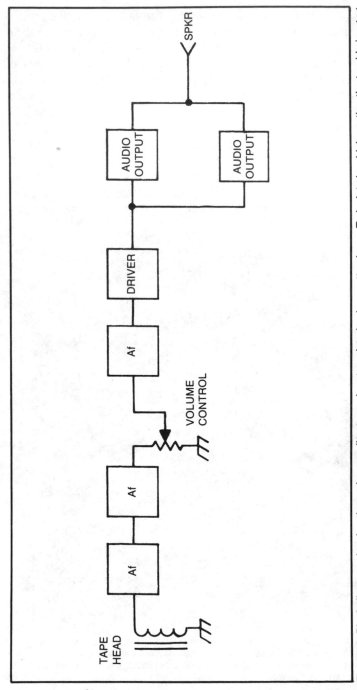

Fig. 5-13. Block diagram showing the various audio stages in a transistorized cassette player. To isolate in which section the trouble is, start at the volume control and work both ways.

with those found on the equivalent components in the good channel. Since both stereo channels are the same, the gain and voltage measurements can be compared at any given point.

When IC components are found as amplifiers in the cassette player, signal-trace in the same manner (Fig. 5-14). If no hum is heard with the screwdriver at the volume control, suspect a defective output IC. Measure the voltage at each terminal and compare it with the normal channel. If the voltages are way off on some terminals, suspect a defective IC. Replacing all the audio output circuits with one IC saves a lot of stage-to-stage troubleshooting.

INTERMITTENT AUDIO

Inspect the tape-head wires when the cassette cuts in and out but the radio section is normal. Look for broken or torn off wires lying against the head terminal. Because the cassette carriage shifts up and down when loading the tape head, the cable is constantly moving up and down. In time, the tape-head wires break off (Fig. 5-15). Sometimes both stereo channels can be intermittent with poor tape head connections.

Cut back the insulation from the small cable wires with a pocket knife. You can place the soldering iron tip against the flexible wire and melt the insulation off. Tin the end of wire cable and hold it against the connection while soldering it. Make a good solder joint, but not with a lot of solder. Make sure the ground or common wire is secure. In some players, the shield of the cable is common ground for both channels. Check the head winding with the ohmmeter and compare it with the other channel. When the cassette reverses direction and there is sound in only one direction, suspect a broken ground wire of the tape-head assembly.

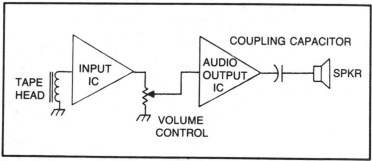

Fig. 5-14. Here is a block diagram of a cassette player with only two separate ICS. In a stereo player these are two identical circuits with a total of four ICs.

TAPE TEARS OR SPILLS OUT

First clean the tape heads, capstan, and pressure roller after tape has pulled out of the cassette. Inspect the rubber pressure roller for worn edges. Does the rubber roller turn freely? Note if the pressure roller has a worn bearing. Check the pressure roller tension spring.

In the cassette tape player, if the take-up reel or turn-table appears sluggish or stops, the tape will pull or roll out of the cassette (Fig. 5-16). Some of the loose tape wraps around the capstan and pressure roller. No fast-forward action also indicates the take-up reel is not operating. Inspect the take-up reel for dry or frozen bearings. A drop of oil on the bearing can cure the slow or erratic take-up reel.

Check the rubber drive pulley at the other end of the take-up reel. Some players use a rubber drive pulley or a belt assembly to turn the take-up reel. If the "C" washer drops off the drive pulley, you might find it down inside the metal chassis, preventing the take-up reel from moving. Note if the drive pulley is engaging the fly-wheel drive assembly.

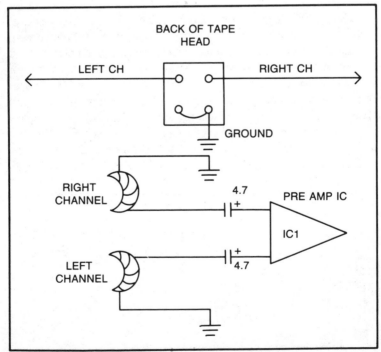

Fig. 5-15. Check for broken tape-lead wires if sound is intermittent in the cassette player. Measure the tape-head resistance.

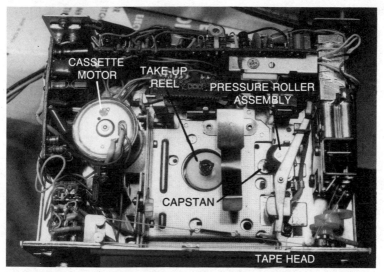

Fig. 5-16. Note if the take-up reel is erratic or stops if the tape spills out of the cassette. Inspect the pressure roller for excess tape wrapped between rubber roller and the metal frame of the pressure roller.

Sometimes the black hub-keeper at the top of the take-up reel or turntable will ride high or come off with a missing "C" washer, causing the reel to slow down and spill out tape. Note if the cassette is seating properly. Check the metal keeper at the top of the cassette to hold it in place. Do not overlook a defective cassette.

Double check the pressure-roller assembly for excess tape wrapped around the rubber roller. The excess tape gets down around and between the rubber roller and metal brace. Try to pull out as much loose tape as possible. Secure the piece of tape with a pair of long nose pliers and pull. Rotate the rubber roller in the direction opposite of normal rotation and pull on the tape. Remove all tape from around the pressure-roller bearings. Clean the brown oxide from the pressure roller with alcohol and a cleaning stick.

6

Common Portable
Tape Player Tips

Portable tape players come in all shapes and sizes. The portable player can be either an eight-track stereo or a cassette player with mono or stereo operation. In some units you can get an AM/FM portable radio combination. Regardless of what you have, they are all serviced the same way (Fig. 6-1).

When attempting to service a portable tape player, you must first isolate the problem in the defective section (Fig. 6-2). Slow speed problems can be rectified in the tape mechanism. A distorted right channel can be caused by a defective transistor in the right amplifier section. A dead condition might be caused by a defective power supply or battery circuit.

CHECK THE BATTERIES

Suspect defective batteries if the tape will not turn and you have no sound. Slow tape speed might be caused by weak batteries. Even one dead battery can prevent operation of the tape player.

Check batteries with a battery tester or VOM (Fig. 6-3). When checking the batteries with a VOM, measure the total voltage across all of the batteries with the player in operation. Place the VOM on 15 Vdc. If a cell measures 1 volt or less, discard it.

The batteries last only a week or two with constant operation. Intermittent operation of any tape player will increase battery life. Always remove the batteries if the player is not going to be used

Fig. 6-1. Always use a small soldering iron with a pc board.

for several weeks. If you don't, they might leak and corrode the battery terminals or ruin the tape player. Wipe off the battery terminals when installing new batteries.

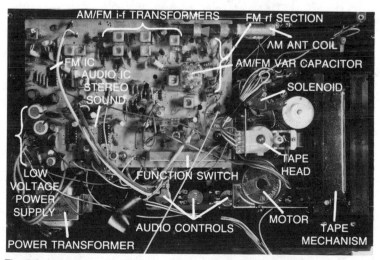

Fig. 6-2. Isolate the trouble to a specific section of the tape player. Here we find the portable tape player divided into several sections.

Fig. 6-3. Check the batteries when the tape player will not function in battery operation. Follow the arrows on the battery compartment.

CLEAN THE TAPE HEADS

A dirty tape head can cause a weak, distorted, or dead channel in the tape player. Clean the tape head with alcohol and a cotton swab (Fig. 6-4). Use a cleaning stick so you can clean inside the head area. A tape-head cleaning cartridge can be used to keep the head area clean.

You might find that after cleaning the tape head the weak or dead channel is now normal. Sometimes the excessive oxide from the tape packs against the tape head, causing sound problems. It's possible to have a dead channel caused by packed oxide dust. The oxide gets inside the tape-head gap area and prevents tape contact. This is especially true in portable cassette player tape heads. When you see dark brown marks on the tape head, clean it to improve the performance of the tape player.

Also clean the program switch and capstan area with alcohol. Sometimes the brown oxide builds up on the capstan drive area and can produce wow or speed problems. When excessive oxide builds up on the capstan drive area, the tape may be pulled from the cartridge and end up wrapped around the capstan.

When excessive tape is wound around the capstan, the plastic back cover must be removed to get to the capstan drive assembly.

112

Remove all pieces of tape and clean the capstan with alcohol. Rotate the capstan/flywheel with the cotton swab pressed against the drive area. Rotate the flywheel to clean the capstan drive area.

SLOW OR UNEVEN SPEED

Check for a loose motor-drive belt when the tape speed is slow. Turn the unit on and hold the flywheel. If the motor pulley turns inside the drive belt, replace the belt. You should also install a new belt if it keeps slipping off the motor pulley or flywheel. The drive belt might not stay on the motor pulley if the pulley is not in line with the flywheel (Fig. 6-5).

If the motor drive belt is excessively worn, it must be replaced. You might be able to buy a drive belt where you purchased the tape player, but the drive belt can also be ordered from the manufacturer.

Take the old drive belt with you when attempting to buy a new one locally. Always select one a little smaller in diameter than the old one. These belts stretch and become loose with age. Select a belt of the same width. Never replace a round belt with a flat one.

Slow or uneven speeds can be caused by a dry or sluggish capstan/flywheel bearing. Remove the bottom bracket and pull the

Fig. 6-4. Clean the tape heads with alcohol and a clean swab. A dirty tape head can cause distorted, weak, or no sound.

Fig. 6-5. Check the motor pulley, flywheel, and capstan for slow speeds.

flywheel out. Clean the capstan drive and bearing area with alcohol. Slip a cleaning stick inside the bearing support area and clean it. Remove the excessive grease and tape oxide around the capstan bearing. Apply a drop of grease or light oil to the bearing support area and replace the capstan/flywheel. Wipe any excessive oil or grease off the capstan drive area with alcohol and a cloth. Read the next section for proper lubrication methods. Replace the bottom support bracket. Make certain all parts are in position.

Clean the flywheel drive area and the motor pulley with alcohol. After the motor belt is installed, rotate the flywheel by hand. Note if the belt rides in line. Suspect a defective motor if you encounter slow speed after a good cleaning.

CORRECT LUBRICATION

The capstan/flywheel bearing should only be lubricated after cleaning. You can't oil the capstan from the top—the oil might drip on the drive area and ruin a good cartridge. For good lubrication, remove the bearings from the flywheel assembly. The capstan/flywheel bearings should be lubricated at the top and bottom of the capstan bearing area. When lubricating the capstan bearings, use only a drop of oil (Fig. 6-6).

Do not place oil on the belt area. Any grease or oil on the motor belt will cause slow speeds and wow effects. When grease is suspected of causing slow speed problems, clean off the belt and all rotating areas thoroughly with alcohol and a cloth.

The slide and cam areas should have a light coat of grease. A drop of oil on the plastic cartridge slide areas will allow the cartridge to be loaded easily. Wipe all grease from the tape head and capstan drive areas with alcohol.

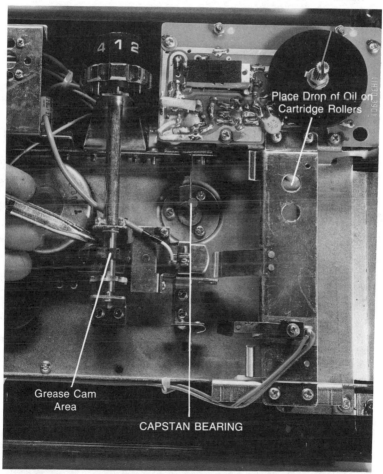

Fig. 6-6. Here are the various areas for correct lubrication of the portable eight-track tape player.

EIGHT-TRACK PLAYER—WON'T CHANGE CHANNELS

Suspect a defective switch button or solenoid when the manual button will not change channels. If the program switches to another channel at the end of the tape, you know the automatic portion of the channel changer is functioning (Fig. 6-7). You can quickly check the automatic changer by shorting the automatic switch blades with a screwdriver. Hold the cartridge switch on with a pencil or pen; then short the automatic channel switch. Note if the head shifts position.

In some portable battery-operated tape players, you might find a manual-type channel changer. Simply rotate the knob to a different channel. This type of manual changing mechanism usually doesn't cause very many problems. If the manual changer rotates very hard, suspect dry bearings. A drop of oil on each end of the bearing might help.

Clean the switch contacts when the automatic switch functions and the manual switch does not. You might find a broken manual switch. Check for poorly soldered contacts on the switch terminals.

Fig. 6-7. When the program switch will not change channels, in an 8-track player check the solenoid to see if it's energizing. Check for continuity across the program or cartridge switch.

These switches should be replaced with the original (not generic) part numbers.

When the channel changer appears intermittent, suspect the small lever of overriding the plastic arm in the head assembly. Bending the lever slightly downward corrects this situation. Extra tension on the solenoid arm level might help. A burned or overheated solenoid should be replaced.

Inspect a suspected program switch for broken or dirty contacts. Check for continuity across the program switch terminals. Place the VOM on the R×1 scale (Fig. 6-8). If the switch is normal, a short should occur. When the ohmmeter reading is erratic, suspect dirty contacts. Clean the switch contacts with a cleaning stick and alcohol.

To check the solenoid of the channel-changing mechanism, shunt across the switch with an alligator test lead and note if the solenoid energizes. (The tape player must be plugged into the power line.) If the solenoid doesn't energize, suspect a defective solenoid or broken wiring connections. Check all wiring connections near the solenoid coil. If the solenoid still doesn't change channels, check for voltage across the solenoid terminals. Most of these solenoids operate directly from the dc power supply. Place the VOM to the 60 Vdc scale. Remember, this voltage should equal the total battery voltage or dc power supply voltage—somewhere between 9 and 20 volts.

If supply voltage is found at the terminals of the solenoid and it still does not energize, suspect an open coil winding. Check for a poor coil soldering connection where the coil wire is bonded to the solenoid terminals. The coil wire could be broken off. If the coil wire is broken, pull out or unwind it a turn so it can be soldered back to the original terminal. Scrape the coil wire to remove the enamel wire insulation. Dip the end in rosin soldering paste and apply solder. Reconnect the broken coil wire to its original terminal.

A defective switch or solenoid should be ordered from the manufacturer. You must locate the original part number. Sometimes the channel switch can be replaced with another type, but usually the solenoid is specially built for a particular model. Order it from your local dealer, distributor, or the manufacturer.

NO TAPE MOTION

A tape player with no tape motion can be the result of a defective cartridge switch, broken motor-drive belt, defective motor, or improper voltage to the motor circuit (Fig. 6-9). First determine if power is applied to the radio and audio amplifier circuits. If a radio

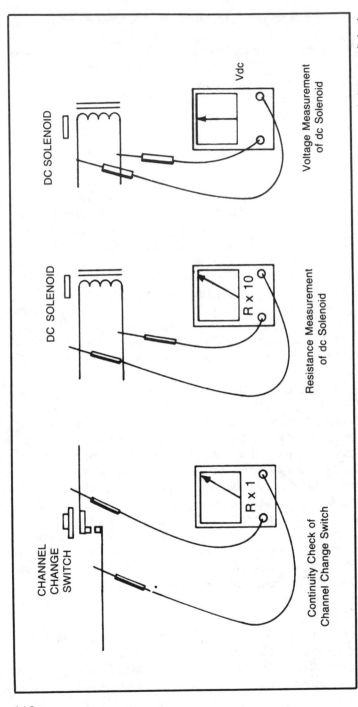

Fig. 6-8. Three VOM tests to make when checking the channel-changing function. Check continuity across the channel-change switch, dc voltage across the solenoid, and do a resistance measurement on the solenoid.

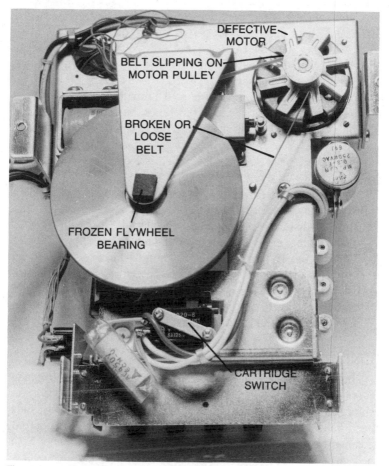

Fig. 6-9. Here are the various areas to check when tape doesn't rotate.

is enclosed with the portable tape player and is working normally, you can assume the power and audio circuits are functioning. When switched to tape, note if one of the channel lights is on. Lighted channel bulbs usually indicate voltage is being applied to the tape circuits.

Place your ear close to the tape player when inserting the cartridge. You should be able to hear the tape motor motion. If not, check for a defective cartridge switch. This switch might be a leaf or micro type. Sometimes the copper or brass leaf prongs get bent out of line and will not press together when the cartridge is inserted. Determine if the cartridge switch assembly is in line.

Next take a VOM continuity reading across the cartridge switch terminals. Make this test with player turned off. Set the VOM to the $R \times 1$ scale. With the cartridge inserted, you should have a short across the switch terminals. If the cartridge switch is normal, move on to the other components.

If the motor is running and there is no tape motion, suspect a broken or loose motor drive belt. Sometimes these belts simply come off. If too loose, the belt will not stay in place. Check for oil or grease on the flywheel drive area and motor pulley. You might find the motor is running slow because the rubber belt is lodged between motor and pulley.

To check for a defective motor, first try to spin the motor pulley with your fingers. If the motor starts, suspect a dead spot on the armature. A defective motor must be replaced. Check for dc voltage at the motor terminal wires when the motor will not rotate. Set the VOM at the 15 Vdc scale. If the meter hand hits the peg, go to the 60 Vdc scale. No voltage measurement at the motor terminals might indicate a defective dc power supply circuit. The dc voltage should be between 10 and 20 volts. Replace the motor if normal dc voltage is found on the motor terminals and the motor doesn't run.

RUNS TOO FAST

Improper tape speed can be caused by the motor belt running on the high side of the pulley or by a defective motor. Note if the motor belt is riding high on the flange of the motor pulley. Sometimes these belts will fly up on the motor flange without any apparent reason. Make sure the motor pulley and flywheel are in line. Spin the flywheel around several times. If the belt is riding high or low on the flywheel, the motor pulley is out of line.

Check for a motor pulley set screw. Some are located in the metal pulley. In most plastic pulleys, they are just pressed on and set with a little dab of glue. If the belt is riding high on the flywheel, press the plastic pulley toward the motor assembly. However, in case the belt is riding low on the flywheel, pull the plastic pulley outward. Rotate the flywheel several times. The belt should ride right in the center of the flywheel (Fig. 6-10).

Before attempting to replace a possibly defective motor, check the capstan drive area for extra tape wrapped around the capstan. You might find a couple of turns of tape pressed firmly in place, causing the tape to run faster. Sometimes the tape will tear out of the cartridge and wrap around the capstan drive area. Try to remove

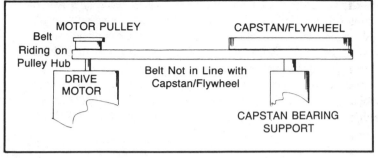

Fig. 6-10. When the tape runs too fast, check to see if the belt is riding up on the hub of the motor pulley. Check for excess tape around the capstan drive area. A defective motor can also cause fast speeds.

the excess tape from the cartridge opening. If this can't be done you might have to remove the capstan flywheel assembly. Clean off the capstan drive area with alcohol and a cleaning stick.

Suspect a defective motor if the belt is in line but the tape is rotating too fast. Check for correct dc voltage at the motor terminals. As a last resort, tap the motor with the handle of a screwdriver. Sometimes the motor will resume normal speed. If this happens, replace the motor as it could cause erratic speed conditions at any time.

Determine if the portable tape player really warrants motor replacement, because some of these motors are expensive. Take the model number of the tape player and the motor number to your nearest dealer. You must have the motor number to order a new one. Usually this number can be found in the manufacturer's parts list. Also, replacing the motor yourself will make the repair less expensive.

CAN'T CONTROL THE VOLUME

Sometimes the volume control is disabled. This problem can occur even in new tape players. Sometimes the problem occurs after the player is used only a couple of times. This problem might be caused by a defective volume control or poor wire connections.

Determine if the volume control is the round or sliding type. Check all of the wires going to the control terminals. The sliding type control can have four to eight separate wires going to it. Most stereo players have a dual-type volume control. You might find a separate volume control for each channel in the smaller, inexpensive players.

121

In the round-knob control, note if the wiper blade is rotating. The center terminal ties to the rotating blade of the volume control. If the blade is bent out of line or broken off, the volume will remain the same. However, with the flat sliding control it's difficult to determine if the wiping contacts are in line.

Check for a broken or poor common ground wire at the lower control terminal (Fig. 6-11). When the ground wires break off, very little volume change will be noticed as the control is turned. Then

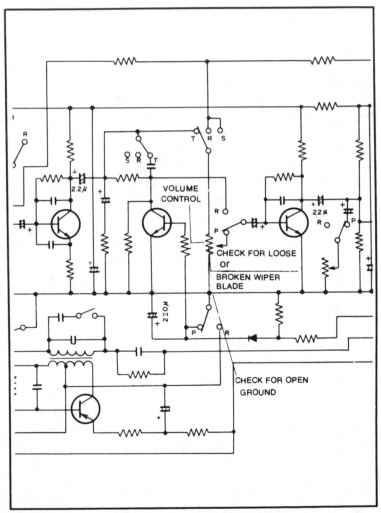

Fig. 6-11. When the volume can't be controlled, check for a poor or broken ground connection on the volume control.

check for correct control resistance across the two outside terminals. Most of these volume controls have a resistance of 25 to 100 K ohms. Remove one of the outside terminal wires for accurate resistance measurements. Set the VOM at R × 1 K. Don't attempt to measure the resistance of a flat, sliding volume control unless you take the time to check where every wire goes in the circuit.

After the control is determined to be defective, replace it with the same type, if possible. Dual or single round-type controls can be substituted, but the flat sliding control should be an exact replacement. When volume control substitution is needed, you might have to cut the control shaft to the correct length. Also, the mounting hole might require a little enlarging for correct replacement. Always mark down on a piece of paper where each colored wire goes— don't trust your memory.

DEAD CHANNEL

It's possible that either channel will appear dead with just about any defective component in the audio circuit. When the two speakers are separated in the portable tape player, check the cable and plug for dead or intermittent sound. Turn on the player and flex the connecting cable. If the sound comes and goes, suspect a broken cable wire or plug.

Hold the plug tight in the socket while moving the cable. Determine if the plug or cable wire is broken. The cable wires tend to break where they go into the speaker cabinet or socket. Because the sockets and plugs are difficult to obtain, try to repair them. The cable wires can be easily spliced together, except the wires broken inside a male or female multi-plug socket are a little more difficult.

If the break is where the wires enter the connecting plug, determine which wire is broken. Take a resistance reading between the suspected cable wires and metal plug connector. First cut into the cord where it enters the plug area. Sometimes you can pull tightly on the wires and they will pull out, but don't pull too hard. If you can't get the wires out, place a large darning needle into each wire and measure the resistance between the needle and the corresponding plug connector (Fig. 6-12).

Set the VOM at R × 1. Clip one lead to the darning needle and the other at the metal plug connection. When the continuity of each wire is located, the meter should read zero ohms. If the cable is intermittent, flex the cable while under test. The VOM will have an erratic reading when the cable is moved.

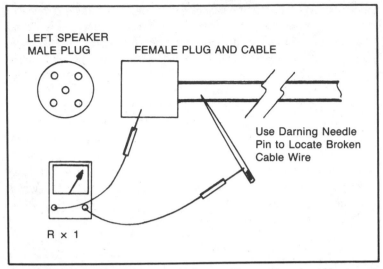

LEFT SPEAKER
MALE PLUG

FEMALE PLUG AND CABLE

Use Darning Needle
Pin to Locate Broken
Cable Wire

R × 1

Fig. 6-12. A dead right or left speaker in the portable tape player could be caused by a broken extension cable or plug. Flex the cable to check for intermittent speaker operation.

After locating the exact break at the cable plug, see if you can locate the end of the metal connector or broken wire. You might locate more than one broken wire in a speaker cable. Check each wire and plug for continuity. Locate the break and repair it. Solder and tape the connection. Use rubber silicone cement to seal the rubber plug connection.

A defective transistor or IC can produce a dead right or left channel (Fig. 6-13). Both channels might be dead or distorted by a single defective IC component. Some portable tape players use only one IC for both channels. Simply replace the defective IC.

To isolate the correct channel, trace the wires from the speaker to the large electrolytic coupling capacitor. These capacitors range from 100 to 470 μF and are located near the corresponding IC. Use solder wick to remove all solder around the IC terminals. Then lift the component off the pc board. Use a small pencil soldering iron to solder the terminals of the replacement IC. Refer to Chapter 1 for information on how to remove and replace ICs.

When only transistors are used in the audio output channels, you must isolate the correct channel and the defective component. It's possible to have one or more defective transistors and bias resistors in a dead output channel. Use another amplifier or the other good stereo channel to signal-trace the defective one. Improper volt-

Fig. 6-13. When one channel is dead or intermittent, suspect a defective transistor or IC. Here there are two separate ICs, one for each channel.

age measurements on the suspected transistor indicates that the transistor is defective.

NO AM BUT NORMAL FM

Go directly to the AM section when the FM radio reception is normal. When the FM is normal, you know that the i-f stages are functioning. Most AM receivers have one oscillator or converter transistor ahead of the i-f stages (Fig. 6-14). Locate the AM converter transistor, which is usually mounted close to the variable tuning capacitor. Secure a service manual or component layout guide to locate the suspected AM transistor.

After the AM transistor is located, take voltage measurements (Fig. 6-15). Compare these voltage measurements to those on the

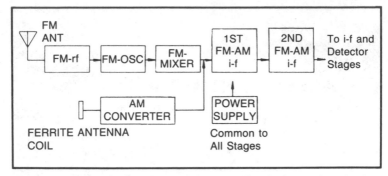

Fig. 6-14. With no AM reception, isolate the problem in the receiver circuitry. Here a block diagram illustrates how the AM and FM stages are connected in the portable AM/FM tape player combination.

schematic. An in-circuit transistor tester might indicate if the transistor is defective. If an in-circuit tester is not handy, remove and check it out of the circuit.

Cut the transistor leads about ¼ inch above the pc board. If not marked on the pc board, mark down each transistor terminal.

Fig. 6-15. Locate the AM transistor on the pc board. Use the service literature or parts layout chart for identification. The AM transistor is usually near the tuning capacitor.

Connect the new transistor to the pc board. Solder each terminal in place and use a pair of needle nose pliers for a heat sink. Always use a low-wattage type iron when soldering transistor and IC terminals.

Weak AM reception can also be caused by a broken antenna wire or antenna ferrite core. If the ferrite core is broken, replace the entire antenna coil. There might be an rf transistor ahead of the converter transistor. An open or leaky rf transistor might cause only local stations to be received.

See also Chapter 4, "Car Radio Repairs" under the heading "No AM But Normal FM."

NO AC OPERATION

When the tape player operates with the batteries but not in ac operation, suspect a defective power supply. Check for low dc voltage at the cathode terminals of the silicon rectifiers. Usually the cathode terminal is marked with a white ring (Fig. 6-16). Set the VOM on the 60 Vdc scale. If the voltage is below 15 volts, turn the VOM to the 15 Vdc scale. If no voltage is found here, check for low ac voltage at the anode terminals of the silicon diodes. Turn the VOM to the 60 Vac scale. If you find a voltage, unplug the tape player and measure the resistance of the ac power transformer. Set the VOM to the R×1 scale. Check the ON/OFF switch terminals for continuity. Infinite reading will indicate the primary winding is open. When the primary winding goes open you will usually find shorted or leaky silicon rectifiers.

Check the power plug and cable for possible breaks. Sometimes interlock cords are used in the portable tape players. Check for a broken plug or wire at the male socket. Turn the VOM to R×1 scale for continuity tests. Trace each wire to the power transformer primary winding before determining if the transformer winding is open.

Low voltage at the terminals of the silicon diode indicate an open filter capacitor or circuit leakage. Cut the foil leading to the various circuits to locate the overloaded circuit. Remove one circuit at a time and check the voltage. Leaky power-output transistors and filter capacitors cause most of the overload conditions. Shunt a known electrolytic capacitor across the main filter to eliminate hum or to restore the normal supply voltage.

DEAD SPEAKER

Don't overlook the possibility that a small speaker could have

FILTER CAPACITORS

LOW-VOLTAGE
SILICON DIODES

Ac POWER
TRANSFORMER

Fig. 6-16. Check for dc voltage at the cathode terminals of the silicon diode rectifiers when the player will not operate from the power line.

an open voice-coil winding. When one speaker is dead in stereo operation, suspect the speaker or amplifier section. Remove one speaker terminal wire and check the speaker terminals for continuity. The resistance should be somewhere from 1 to 10 ohms, depending on the size of the speaker (Fig. 6-17). Clip another speaker across the suspected terminals for a quick check.

If the speakers plug into the tape player, try exchanging the two speakers. When both speakers appear dead in one given channel, check the amplifier circuitry. If one speaker appears dead, check

Fig. 6-17. Check the continuity of a suspected defective speaker with the VOM, set to the Rx1 scale. For quick results, clip another speaker across the suspected speaker terminals.

the plug and speaker cable. Most cable breaks occur where the cable enters the speaker baffle or right at the speaker male plug. Check the female speaker jack for poor or intermittent reception.

DISTORTED SOUND

First check the tape head for excess oxide that might cause weak sound and distortion in one or both channels. Clean off the packed oxide with a plastic rod if it will not wipe off. Be careful not to damage or scratch the front of the tape head. While you are at it, clean all tape heads and guide assemblies of oxide dust.

Next check the speakers for possible distortion. Clip another PM speaker across the suspected one. Pull the new speaker away from the player and listen for distortion. Check all speakers for distortion. Remove one speaker wire if it's difficult to determine whether the old speaker is defective. If the distortion is still present, check the amplifier sections.

Start signal-tracing the audio circuits for distortion with the external audio amp. Note if the distortion is coming out of both speakers. Suspect a dual IC audio output component or a defective

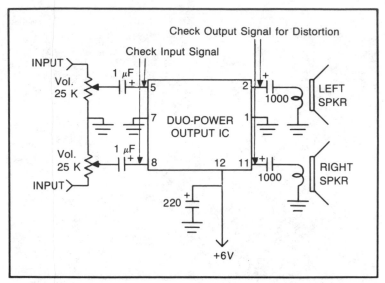

Fig. 6-18. Signal tracing with the external amp can quickly locate a distorted transistor or IC. Check the input signal and output terminals for distortion in the IC power amp.

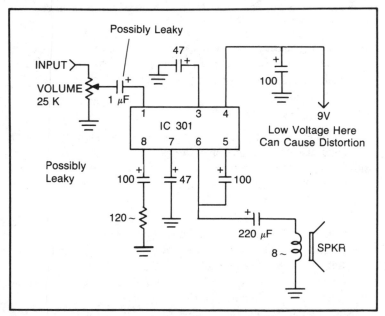

Fig. 6-19. Leaky or open electrolytic coupling capacitors can cause weak operation and distortion at the IC terminals. Replace the suspected IC when the supply voltage is low for both signal-in and signal-out tests.

power supply when both stereo channels are distorted (Fig. 6-18). Signal-trace the left stereo channel if distortion is found in the left speakers. Most distortion problems are caused by leaky or open output transistors and IC circuits.

WEAK SOUND

After cleaning the tape head, determine if the weak audio occurs in the left or right channel. The mono player will have only one set of speakers. A weak audio stage can be located with the external audio amp. Begin at the first af amp and check the signal on the base and collector terminal of each transistor. When the signal drops down, you have located the weak stage.

Now check each transistor in the circuit for open or leaky conditions. Signal-trace the audio on each side of an electrolytic coupling capacitor because these capacitors have a tendency to cause weak audio. Shunt another electrolytic capacitor across each bypass capacitor. When the signal pops up, you have located the dried-up capacitor. Check emitter and bias resistors for the correct resistance.

You might find IC audio components in the latest portable players. Signal-trace the audio at the input and output terminals for a loss of audio (Fig. 6-19). If normal audio is found at the input terminal but is very low at the output, suspect a defective IC. Check the signal all the way out to the speaker terminals with the external amp. You might also locate an open speaker coupling capacitor between the IC output terminal and speaker.

7

Portable Cassette Player and Boom Box Repair

Although the cassette tape player might look a little complicated, don't be afraid to open it up and make a few repairs. The tape head and pinch-roller assembly can be cleaned from the top. For other repairs, you must take off the bottom or back cover to get at the mechanism (Fig. 7-1). Here are some of the different problems you may encounter in a portable cassette player.

NO ROTATION

A dead cassette player can be a result of several different situations. Let's start at the beginning and eliminate each problem one by one. First determine if the portable player will function in battery or ac operation. If the player operates with ac operation and not with the batteries, suspect weak or dead batteries. Check to see if they are inserted properly. Problems with ac operation are usually found in the power supply (Fig. 7-2).

Check the pause control. Some of the small portable cassette players do not have a pause control, but if your model has one, make sure it's turned off. The pause control might turn off both the motor and tape operation.

Check the fuse. Some of the larger tape players have a small fuse to protect the internal circuits. Set the VOM to the R×1 scale. Check for continuity across the fuse terminals. If the fuse is open, a short circuit might have occurred in the motor or amplifier circuit.

Fig. 7-1. Radio-TV technician repairing a small tape recorder. For many repairs, the top and bottom covers must be removed.

PINCH ROLLER   CAPSTAN

CAPSTAN
FLYWHEEL

TAPE
MOTOR

BATTERIES   POWER TRANSFORMER

Fig. 7-2. Various areas to check for rotation problems. Check for poor battery connections or an open power transformer in the portable radio-cassette player combination.

Try another fuse. Sometimes transistors or IC circuits overload for no apparent reason. Check the wiring going from the player switch to the amplifier for overloaded conditions.

Locate the ON/OFF switch. This is a lever-type switch with long tongs in a small tape player. You might find it slightly ahead of the cassette holder. When one of the function buttons is pushed, the mechanism slides against the switch, applying power to the motor and amplifier. Check for poor switch contacts or broken tongs. Clean the switch contacts with alcohol. You can also clean the contacts with a cardboard fingernail file. Note if the switch assembly is broken or out of line. You might be able to repair these broken switches by putting everything back together and applying a coat of epoxy cement to hold the switch in position.

Next determine if the motor is defective. Measure the voltage at the two motor terminals. Set the VOM on the 15 Vdc scale (Fig. 7-3). No voltage at the motor terminals indicates a defective switch or power supply. If voltage is found at the motor, remove the motor belt and spin the motor pulley. If the motor takes off, either the motor is defective or it has dry bearings. The motor pulley will usually turn inside the belt when the drive system is jammed.

Lubricate the motor bearings with a light machine oil. Note if the bearing seems noisy. If the bearings are very noisy and worn, the motor should be replaced. Be sure to check the replacement cost as some of these small motors can cost more than the value of the player.

If the motor is running and the tape does not move, visually inspect the drive system and the various belts and pulleys. Note if the belt is off or rotating. Push the play button (without a cassette) and see if the capstan/flywheel is moving. A defective pressure-roller assembly or frozen pulleys can prevent the tape from moving across the tape head.

TAPE TURNS BUT NO SOUND IS AUDIBLE

Dead reception with the tape rotating might indicate a defective amplifier or tape head, dirty head, or broken head cable wires (Fig. 7-4). To check the playback function, push the play button without a cassette in the holder. Turn the volume wide open. Pass the blade of a small screwdriver over the front of the tape head area. You should hear a fluttering noise each time the blade goes across the tape head. If not, either the tape head or amplifier is defective.

The top plastic cover must be removed before you can check the tape-head wiring assembly. Usually four or five small screws

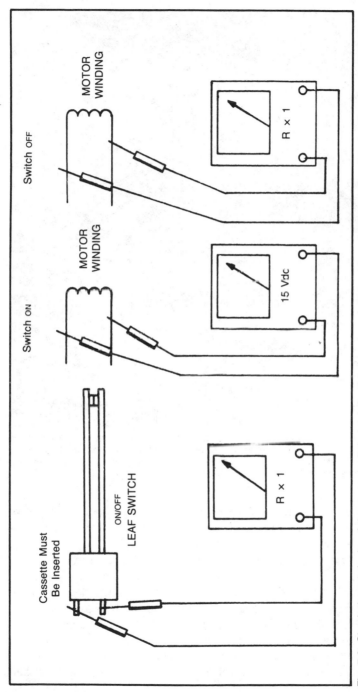

Fig. 7-3. Check the continuity of the ON/OFF switch. Look for this lever-type switch on top of the cassette chassis. Measure the voltage at the motor terminals. Shut the player off and check for continuity across the motor terminals with one lead disconnected.

Fig. 7-4. Sound problems can be caused by an oxide-packed tape head. Clean with alcohol and a cleaning stick. You can clean most tape heads from the front cassette opening. Push the play button down so the head will stick out, but keep the power off.

hold the chassis to the plastic cover. Be careful not to take out screws that are holding other components to the chassis. Only remove the screws or bolts going into the plastic cover.

After removing the top cover, check the cable from the tape head to pc board. Keep the volume wide open. Touch the screwdriver blade to each ungrounded wire of the tape-head cable. You might have two separate cables with a stereo-cassette player. With the amplifier functioning, you should hear a loud hum. If not, the amplifier section is defective.

Be certain the tape head is touching the tape area. Visually inspect the tape-head assembly. If the tape head is loose or pushed back in its holder, the tape will not pass over it. Check for a missing tape-head mounting screw. Sometimes the tape head can break loose from its mounting. Scrape the sides of the tape head along the bottom area. Solder the tape head back in place. If it is not repairable, order a new tape-head assembly. Be sure to demagnetize the tape head after working on it.

SLOW AND ERRATIC TAPE SPEED

Slow and erratic tape speed might be caused by a dirty or dry pressure roller. Clean the tape head and pressure roller with alcohol. Turn the pressure roller with your fingers. If sluggish, clean and lubricate it with a drop of light oil. Check for pieces of tape around the pressure-roller bearing. Suspect a worn pinch roller if the tape pulls upward at the capstan pinch-roller area. If it's worn, the pressure roller assembly should be replaced.

Check the motor drive belt, which runs from the motor to the capstan/flywheel (Fig. 7-5). If the belt is worn, replace it. A loose belt will cause poor tape speed. First remove the drive belt and clean it with alcohol and a cloth. Clean the motor pulley and capstan/flywheel with a cleaning stick dipped in alcohol. Then replace it and check the tape speed.

The capstan/flywheel can also produce tape drag. To correctly lubricate and clean, remove the capstan/flywheel assembly. Clean all surfaces with alcohol and a cloth. Apply a dab of phonolube or light grease to the capstan bearing area. A good cleanup and lubrication will solve most tape drag problems.

NO SOUND BUT ONLY A LOUD RUSH

If the tape is turning and the only sound is a loud rush with no sound reproduction, suspect a broken wire to the tape head. This occurs after the tape player has been used for some time. With the tape head assembly moved to the play position, excessive strain might be applied to the tape-head cable. After awhile, either one or both wires might break off from the head connections.

Remove the top cover and inspect the tape-head assembly. The head cable consists of a center wire inside a shielded or braided cable. Usually the shield wire remains in place, but not the center one. Strip and tin the connecting wire. Solder the broken connection with a small soldering iron.

Erratic or intermittent music might be caused by a defective tape head. With the tape playing, apply pressure to each tape-head

Fig. 7-5. Check for oil or grease on the belt for erratic or slow speeds. Clean the belt, capstan, and motor pulley with alcohol. Slow speed might be caused by a stretched or loose motor belt.

terminal with the rubber eraser of a pencil. If the sound cuts in and out, suspect a broken internal connection. Sometimes you can temporarily repair the condition by applying a wooden wedge between the two head terminals. Hold the wedge in place with glue or silicone rubber cement.

The tape head may have an open winding. Check the continuity of the tape head with the VOM. Set the meter to the R×1 scale. Remove the ungrounded lead from the tape head. The resistance of the tape head should be between 200 and 2 K ohms (Fig. 7-6). If open, replace the tape head.

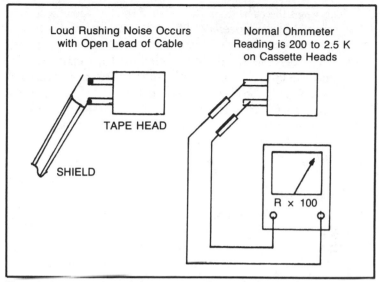

Fig. 7-6. A defective tape head can cause a loud rushing noise or no sound at all. Remove one terminal lead from the tape head and check for continuity with the VOM across the tape terminals.

KEEPS EATING TAPES

In most tape players, tape pulling is caused by a sticky capstan, worn pinch roller, or a defective cartridge or cassette. An erratic or nonrotating take-up reel can pull the tape from the cassette. Note if the take-up reel (the one to the right) is moving. When the take-up reel stops or slows down, the pinch roller keeps feeding tape. The excess tape can wrap around the capstan or pinch roller.

First clean the pinch roller, capstan, tape head, and all tape guide posts. Use alcohol to clean the rubber pulley on the bottom of the take-up reel. Check the friction drive tension of the take-up reel. Turn the player on without a cassette in the holder. Watch the take-up reel rotate. If the take-up reel operates erratically with a cassette playing, remove the take-up reel. Clean the bearings with alcohol, then lubricate and replace them.

A worn or dry pinch roller can cause the tape to pull or drag. Check the rubber roller for worn outside edges. If the pinch roller appears normal, remove it, clean out the bearing, and lubricate it with a drop of light oil. While the pinch roller assembly is apart, clean out all pieces of broken tape. Sometimes the tape wraps tightly around the capstan bearing, causing drag during playback.

Sometimes the cassette pushes against the take-up reel or turntable, causing erratic movement. When the take-up reel is slowed or stopped, tape can be pulled from the cassette. Check for proper seating of the cassette. If the cassette seems to place extra pressure against the take-up reel, suspect a bent spring clip (Fig. 7-7). In some models, a top spring clip holds the cassette in line with the tape head. If the spring clip is jammed downward and goes inside the cassette opening, suspect extra pressure against the take-up turntable. Simply bend the spring clip up so the cassette fits snugly underneath. This clip is fastened directly to the tape-head assembly.

NO FAST-FORWARD

When the fast-forward mode appears sluggish or doesn't move, suspect problems with the drive or take-up turntable. In the fast-forward mode, the cassette tape should be released from the capstan and pinch-roller assembly. The tape runs directly from supply reel to the take-up turntable or reel.

Note if the cassette operates normally in play mode. If it does, suspect that the drive pulley is not engaging the take-up turntable in fast-forward operation. Check for oil or grease on the rubber drive area. Clean all working pulleys and drive areas with alcohol. If the fast-forward operation is still erratic, remove the take-up turntable (Fig. 7-8). Clean off the old grease and apply a drop of light oil to the reel bearing.

Erratic fast-forward can be caused by improper idler pulley tension. In some models, there is a small spring and others have a pressure adjustment. In the model shown in Fig. 7-9, a small adjustment screw is located in a hole. Improper tension adjustment

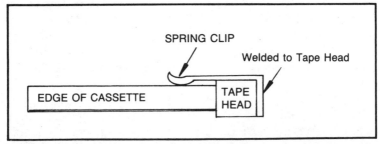

Fig. 7-7. Tape pulling can be caused by extra pressure against the take-up reel, producing erratic operation. In some models a spring clip is found to line up the cassette with the tape head. Sometimes the clip gets bent downward placing extra pressure on the cassette and take-up reel. Simply bend the clip back to the original position.

Fig. 7-8. Remove the take-up reel and clean off the old grease with alcohol and a cloth. A gummed up take-up turntable or reel might cause erratic fast forward motion. Be careful not to misplace the small C clip.

Fig. 7-9. Erratic fast-forward can be caused by improper idler pulley tension. This model has a pressure adjustment screw. Applying more tension to the take-up reel might prevent erratic fast-forward or tape pulling in PLAY position.

applied to the take-up reel can cause erratic fast-forward or tape pulling. Check the manufacturer's literature for proper adjustment.

WON'T RECORD

Recording problems can be caused by a clogged tape head or dirty play/record switches (Fig. 7-10). Clean the tape head with alcohol and a cleaning stick. If the oxide is packed on the tape head, the audio will be distorted or the player won't record at all. Spray cleaning fluid inside the play/record switch area. Move the switch back and forth to clean the contacts. Inspect the play/record switch for incorrect switching or a broken plastic lever. When in RECORD mode, the switch is fully engaged.

Don't forget to check the small cut-out at the rear of the cassette. This cut-out or indentation is in the rear left corner of the cassette. If the small piece of plastic is broken out, the cassette will not record. Simply place a piece of tape across the opening. The cut-out is made so the recording cannot be erased or recorded over. You will find a deep indentation on recorded cassettes that you purchase at the local stores.

Fig. 7-10. Erratic recording can result from a dirty or broken play-record switch, where noisy or poor recording can be caused by an oxide-clogged tape head.

CROSS-TALK

When two different recordings can be heard at the same time, it is called *cross-talk*. When this happens, suspect erase problems. Cross-talk found in an eight-track player is caused by improper head adjustment, but in the cassette player the tape head is in a fixed position, so a jumbled cassette recording is the result of another recording on top of the original.

To check the erase head, make a recording without feeding anything into the recorder. Disconnect or pull out the microphone plug. Let the player record for a couple of minutes and then rewind. Play the recorded area. If the erase head is operating properly, the previous recording should be erased completely.

If it's not erased, suspect a defective erase head or circuitry. Check for a wire broken off the erase head terminals (Fig. 7-11). The erase head is the farthest one to the left. If the wires are intact, check the continuity of the erase head. Set the VOM at the $R \times 1$ ohm scale. Any reading below 250 ohms indicates normal continuity.

Some of the cassette erase heads are fed by a dc voltage, while others are excited with an internal oscillator circuit. Check for dc voltage across the erase head. A voltage measurement of the erase oscillator transistor can indicate a defective transistor or other component.

DEFECTIVE CASSETTE

It's possible to purchase a new cassette that is also defective. Noisy or erratic recordings can be caused by a bad cassette. Choose a good brand for recording purposes. In addition to excessive noise, the cassette might run slow, drag, or keep losing tape. A warped spider (seats the reel or turntable) can produce a mechanical noise. This noise usually occurs toward the end of the tape.

Sometimes the tape is wound too tight, producing drag or wow conditions. Substitute a new cassette to determine if the cassette is defective (Fig. 7-12). If possible, play the suspected cassette in another player. When a new or recorded cassette is found to be noisy or drags, return it for another cassette. Stay away from the cheap cassettes, because you get what you pay for in cassettes or cartridges.

LOSS OF HIGH FREQUENCIES

The loss of high-frequency notes in a cassette can result from improper azimuth adjustment or a worn tape head. Check the front

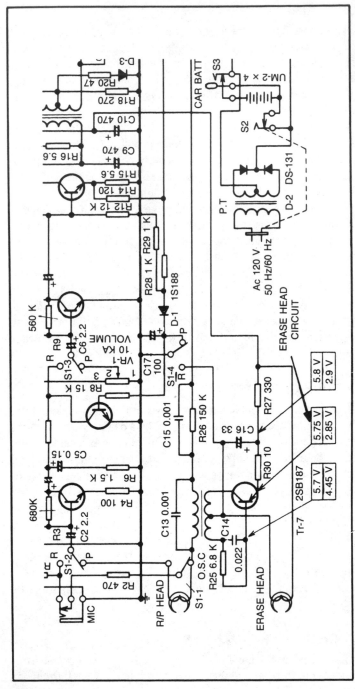

Fig. 7-11. Visually inspect the erase head terminal connections for broken or poorly soldered joints. Notice if the erase head is loose or not in position. Here is a typical erase head circuit in a portable cassette player.

144

Fig. 7-12. A defective cassette can appear noisy both mechanically and when recording. The defective cassette might drag or have wow sound. Substitute a new cassette to determine if one appears defective.

of the tape head for a very worn surface. Clean off the oxide for a good look. If the front head gap area is not worn, check the level of the tape head. The tape head should be level with the tape as it rotates.

You might find the tape head tilted to one side with a loose or missing adjustment screw (Fig. 7-13). The cassette tape assembly must be removed from the case to get at the tape head. You should be able to locate the azimuth adjustment screw to one side of the tape head. Adjust the screw until the tape head appears level and will then be turned for maximum sound output.

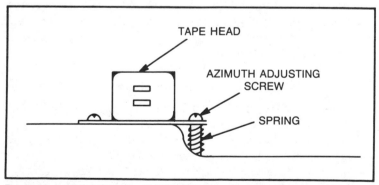

Fig. 7-13. Look for the azimuth adjustment screw located to one side of the tape head. Adjust this screw for maximum volume at the speaker.

If a 6- or 10-kHz test tape and VTVM are handy, connect the VTVM across the speaker terminal for an indicator. Insert the test tape and adjust the azimuth screw for maximum voltage upon the VTVM. You can connect an 8-ohm, 2-watt resistor across the external speaker jack and connect the VTVM across the 8-ohm resistor. Now adjust the azimuth screw for maximum voltage.

DEMAGNETIZING THE TAPE HEAD

You should demagnetize the tape head when a low hissing noise is heard in the background. The head demagnetizer removes residual magnetism, restores high frequency response, and reduces tape hiss. While working around or servicing the cassette player, the tape head might get magnetized by magnetic screwdrivers or nearby bench speakers. The cassette demagnetizer is ideal and just slips into the player. A small hand-type demagnetizing tool with a small probe gets right down into the cassette opening to do the job.

SERVICING BOOM BOXES

The boom box provides high-power output in a small package. The "earth shaker" or ghetto blaster gets carried to football games, picnics, and camping trips. You might see one riding on the shoulder of a roller skater or blasting away in the midst of a group of teenagers (Fig. 7-14). In addition to a cassette player, the portable boom box has an AM-FM-MPX radio with stereo sound.

Many of the boom boxes have large 5- to 7-inch woofer speakers with small 1-inch tweeters, with up to six speakers in the larger boxes. For example, the Magnavox Model D8843 has an 8-inch center subwoofer, two 5⅓-inch wide-range woofers, and two piezo woofer horn tweeters. In some portables, you might find a sound graphics equalizer, programmable search system, recording level meters, and soft-touch cassette operation. You can keep that boom box playing with the following repairs.

Checking the Speakers

Determine if the sound is disabled in the speaker or the entire channel (Fig. 7-15). Many boom box machines are operated at high volume, and in time a speaker or two becomes damaged. The speaker operated at high volume can have a loose or damaged voice coil. The voice coil might be blown, or the cone is torn or vibrating.

Remove the back plastic cover to get at the speakers. You might find the front cover comes off by removing several screws in the

Fig. 7-14. The boom box has high output wattage in a small package. You can get from two to six speakers in these players.

back cover. In some portable players, large speakers are hooked to the ends of the radio-player case for transporting and can be removed for greater music separation (Fig. 7-16).

Check speaker continuity of the voice coil with the ohmmeter. An accurate resistance measurement of the speaker might equal the speaker's impedance (Fig. 7-17). Next remove the speaker from the front panel and check the cone for torn or loose particles. Inspect the cone where it is glued around the rim area. Excessive volume can loosen up the cone or tear loose the spider ring next to the voice coil, producing a "blatting" sound. Press down on the cone to see if the voice coil is rubbing against the magnet. A "mushy" speaker has the voice coil rubbing against the center piece. If it won't move, the voice coil is frozen against the center magnet.

The defective speaker should be replaced with one having the original characteristics whenever possible. Take the model number of the player and speaker to the parts depot or service department of the dealer where it was purchased. A universal speaker replacement is sometimes a better speaker than the original one. When replacing the bad speaker, choose one with the same size, wattage, impedance and weight of magnet. Remember, these speakers take a lot of power and must withstand unusually heavy punishment.

147

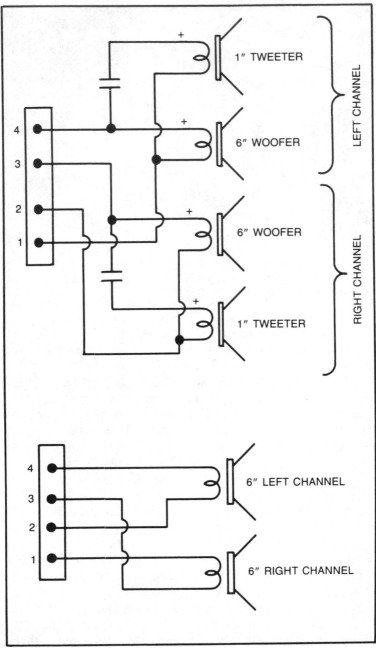

Fig. 7-15. In this speaker arrangement there are four six-inch and two one-inch speakers in a woofer and tweeter system. The two center speakers are fed from another IC component.

Fig. 7-16. The large boom box player might have two speakers that can be detached for added speaker separation.

WORKS ON BATTERIES BUT NOT AC

Check the low-voltage power supply, ON/OFF switch and the 120-volt input terminal switch located in the female ac plug when the player does not operate from the power line (Fig. 7-18). Insert the ac cord to the unit (not the power outlet), turn the unit on, and

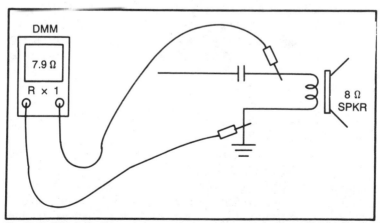

Fig. 7-17. Check each speaker cone for continuity. You might find the speaker resistance is normal but the voice coil is frozen against the center magnet.

Fig. 7-18. Check the fuse and low-voltage power supply when the player and radio are dead. Measure the resistance of the primary winding of the power transformer at the ac male power plug with power plug pulled to check the ON/OFF switch and primary winding of the transformer.

measure for continuity across the ac plug. You are measuring the continuity of the primary winding of the power transformer. If infinite, suspect the primary winding is open.

Although most power supplies are not fused, take a peek and see if one is located near the rectifiers. If open, replace with the exact amperage. Now measure the dc voltage at the main filter capacitor (Fig. 7-19). If the voltage is low or there is no measurement, inspect the low-voltage diode. These bridge diodes can be mounted singly or in one large bridge component. Measure the ac voltage of the bridge circuit.

Very low ac input or low dc output voltage can result from a leaky diode. Sometimes a shorted diode will blow the fuse or open the primary winding of the power transformer. Remove the end of each diode for a correct diode test with the DMM. The open diode will have an infinite and a shorted diode will have a low-ohm measurement in both directions. You might find one or two diodes

150

leaky in a bridge rectifier circuit. Replace the leaky diodes with 1-amp replacements.

Won't Work on Batteries

Before replacing the batteries, inspect the battery terminals for corrosion or dirt. Clean the terminals with sand paper and/or cleaning fluid. Check the battery terminals for torn or loose wires. If after battery replacement the boom box doesn't work, check the ac/dc selector switch (Fig. 7-20). This switch is usually found in the ac female plug assembly. Spray cleaning fluid down into the switch points. Inspect the plastic plug assembly for cracks or breakage. Repair the broken plug assembly with epoxy cement.

WEAK AND DISTORTED SOUND

Today boom-box audio circuits consist of one or two IC circuits. In smaller players, the tape deck pre amp and recording circuits can be contained in one IC, while the complete audio circuits contain one large IC for both channels (Fig. 7-21). Suspect a leaky audio-amp output IC for weak and distorted sound.

First determine if both or only one channel is weak or distorted. If both channels are distorted, suspect a leaky output IC. When one channel is weak and distorted, check the speaker, audio amp and one-amp circuits (Fig. 7-22). A dirty tape head might create a

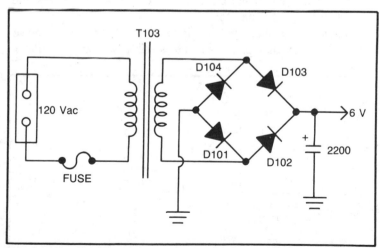

Fig. 7-19. The bridge rectifiers may be mounted singly or in one integral component. Check each diode for leaky or open conditions with one lead removed from the circuit.

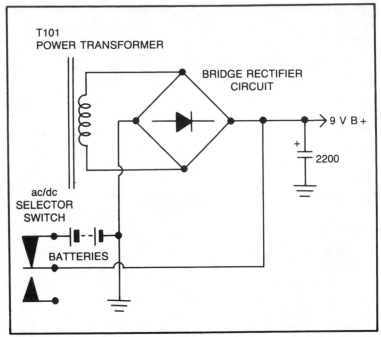

Fig. 7-20. A dirty or defective ac/dc selector switch can prevent the portable from battery operation. Spray cleaning fluid inside and check the switch continuity with the ohmmeter.

distorted and weak symptom. Signal-trace the audio circuits with the external signal generator.

A defective audio output IC can be located with voltage and resistance measurements. Locate the possibly defective IC on the

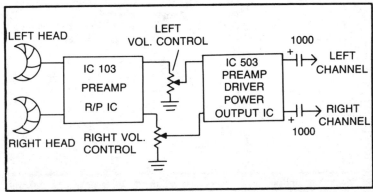

Fig. 7-21. The audio circuits in the newer large players might consist of only two IC circuits. With a weak or distorted symptom, suspect a leaky duo-audio IC.

Fig. 7-22. In this boom-box, two separate power output ICs are mounted on separate heatsinks.

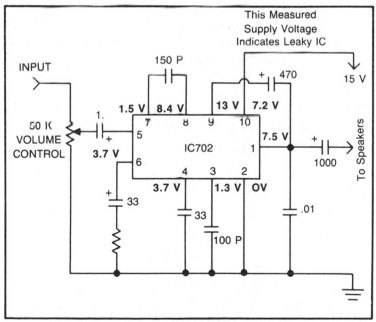

Fig. 7-23. Measure the voltage on all terminals of the suspected IC for leakage or open conditions. Here a low supply voltage on terminal 10 indicates a leaky IC 702.

chassis. Check the voltage at all terminals and compare them to the schematic (Fig. 7-23). Make sure the supply voltage is right on the nose. If the supply voltage is very low, suspect a leaky power IC or defective power supply circuits.

Sound From Only One Speaker

Sound from only one speaker in a two-speaker portable stereo might indicate a dead channel or speaker. Clip another speaker across the dead speaker terminals or interchange the speaker leads. Measure the resistance of the defective speaker. If the speaker is normal, check the headphone-jack assembly for poor or shorting contacts. Clip another speaker through a 470-μF capacitor to the output terminal of the dead IC component (Fig. 7-24). Poor wiring or an open speaker coupling capacitor can produce a dead channel. No sound from the test speaker at the IC output terminal might indicate a defective integrated circuit.

Intermittent Music

Intermittent sound in the audio circuits can be caused by loose tape-head wires, IC components, worn volume controls, or speakers. First make sure the speaker and tape heads are good. Spray cleaning fluid down inside the volume control. A broken or worn volume control can of course cause erratic music. Signal-trace the signal at the input and output terminals of the IC with the external amp (Fig. 7-25).

Monitor the audio signal at the volume control with a scope or external amp. Do you still have audio at the volume control when

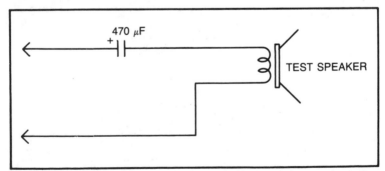

Fig. 7-24. Clip the test speaker through a 470-μF electrolytic capacitor to the output terminal of the suspected IC component to determine if the IC or the speaker is defective. Check the speaker coupling capacitor for open conditions with the test speaker.

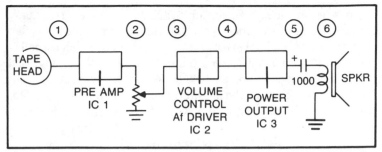

Fig. 7-25. Check the numbered test points with the external amp to locate the intermittent stage.

the music drops down, or does the volume at the control drop out with the speaker? If the music is still heard at the volume control but not at the speaker, monitor the output circuits. Monitor the supply voltage at the power output IC. Spray the suspected IC with coolant after the volume drops down. Sometimes the volume will "pop" up after coolant has been applied. Hence, between audio signal and voltage monitoring, the defective IC or component can be located.

Frozen Function Switch

The selector switch can be broken or frozen in the AM/FM radio section. In some units a large rotating function switch selects AM-FM-MPX radio and player operation. In others, a push-button assembly selects the different player/radio selections (Fig. 7-26).

Fig. 7-26. Suspect a broken or frozen pushbutton assembly or selector switch when there is no tape action or the radio is dead. Replace it with the exact part number.

155

In some models, the selector switch can become dirty. Spray the selector or push button switches with cleaning spray. Inspect the wafers or switch terminals for breakage. The switch assembly often cannot be fixed if there are broken wafers. When any band or operation will not work, suspect broken switch contacts. Do not overlook a break around the pc wiring where the switch is mounted. Order a complete switch assembly if it is broken beyond repair.

Defective Headphone Jacks

One channel can be dead or intermittent with a defective headphone jack. Either the speaker has no sound or the headphone channel is dead. Check the audio sound ahead of the headphone jacks with a speaker clipped across the jack terminals (Fig. 7-27). If the signal is normal in both channels, suspect dirty internal headphone contacts or broken jack terminals.

Clean the shorting jack terminals with the plastic cleaning spray tube inserted into the open end of the headphone jack. After several coats of spray, insert the male headphone jack and work the plug in and out to clean the terminals. The headphone jack must be replaced if the cleanup does not clear up the problem (Fig. 7-28). Most of these headphone jacks are specially made for each player and must be ordered from the manufacturer or service depot.

Slow Cassette Player Speed

Improper or erratic speed in the cassette player might be caused by a dirty or worn pressure roller, excess tape wrapped around the pinch-roller bearing, or improper adjustment of the take-up reel (Fig. 7-29). Inspect the pressure roller for tape wrapped between the roller and brace-bearing area. Clean all oxide from the capstan and rubber roller areas. Make sure the pressure roller spins freely.

Re-adjustment of the pressure-roller spring and the take-up reel tension can restore the cassette speed. Usually the take-up reel adjustment is found on the front of the take-up reel. Move the metal spider to a higher level to apply more take-up pressure. In most cases, the player must be removed from the cabinet, or the front cover must be removed to get at the take-up reel adjustment. In the dual tape players, check the take-up adjustment of both the record/play side and the separate play side (Fig. 7-30).

Broken Levers

Too much pressure or a dropped player might break the plastic

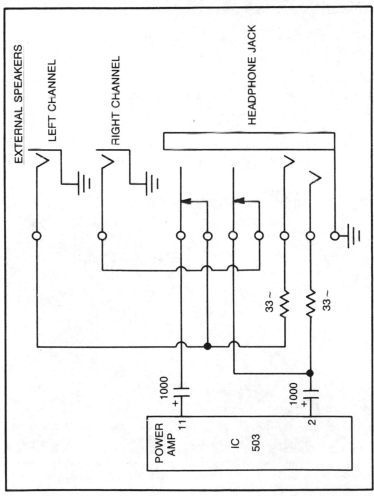

Fig. 7-27. A dirty or broken headphone jack can produce an intermittent or a dead channel. Signal-trace the audio with the test speaker ahead of the earphone jack.

Fig. 7-28. Replace a defective earphone jack with the exact part number whenever possible.

levers off at the very end or at the moving axis (Fig. 7-31). These broken buttons or levers should be replaced and not repaired. Dismantle the entire assembly. Remove the end "C" washer and metal rod. Pull out the metal rod until the broken lever or button is free. Replace the new lever and fasten the metal rod with the "C" washer. These plastic buttons or levers must be obtained from the manufacturer.

Fig. 7-29. The tape cassette assembly might have to be removed to get at the take-up reel or turntable assembly adjustment. Move the metal spider ring to a higher level for greater pressure.

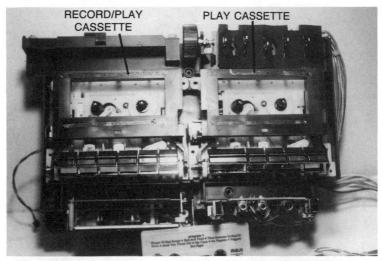

Fig. 7-30. Both the dual cassette decks' take-up must be adjusted when separate record/play and play cassette decks are combined in one boom box.

Fig. 7-31. Remove the entire cassette deck to remove and replace a broken lever or button. Pull the rod to the broken lever and replace it with a new one.

Fig. 7-31. The plastic doors of the cassette are easily broken and must be re-placed with the original. Make sure the metal trim plate is attached or comes with the plastic door.

Broken Cassette Door

The hinges on the front plastic door are easily broken when removing the door (Fig. 7-32). Some of these plastic doors snap down into place, while others are hinged at the outside ends. Carefully inspect the plastic door for mounting. First order the plastic door from the dealer, manufacturer, or service depot. Some of the plastic doors come with the metal trim plate, while in other models both plastic door and trim plates must be ordered. Use extreme care when mounting the door into position.

8

Cassette Deck Problems

The cassette tape deck can be found in the larger AM-FM-MPX combination or in a compact model. Features might include special slip clutches, automatic shut-off, and other special circuits. Most compact tape decks are front loaded (Fig. 8-1). Problems with the larger cassette tape decks are very similar to those of the portable player. Here are some of the most common troubles that you might encounter in your cassette tape deck.

KEEPS BLOWING FUSES

Most compact tape decks have a separate ON/OFF switch along with a line fuse. When the dial lights will not light or the amplifier hums, suspect a blown fuse or defective power transformer. Try to locate the fuse holder on the rear apron or close to the power transformer.

If the fuse blows again, suspect an overload condition in the low-voltage power supply or the audio output circuits (Fig. 8-2). First check for leaky silicon diodes in the power supply. Remove one end of each diode to check continuity. Only a 10-ohm reading should be noted with reversed test leads. Check the continuity of the primary and secondary winding of the power transformer. With the diode out of the circuit, the ohmmeter should read below 20 ohms in each winding. In case the low-voltage power circuits are normal, check the regulator and audio circuits.

Fig. 8-1. This Realistic Model SCT-15 cassette tape deck comes with front loading.

You might find a small voltage-regulator circuit in some models. In the power supply shown in Fig. 8-3, there are actually two different voltage sources. One source supplies power to the motor circuit, while the bridge rectifier system provides regulated voltage to the audio and recording circuits. A leaky voltage regulator transistor can keep blowing out the line fuse. Remove the transistor from the circuit

FILTER CAPACITORS

LOW-VOLTAGE POWER SUPPLY

POWER TRANSFORMER

Fig. 8-2. At bottom left is a typical low-voltage power supply.

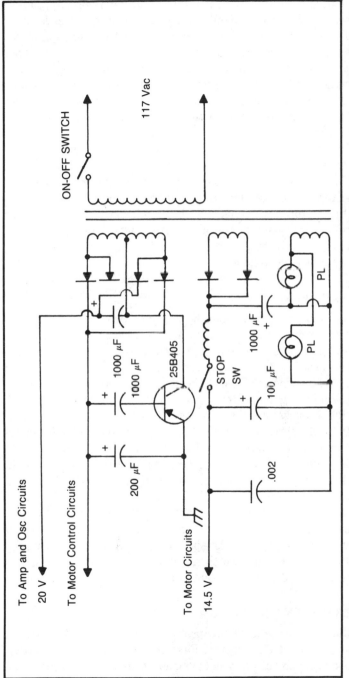

Fig. 8-3. Here two separate voltage sources are included. The 20-volt source has a transistor as the voltage regulator, and the 14-volt motor circuit uses two transistors in a speed-control circuit.

and test. If a flat-type regular transistor is used here, replace it. These thin transistors seem to break down easily under load.

Determine if the unit is overloaded only when the tape player begins to run. A separate on/off switch usually turns on the amplifier circuits, and when the play button is engaged the motor is already operating. If this is the case, suspect a defective motor or switch assembly. You may find a pinched wire going to chassis ground in the tape player. Inspect the wiring connecting the small motor and switch assembly.

Remove the amplifier circuits from the power supply to determine if the overload condition is in the amplifier section. Unsolder the B + lead from the power supply. Suspect leaky output transistors if the fuse does not blow and the pilot lights come on and the motor is rotating. Check for a leaky transistor and/or electrolytic capacitor in the amplifier circuits. You might find a mounting screw holding the pc board to the metal bracket is shorting out the dc supply voltage.

NO TAPE MOTION

The tape might not rotate because of a defective switch, broken belt, broken switch lever, torn connecting wires, or defective motor. Before tearing into the tape player, inspect the pause control button—make sure the pause button is off. Check for lighted dial lights, and turn the volume up to hear amplifier noise in the speakers.

Go directly to the motor when you can hear hum in the speakers with the dial lights on. If the motor is on, check for a loose or broken belt. Measure the voltage (12 to 14 V) at the motor terminals if the motor is not rotating (Fig. 8-4). No voltage measurement might indicate poor motor connecting wires or a defective play switch. Check for dirty switch contacts. Clean off the contact with alcohol and a small fingernail file.

Remove the small motor belt and spin the motor pulley if correct voltage is found at the motor terminals. If the motor starts, suspect frozen motor bearings or a flat spot on the armature. Generally, the small tape motor is not worth repairing. Replace the drive motor if you have dead or intermittent conditions.

INTERMITTENT ROTATION

Most intermittent rotation problems are caused by dirty switch contacts or a defective motor. First determine if the intermittent rotation problem occurs in all functions. If the tape is erratic in the

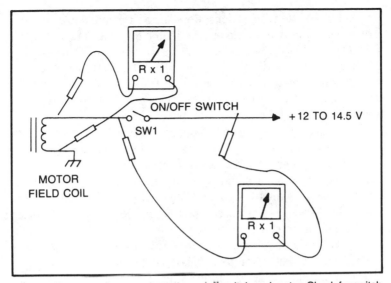

Fig. 8 4. If tape won't move, check the on/off switch and motor. Check for switch continuity across the switch terminals. Remove one lead from the motor and measure the field resistance with the ohmmeter on the R×1 scale.

play mode, suspect a dirty switch or defective motor (Fig. 8-5). Sometimes when any function button is pressed, the switch contacts that supply power to the motor might not make good contact. Clean the switch contacts with a fingernail file and alcohol.

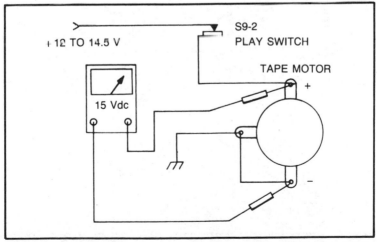

Fig. 8-5. An erratic motor can cause intermittent rotation. Monitor the voltage at the motor terminals and note if the voltage measurement is constant when the motor stops rotating.

For intermittent operations, determine if the motor is on or not. For instance, in rewind mode, the motor belt might turn but the rewind turntable won't move. Suspect the belt is too loose and is slipping over the rewind pulley (Fig. 8-6). If this is the case, simply install a new motor drive belt. If it takes a while to order a replacement, temporarily repair the slippage with a coat of non-slip liquid such as rosin on the plastic pulley drive surface.

Take-up or rewind slippage can also be caused by a poor friction clutch. Look for a spider-type spring at the bottom of the turntable. To add more pressure and prevent possible slippage, turn the spider spring clockwise. You must pull the spider spring up to the next notch. This raises the turntable, adding more pressure to the friction clutch. If the clutch is too loose, tape can be pulled from the cassette.

Suspect an intermittent motor if voltage is found at the motor terminals but the motor will not rotate (Fig. 8-7). Monitor the supply voltage on the motor terminals to determine if the motor is intermittent. Sometimes the intermittent motor won't rotate if the motor pulley is held in the PLAY mode. Grasp the motor pulley and hold it for a few seconds. If the motor will not start or is erratic,

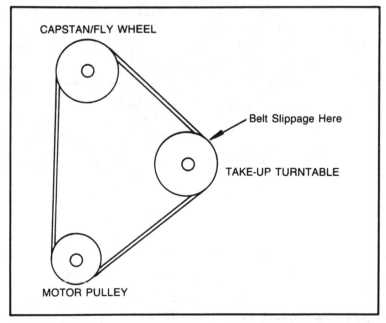

Fig. 8-6. An erratic rewind turntable can cause tape pulling or intermittent operation. Check for a loose belt or a defective clutch. Adjust the tension screw or spring on the turntable clutch.

Fig. 8-7. Suspect a defective motor if you have intermittent or erratic rotation. Grasp the motor and stop it—then see if the motor will start up again. Do this several times.

replace it. Also check the motor regulator circuits for intermittent conditions.

NO SOUND BUT SPINDLES ROTATE

No sound from the tape deck can be caused by a defective amplifier, tape head, or loading mechanism. Note if the pinch roller is turning with the capstan drive shaft. Does the loading mechanism lock when the play button is pushed? Sometimes the loading assembly won't allow the cassette to touch the pinch roller and capstan area (Fig. 8-8). Check for a broken lever at the rear of the push-button assembly.

Determine if the VU meters are moving with the sound of the music. Although you cannot hear the music from the cassette, the

Fig. 8-8. Check for a frozen loading platform or broken play-lever assembly if the cassette will not engage the pinch roller and capstan.

amplifier circuits might be functioning with movement of the VU (or level) meters. If the meters are indicating, check for broken connecting cables. Two output cables are used in a preamp cassette tape deck. A broken or shorted cable could prevent sound from coming from either channel.

A broken wire connection on the tape head or a defective tape head will inhibit sound. Check the VU or level meters for indication. If the meters are not indicating, the no-sound problem might be in the tape head or the first two preamp transistor circuits. Usually one channel is defective but not both. Signal-trace the audio circuits with an audio-signal generator or separate amplifier. Voltage measurements should indicate a defective transistor.

TAPE AUTOMATICALLY STOPS

When the cassette stops automatically while depressing the play button, suspect problems within the loading mechanism, automatic shut-off, or APSS (automatic program search system) circuitry. Sometimes the small sliding bar lever right under the push-button assembly will not lock properly. Inspect the slide-bar assembly, but don't align the cassette to play to the end. Try another cassette. The cassette might be wound too tight. This extra pressure can cause the mechanism to kick out.

In units with automatic program search system (APSS), determine if these circuits or the loading mechanism is defective. Inspect the APSS solenoid assembly when the unit stops playing. If the solenoid does not energize or the solenoid lever does not move, suspect the mechanism assembly. When the solenoid lever is pulled with the solenoid energizing, the APSS circuitry is activating and kicking out the loading mechanism. Because the APSS circuitry is quite involved and complicated, it's best to take the player to a qualified sound technician.

In some APSS models, when the motor stops, the loading platform will kick out after a few seconds. Each time you push down the play button, the cassette automatically unloads. Check the motor circuitry. Measure the voltage at the motor terminals. No voltage at the motor with the play button depressed indicates poor wiring connections or dirty switch contacts.

Locate the switch that activates when the play button is depressed. The switch terminals might be dirty, preventing applying voltage to the motor. Spray cleaning fluid inside the switch assembly. Move the switch lever up and down to clean the contacts. Now plug in the power cord and see if the motor starts. In fact, it's not a bad idea to clean all moving switches the same way.

Automatically stop circuits are a lot easier to service (Fig. 8-9). Dirty switch contacts or faulty transistors or diodes usually cause most of the problems. Remove the transistors from the pc board

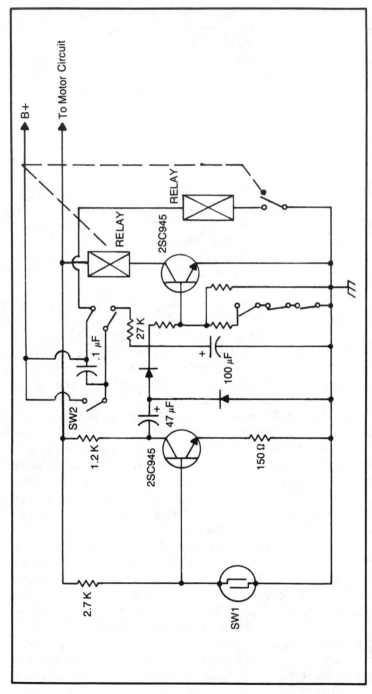

Fig. 8-9. Check each component in the automatic stop circuitry. Remove the transistor and one terminal of each diode for correct tests.

for leaky or open tests. Pull one end of the diode from the circuitry for ohmmeter tests. Check each relay field coil for continuity.

WON'T ERASE

When more than one recording is heard after several recordings, suspect a defective erase head. First make a few minor tests before tearing into the tape player.

Turn down the volume control. Keep the balance control in the center position. Disconnect any microphones or extension cables for outside recording. Set the tape counter at zero if one is located on the front panel. Insert a cassette that has a recording on it. You are going to erase a small portion of the tape, so choose a recording that can be erased.

Push RECORD. Let the tape record until 50 shows on the tape counter. Stop the player and rewind. Now listen for any signs of music or noise. With the volume fairly high, you should hear only a rushing noise. The erase circuits are not functioning if any signs of music are heard.

Clean the erase head with alcohol and a cleaning stick (Fig. 8-10). Check the erase head for a loose mounting. If the head does not

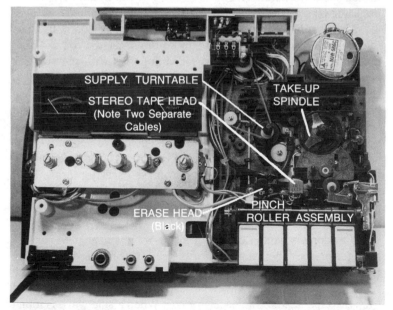

Fig. 8-10. An oxide-packed tape head can impair recording. The tape might work in play mode but not in recording. The erase head is always to the left of the play/record head.

meet the tape, the previous recording cannot be erased. Clean the record/play switch with contact spray. Spray the liquid inside the switch area. Move the record switch back and forth to clean the switch contacts. Check the erasing procedure again. If the erase head does not remove the previous recording, suspect a defective tape head or circuit. Remove the top panel. You may have to remove the whole front panel to get at the erase head if you have a front-panel cassette loading system. Check the tape head connections. A broken or loose ground can impair tape erase.

Follow the erase head cable to where it connects to the pc board. The erase-head cable is usually the smallest shielded cable coming from the tape-head area. Inspect the connection on the pc board. If all connections seem normal, remove the cable at the pc wiring and check the resistance of the erase head.

In small battery-operated portable tape players, the erase head can be excited by a dc voltage. Generally, the resistance of this type of erase head is below 200 ohms. With larger cassette decks, the erase and recording heads are excited by a bias voltage supplied from an oscillator bias circuit (Fig. 8-11). The bias signal frequency depends on the erase oscillator frequency and might differ from one manufacturer to another. The resistance of the erase head in the oscillator bias circuit is less than 10 ohms.

Always remove the erase head cable from the pc board, because the erase head is connected directly to the oscillator coil winding. Sometimes a 10-ohm resistor is found in series with the two coil windings. Now check the resistance of the oscillator coil windings. Usually the coil resistance is about double the resistance of the erase head. Resolder all terminals and check the recording mode again.

Check the voltages on the oscillator transistor. Improper voltages can indicate the transistor is defective. Remove the suspected transistor and test it out of the circuit. Check for supply voltage at the oscillator circuitry. In most oscillator erase-head circuits, the negative or ground terminal of the circuit is switched in the RECORD mode, so make sure this side of the circuit is grounded in the recording mode.

If a scope is handy, check for a sine-wave signal at the erase-head terminals. The frequency of the sine wave is determined by the manufacturer's circuitry. The cassette player must be in the recording mode. The sine wave or oscillator signal can be checked from the tape head to the oscillator coil. When a sine wave is found at the erase head terminal and the head is not erasing properly, re-place the erase head.

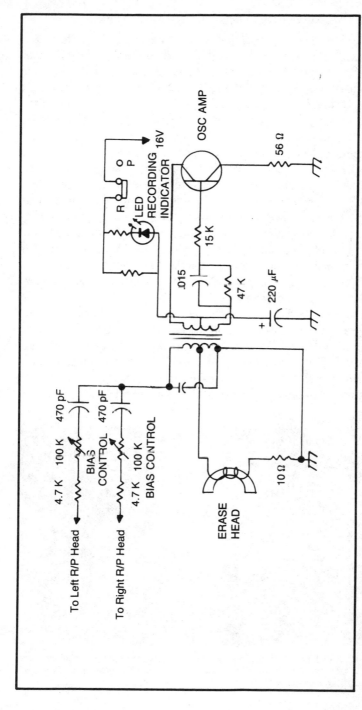

Fig. 8-11. Here is a typical oscillator erase-head circuit found in many tape decks. The oscillator bias frequency is also fed to each R/P tape head in the stereo tape deck.

173

WON'T PLAY OR RECORD IN ONE CHANNEL

If the deck has play or record problems, suspect a defective tape head or amplifier problem. Isolate it to the defective channel if only one channel operates normally in the play and record mode. Also suspect a bent recording lever or dirty play/record switch assembly (Fig. 8-12). Again check the movement of the VU meters. If both meters are indicating with a cassette playing, suspect problems after the meters or in the connecting amplifier cables.

Remove the top and front panels to gain access to the tape head. You will find two separate cables coming from a stereo tape head. Turn the volume up without a cassette loaded and press the PLAY button. You should hear a loud hiss in the normal channel. The defective channel might be entirely dead or have a low hum sound. Touch each ungrounded head terminal at the rear of the tape head. If both amplifiers are functioning, you should hear a loud hum in each stereo channel. Low or no sound from the defective channel indicates defective amplifier circuitry. Check each transistor stage and compare the gain to the good channel.

A loud hum indicates both channels are active. Check for a broken wire on the tape head. If both wires are intact, suspect an open tape head. Remove both wires from the dead tape-head terminals. Check the tape-head continuity with the VOM on the R × 100 scale. Compare the ohmmeter reading with the normal tape-head winding. Most tape-head coils open rather than short.

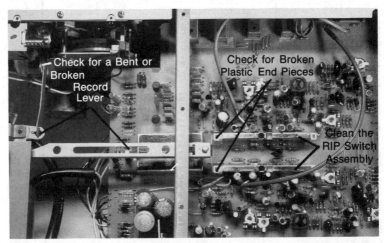

Fig. 8-12. One channel might not play or record with a bent or broken play/record level. Check for a broken plastic piece on the switch assembly. Clean all contacts within the PLAY/RECORD switch.

174

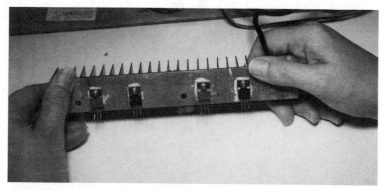

Fig. 8-13. Power output transistors are often mounted on separate heatsinks while others use the metal chassis as the heatsink.

DEAD LEFT CHANNEL

Suspect the audio output transistors or IC when only one channel is dead. Turn the balance control to the left side. Quickly rotate the volume control up and down. Is there a scratchy noise in the left speaker? Check the audio output circuits with no signs of audio or noise.

Measure the voltage at the collector terminals of the audio output transistors or the supply voltage pin of the power IC. Check the voltage at the insulated metal terminal of the power output transistors. The power transistors might be mounted on a separate heat sink (Fig. 8-13). Very low voltage might indicate a leaky transistor or IC.

Proceed to the audio input circuits if the output transistors and ICs seem to be normal. Check for pick-up hum at the volume control center terminal with volume wide open. A loud hum indicates the audio output stages are good. No or very little sound might indicate a defective af or driver transistor and IC component. Injecting an audio signal into the base terminal of each transistor can locate the dead stage. Test each suspected transistor in the circuit with the diode test or transistor tester. Take crucial voltage measurements on the transistor terminals.

DISTORTED RIGHT CHANNEL

Go directly to the audio output stages with distortion in either channel. Check the power supply voltage on the large power IC with distortion in both channels (Fig. 8-14). Measure the supply voltage on pin 8. If the voltage is very low, suspect a leaky IC. Distortion

175

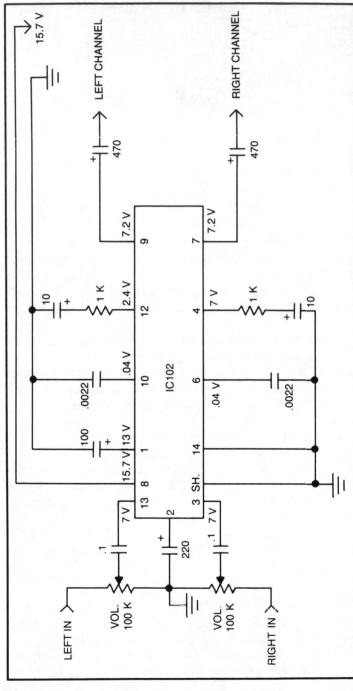

Fig. 8-14. Check the supply voltage pin on the large power IC when there is excessive distortion. If the voltage is low, replace the leaky output IC.

Fig. 8-15. If no schematic is available, compare the voltage and resistance measurements of the suspected transistors in the bad channel to those in the good channel.

in the IC output circuit might be caused by broken pin resistors or leaky electrolytic capacitors.

Excessive distortion in transistor circuits occurs with leaky or open output transistors. Test all output transistors in the distorted output channel for leakage. Remove any output transistor suspected of leakage and test it out of the circuit. Compare the voltage and resistance measurements to chassis ground with each transistor terminal (Fig. 8-15). Compare these measurements with the good channel when a voltage chart or schematic is not available. Universal power output transistors can replace the original transistors without any problems.

9

Phonograph Repairs
and Adjustments

A wide variety of problems can occur in portable or in record players. Some of the problems are very simple, while others are a bit more complex. Here are some of the most common problems possible.

CHANGING THE STYLUS OR NEEDLE

When the pickup arm skips across the record, suspect a defective stylus needle (Fig. 9-1). A defective needle might produce a scratchy sound. Dull or broken stylus points can damage the grooves in your records. To prevent this, clean out all dust and dirt with a small brush.

First be sure the stylus is not turned to the 78 rpm side (styluses are usually double-sided). The 78-rpm stylus point is too big and might not stay in the smaller 33⅓ record groove. Hold the stylus under a magnifying glass to determine if the point is broken, worn, or rounded off. Replace the stylus if small black chips or a duller appearance is noted after playing a small portion of the record. Hold the record under a strong light and check the area played. The defective stylus can dig out the groove and it will appear very dull.

Most needles are held in position with a small clip or keeper. Hold the pickup arm as high as possible. Lift up on the clip and the stylus will slip out. Some lower priced units might have a small screw holding the stylus in place. Others just clip in over the cartridge body. In larger units, the whole cartridge assembly might have to be removed to get at the stylus. Be very careful not to damage the saddle

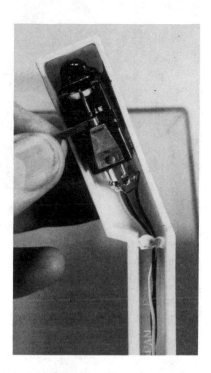

Fig. 9-1. When the pickup arm skips across the record, suspect a defective stylus.

the stylus rests in. Reverse the procedure in replacing the new stylus.

DEFECTIVE CARTRIDGE

The cartridge is the housing for the stylus. The defective cartridge can create a mushy, weak, or distorted sound. When only one channel operates intermittently, suspect a defective crystal cartridge. In stereo units you might find only one channel defective. Most cartridges will be damaged if the pickup arm is dropped or placed in excessive heat (Fig. 9-2). Don't leave a portable phonograph out in the hot afternoon sun.

To determine if the cartridge is intermittent, play a record at normal volume. Place extra pressure with thumb and forefinger on the cartridge area. Now push the arm from side to side or up and down—not enough to jump the record grooves, but with enough pressure to cause the intermittent condition to act up. If the cartridge is defective, the volume will cut up and down in that channel.

A defective cartridge can also cause very low distortion or no sound. At the back of the cartridge, touch the ungrounded lead with a pocket knife or screwdriver point. Turn the volume up for this

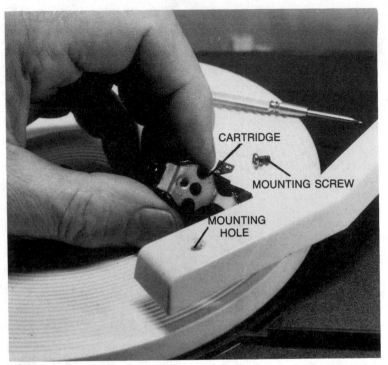

Fig. 9-2. The phono cartridge can become damaged from being dropped or from too much heat. Suspect a defective cartridge when you have a mushy, distorted, or weak sound. You can also have a weak or dead channel due to a defective stereo cartridge.

test. You should hear a loud hum on each side of the stereo cartridge. If one side is weak, suspect problems in the amplifier circuits.

Check the small wire terminals at the rear of the suspected cartridge. Sometimes these wires break off or have poor connections. Always remove the small prong clip before making any soldering connections to prevent damaging the cartridge. Only a drop of solder is needed.

The defective cartridge might be removed by turning a clip at the front or by loosening small mounting screws. If no screws are visible, look closely at the front of the cartridge for a small metal clip. Pry outward with a pocket knife or small screwdriver blade. Some cartridges are held in position with two side-mounting screws. You may also find only one screw on top of the cartridge holding it in position.

Before removing the cartridge, mark down where each colored wire goes. The red and green wires are usually on one side and the black and white wires are on the other side of the stereo channel. The green and black wires are ground or common shield terminals. Replace the new cartridge in the very same manner. Be very careful when handling each wire—don't break them off or damage the new cartridge. Keep the soldering-iron tip away from the front of the cartridge.

RUNS TOO SLOW

Slow speeds can be caused by a worn idler wheel. Check the rubber idler wheel for worn or rounded areas. A slick idler wheel indicates slippage between the wheel and motor drive area. Excessive oil on the rubber drive area can cause slow speeds (Fig. 9-3). Clean the idler wheel with alcohol and a cloth. If you hear a bumping noise as the turntable rotates, this indicates a burned area in the rubber wheel caused by the motor drive shaft. Replacing the idler wheel will solve a lot of slow or erratic speed problems.

Check the turntable drive area for possible signs of slippage. Excessive rubber tire marks on the drive surface can be repaired with surface compound. Clean off the drive area with alcohol and a cloth. Apply liquid rosin or regular turntable dressing. Some of the turntable dressing compounds have a small gritty iron substance

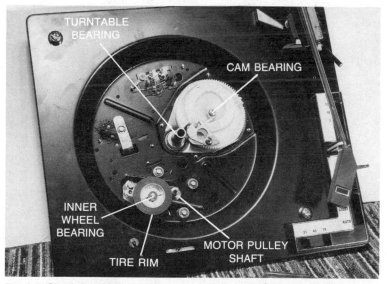

Fig. 9-3. Check these areas for slow or erratic speed. Clean all rotating areas with alcohol and a cloth, because oil or grease on any contact area can cause slow speeds.

in the liquid. When applied, it gives greater traction to the rubber idler wheel against the turntable rim area.

A defective motor can cause slow speeds. Proper cleaning and lubrication solves most motor speed problems. Clean the motor drive pulley with alcohol and a cloth. As a last resort, when all other components are checked for slow speed problems, a coat of slip compound on the pulley drive area might help.

TURNTABLE WON'T SPIN

If the turntable will not move and a loud hum comes from the turntable area, suspect a frozen motor assembly (Fig. 9-4). The frozen motor can be caused by dry or gummed-up motor bearings. Lift the turntable off and try to spin the motor pulley with your fingers. If the motor starts very slowly, suspect gummed-up bearings. When

Fig. 9-4. When the turntable won't turn, suspect a frozen motor. Check for gummed-up or dry motor bearings. Turn the motor shaft with your fingers. If the motor then starts to run, remove it and clean the motor bearings.

a squeaky noise is heard, the bearings are badly worn or very dry. In either case, the motor should be removed and cleaned. Pull off the bottom bearing assembly and wash with tuner lube or cleaning wash. Generally, the top bearing assembly remains with the armature of the motor. Wash out all the old oil or grease. When the armature bearing area begins to shine, you have removed all the old oil. Now apply several drops of oil to each bearing or cup area. Reassemble the small motor.

Spin the motor shaft with your fingers. If the motor will not turn freely, you might have to realign the mounting bolts. Now let the motor run for an hour. If the motor appears very hot, the motor's field coil might have some shorted turns. Sometimes if the motor freezes up a week or two after a good cleanup, replace the defective motor.

If the motor will not rotate and no hum is heard, suspect an open motor winding or ON/OFF switch. Set the VOM at the R×1 scale. Check for continuity across the ON/OFF switch, then check the motor field winding (Fig. 9-5). You should have less than 50 ohms across the motor terminals. If open, check for broken wires coming from the motor winding to the motor terminals. You must replace the defective motor with the exact replacement from the manufacturer.

A dry or frozen center turntable bearing might not allow the motor to rotate. Suspect the bearing if the turntable is difficult to remove. Wash out the gummed-up bearings with alcohol and a small brush. The turntable should now rotate freely. Apply phonolube or light grease to the center hub bearings.

Suspect a broken or worn idler wheel if you have no turntable rotation. Remove the turntable. Note if the motor is running. If so, check for a frozen idler wheel. Remove the idler wheel. Clean out the bearing with alcohol. Apply a light oil on the bearing area; then check the idler wheel rotation. The idler wheel should engage the motor pulley.

BELT WILL NOT STAY ON

The belt can come off in motor-driven turntables. Remove the turntable platter and check the motor belt (Fig. 9-6). The belt might not stay on the motor pulley and turntable if the belt is too large. Check for a cracked or broken belt. The normal belt should fit snugly around the drive rim of the turntable. Clean the belt off with alcohol and a cloth if it appears oily.

If the belt is broken or too large, replace it. Lay the old belt or the pieces alongside a ruler and measure the length of the belt

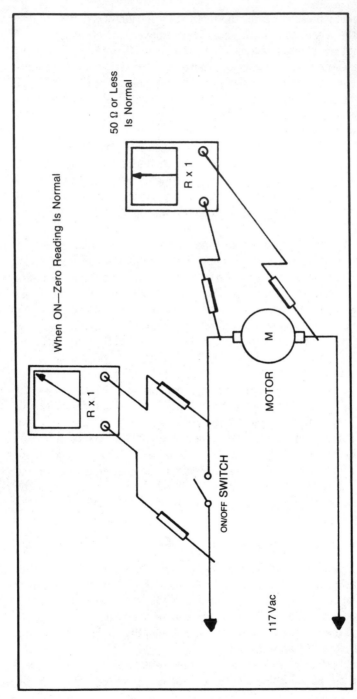

When ON—Zero Reading Is Normal

50 Ω or Less
Is Normal

R x 1

R x 1

ON/OFF SWITCH

MOTOR

M

117 Vac

Fig. 9-5. Check the continuity across the ON/OFF switch and motor field winding. If the motor winding reading is greater than 50 ohms, suspect a defective field winding.

Fig. 9-6. Remove the turntable platter and check the motor belt when there is no rotation. Check the belt for loose or broken pieces.

(Fig. 9-7). Take this measurement or the old belt to your electronics dealer for a new one. If the belt or some pieces are missing, take the turntable in so the belt rim can be measured for a replacement. To replace, hold the belt with left finger through the platter cut-out and place it over the motor pulley.

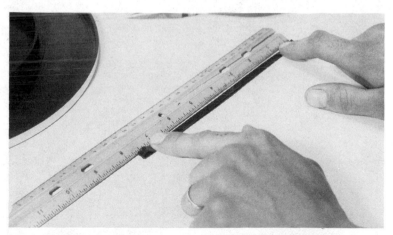

Fig. 9-7. Lay the old belt alongside a ruler to get the correct length. The good belt should fit snugly around the belt drive rim before being placed around the motor pulley.

SOUND IS UNEVEN

Uneven music may be caused by oil on the drive surfaces or improper idler-wheel adjustment. If handy, place a record strobe disk on the turntable and note if the speed changes. First clean the idler rubber drive area with alcohol and a cloth. Clean off the inside turntable rim and motor pulley.

If the speed is still jerky, inspect the area where the idler wheel rides against the motor pulley (Fig. 9-8). The rubber tire rim might be riding part way up on the 33⅓ section and sometimes on the 45 rpm area. This causes uneven or jerky motion. Look for a small, screw adjustment beside the idler wheel assembly. Turn the screw (with the speed set at 33⅓) so the tire rim runs about halfway up on this drive area. Now turn the speed indicator to 45 rpm and see if it's tracking properly. The faster the speed, the bigger the diameter of the motor drive area. Check all speed functions for any erratic motion.

Fig. 9-8. Jerky turntable motion can be caused by the idler wheel riding partly on the corresponding speed drive area. Set the adjustment screw so the idler wheel rides in the center of each speed area.

Fig. 9-9. Tonearm adjustments. The tonearm set-down and arm height are the most important. After making each adjustment, test several times with a good record.

TONEARM SLIDES OFF RECORD

Improper setdown adjustment can cause the tonearm to hit the edge and slide off the record. Adjust the pickup arm set-down adjustment when the pickup arm lands just off the record or too far inside the landing area. Turn the small screw under (or alongside) the base of the pickup arm assembly. For correct adjustment, turn the screw so the stylus will land ⅛ inch from the edge of a 12-inch record. You might have to load the record several times before correct adjustment is achieved. Sometimes only a quarter of a turn is sufficient (Fig. 9-9).

For tonearm height adjustment, a small hex screw is located under the tonearm. On some models, hold the nut firmly and turn the screwhead counter-clockwise. To lower the tonearm, reverse the procedure. Adjust the tonearm to clear its arm rest by ⅛ inch. In older models, a small screw with a metal flange was used inside the tonearm for height adjustment. If the arm is adjusted too high, the tonearm might hit the top-loaded records.

Stylus pressure should be set with a stylus pressure gauge, found in most local hi-fi stores. The stylus pressure indicator on the side of the tonearm is for reference only and indicates an increase or decrease in stylus pressure setting. When the arm glides across the record or flies up, not enough arm pressure is applied. Most tonearms are adjusted between 3.5 and 5.5 grams. When in doubt, always follow the manufacturer's adjustment procedure.

TONEARM DOESN'T REJECT

If the pickup arm will not reject at the end of the record, reject it manually. Grab the tonearm and move it towards the inside of the record. If the tonearm will not reject in either case, remove the top turntable. Most of these turntables are held down with a large "C" washer. Suspect the small tripping lever on the plastic cam gear assembly (Fig. 9-10).

If the trip lever is frozen, remove the small "C" washer, pull off the cam gear assembly, and wash out the bearing area. Work

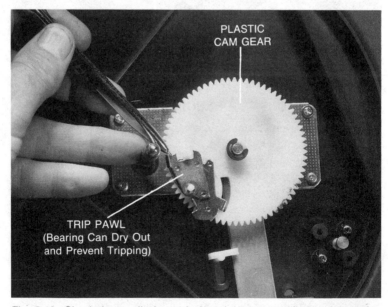

PLASTIC
CAM GEAR

TRIP PAWL
(Bearing Can Dry Out
and Prevent Tripping)

Fig. 9-10. Check the small trip pawl when the tonearm will not reject at the end of the record. This small lever is located on the cam assembly under the turntable.

the trip lever back and forth. Intermittent rejection can be caused by an old or gummed-up trip-lever bearing.

Replace all components and play another record. The tonearm can be started about one inch from the inside trip groove of the record. If the tonearm will not trip by itself, check for a dragging tonearm slide lever. The lever might be bent and out of line. Check for friction and free movement of the tonearm. Note if a tight cartridge cable is holding the arm at the rear of the tonearm.

Improper stylus set-down adjustment may prevent the tonearm from playing the previous record. Readjust the stylus set-down at the center of the lead-in groove (at the beginning of the record). Suspect a defective record if only that record will not reject or play the entire record. The record might have a worn groove or scratch, causing the arm to keep repeating.

TONEARM DOESN'T MOVE

The tonearm cannot move off of the resting post if the holding clip is over the tonearm! Before turning the phonograph on, remove the tonearm holder clip (Fig. 9-11). In some players, the tonearm is held in the rest position by two plastic clamps. The tonearm is clamped in position automatically after the record player shuts off.

If the arm must be picked up off the rest area and placed on the record, suspect improper arm height adjustment. If the height adjustment is too low, the arm can't lift off the rest. The height adjustment is located underneath and at the rear of the tonearm.

Check for broken linkage or a jammed cycling mechanism under the turntable. Rotate the turntable by hand away from the stylus. If the turntable rotates easily, the tonearm should follow. If the turntable is jammed, remove it to see if the cycling cam rotates. Turn it by hand. An excessively dry cam or tonearm pivot bearing can freeze, preventing the arm from cycling.

TONEARM DOESN'T RETURN

The tonearm should automatically return at the end of the record to the arm rest (in a semi-automatic turntable). Check for a bent trip-clutch assembly. Re-align the clutch plate or replace it. Inspect the auto lever for poor alignment. In some models, the auto lever strikes the micro switch and shuts the player down after the arm returns (Fig. 9-12). Turn adjustment screw C clockwise if the tonearm automatically returns before the end of the record.

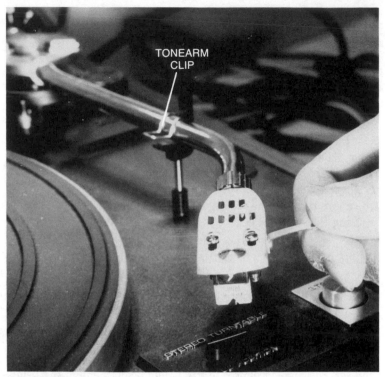

TONEARM
CLIP

Fig. 9-11. Remove the tonearm clip before attempting to play a record. This clip holds the arm in place and prevents any damage to the stylus or cartridge.

TONEARM DOESN'T TRACK ON RECORD

First check the stylus for a chipped or broken point. If the stylus is clogged with dirt and lint, the needle might jump the record groove. Clean it with a small brush and see if the tonearm tracks properly. If not, shut the player off and place the function switch on the manual or start position. Pick up the tonearm and move it towards the center spindle (Fig. 9-13). Note if the tonearm seems to drag or if it stops at any point before the trip area. The tonearm might be binding. Lubricate the pivot bearing with light oil. Check the cartridge cable at the end of the tonearm. The cable might not have enough slack and is keeping the arm from going to the center of the record. Pull out some extra cable from underneath the turntable area.

The activating pawl is located underneath the turntable on a plastic or molded cam. If the pawl is sluggish, remove it from the cam assembly. In many cases the grease builds up on the activating pawl bearing and will not let it move. Take the activating pawl

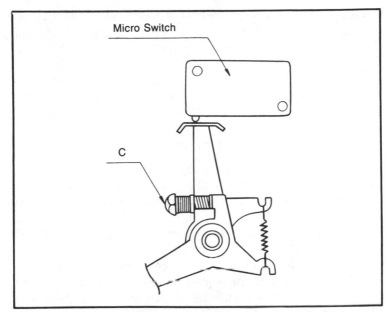

Fig. 9-12. Check the clutch plate and arm adjustment if the tonearm does not return (in a semi-automatic turntable). Adjust screw C clockwise if the tonearm returns before the music has finished.

Fig. 9-13. Pick up the tonearm and move it toward the center spindle. Note if the tonearm seems to drag or stop at any point before the trip area.

assembly apart, clean it with alcohol, and lubricate it with light oil. Reassemble and replace it on the cam assembly. Now take hold of the tonearm and note if the pivot assembly trips the rotating cam assembly.

Check also for insufficient stylus pressure. The arm tension might be set too close, lifting the arm up from the record. Adjust the stylus pressure according to the manufacturer's literature.

TONEARM GOES TO THE CENTER OF THE RECORD

When the tonearm automatically goes to the center of the record while attempting to play a 12-inch record, suspect the record control lever is not set correctly. The function lever might be turned to the 7- or 10-inch record location. If not, move the control lever back and forth. Check for a missing screw from the plastic control lever.

In older players, a trip lever is located close to the tonearm post. When a 12-inch record is played, the record comes down and trips the mechanism. Then the tonearm sets down at the beginning of the 12-inch record. In checking the turntable operation without a record, the trip lever must be tripped by hand. If not, the arm will drop close to the middle of the turntable.

You might discover a piece of missing linkage between the control lever and the record size mechanism. With the record player removed from the cabinet, rotate the turntable slowly by hand. Note how the tonearm drops down. If the set-down adjustment is off, the arm might miss the record edge or go towards the center of the record. The function lever mechanism might be gummed up. Clean out with alcohol and lubricate with light oil.

RECORDS FAIL TO DROP

Note if the center spindle is not completely seated or is bent when records fail to drop. In some turntables, the center spindle is stationary and cannot be removed, while in others it can be removed (Fig. 9-14). This type of spindle must be pushed all the way down and lined up with a small notch at the base of the turntable bearing area for correct function.

Without a record on the turntable, rotate the turntable by hand and check the record feed lever. This lever is inside the record spindle. The lever could be bent and unable to push off the next record. If so, the whole spindle assembly should be replaced.

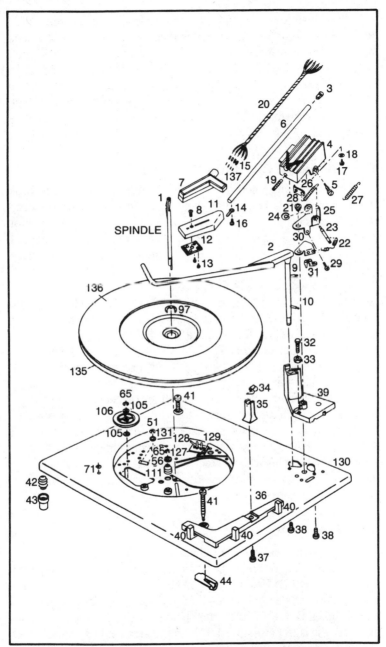

SPINDLE

Fig. 9-14. The center spindle can be removed in some models. Make sure the spindle is in tight and pressed down against the turntable bearing area.

If the feed lever and spindle seem normal, but the feed lever does not come out far enough to push the record off the post, check for a spring missing from the link feed lever. This is located underneath the spindle area. Replace or reposition the spring. In some models, a spring-type clip pushes the feed lever upwards as it engages the record. If the feed lever does not come up high enough, it will not push off the next record. Simply bending the foldover spring clip will solve this problem.

TWO OR MORE RECORDS DROP AT ONCE

Check the center hole of the records when two or more records fall at once. The hole could be worn out, letting the records drop with the preceding record. When only one record seems to do it every time, check its center hole area. This same record might not push off the spindle post when played singly. At any rate, replace the record.

Several records might drop at once if the control arm (or record keeper) is not fully down, due to incorrectly loaded records. Remove the records and note if the control arm falls into position under its own weight. If not, clean the shaft area with alcohol and a cloth. The control arm might be slightly bent, preventing the records from sitting level. Twist or bend the control arm until the record stack is parallel to the top surface of the turntable.

Two or more records might fall when the record keeper lever is out of place. This small lever is located at the top of the spindle. The lever must fall in place so that only one record will be pushed off the spindle post. If not, two or more records might drop at once. This usually happens when a stack of records is played. To prevent this, always pull the whole stack of records completely off the turntable and then reload.

TONEARM REPLACEMENT

A broken or bent tonearm should be replaced with the original part number. To remove the complete tonearm assembly, first unsolder the pickup lead assembly from the phono socket or terminal strap. Loosen the set screw on the pickup hinge assembly. Sometimes a C washer holds the spindle assembly in place. If only the tone arm is to be removed, loosen the small outside pivot screw and lift the arm off. Be careful not to loosen the balance or spindle spring. Pull out the cartridge wires through the slot in the base of the metal turntable plate. Reverse the procedure when installing the new tonearm. Write down what components are removed and lay them out in line so they can be returned in the correct order.

WON'T SHUT OFF AFTER LAST RECORD

After the last record has played, most turntables will automatically shut off. A few older models might not have this provision. Note if the tonearm has returned to the rest stop. Check for a faulty switch. Place the ohmmeter leads across the ac phono switch (with power cord pulled) and work the switch back and forth. Sometimes the switch lever binds or the switch leads are too tight, resulting in poor switching action.

If the turntable shuts off before the last record is played, check for a bent arm keeper. The tone arm might be bent up from grasping the front end of the keeper to load records. In some changers, the thickness of the last record governs the playing of the last record. Simply bend the arm keeper down and level with the loaded record. Be very careful not to break off the arm keeper.

If the arm keeper will not go down completely, clean and wipe off the round arm-keeper shaft. Lubricate the shaft area. Check the top arm keeper screw at the back. The arm keeper might be loose, preventing last-record shut-off. Also check for a worn or out-of-place shock rubber on the arm keeper shaft.

In some portable changers, a small lever at the bottom slide assembly can be frozen or sluggish. When the small lever becomes frozen or sluggish because of old grease, the lever will remain inside and not trip the arm mechanism to shut off the last record (Fig. 9-15). Clean and lubricate the lever bearing until the small spring keeps the lever pushed outward.

BUMPING NOISE

A worn or burned tire on the idler wheel can produce a bumping noise. Suspect a burned groove in the rubber tire if the turntable or idler wheel will not rotate. The motor pulley can keep running and wear a groove in the rubber tire. As the idler wheel rotates against the turntable rim, you might hear a bumping sound. Replace the worn idler wheel.

Check for foreign material inside the turntable rim for a thumping noise. If the thin spacer is missing from the turntable bearing, you might hear the turntable rim scrape against the sides. This small

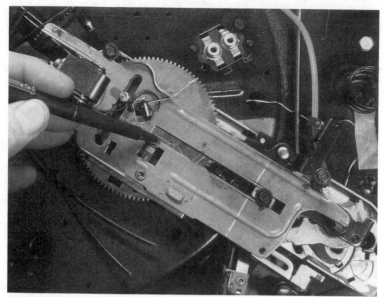

Fig. 9-15. If the record player will not turn off after playing the last record, suspect a defective ac switch. Check for a possibly stuck lever located in the slide assembly of some older changers.

bearing spacer can come off when the turntable is lifted out of the player area. Look for it inside the bearing area or loose on the workbench.

NOISY TURNTABLE

Excessively dry turntable bearings can produce a grinding noise in the turntable area. Remove the turntable and note if the noise stops. If so, wash out the bearings with alcohol. Lubricate with phono lube or a light grease. Be sure all space washers are in the correct place.

A rumbling noise can be caused by defective motor grommets. The motor must float freely on the mounting grommets. Replace them if the rubber grommets are cracked and old. Check for a missing grommet in the motor mount. Most phono motors have at least three rubber motor mounts.

Dirty or worn turntable bearings can cause motor rumble. Clean and lubricate the bearings. If the ball-bearing rack is worn or several ball bearings are missing, replace the bearing assembly. Lubricate the turntable bearings with phono lube or use light grease on the ball-bearing assembly.

Dry or worn motor bearings can cause a high-pitched squeal or turntable noise (Fig. 9-16). Remove the turntable and note if the noise continues. Pull the idler wheel away from the motor pulley to determine if the idler wheel is causing the noise. Grab the motor pulley and stop the motor. Suspect defective motor bearings if the noise stops. Remove the motor and wash out the bearings with alcohol. Apply light oil to the motor bearings. If the noise continues, the motor should be replaced. These motor replacements are fairly expensive so check the price before ordering a new one.

DEFECTIVE 45 RPM SPINDLE

When the 45 rpm records will not play or load properly, suspect a defective 45 spindle. These spindles come in various sizes and shapes. The older units consist of a large body with extended plastic fingers to drop the record down (Fig. 9-17). A pair of thin levers comes out to hold up the stack of records while the bottom record falls down ready to play. Other 45 rpm spindles are simply a piece of molded plastic that fits over the regular spindle.

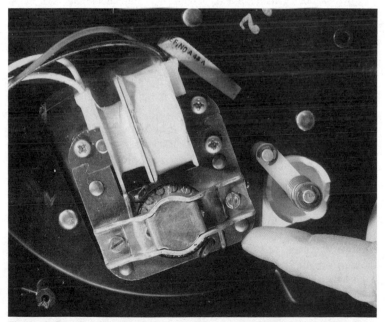

Fig. 9-16. Dry or worn motor bearings can cause a high-pitched squeal. Stop the motor pulley by hand to determine if the motor is causing the noise. Clean and lubricate motor bearings. The motor should be replaced if the bearings are excessively worn.

Fig. 9-17. A defective or improperly seated 45 rpm spindle may not play the 45 records. Make sure the spindle is down against the turntable.

The 45 rpm spindle fits down over the regular 33⅓ record spindle. Make sure the spindle sets completely down on the turntable. Check to see if the slotted area fits over the regular record spindle. Improper seating of the 45 spindle can cause damage or prevent it from dropping the records.

Apply talcum powder around the body of the 45 spindle if the records seem to be binding. A drop of oil inside the lever and finger areas can help provide proper 45 rpm record loading.

CLEANING AND LUBRICATION

A good cleanup and lubrication solves a lot of turntable speed problems (Fig. 9-18). Any sign of grease or oil on the idler wheel, motor drive area, or turntable rim can produce speed problems. For slow or erratic speed conditions, clean off the idler wheel, tire, and turntable rim with alcohol.

A dirty or gummed-up motor might need the bearings washed out to restore the correct turntable speed. Use a light machine oil on the upper and lower motor bearings. Only a drop will do. If the turntable speed is still slow with idler wheel replacement and cleanup, suspect a defective motor.

Slow speed might be caused by the idler wheel slipping on the turntable rim. Clean the inside with alcohol. Apply a coat of liquid rosin or turntable dressing. Some types of turntable dressing have small grit inside the liquid for greater traction. Brush an even coat on the turntable rim. Let it dry for a half hour before replacing the turntable. Check for correct speed with a strobe disc.

Apply a drop of oil to the idler wheel bearing. Only light oil should be applied to the tonearm raising spindle. Be very careful not to overdo it. Excessive oil or grease may run down on the rubber tire of the idler pulley or inside of the turntable rim. Use a light grease or regular phono lube in sliding areas. Apply grease to the speed-change and idler-pulley arm. A light coat of grease can be applied to the large turntable bearing after cleaning it with alcohol. Also apply a light coat of grease to the bearing surfaces of the operating plate and glide mechanism. Use only a small amount when lubricating to prevent further speed problems.

DEAD CHANNEL

When the sound is dead or weak in one channel, suspect a defective cartridge or amplifier. Turn the volume wide open and turn

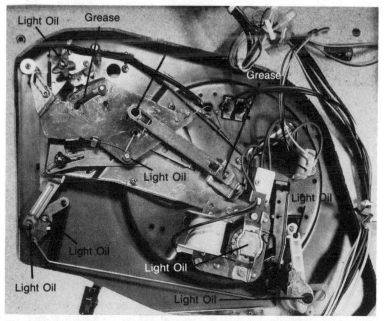

Fig. 9-18. Check these areas for correct turntable lubrication. Be very careful not to use two much oil or grease—only a drop is needed.

the balance control to the weak or dead channel. When you thumb the needle, a loud hum should be heard. If the other channel is normal, check at the rear of the cartridge.

Touch a knife or screwdriver blade against the small terminals of the cartridge. Try both cartridge terminals. You should hear a loud hum. If not, the amplifier section is defective. If a loud hum is heard, one channel of the cartridge is defective. Replace it with an exact replacement cartridge.

When very little or no hum is heard at the cartridge terminal, go right to the amplifier section (Fig. 9-19). Try the hum test at the center terminal of the volume control. A louder hum at this point

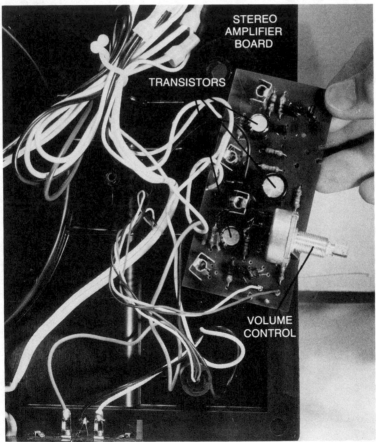

Fig. 9-19. A defective transistor can cause a weak or dead condition. Check for a humming sound by placing the screwdriver blade on each terminal at the rear of the cartridge terminal. If no hum is heard, suspect a defective audio section.

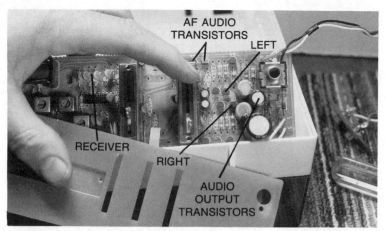

Fig. 9-20. A weak sound condition may be caused by a defective transistor, coupling capacitor, or IC. Very weak conditions may be located with an audio-signal generator.

might indicate the circuit is normal from the volume control to the speaker. Then check for a defective transistor or coupling capacitor ahead of the volume control.

The small amplifier can be checked with signal injection, separate amplifier, or voltage tests. If an audio-signal generator is handy, inject a signal at the input of the amplifier to the first transistor stage. Start at the volume control and go to the base of each transistor until the noise is lost. Now take voltage measurements on the suspected transistor. A separate amplifier can be used to signal-trace the lost signal with a record playing. This method is very effective in larger amplifiers where weak conditions are noted. Weak conditions can be caused by open coupling capacitors, transistors, or ICs.

WEAK CHANNEL

A weak or mushy channel might be caused by a defective cartridge, coupling capacitors, transistor, or IC. For weak and noisy sounds, suspect a defective cartridge. Simply exchange the small leads at the cartridge terminals. A mushy channel sound might be caused by a defective speaker. Exchange the speaker connections to determine if the speaker is defective.

When the weak condition is found inside the amplifier section, use an audio-signal generator and self-contained speaker as an indicator. If a scope is handy, use it as the indicating instrument.

Start at the cartridge terminals and inject the audio signal. Go from base to base of each transistor (Fig. 9-20). When the audio tone is heard in the speaker, back up a stage—the weak stage is close by. Improper voltage measurements on the suspected transistor can indicate the transistor is defective.

Inject the signal on both sides of a suspected coupling capacitor. The strength of the signal should be the same. Use the schematic to identify each coupling capacitor. You might find a small diagram on the bottom side of some portable phono players. When the large electrolytic speaker coupling capacitor is suspected, shunt a known capacitor across it. Signal injection is not amplified at this point.

Audio signal injection and voltage tests will uncover a defective IC. Inject the signal at the input terminal. Compare the signal at this point to the good channel. Now inject the audio signal at the volume control. Some portable players have a preamp IC with several output transistors. In this case, inject the signal at the input and output terminals of the IC.

10

Compact Disc Players

The compact disc player provides noiseless, scratchless music with exceptional high fidelity sound. Features might include automatic music scan, A/B repeat, index program, search, and keyboard programming, to name a few (Fig. 10-1). Like the VCR or TV set, you can control many different functions with the remote-control unit.

Although the CD player has many complicated circuits, there are many the average homeowner or hobbyist can maintain. For example, replacing the fuse and repairing the power supply circuits can correct a lot of service problems in the disc player. Broken belts and broken track-loading gears can occur if the loading door is grabbed or pulled accidently. Improper motor rotation of the loading, disc, and SLED motors frequently causes problems. Locating a defective audio IC component in the audio output stage is no different than in the car radio or cassette player.

WHEN YOU GET YOUR NEW PLAYER

Transportation screws that are used to disable and protect units during travel must be removed before use. Do not plug the compact disc player into the power outlet until you have located the transportation screw on the bottom of the player. In most players, the transportation screw locks down the laser pick-up assembly, so the compact disc player will not operate until this screw is removed. Scotch tape the screw to the back side for future shipping, if necessary.

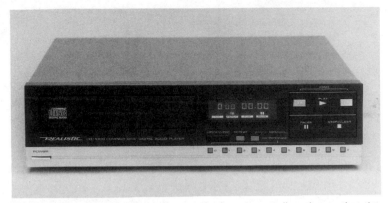

Fig. 10-1. There are many service repairs in compact disc players that the average hobbyist can do. Simply knowing how the CD player operates can clear up many trouble symptoms.

KNOW HOW TO USE THE CD PLAYER

Although the compact disc player is very easy to operate, improper operation can produce trouble when nothing is really wrong with the player. The following describe the basic functions of most compact disc players.

- ⊙ **POWER Switch**—Press to turn power to the unit on and off.
- ⊙ **Disc Tray**—When power is turned on and the open/close switch is pressed, the disc tray opens outward. Compact discs are loaded here. To close the tray, press the open/close switch again.
- ⊙ **PLAY Key**—Press to begin PLAY mode.
- ⊙ **PAUSE Key**—Press to temporarily interrupt PLAY mode; press again to release from the PAUSE mode.
- ⊙ **STOP/CLEAR Key**—Press to stop PLAY. When pressed, all operations stop. Additionally, when the player is in the STOP mode, pressing the key again cancels any memorized contents of programmed play.
- ⊙ **TRACK SEARCH Keys**—When the player is in the normal play or programmed modes, these keys are pressed to perform a search for the desired track. When pressed in forward direction, the disc will advance to the next track; in reverse direction, the disc returns to the beginning or end of the previous track, depending on the player.

- ⊙ MANUAL or SKIP SEARCH Keys—These keys are pressed to perform fast forward and fast reverse when the player is in the PLAY or PAUSE modes.
- ⊙ INDEX SEARCH Keys—When the player is in the PLAY or PAUSE modes, these keys are used to search for divisions (index numbers) within the individual tracks. When pressed, the player returns the disc to the previous, or advances to the next, index number.
- ⊙ TIME Key—Press this key to change the display mode of the time indicator. Each time the key is pressed, the display mode changes alternately in the order of TIME, REMAIN, and TOTAL.
- ⊙ REPEAT Key—Press to perform repeat playback.
- ⊙ PROGRAM Key—Use to memorize desired programs for programmed playback. After designating a desired track number with the number keys, press the program key to memorize the track.
- ⊙ PHONE LEVEL Control—Although some compact disc players do not have headphone listening jacks, the phone level control can be adjusted for easy listening of the headphones.
- ⊙ Remote Control—Some compact disc players can be operated from your easy chair like a VCR or TV set. Most of the controls on the front of the disc player can be operated with the remote control unit.

DISC CARE

Because compact discs are made of plastic, they can be easily scratched or damaged. Keep the compact disc inside the plastic container it comes in and store it in a disc cabinet. If left out, they can get dirty, dusty, damaged, or warped and the signal won't get picked up properly. The damaged discs can cause the player to malfunction. Music *dropout* (digital information loss of a magnetic storage device) can occur with smudged or damaged discs.

Handle the compact disc by the outside edges or with the forefinger in the hole area and the thumb at the outside edge. Do not touch the surface to be played (reflected silver or rainbow side). Finger marks or grease can prevent accurate tracking. The reflected surface must go down while the label side is upward (Fig. 10-2).

When fingerprints, dust, and dirt adhere to a disc, wipe it off with a soft dry cloth. If it does not come clean, wipe off with a cloth

Fig. 10-2. Be especially careful when taking voltage and resistance measurements on the crucial ICs, microprocessors and LS1. A slip of a test prod can damage the component.

moistened with water. Do not use record cleaners, benzine, or alcohol or clean the disc. Do not write on the label or stick paper or adhesive tape to the disc. There are several compact disc cleaners on the market that can be found at music, electronics, and other stores.

Keep compact discs in their plastic cases. Do not place the discs near a window or anyplace they might be exposed to direct sunlight. Keep them away from high temperatures and humidity.

Condensation. When moving the compact disc player from a cold to a warm place or into a room with high humidity, condensation can cover the optical lens. Condensation could prevent the light from the lens from reaching the disc and cause a noise or malfunction. Some disc players will operate erratically and shut off. If dew or condensation is present, allow the player to sit for several hours with the power off to permit drying.

SAFETY PRECAUTIONS

When working on the CD player, make sure the player is on an insulated table or bench. All test equipment that plugs into the ac power line should be properly grounded or operated from an isolation power transformer. Do not make any control adjustments unless specified by the manufacturer. Be especially careful when taking voltage and resistance measurements on crucial ICs, microprocessors, and LS1 (large scale integration ICs) components (Fig. 10-3).

Extreme care must be exercised when working around the laser-beam assembly with the power on. Usually there is a warning label to warn against direct exposure to the laser beam. Do not look

Fig. 10-3. Handle the compact disc with extreme care. Keep the shiny or rainbow side clean of dirt, dust, and scratch marks to prevent dropout.

directly at the laser for any length of time. Keep your eyes at least eighteen inches away from the beam. This does not mean you cannot glance at the meter to see that it is lighted. However, when the compact disc is properly loaded and in place, the laser beam cannot be seen. The metal-sided part of the disc is mounted downward to prevent direct radiation while servicing the player. Do not short out any radiation interlock safety switches (discussed subsequently).

Be careful when soldering components on the pc board. Always use a low-wattage (25 W) iron on ICs or microprocessors. The battery-operated iron is ideal because it operates at low wattage and has a thin iron tip. Use 60/40 rosin core, small diameter solder when soldering components on the pc board.

INTERLOCK PROBLEMS

In many CD players, some type of interlock system is used to lower the laser beam when the tray door is opened and loaded. The loading limit switch controls the supply voltage fed to the laser diode (Fig. 10-4). The laser outputs are controlled by the injection or cut-off of the constant voltage source to the laser diode pin number of the system control IC. When the loading limit switch is set to the CLEAR side, the disc tray is closed and the laser emits a beam at the high level. When the loading switch is in the OPEN position and at the low level, the laser does not emit a beam.

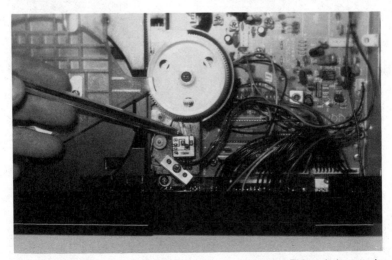

Fig. 10-4. Check the limit loading switch for good contacts. This switch controls the laser beam when the disc is loaded.

A malfunction of the switch contacts could keep the laser beam on all the time, emitting radiation whether the door is open or closed. Make sure the switch contacts are clean and making positive contact. They can be checked with the unit schematic for proper contact positions.

ISOLATING SERVICE SYMPTOMS

Scan the block diagram to determine what section the trouble might be in (Fig. 10-5). Then go to that section with the regular schematic and take signal, scope, voltage, and resistance measurements. For instance, if the problem is improper loading (or no loading-motor action), check the loading motor, drive amplifier, and servo-control system IC. Disc motor failure can be caused by a defective disc motor, drive amplifier, or servo IC, or the feed or SLED motor could have an open motor, leaky drive amplifier, or bad servo-control IC. Poor or improper display and button operations could result from a defective system control IC.

Check the audio output circuits for weak or distorted sound. Distortion in both channels can result from a defective dual-power IC or digital-to-analog converting (DAC) IC. A weak or dead channel in the headphones can be caused by a defective IC. Erratic or intermittent channel sound can result from poor output cables or cable connections. After locating the defective section, take transistor, voltage, and resistance measurements to locate the defective component.

NO-OUTPUT CONDITION

With no panel lights or a dead chassis, go directly to the low-voltage power supply. Inspect and check the fuse with an ohmmeter (The fuse is often located on the same board as the power switch). With the ON/OFF switch ON, test the primary circuit of the power transformer with the low scale of the ohmmeter (Fig. 10-6). Remove the power cord from the ac outlet and measure the primary resistance at the ac plug. If infinite, suspect an open transformer primary winding, power switch, or ac cord. Take a quick continuity test on the ON/OFF switch. This power switch is at the rear of the chassis (Fig. 10-7).

Check the bridge and single rectifiers for open or leaky conditions. You might find two or three bridge rectifiers, single or dual components, in the bridge, full-wave, or half-wave rectifier circuits (Fig. 10-8). If any diode shows leakage with an in-circuit test

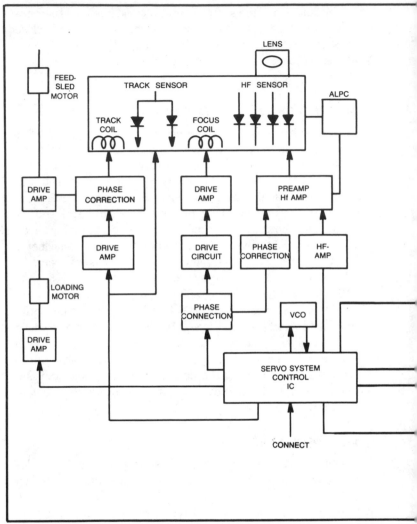

Fig. 10-5. Locate the possible defective section on the block diagram. Then go to that section with the schematic and take voltage, resistance and in-circuit transistor, tests.

on the diode test of the DMM, remove one end for a more accurate leakage test.

Next check the transistor, IC, or zener-diode regulators in the output of each bridge-rectifier circuit. You might find a combination of transistors and zener diodes in each voltage circuit (Fig. 10-9). Measure the voltage on each regulator transistor and compare this

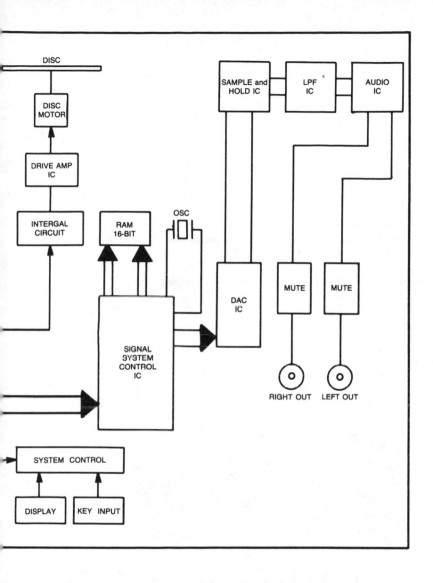

voltage with the other positive or negative voltage. You will find a positive and negative voltage source is fed to each motor amp (or drive circuit), tracking amp, and focus-coil drive amp.

Test each zener diode with the diode test. Usually, a leaky zener diode will show a lower voltage on the base of the regulator transistor. These leaky diodes may be warm or discolored. Remove

211

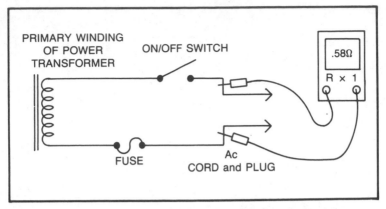

PRIMARY WINDING OF POWER TRANSFORMER

ON/OFF SWITCH

.58Ω

R × 1

FUSE

Ac CORD and PLUG

Fig. 10-6. Test the components in the primary winding circuit of the power transformer with an ohmmeter.

one end of the diode for accurate leakage tests. Replace each diode with the correct voltage and wattage. Check the schematic for the voltage and the parts list for the wattage.

DEFECTIVE ON/OFF SWITCH

In addition to checking for open or dirty contacts, the ON/OFF switch might have poorly soldered terminals on the pc board. Spray the switch with cleaning fluid to clean the dirty contacts. If the switch

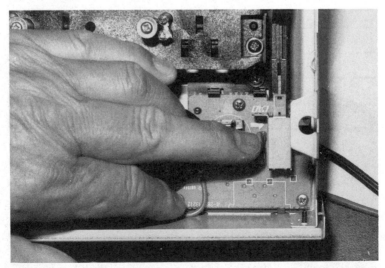

Fig. 10-7. The ON/OFF power switch is often found at the rear of the chassis. Check the switch contacts with the ohmmeter.

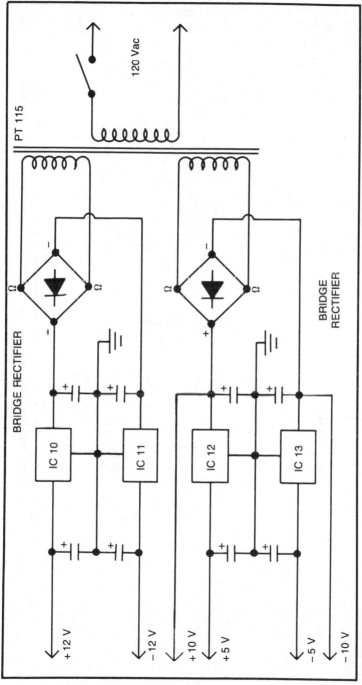

Fig. 10-8. Check the diodes in one bridge rectifier component for leaky conditions. Replace the entire bridge circuit even if only one diode is leaky.

213

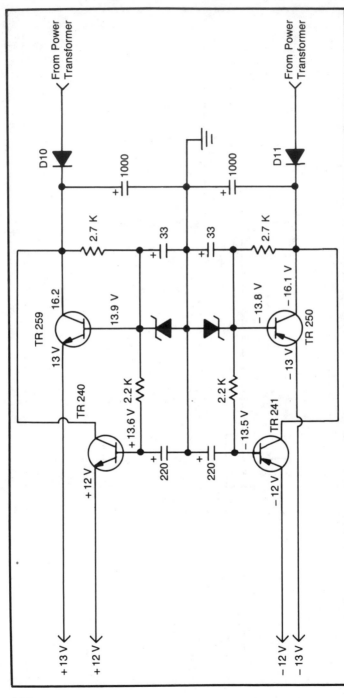

Fig. 10-9. Test each transistor and zener-diode regulator for shorted conditions. First check for leakage between collector and emitter terminals of the regulator transistors.

pops and cracks when pressed, check the terminals with the low (R×1) range of the ohmmeter (Fig. 10-10). A dead short should exist across the switch terminals. Replace the switch if any type of resistance is measured with the switch ON. Most of these switches must be replaced with the exact part number.

KEEPS BLOWING FUSES

If the fuse keeps blowing after replacement, suspect a shorted rectifier, regulator transistor, or a combination of both. Take a resistance measurement across the main filter capacitor. A very low resistance measurement indicates a leaky diode, regulator, or filter capacitor. Check each diode in the circuit for leakage, remembering to remove one terminal if a leakage measurement is found and recheck it.

Because most transistors short between emitter and cathode, take an in-circuit transistor test. Check all terminals on each regulator transistor for leakage. Measure the resistance across each zener diode. The zener diode can be checked with the diode test of the DMM like any ordinary silicon diode.

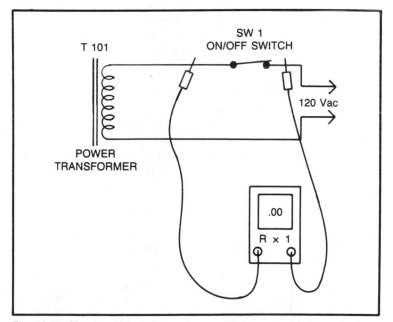

Fig. 10-10. Measure the resistance across the ON/OFF switch terminals. A normal switch should have no resistance. Replace it if any resistance is measured, indicating burned or worn contacts.

Additionally, a directly shorted component in the secondary side of the power transformer can open the fuse. Sometimes a leaky component tied to any voltage source will open the small fuse. Check the emitter terminal of each regulator to ground for a connected leaky component (Table 10-1). Do not overlook a possibly defective power transformer.

NO AC VOLTAGE

Suspect an open or leaky power transformer if no ac voltage is measured at the main silicon diode rectifier. The primary winding of these small transformers often opens, along with a shorted diode in the secondary, and can occur from lightning damage (Fig. 10-11). Take a continuity measurement of both windings. Feel the transformer covering to see if it is running very warm. Sometimes after replacing shorted diodes in the secondary, the transformer winding can become red hot and short out several turns. This shorting occurs because many CD players are not fused in the primary winding.

Replace the defective power transformer with the exact part number. Write down the color-coded terminal wires and where they go for easy replacement. Clip the transformer wires ½ inch from the terminal connection. Some of these small transformers can have from seven to ten color-coded wires.

LOW HUM NOISE

Loud or low hum noise could come from the audio or low-voltage power supply circuits. First check for poor filtering in the low-voltage source. A leaky regulator transistor and zener diode can produce hum in the sound. Besides the main filter capacitors, check for a defective decoupling or small filter capacitor in the base circuits of the regulator transistors (Fig. 10-12).

Test each filter capacitor in the circuit with a digital capacity

Voltage	Resistance
− 5 volts	2.42 K ohms
− 9 volts	6.6 K ohms
+ 5 volts	672 ohms
+ 9 volts	1025 ohms

Table 10-1.

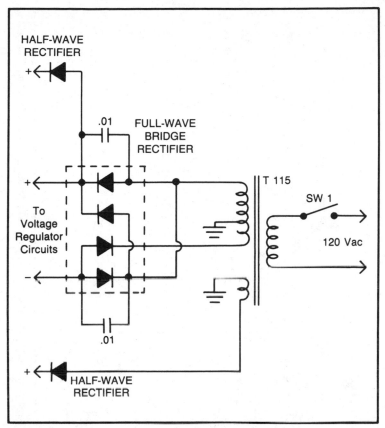

Fig. 10-11. The primary winding of the power transformer can open with a shorted diode in the bridge or half-wave rectifier circuits.

tester. Shunting another known filter capacitor across the suspected one might eliminate the hum problem if a capacity meter is not handy, but do not shunt the filter capacitor while the player is operating. Pull the power plug and discharge the main filter capacitor with a wire clip. These capacitors are usually from 1000 to 2000 μF at 16 or 25 volts. Observe polarity and clip another 2200 μF capacitor across the suspected one. In some of these chassis, the main filter capacitor terminals cannot be seen until the main pc board is removed from the chassis (Fig. 10-13). You can clip the positive terminal of the capacitor in the circuit by locating the cathode terminals of the bridge or single rectifiers, and connect the negative terminal to chassis ground.

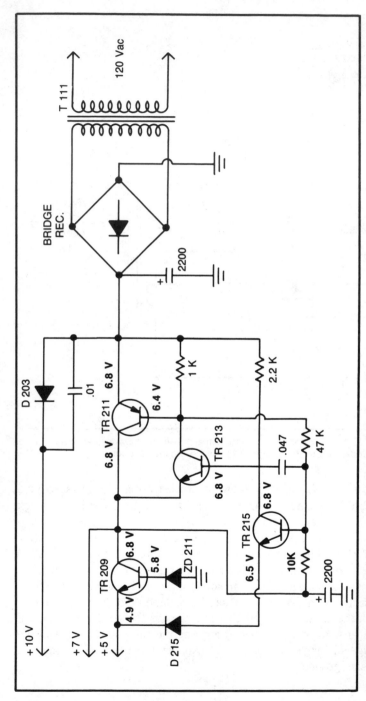

Fig. 10-12. Check the main filter capacitors, regulator transistors, and diodes that can cause hum in the audio circuits. Shunt each capacitor with the power off so transistors and IC components are not damaged.

Fig. 10-13. Because the terminals of the main filter capacitors might be difficult to get at, locate the cathode terminal (+) of the bridge or single diodes
and clip the filter capacitor from the terminal to chassis ground.

POOR SOCKET CONNECTIONS

If one section of the CD player is dead or intermittent, check
all the socket connections, especially those of the components that
are not mounted on the main circuit board (Fig. 10-14), such as the
power transformer, all motors, the laser assembly, protection switches, and diodes. Move the connections around with the player plugged
in and note if it begins to operate.

Most of these sockets are pressed-clip wire terminals which can
have a poor contact. If one of the motors is not operating, do a
continuity test from the top of these socket terminals. Likewise,
check continuity of the tracking and focus-coil socket connections.
If one wire is making a poor contact, strip the end back and solder
it to the top metal terminal clip, being careful not to melt the plastic
socket.

SAFETY PROTECTION DIODE

In some models, an LED safety protection diode lights up to
lower the laser beam when a disc is not in play position or when

Fig. 10-14. Poor socket and jack connections can cause intermittent operation when the components are not mounted on the main pc board, including motors, tracking coils and focus coils.

the door of the loading tray is open (Fig. 10-15). When illuminated, the light is transmitted from the LED to a photo (light sensitive) transistor that turns off a microcomputer chip. With no power to the microcomputer chip, the laser beam is lowered, providing protection to the operator.

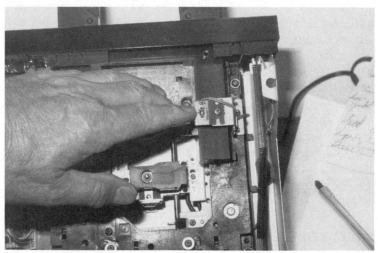

Fig. 10-15. The LED safety diode shuts down the laser when a compact disc is not in position to play.

Opposingly, when the disc is loaded and ready to play, the light from the LED is cut off because of the metal side of the disc. This in turn turns off the photo transistor, which turns on the microchip, providing power to the laser beam assembly. The safety protection diode can be checked in the same manner as any other diode.

IMPROPER LOADING

The loading-gear assembly can be damaged if the loading tray is pulled or held during operation. Do not pull or pry on the loading tray if it seems stuck or will not come out. Broken plastic teeth in the loading tray and gear drive assembly might prevent the tray from loading. Inspect the gears and plastic teeth for breakage.

Remember, the laser beam assembly is mounted under the plastic "flapper" assembly that is raised by a cam gear. The flapper assembly must be raised to load the disc to be played. The whole loading mechanism must operate smoothly. Inspect the plastic cam teeth for breakage or jammed gears (Fig. 10-16). These parts must be ordered from the manufacturer. Finally, improper loading could be caused by a defective tray loading switch.

CLEANING THE LENS ASSEMBLY

Weak audio or disc dropout can occur with a dirty optical lens

Fig. 10-16. Improper loading can be caused by broken or jammed gears in either the loading tray or the plastic cam assembly, which raises up to load the disc.

system. The loading mechanism, flapper assembly, and/or disc pressure assembly must be removed to get at the laser assembly. Dust or dirt should be cleaned from the lens by using a small air brush as used for a camera lens (Fig. 10-17). The lens can be cleaned with cleaning fluid on a cotton stick or similar soft material. Take care not to push down hard against the lens assembly. After cleanup, replace the disc pressure and flapper assembly.

CHECKING LASER CURRENT

Measure the laser current after replacing a new laser assembly or when it is suspected of malfunction. Some manufacturers recommend a laser power meter to measure the laser current, while others use a voltage measurement developed across the output circuit of the laser diodes. Do not look at the sensor or lens assembly in taking this measurement. You may find a semi-fixed resistor for laser current adjustment in some models. The sensor cap of the optical power meter is placed over the lens opening of the optical laser pickup. The normal reading of the laser power meter should

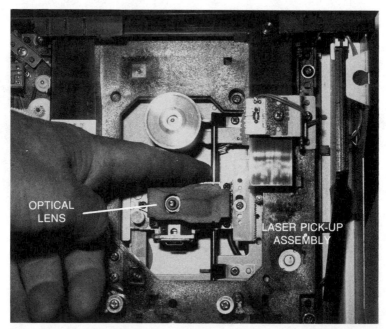

Fig. 10-17. The laser-head pick-up assembly travels outward from the spindle or disc motor on a metal rod track. Clean off the lens assembly with cleaning fluid and a soft cleaning stick.

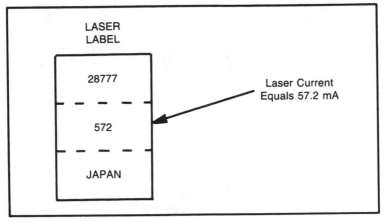

LASER
LABEL

28777

Laser Current
Equals 57.2 mA

572

JAPAN

Fig. 10-18. The laser current might be posted on a label attached to the laser assembly.

he between 0.26 mW and 0.3 mW ±5 percent. If the measurement is under 0.1 mW, you can assume the laser diode has expired.

The laser current is normally driven between 40 and 70 mA. Measure the laser driving current in the circuit. The laser unit might be defective if over 100 mA. The laser current might be posted on a label on the pickup (Fig. 10-18). Note that in this laser unit, the correct operating current is 55.2 mA.

For the voltage method, the laser current can easily be checked with a voltage measurement across the emitter resistor of the servo-control transistor (Fig. 10-19). This resistor might be a 10- or 12-ohm resistor. In the figure, the normal voltage measurement should be from 0.48 to 0.84 volts across R160. The electric current of the laser equals the voltage measure divided by 10. If the electric current of the laser exceeds 10 percent of the recommended value, the laser pickup should be replaced.

POOR CABLE CONNECTIONS

After the compact disc male cable plugs have been removed and inserted many times, a broken or defective male plug can cause intermittent or erratic sound (Fig. 10-20). Check the cables from disc players to the amp jacks with the low-ohm range of the ohmmeter. Clip the ohmmeter to each male end and flex the cables for a possible broken cable or wire. If the meter measurement is unresponsive or erratic, try to repair the cables. Most cables break right where they enter the plug. Inspect the male tips for good sol-

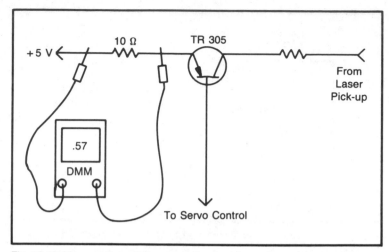

Fig. 10-19. Measure the voltage across the dropping resistor of the servo-control transistor to determine the operating current of the laser head. Actually, the small voltage shown here equals 48 to 84 mA of current.

der connections. You can interchange the cables to find the defective one (with the player operating). You can replace the intermittent ones with a new set of audio cables, available at most audio or electronics supply stores.

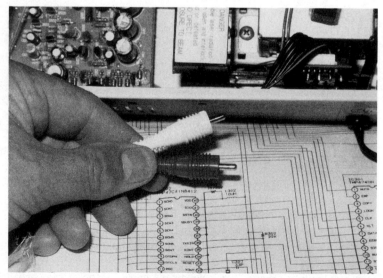

Fig. 10-20. Check the male plugs of the audio cable for broken or erratic connections. Flex the cord while the compact disc is playing.

224

LOADING MOTOR PROBLEMS

The loading motor operates the tray assembly in moving it in and out to load and unload discs. The loading motor can be operated directly from an IC or from a balanced transistor circuit (Fig. 10-21). The IC or transistor loading motor circuits are ultimately controlled by a large system-control IC.

Check the voltage across the motor terminals with the load button pressed. There is zero voltage on the motor in either the transistor or IC circuits (Fig. 10-22). Measure the continuity of the motor at the motor terminals. Infinite reading indicates the motor is open. The average loading-motor continuity resistance is under 10 ohms. If no voltage is at pin 10, suspect a defective IC 305 or system-control IC. Take a voltage measurement on each IC or transistor terminal and compare each with the schematic. These motors should be replaced with the exact part numbers.

SLED (OR SLIDE) MOTOR ERRATIC

The *sled* or *slide* motor moves the optical laser assembly across the disc from the inside to the outer rim. Sometimes it is called a

Fig. 10-21. The loading motor can be controlled by two balanced transistors or an IC component. Locate the IC on the pc board and take voltage measurements.

225

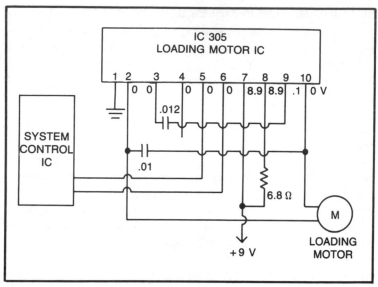

Fig. 10-22. Check for loading-motor continuity at the motor terminals. Accurate voltage and resistance measurements on IC 305 can locate a leaky control IC.

feed motor. The slide motor can operate from an IC or transistor circuit or a combination of both (Fig. 10-23). The two motor-driver transistors should look like any ordinary transistors.

Check for motor continuity at the motor terminals with the ohmmeter; then proceed to the output transistor. There should be a positive supply voltage at the collector terminal of one transistor, and negative supply voltage at the other (Fig. 10-24). The balanced output circuit is controlled by IC 511, which in turn is controlled by the master servo-control IC.

SPINDLE MOTOR PROBLEMS

The spindle or drive motor rotates the disc during play. The disc starts out very fast but sets slower as the laser pickup is moved out toward the rim of the disc by the feed motor. The spindle motor can be controlled with two output-type transistors or the IC circuit (Fig. 10-25). In the figure, Q311 and Q312 are in turn controlled by the spindle servo, IC 310.

If the drive motor fails, check output transistors (in Fig. 10-26, Q311 and Q312). Measure the motor continuity for an open motor. Zero voltage is at the motor terminals until the play button is pushed. Check for +10 volts at the collector terminal of Q311 and −10 volts

Fig. 10-23. The slide motor can be directly controlled by two balance output transistors. Locate them on the pc board and take in-circuit transistor tests.

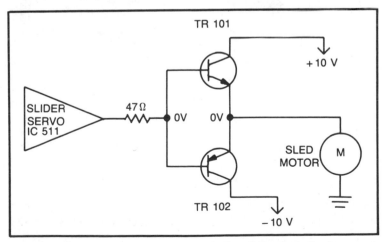

Fig. 10-24. Zero voltage is at the motor terminals until the play button is pressed. Check the collector voltage of each transistor to determine if transistors or the low-voltage source is defective.

227

Fig. 10-25. Locate the two balanced spindle (or drive) motor transistors on the pc board. Take in-circuit transistors and voltage measurements. Replace both transistors if one if leaky.

at the collector terminal of Q312. Go directly to the low-voltage regulator circuits with no or improper supply voltage. If the output transistors and motor appear normal, check the voltage on the spindle servo IC (IC 310).

WEAK OR DISTORTED SOUND

Weak and distorted sound can occur in the audio output stages and between the sample/hold IC and the first audio stage. Both audio circuits can be combined in one IC component (Fig. 10-27). Sometimes when one section is distorted, the other might be weak because of a duo-audio IC. The signal can be signal-traced to input

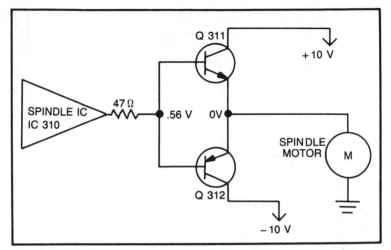

Fig. 10-26. The drive motor can be controlled by an IC or two output transistors. Take voltage and resistance measurements on the IC and transistor terminals.

terminal 4 and at pin 2 of IC 224. If the signal is normal going in but distorted at pin 2, suspect a leaky IC 224. Take voltage and resistance measurements on each IC pin to determine if the IC is defective.

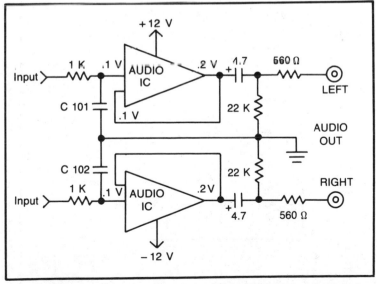

Fig. 10-27. Weak or distorted audio can result from a leaky duo-audio IC. Isolate the audio IC with voltage and resistance measurements.

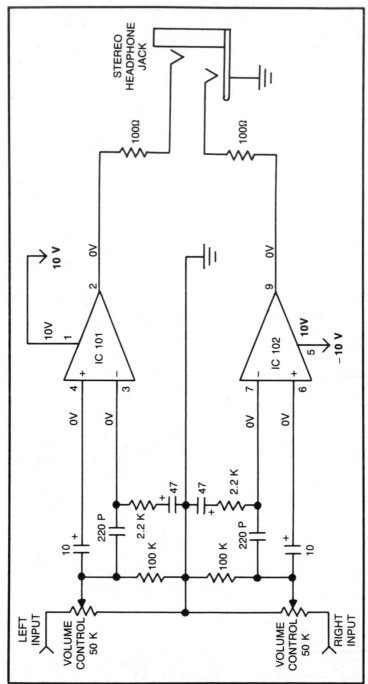

Fig. 10-28. Besides voltage and resistance measurements on the headphone audio IC, check the headphone stereo jack for poor contacts.

HEADPHONES DEAD OR WEAK

Many CD players have a headphone jack for easy, quiet listening. Often there is a separate headphone volume control ahead of the audio IC (Fig. 10-28). Check the audio signal ahead of the headphone jack. Sometimes a broken or poor contact connection of the jack causes dead or intermittent headphone reception. If the audio is normal at the compact disc stereo jacks, suspect a defective IC or connecting components.

Weak reception can be caused by the electrolytic coupling capacitors between the volume control and audio IC. Signal-trace the audio signal from the volume control to the phone jacks. If the signal is good going into the IC and weak coming out, suspect a defective IC. Test each electrolytic capacitor and resistor tied to the audio IC before attempting to replace it. Replace the new audio IC with the original or a universal replacement, and solder the small terminals with a low-wattage (25 W) soldering iron.

Part 3

Video

11

Questions and Answers about TV

These are some of the most common questions asked about color TV receivers. Although some of them might seem rather obvious to you, to others it may be a serious problem. These questions are broken down into four different sections: general questions, the TV antenna, TV operation, and the TV chassis.

GENERAL QUESTIONS

■ *Do I have to pay for a service call just to adjust my TV?*
Yes, it costs money to send a TV technician to your home. Someone has to pay the technician's wages and the travel expenses for the house call. A house call can take over an hour for the adjustment and round trip. Sometimes a TV adjustment involves more time and expense than you might think.

■ *What is the difference between a trip charge and a house call?*
Some TV shops have a set fee called a trip charge. This charge is for just going to the house and back. You will be charged extra labor for each repair or adjustment the technician does to get your color TV back in operation. The price of a house call varies from $8.95 to $24.95 or even higher. This charge represents getting to the house and labor for the first half hour. Some shops charge for the extra time it takes to complete the call while others do not. Beware of TV servicemen who make service calls for under $7.95.

You might have a low labor charge, but extra unnecessary parts could be installed to make up for the difference.

■ *How do I know the TV shop has honest men working there?*
You can bet that over 90% of all TV men are honest people. Like any other profession, you have a few who take advantage of the customer. If you are new in town, check with the Better Business Bureau. Ask how many years the TV establishment has been in the business. You can assume the shop is honest and does a good job if it's been in business 15 years or more. They probably wouldn't be in business that long if they weren't honest.

■ *Should I trust the TV technician to take my TV to his shop?*
If the technician cannot repair the TV in your home with tube and module replacement, it should go to the repair shop. Most qualified TV technicians can determine within a half hour what's wrong with a TV. Like a car mechanic, he has all the test equipment and tools to do a good job at his place of business. You wouldn't want him to lug all that expensive test equipment over and put it on your living room rug. In the first place, it would cost you too much money. Secondly, a better overall repair can be made at the TV shop.

■ *Can I ask for a TV repair estimate before having my TV repaired?*
Yes, most TV shops will give you an estimate before completing the repair. However, the technician might have to practically repair the TV chassis before he can give you a correct estimate. Be prepared to pay for an estimate charge if you decide not to have the TV fixed. It takes more time to locate the defect than to replace the defective component. In some stores, you might have to pay for an estimate charge before they even look at the TV. Of course, the estimate charge is credited to the cost of the repair if you decide to have the TV repaired.

■ *Can't the TV technician give me an estimate in the home before he takes my TV set?*
He might be able to give you a rough estimate, but do not hold him to the quoted price. At least it will give you an idea in round figures what the repair could cost. It's best to have an estimate made after the TV chassis is thoroughly checked.

■ *Should I ask for an itemized statement?*

Always ask for an itemized statement when any unit is re-ired. If you like, ask the TV technician to save the defective parts. Some shops have a defective parts bag for this very purpose. If in doubt about any component or charge, feel free to ask the service technician.

■ *Can I save any money by dropping my TV off at the shop?*

Yes—you can save a house call or pickup and delivery charge. Most shops have a separate charge for pickup and delivery service. Usually, the shop labor is charged by the hour but some have a flat rate charge.

■ *Why can't the TV man work on my TV at once when I drop it off?*

Today most shops are very busy and it's just about impossible to quit the job they are working on to take a look at another TV set. It wouldn't be fair to other customers to drop what they are doing and work on your TV. You wouldn't want this to happen to you, either. Some shops do have a technician handy who does nothing but rush jobs. Remember, a busy shop is doing something right or they wouldn't have all the business.

■ *Should I tell the serviceman how the TV set is acting or let him find it out?*

Tell him everything. It will save you money in the long run. The more hints and clues you can give him, the quicker he can make the repairs. If you don't tell him what actually happens and there is more than one problem, he may repair the most obvious, resulting in a call-back, which is always unpleasant both to the owner and service technician.

THE TV ANTENNA

■ *Does it make any difference which wire of the flat lead-in goes to either one of the antenna screws?*

No, it doesn't matter which wire of the flat lead-in goes to which screw. But make sure the lead-in wire is bare and wrapped around the metal screw. Tighten the screw so the stations will not get snowy as with a bad lead-in connection. You might want to add an antenna plug so the lead-in wire can be easily disconnected if a storm approaches.

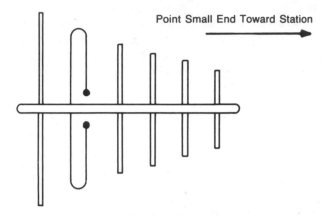

Point Small End Toward Station

Fig. 11-1. All channel antenna. Always point the narrow end of the antenna in the direction of the TV station.

■ *Should I disconnect my TV lead-in or just the ac cord when it begins to rain and thunder?*

Remove the lead-in wire from your antenna *and* pull out the ac cord when a storm approaches. A TV set can be damaged by lightning coming in the antenna lead-in or the power line. Be sure to disconnect both the lead-in and the power cord before going on vacation.

■ *Which antenna wire is the best, round, or flat?*

Both types of lead-in wire are good. Shielded 75-ohm lead-in is usually used in noisy areas. It will help keep man-made noise and standing waves from being picked up by the lead-in cable. Very long lead-in wires will cut down on TV reception when living in extreme rural areas. Flat lead-in must be insulated away from the TV mast, metal eaves, and siding, while the shielded lead-in can be stapled or taped to the metal tower, pole, or siding. Shielded lead-in costs about twice as much as flat lead-in.

■ *Why are there so many different types of antennas in my neighborhood?*

There are many good TV antennas on the market. Each TV shop feels it sells the best. Hence, there are many different kinds. Go to the retail store where you purchased your TV set. They will tell you what type of antenna works best with the set you purchased.

■ *A different TV man said my antenna wasn't strong enough to pick up distant stations; is this true?*

238

The gain of a TV antenna is determined by how many elements are on the TV mast. An antenna with 14 elements will pick up more signal than one with only six elements. It's like collecting rain in a bucket. You can collect more rain in five buckets than one. Look around the neighborhood. If most families use a large antenna you probably should too.

■ *I just purchased an all-channel antenna; which way should I point it?*

Always point the smallest end of the antenna towards the station you want to receive. If there are several stations in one given direction, point the tapered end element in that direction. If you are trying to pick up several stations in different directions, with a directional TV antenna, you must install a rotator to point the antenna to each station.

■ *To which antenna terminal should I hook my antenna lead-in? One is marked* VHF *and the other* UHF.

If you have only one lead-in wire and no uhf station in your vicinity, connect the lead-in wires to the vhf terminals. When two separate lead-ins are coming into the house, make sure they are connected properly. In case they are not marked, turn your TV to the lowest channel in your area (let's say it is channel 5). Now connect each cable and see which one gives the best TV picture. Connect the other wire to the uhf terminal. Now check stations on both vhf and uhf channels.

■ *Should I leave the built-in lead-in wire connected when I connect the outside antenna?*

No. Leave these two wires disconnected when using the outside antenna. In extreme rural areas, a built-in antenna might produce a snowy picture.

■ *Someone said I should have a lightning arrestor on my TV lead-in wire.*

A lightning arrestor can indeed help to protect your TV receiver when lightning hits the antenna or strikes in your area.

■ *Should I have my antenna mast grounded even if I live in a mobile home?*

Yes, all TV antenna masts or pipes should be grounded. A ground wire should be connected from the metal TV mast to earth ground.

Either install an 8-ft ground rod or connect the ground wire to a metal water pipe. This prevents electric charges from collecting and building up on your mobile home or house during a thunderstorm. A good ground keeps these charges at ground potential.

TV OPERATION

■ *What can I do when heavy lines go across the screen and I have no picture? The sound is okay.*

Heavy horizontal or color bar lines at an angle indicate the horizontal hold control is not adjusted properly. Adjust the horizontal hold control until the lines become farther apart and the picture comes in. If you go too far, the picture will go out of horizontal sync in the opposite direction. If the picture will not lock in horizontally, you could have sync problems in the horizontal circuits. When the picture will not hold either horizontally or vertically, the trouble could be in the sync circuits.

■ *My TV set keeps flipping upward and after it warms up it won't stand still. What is wrong?*

Flipping or vertical rolling can be caused by improper setting of the vertical hold control. Simply adjust the control so the picture will lock it in. If turned too much, noise can cause the picture to flip or roll. In older TV chassis, readjustment of the vertical linearity and height controls should be made. Sometimes these controls are overadjusted, causing poor vertical lock. When the vertical hold control will not keep the picture from flipping or rolling, suspect vertical sync problems. The vertical sync and vertical output tube should be replaced. Vertical problems within a transistorized chassis can be caused by a leaky vertical sync transistor.

■ *My TV is dead and the dial light is off. Should I push in the little red button in the back?*

First make sure the ac cord is plugged in properly. Try it in another socket. Check the interlock where the cord goes into the TV set. Sometimes when the set is moved for cleaning, the interlock can get pulled out. Now turn on the ON/OFF switch. If the TV receiver doesn't come on, push in the red circuit-breaker button found in the rear of most TV chassis. Of course, there are some TVs that use fuses instead of a circuit breaker. Push the button clear in and release. You may find the TV receiver comes on and is normal, but if the overload button kicks out, you have an overloaded condition in the chassis.

240

■ *I have black and white dotted lines going across my picture on channel 5. How can I get rid of them?*

This is usually man-made interference and you cannot adjust anything on your TV to eliminate this type of noise. Man-made interference such as automobile ignitions, neon signs, flashing signs, and power-line interference usually occurs on channels 2 through 6. Very seldom does it exist on channels 8 to 13, unless it is very strong interference.

You can install shielded 75-ohm lead-in cable and raise the outside antenna as high as possible to overcome this type of interference. You need to pick up more TV signal to override the interference.

■ *What is wrong when all the other stations are good but on channel 3 I can only hear the sound?*

Generally, when only one station is not tuned in and the others are normal, the fine-tuning control is not adjusted properly. Try adjusting the fine-tuning knob, located behind the selector knob. Rotate the knob three or four turns each way to tune the picture in with the sound.

Today most TV receivers have an automatic fine-tuning button which when activated will automatically fine tune each station. If this button is pushed in and left on, each station will automatically be tuned in. In the color receiver with a push-button TV selector, a synchronizer circuit is used for automatic station control.

■ *On channel 8 and 11, I seem to get another station in the background. What control can I adjust?*

The only control to help eliminate co-channel interference is the fine tuner control. If you cannot tune out the interfering station or eliminate some of it, there's nothing more you can do. Co-channel interference is usually found when you are connected to cable TV. This is one of the problems with cable TV. Anytime you have a signal on every channel, some of these stations can interfere with one another. Of course, a lot of this depends on the construction of your TV receiver. It depends on how many traps are located in the tuner. You might find a low-priced TV will not reject the interfering station, while a well-constructed TV will. Perhaps the next time you purchase a new TV, you should try out several models on cable before you decide which one performs the best.

■ *What can I do to keep my neighbor's CB station from interfering with my favorite program?*

CB interference can be eliminated or at least lowered if both parties try to correct the situation. The party operating the CB station can place a trap on his or her equipment. Also, you can install a trap at the antenna bay and one behind your TV set. If this doesn't cure the problem, or at least help, try installing shielded lead-in from the antenna to your color receiver.

THE TV CHASSIS

■ *My husband tried to fix the TV set and really messed it up. Should we tell the TV serviceman?*

Yes. When the serviceman opens the chassis he will know that the set has been tampered with anyway. You can save yourself some added expense by simply stating the facts.

■ *We took our portable color TV to another shop and they couldn't fix it. Should we mention this when we take it to another shop?*

Yes. If possible, you should state what the other TV shop actually did. You don't have to mention the name of the other repairman, just what repairs were made. State exactly what was wrong when you took it to the shop for repair. You might even have to pay more to have the set repaired, since the other repairman may have added a problem or two.

■ *My TV set has no picture, but the sound is good. Is my picture tube gone?*

Not necessarily. It's possible your picture tube is defective, but in most cases the problem is in the horizontal sweep circuits. The problem could be a blown fuse in the horizontal circuit, shorted or open horizontal tubes, defective horizontal transistors, or defective high-voltage circuits.

In the newer transistorized TV chassis, when the horizontal section is defective, the sound is also dead. Today the voltage source for many other circuits comes directly from the horizontal output transformer circuitry. Repairing the horizontal circuits might solve both picture and sound problems.

■ *My picture tube takes a long time to come on. Is the picture tube about ready to go out?*

This could be a sign of a weak or old picture tube. Most picture tube defects involve open heaters, poor focus, intermittent picture, or the tube takes a long time to brighten. When the heater opens, you will have no brightness or picture. Poor focus or a fuzzy picture is caused by a weak or old picture tube. An intermittent or negative raster could be caused by a short in the gun assembly of the picture tube. With this condition, you can tap lightly on the end of the picture tube and the condition might clear up. The tube might also take a long time to come on with a defective high-voltage or horizontal stage.

■ *Should I have a rebuilt picture tube installed in my TV set?*
   A rebuilt picture tube consists of using the original glass with a new gun assembly. the rebuilt picture tube can last just as long as a brand new tube. Check the warranty on the picture tube. You can now have tubes installed with a 5-year or indefinite warranty. Of course, you pay a little more money for it.

■ *Should I have a new picture tube installed if my TV is eight years old?*
Most manufacturers say the life of a tube chassis TV is between six and eight years. The life of a transistor chassis is from ten to eleven years. Don't exceed the life of the TV set. If your set has an eight-year-old tube chassis, don't install a new picture tube. Just purchase a new TV.
   Many picture tubes have been installed after the life of the TV set has been exceeded, but experience has shown that within a few months after installing a new tube in an older TV, you could have filter, transformer, or other problems.

■ *My screen has horizontal colored lines in it. What control should I turn?*
Try adjusting the horizontal hold control. This control is located either on the front or rear panel. In some of the newer TVs, you may have neither a horizontal nor vertical control—this is because an IC automatically adjusts these circuits.

■ *My TV screen has only a horizontal white line. Is the problem in the horizontal circuits?*
People sometimes get the horizontal and vertical sweep circuits confused when trouble occurs in either one. A horizontal white line is actually vertical sweep trouble. The vertical sweep has collapsed to a white horizontal line. This trouble might be caused by a defective vertical tube or transistor in the vertical circuit. Sometimes the vertical trouble can be cured by vertical linearity and height-control

adjustments. If neither one of the vertical controls has any effect on the vertical raster, the trouble exists inside the TV chassis.

■ *The sound cuts in and out of my portable TV. What can I do?*
Intermittent sound cannot be fixed with any outside control. The sound problem is in the sound circuit. Intermittent sound can be caused by defective tubes or transistors. In the transistorized chassis, a "popping" sound is caused by a defective output transistor.

■ *Can I have a new TV chassis installed in my TV cabinet? The cabinet is as good as new.*
No, there are no television manufacturers who make only a TV chassis to slip into your old TV cabinet. Sometimes it's possible to put a new portable or table model TV in the old cabinet if there is room. So far, TV manufacturers do not make a chassis replacement.

12

Portable Black and White TV Repairs

About half of the TV receivers in homes still have a tube or hybrid chassis. So if you have three TV receivers, one of them probably contains some tubes. The hybrid chassis might have tubes only in the horizontal and vertical sweep areas, the remaining circuits being transistorized. If any of the TVs are less than five years old, they should have a completely transistorized or IC chassis.

In this chapter, I discuss some of the most common portable black and white (B&W) TV repair problems. These same repair problems are found in B&W consoles. First you will find the transistorized chassis symptoms listed with the same tube-related problems. Although the tube chassis is slowly fading out of the picture, I did not leave it out entirely. You will find that many symptoms and repairs are common to both.

SET DEAD

The following problems can cause a no-output condition in your TV set.

Blown Fuse

Always look for a blown fuse or fusible resistor when the set is entirely dead. The fuse might open because of an overload in the chassis or a component is temporarily causing an overloaded condition. Unstable power lines or lightning can cause the fuse to blow. So simply replacing the blown fuse can restore the portable TV to operation.

Transistor Chassis. You might find one or two protecting fuses in the B&W chassis. Usually either a fuse, fusible resistor, circuit breaker, or a combination is found in the power line circuits (Fig. 12-1). Sometimes a small fuse is used to protect the horizontal output circuit. Always replace the defective fuse with one having the same current rating—otherwise you are defeating the fuse protection. Too large a fuse can cause a fire in the chassis.

Check for an open fuse, fusible resistor, or circuit breaker with the $R \times 1$ scale. Place the VOM leads right across the suspected components but make sure the power cord is unplugged from the power line before attempting any ohmmeter measurements.

When the circuit breaker is not properly seated, the circuit will remain open. If the TV chassis contains a circuit breaker, push in on the red button and release. The chassis might not come on if there is an overload condition. The circuit breaker might have dirty contacts or be weak, and after on a few seconds, kick out. These circuit breakers can easily be damaged after being reset several times on an overload condition. Replace the circuit breaker with one having the exact current rating as marked on the body of the circuit breaker or in the data in the service literature.

Tube Chassis. All of the above mentioned defective components can be found in the tube chassis. Usually a low-ohm, fusible resistor is found ahead of the silicon rectifier in the filament string hybrid TV chassis (Fig. 12-2). These tubes are wired in series and equal the power line voltage. When the filament or heater element of any tube opens up, the chassis is dead. None of the tubes will light up. To quickly locate the defective tube, remove each tube separately and check the heater terminals with the $R \times 1$ scale. No

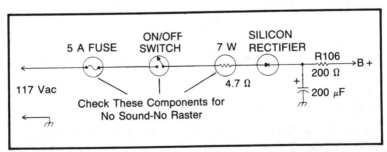

Fig. 12-1. Check for an open fuse if the portable B&W TV is completely dead. Also check for a leaky silicon diode. Replacing the fuse may be all that is needed.

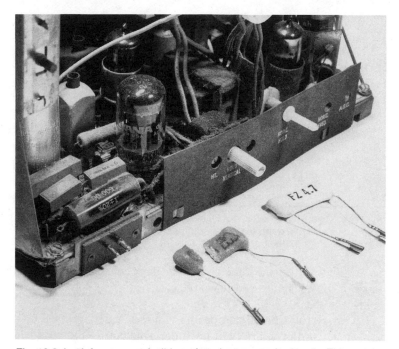

Fig. 12-2. Look for an open fusible resistor in some early chassis. This resistor operates fairly warm and can open with an overloaded power supply. Replace the fusible resistor with one of the same value. There are 1-, 4-, 5-, and 7.5-ohm types.

reading indicates the tube has open internal heater connections. If a large heater voltage dropping resistor is found in the series string, check the resistor for open conditions.

An open fusible resistor can be caused by a shorted silicon rectifier or an overloaded component within circuits supplied by the low-voltage power supply. Replace these fusible resistors with ones having the same ohm and wattage ratings. You might find after replacement that these fusible resistors run quite warm—this is normal.

Defective Switch

The ON/OFF switch can be the same type in either the tube or transistor chassis. The switch is usually located at the rear of the volume control. Check the ON/OFF switch with the R×1 scale across the switch terminals (Fig. 12-3). A defective switch might have an erratic, shorted reading or no reading at all. Rapidly click the switch

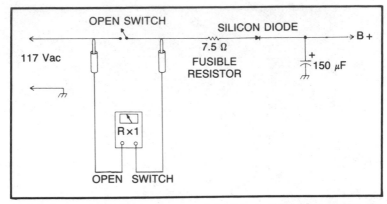

Fig. 12-3. Check for an open ON/OFF switch after checking the fuse. Use the R×1 scale and place the test leads right across the switch terminals. With the switch on, the meter should read a short.

on and off to determine if the switch has dirty contacts. Sometimes tuner or contact spray used inside the switch area can solve the poor contact problem.

Transistor Chassis. A dead TV chassis can be caused by a broken ac cord or interlock. Check the condition of the cord and interlock with the R×1 range. Clip a test lead across the ac power plug and check for a low-ohm reading at the interlock terminals. An open reading indicates a broken cord or poor interlock connection. Poor or open soldered connections in the power line wiring can cause a dead TV chassis.

Tube Chassis. First, all of the above problems should be checked in the tube chassis. You might find a set of dual terminals on the ON/OFF switch in the tube chassis (Fig. 12-4). The ac power line can be switched as in the transistor chassis with separate heater switching terminals. Both the tube heater string and power is switched on with this type of switch.

When you cannot turn off the receiver with the ON/OFF switch, suspect a defective switch or shorted silicon diode across the switch terminals. In instant tube warm-up circuits, the diode is used across the switch terminals to keep the tubes warm so when the switch is turned on, the chassis will come alive. This diode can become shorted when lightning strikes close by or on the power line. Replace the defective diode with one having a 2.5-amp rating.

Bad Silicon Rectifier

Defective silicon diodes cause more fuses to blow than any oth-

Fig. 12-4. In the tube chassis, you might find more than two terminals on the rear of the ON/OFF switch. One circuit might be used to apply power to the power supply and the other to apply voltage to the heater string of tubes. Sometimes one circuit is used to short out the brightness circuits so that you will see a small, round circle when the set is turned off. Make sure you have the correct terminals when connecting the new switch.

er component in the transistor power supply. When you find a blown fuse, connect the test probes of the ohmmeter across the diode terminals. A low reading in both directions indicates a leaky or shorted diode. Remove one end of the diode for accurate tests.

Transistor Chassis. In some low-voltage power supplies, you find two silicon diodes in a full-wave rectification circuit (Fig. 12-5).

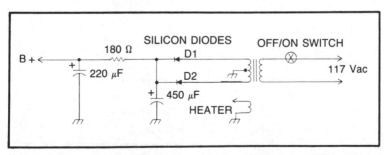

Fig. 12-5. In a full-wave rectification circuit, you will find two silicon diodes. Remove one end from each diode for correct continuity tests. A leaky diode will show a low reading in both directions.

To check accurately, remove one end of each diode. Both diodes might be defective. Each diode leg should be checked in bridge rectifier components. There are four single diodes in the bridge rectifier circuit. Some bridge rectifiers are one molded component. Check each diode for open or shorted conditions. A normal diode will have a resistance of around 10 ohms and infinite reading with reversed test leads. These diodes can be replaced with ones having a 2.5-amp rating unless otherwise stated.

Tube Chassis. The very same half or full-wave low-voltage diode rectifier can be found in the tube chassis. Sometimes a silicon diode is used in the heater string of the tube setup. With the instant warm-up chassis, check the warm-up diode for possible leakage or open conditions. An open warm-up diode or switch might take the TV chassis a little longer to come on. These warm-up diodes are found in the early B&W TV chassis. Since the energy crisis, they have been left out.

Other Causes

Suspect a dirty or defective interlock switch when a portable TV operates on batteries but not ac.

Transistor Chassis. First check the interlock switch with the R×1 scale. Clean the switch contacts with tuner or cleaner spray. These small switches generally make contact when the ac cord is plugged into the TV chassis (Fig. 12-6). If the switch is normal, check for possible wire breakage or poorly soldered terminals. A leaky

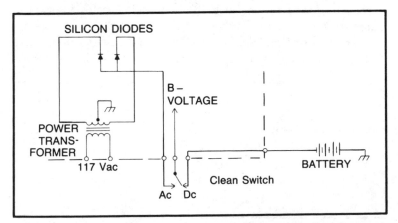

Fig. 12-6. A dirty ac/dc switch can prevent the TV from operating from the power line. Spray the switch terminals with tuner lube or cleaner. Check the switch contacts with the R×1 scale of the VOM.

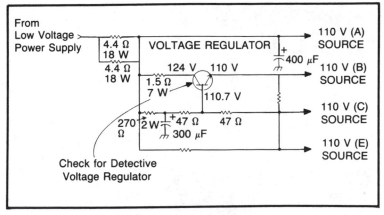

Fig. 12-7. Check for an open or leaky voltage regulator transistor in the power supply of a dead receiver. Measure the voltage from the regulator transistor for low or no voltage.

diode or faulty power transformer can prevent the ac/dc portable from operating off the power line.

A leaky or open voltage regulator transistor may produce a dead transistor chassis. Check the output voltage from the regulator transistor (Fig. 12-7). If low or no voltage, suspect a defective regulator transistor. It's best to replace the regulator transistor, because these transistors have a tendency to open after loading down. Simply locate the regulator transistor near the low-voltage power supply and replace it. Smear silicon grease between the heat sink and the transistor. See Fig. 12-8. Check for a piece of insulation on the old regulator transistor and replace it if found.

A leaky zener diode in the power supply circuits can cause a dead chassis. Replace these diodes with ones having the correct voltage rating. Since most voltages are now derived from the flyback circuits, suspect a horizontal-output transistor for dead conditions in all other circuits.

Tube Chassis. Replace the horizontal output and damper tubes in a dead tube chassis. In some tube chassis, the sound will not come up until the horizontal-output section is functioning. Check the low-voltage power supply for improper or no voltage to the tube circuits. In older tube chassis, a 5U4G tube can be used as a rectifier instead of the silicon diodes used in transistorized chassis.

NO SOUND OR RASTER

A voltage test to isolate the power supply and horizontal-output

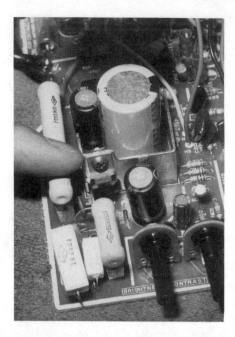

Fig. 12-8. Voltage-regulator transistor mounted on a small metal chassis that serves as the heat sink. Check to see if there is an insulator between transistor and heat sink when replacing.

circuit can be done to the collector case of the horizontal-output transistor.

Transistor Chassis. High dc voltage on the collector terminal of the horizontal-output transistor can indicate an open transistor. Set the VOM on the 300 volt dc range. A lower dc voltage might indicate a leaky horizontal-output transistor or improper drive voltage. Voltage found here at least tells you the low-voltage circuits are probably normal.

The horizontal-output transistor can be removed and a leakage test made between the base and collector terminals. A leaky transistor will give a reading with reversed test leads. It's best to always replace a suspected horizontal-output transistor. These transistors have a tendency to open under load and pull down the low-voltage source when there is internal leakage. Most of these transistors can be removed by removing the two mounting screws (Fig. 12-9).

When a low voltage or horizontal circuit fuse keeps blowing, suspect a defective horizontal circuit. Simply remove the horizontal-output transistor and replace the fuse. If the fuse does not open, suspect the removed horizontal-output transistor is leaky or has no bias (drive) voltage on the base terminal. Because the voltage is very low, the VOM might not provide adequate drive voltage

Fig. 12-9. The horizontal-output transistor is easily removed by removing two mounting screws. On some you might have to unsolder the leads to the transistor before removing, but be sure to mark down where each lead connects.

measurements. Here is where the scope comes in handy.

Quite often the lack of drive voltage is caused by a broken horizontal-oscillator coil. This coil is actually the horizontal-hold control in most transistorized chassis. (Fig. 12-10). Since the coil is placed upon the rear chassis, it is easily bumped and broken.

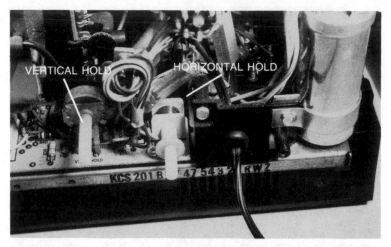

Fig. 12-10. The horizontal-output control shaft sticks out of the rear of the TV and is easily bumped. You might also find the coil connections broken in the process. Repair the coil assembly by reconnecting the broken wires, then mount and solder them to the pc board.

Locate the coil on the rear portion of the pc board chassis. Now take a continuity measurement of the horizontal coil winding with the R×10 range. Usually this coil has a center tap, so measure each leg on the bottom wiring side. The resistance might vary from 30 to 194 ohms.

If one or both sides of the coil are broken, it's possible to repair the broken ends. Unsolder the coil lug terminals from the pc wiring. Now check for continuity. If only one lead shows continuity, look for a broken wire. Sometimes it's necessary to use a small magnifying glass to locate the broken piece.

Scrape the coil wire end to remove the baked enamel coating. Tin the wire end and form a loop. Now take a short piece of stranded hook-up wire and remove one strand of wire. Form a loop on each end to connect to the broken wire. Solder both ends and check both windings for continuity. Then replace the repaired horizontal-oscillator coil.

Tube Chassis. A no sound/no raster symptom in the tube chassis can be caused by a defective horizontal-output tube. Replace the horizontal-output tube before looking any further. If nothing happens, replace the horizontal damper, oscillator high-voltage and rectifier tubes. Other possible defective components in the tube chassis are shown in Fig. 12-11.

REPLACING THE HORIZONTAL OUTPUT TRANSISTOR (TRANSISTOR CHASSIS)

After locating a defective horizontal-output transistor, the proper replacement must be used. Universal horizontal-output transistors work well in the horizontal-output circuits. Check the transistor part number in the universal transistor substitution manual. Practically every TV manufacturer has a transistor replacement manual, such as RCA, General Electric, Sylvania, Motorola, TCG, Workman, and Zenith. TAB BOOKS also has a good one.

The horizontal output transistor can be mounted at the rear of the metal chassis, or there can be a small metal strip with the output transistor mounted on it on the pc board (Fig. 12-12). Remove the metal screws holding the transistor to the metal heat sink. Unsolder the emitter and base terminal wires. Mark down the color coding of each wire for easy replacement. Note if there is a piece of insulating material between transistor and heat sink. Make sure this piece of insulation or a new one is mounted on the new transistor. Sometimes the horizontal-output transistor is mounted directly to the metal strip and the collector terminal is insulated from the pc board.

Bolt the transistor to the metal heat sink. Connect and solder the emitter and base terminal wires. Take a low-resistance measurement between transistor and heat sink if it is supposed to be insulated. When cinching up the metal screws, the transistor might

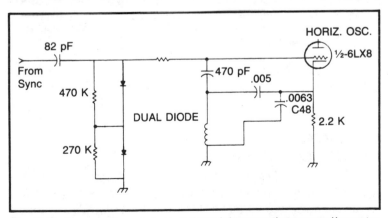

Fig. 12-11. Several other components that might cause the no sound/no raster symptom. Check the horizontal-output tube socket. These tubes run quite hot and the solder can loosen from the pc board. Sometimes soldering all the tube prongs on the horizontal output tube solves the no raster problem.

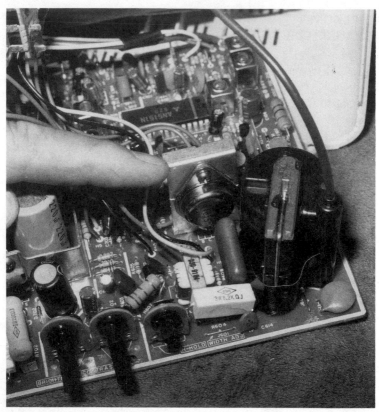

Fig. 12-12. Here the horizontal-output transistor is mounted on a small metal strip, which serves as the heat sink. There is a piece of insulation between transistor and heat sink.

bite into the insulation and ground out the collector terminal. There should be no resistance measurement when the transistor is insulated from the metal heat sink.

SMOKING FLYBACK
TRANSFORMER (TRANSISTOR CHASSIS)

Today most flyback or horizontal-output transformers are molded inside a plastic case. Internal arcover or shorts can cause the transformer to overheat and begin to smoke (Fig. 12-13). These flyback transformers must be replaced. Before obtaining and replacing the transformer, make sure the repairs are not going to cost more than the portable TV is worth. A defective flyback transformer can damage the horizontal-output transistor, along with other components.

Remove the horizontal-output transistor from the circuit for an accurate leakage test. While the transistor is out of the circuit, check the base for the horizontal oscillator and driver waveform to make sure the horizontal circuits are normal. If the horizontal circuits are normal, replace the new output transistor and flyback transformer. A leaky flyback will often destroy the horizontal-output transistor. If the output transistor is replaced before replacing the leaky flyback, the new transistor will be damaged.

POOR HORIZONTAL SYNC

Transistor Chassis. Poor horizontal sync generally occurs in the afc sync and horizontal-oscillator circuits. If the vertical picture is normal, you can eliminate the sync circuit from the possible problems. Replace the afc dual diode found near the horizontal-oscillator circuits. Remove the diode and check resistance with the R×1 K scale. The center terminal of the diode is usually common to the

Fig. 12-13. The horizontal-output transformer might smoke if the transformer is leaky or the output transistor is shorted. Check the horizontal circuits before replacing the flyback.

two outside terminals. The readings on each diode should be quite close to the common terminal.

Tube Chassis. Replace the horizontal oscillator and sync tubes for poor horizontal sync. A leaky horizontal oscillator can also cause poor horizontal sync. Check the sync coupling capacitor between the sync tube and horizontal circuits for leakage (Fig. 12-14). Remove, test, and replace the afc dual-diode component as in the transistorized chassis.

HORIZONTAL PULLING

Transistor Chassis. After replacing the horizontal components mentioned above, if the horizontal picture still wants to pull to one side, suspect a leaky voltage regulator transistor in the low-voltage power supply (Fig. 12-15). Just replace the regulator transistor with a new one. Sometimes voltage measurements on the transistor elements will not indicate a leaky transistor in the circuit. Also, shunt large filter capacitors in this circuit to find the cause of horizontal pulling.

Tube Chassis. Besides replacing the horizontal oscillator sync and output tube for horizontal pulling, check the filter capacitor. Shunt the filter capacitor which supplies the voltage source to the horizontal-oscillator circuits. This capacitor is usually found close to the horizontal-oscillator coil. Check the small capacitor across the oscillator coil for leakage when the horizontal frequency shifts off channel after receiver warmup.

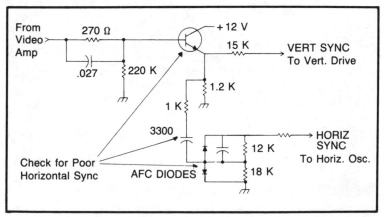

Fig. 12-14. Check the sync coupling capacitor between sync and horizontal circuits for leakage. Remove the low-voltage terminal of the capacitor. Check for leakage across the capacitor terminals with the highest ohmmeter scale.

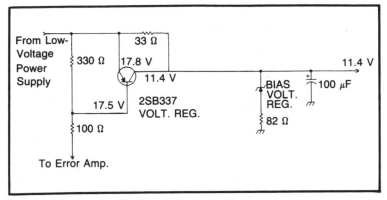

Fig. 12-15. Replace the leaky voltage regulator transistor in the power supply when horizontal pulling is noted in the raster. Also, shunt the large filter capacitor for a possible defective capacitor in the low-voltage power supply.

VERTICAL WHITE LINE

Transistor Chassis. A vertical white line is caused by improper horizontal sweep—the high voltage is near normal except the horizontal sweep system is open. Suspect a broken wire going to the deflection yoke. Note if the yoke plug is properly seated. In some transistor chassis, a defective bypass capacitor might be found at the grounded side. Measure the resistance or continuity of the horizontal winding of the deflection yoke.

Tube Chassis. Check for the same problems in the transistor chassis. You might find a burned resistor in series with one of the horizontal deflection yoke windings (FIg. 12-16). Sometimes the horizontal coupling capacitor on the yoke assembly is open or leaky.

POOR WIDTH

Transistor Chassis. Suspect a leaky horizontal-output transistor or improper voltage from the low-voltage power supply. Check for low voltage at the body (collector) of the horizontal-output transistor. Remove the transistor if the voltage is lower than normal. Check the transistor out of the circuit for leakage. Poor width can be caused by a defective voltage regulator transistor.

When the voltage cannot be varied with the small voltage control found in the low-voltage power supply, suspect a leaky voltage-regulator transistor (Fig. 12-17). In some B&W chassis, the transistor is called the APF or AVR transistor. Remove the transistor and check resistance across all elements. Replace the transistor with an exact or universal replacement. You might have horizontal pulling

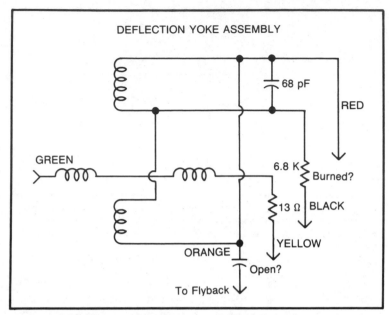

Fig. 12-16. Check for a burned isolation resistor in the horizontal yoke winding in the tube chassis. A shorted or open horizontal coupling capacitor mounted in the yoke assembly can cause a horizontal sweep problem.

or vertical flipping with a leaky regulator transistor. A leaky regulator transistor can also cause the center of the picture to become very dark.

Tube Chassis. Poor width in a true chassis is usually caused by a weak horizontal output or damper tube. Replace the horizontal

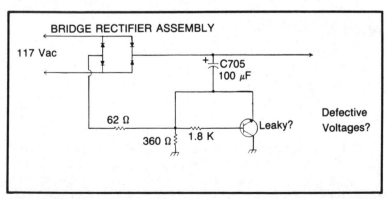

Fig. 12-17. A leaky or open voltage-regulator transistor in the low-voltage power supply can cause poor width. If the transistor is defective, the output voltage is usually lower.

oscillator and high-voltage rectifier tube if the width is still poor. Check the screen grid resistor for improper value. Adjust the horizontal width or linearity control for greater width.

GOOD SOUND BUT VERY LITTLE BRIGHTNESS

Transistor Chassis. Suspect a defective video-output transistor when the brightness control doesn't work. You can have some signs of picture with a leaky video output transistor. Place your arm next to the screen. The hair on your arm should raise up when the high voltage is applied to the picture tube.

You might find a brightness limiter or video control on the TV chassis for greater brightness. Readjustment of these controls can improve the raster. Finally, a simply weak CRT can result in very little brightness and poor contrast.

Tube Chassis. Replace the two video-output tubes for no brightness when the hv is normal. Make sure all brightness, contrast, and brightness limiter controls are advanced. Check for an open contrast control or plate resistor in the video-output tube circuit when there is insufficient brightness.

NO VIDEO OR BRIGHTNESS (TRANSISTOR CHASSIS)

Other than a defective picture tube or no picture-tube heater voltage, a no-video or no-brightness symptom can be caused by an open or leaky video-output transistor or IC component. Make sure high voltage is present by measuring the hv at the anode terminal of the picture tube. You might find one large IC component that takes care of all video, i-f, AGC, and sound circuits (Fig. 12-18).

Make sure all the voltages are normal on the picture tube. Obviously, without a video signal, the voltage at the cathode terminal will not be correct. Simply replace the large IC. Check the transistors in the first and second video amp circuits with the diode test of the DMM. If in doubt, remove the suspected transistor for leakage tests. Take critical voltage tests on each video transistor to locate the defective transistor or component.

AGC TESTS (TRANSISTOR CHASSIS)

Improper automatic gain control (AGC) voltage at the tuner or i-f stages can indicate a defective AGC transistor. The i-f AGC voltage can vary from 3 to 5 volts. This voltage can be measured at a test point or on the base of the first pix (picture) i-f amp transistor.

Fig. 12-18. One large IC component can control the AGC, video pix i-f, and all the video circuits. Take accurate voltage and resistance measurements in each IC pin before replacing it.

First try to adjust the small AGC control. This control should be located close to the i-f and AGC circuits. Note if the AGC control has any effect on the picture. If it does, the AGC circuits might be normal. Test all AGC transistors in the circuit and take accurate voltage tests with the antenna disconnected.

When the AGC circuits are contained in the video IC component, take crucial voltage measurements. A leaky AGC/video IC can cause erratic pulling or an overdriven picture on the raster. The picture might be very dark with horizontal pulling and poor vertical sync. Replace the AGC/video IC component even if the voltages are fairly normal with the antenna disconnected. Take accurate resistance measurements between each IC pin and ground to locate a leaky IC component.

NO SOUND

Transistor Chassis. With a no-sound symptom, turn the volume control rapidly up and down, listening for any type of noise. A noisy or scratchy sound might indicate the audio output stages are normal. Connect another speaker across the speaker terminals when you suspect an open speaker. Check the speaker leads near the audio output transformer or capacitor. Touch the center terminal of the volume control and if the sound stages are normal, you should hear hum in the speaker.

Suspect an open or leaky audio output transistor or IC if no sound can be heard. Voltage measurements of the sound stages can indicate a defective transistor. Low collector voltage might indicate a leaky output transistor. High collector voltage can be caused by an open audio output transistor or emitter resistor (Fig. 12-19). Most audio output transistors can be replaced with a universal replacement.

Tube Chassis. Replace the last two audio tubes for a no-sound condition in the tube chassis. Take voltage measurements on the tube terminals. A shorted audio output tube can cause the cathode resistor to change value. If the sound is distorted after replacing the audio output tube, check for a burned cathode bias resistor. No voltage on the plate terminal might be caused by an open output transformer winding. Check Fig. 12-20 for additional no-sound tube problems.

POPPING SOUND

Transistor Chassis. A continuous or intermittent popping noise in the sound might be caused by a defective audio output transistor. Sometimes the chassis won't begin to pop until it has warmed up for several hours. Let the chassis begin to act up and then spray the suspected transistor with coolant (Fig. 12-21). The coolant should stop the popping noise. Replace the suspected audio output transistor.

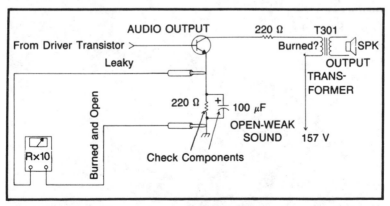

Fig. 12-19. High collector voltage might be caused by an open audio output transistor or emitter resistor. When the output transistor becomes leaky, you might find the resistor is burned or quite warm. Check the resistance with the R×10 scale across the emitter bias resistor.

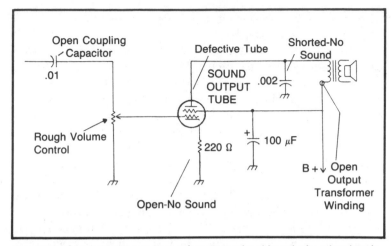

Fig. 12-20. Check these components for no-sound problems in the tube chassis. Don't overlook a possibly bad tube socket or poorly soldered tube terminals on the pc board.

Fig. 12-21. Spray the audio output transistor with coolant when a popping sound is heard in the speaker. If needed, apply several coats of coolant. If it is defective, the transistor should stop the popping when cooled.

Tube Chassis. Normally, the audio output tubes will make a crackling or microphonic noise when jarred or tapped with the handle of a screwdriver. When tapped, the sound might cut up and down in the tube chassis. These tubes might test out as normal in the tester, but should still be replaced.

MUSHY SOUND

Transistor Chassis. There are a number of problems that can cause distortion or mushy sound. A defective speaker with a warped cone will sound mushy. Replace the input and output sound modules in chassis with a sound module. A leaky audio IC or output transistor can produce distortion (Fig. 12-22). Before replacement, check for burned emitter bias resistors. Improper voltage to the output Ic or transistor may cause distortion and weak volume. Weak sound may be caused by a defective emitter bias resistor or bypass capacitor.

Tube Chassis. In the tube chassis, the distortion might not occur until it has operated for an hour or so. This is usually caused by a defective audio output tube. Replace the tube and let the chassis warm up. If the distortion returns, replace or check the cathode resistor and bypass capacitor. Check for a leaky bypass capacitor across the audio output transformer (Fig. 12-23). Weak sound can be caused by weak sound tubes.

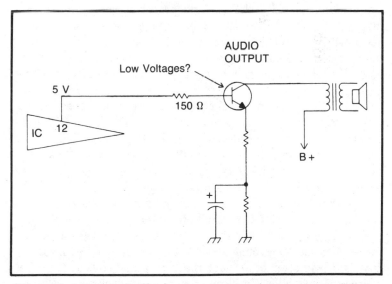

Fig. 12-22. A leaky audio IC or audio output transistor can cause distortion in the sound. Check for lower voltages than those indicated in the schematic.

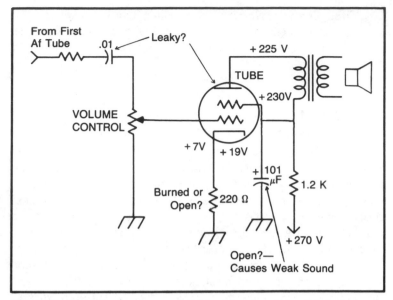

Fig. 12-23. Check these components of the tube chassis for distorted sound. Don't overlook a dropped speaker cone if there is mushy or distorted sound.

NORMAL SOUND BUT NO RASTER

Transistor and Tube Chassis. Other than improper high voltage or defective video stages, a poor CRT socket can produce a no-raster condition. Peer closely between the socket and yoke to see if the picture tube is heating up. If there is no light, simply twist the tube socket and note if the heater begins to come on. If so, resolder the tube pins on the tube socket or replace the defective tube socket.

When the picture tube will not light up, suspect an open internal heater. Remove the picture tube socket. Connect the VOM leads across the heater pin terminals using the R×1 scale. The heater terminals are usually on each side of the small guide pin. When open, the picture tube must be replaced. Before replacing, check the picture tube prices, as they are quite expensive.

Improper voltages on the picture tube can cause no raster, a dark raster, or possibly an intermittent raster. Rotate the VOM voltage range to the 1200 Vdc range. Always use the highest voltage range when checking voltages on the picture tube socket of a B&W chassis. *Never* attempt to check the hv or anode voltage of any TV with a small voltmeter. Check and compare these voltages with those found in the service literature (Fig. 12-24).

266

NORMAL SOUND BUT NO RASTER AND NO HV

Transistor Chassis. In some B&W chassis you might hear a little sound but no picture when you have a leaky horizontal-output transistor. With no horizontal sweep, the sound is usually missing also. The sound voltage source is taken from the flyback transformer windings. Remove the horizontal output-transistor and check for leakage. With the transistor out of the circuit, check the damper diode with the R×10 scale. Simply replacing the transistor might solve the problem.

Check for a leaky or shorted boost rectifier in the flyback secondary. Sometimes these diodes open. Remove one lead to check for leakage. A silicon boost rectifier can be checked the same as any other silicon diode. Germanium boost diodes might not show any reading with the small VOM. A leakage reading with reversed test leads indicates a defective boost diode (Fig. 12-25).

It's very difficult to check the hv rectifier without a hv probe. You may hold an insulated screwdriver blade within a quarter of an inch of the flyback transformer connection, but *be very careful*. Do not touch any part of the hv section when the chassis is operating. Use only an insulated screwdriver. Just place the blade end close to the connection where the transformer lead connects to the rectifier. If you can draw a short arc, you can assume the voltage

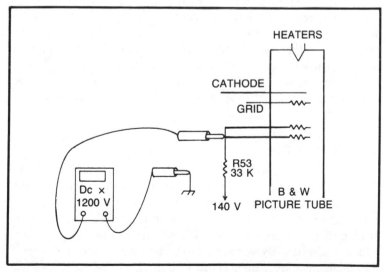

Fig. 12-24. Check for a poorly contacting picture tube socket when the picture tube will not light. Improper voltage on the CRT terminals might reveal a defective component. Use the 1200 Vdc scale for these measurements.

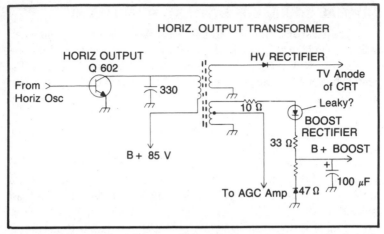

Fig. 12-25. A leaky silicon boost rectifier might show a leakage reading in both directions with the R × 100 scale. In older B&W chassis, a germanium type diode might be found instead. Remove one end for leakage tests.

is normal from the flyback transformer. Sometimes a defective hv rectifier fires internally and produces a sweet smell. Since these units are made up of many separate diodes, continuity tests with the VOM cannot be used. Keep away from the hv anode connections. Never arc the hv lead to chassis ground in a transistorized chassis.

Tube Chassis. Replace the hv rectifier tube for no raster problems. To determine if voltage is present at the cap of the hv rectifier, draw an arc with an insulated screwdriver at the plate cap. No arc here indicates that the flyback circuits are defective. An arc of one-quarter inch indicates the flyback circuits are normal. Check, and if necessary replace, the horizontal-output and damper tubes. However, it's always safest to let a qualified TV technician service the hv section.

SNOWY PICTURE

Transistor and Tube Chassis. A snowy picture on all channels can indicate a defective antenna or lead-in. If you have another set in the house, make sure both sets are snowy before going out on the roof. When the problem is in the TV, suspect burned balun coils or a defective tuner. It's possible for lightning to have struck nearby, damaging the antenna coils or the rf transistor. Check the continuity of the antenna coils with the R × 1 scale of the VOM.

A leaky or open rf transistor in the tuner can produce a snowy picture, especially on very weak stations. This transistor is located very close to the rear and next to the antenna coils. Replacing the transistor is easy when it's located on the top of the tuner. If the transistors are not out in the open, take the tuner to your TV repairman so he can repair it. Don't order a new tuner, because good tuner overhaul is as good as new at less than half the price.

HEAVY HUM AND BLACK BARS

Transistor Chassis. When you hear a loud hum in the speaker and see heavy 60-cycle black bars going up the screen, suspect a defective filter capacitor. These large filter capacitors have a tendency to lose their capacitance after a few years and produce black bars in the raster. If the main filter is defective you might see the raster pull in on both sides (Fig. 12-26). Replacing the electrolytic capacitor may solve the hum bar condition.

Locate a defective capacitor by shunting a known capacitor across the suspected one. It's best to pull the power plug and clip the new capacitor across the suspected one. Make sure of correct polarity and voltage when attaching the new capacitor. The unshielded or open end of the electrolytic capacitor is the positive (+) terminal. The ground or negative terminal is the metal outside end. Shunt each capacitor or section until the hum bars disappear. You might find one or two defective capacitors in one container. If you do, replace the whole unit. If not, very soon each capacitor within the unit will go bad. Always choose a larger capacitor with greater capacity and equal working voltage when shunting across the suspected one. If not, you may damage transistors or ICs in the circuit.

Improper adjustment or a leaky voltage regulator transistor in the low-voltage power supply can produce a black bar across the screen. First try to adjust the voltage control for the required output voltage source. This adjustment is found on the schematic diagram. Measure the output voltage at the low-voltage power supply or collector terminal of the horizontal-output transistor. Simply adjusting this control might eliminate the hum bar without any additional repairs.

Tube Chassis. Beside shunting large filter capacitors within the low-voltage power supply, hum bars can be caused by leaky rf or horizontal-oscillator tubes. If after shunting all of the filter capacitors the hum bar is still present, try replacing the horizontal-oscillator tube. Usually, a leaky oscillator tube will cause horizontal pulling. A shorted or leaky tube will always run quite warm. Replacing the rf tube might cure some hum bar problems.

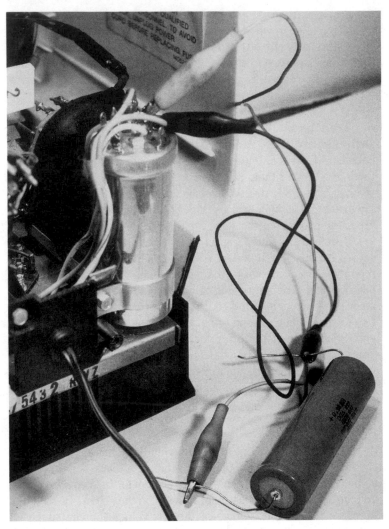

Fig. 12-26. Check and shunt the main filter capacitors in the low-voltage supply when hum bars are found on the TV screen. Shunt each capacitor with a new one until the bars disappear, then replace the defective capacitor.

HORIZONTAL WHITE LINE

Transistor Chassis. Improper vertical sweep is indicated by a horizontal white line. If the horizontal white line appears after the receiver is on for awhile, spray each vertical transistor with coolant. Start at the vertical output transistor and work towards the vertical-oscillator circuits. Most vertical problems are caused by the vertical-output transistors. Replacement of these transistors might solve the vertical sweep problem.

Check the vertical winding of the deflection yoke for an open lead or winding. Set the VOM on the R×1 scale and check each winding. The total resistance of the vertical yoke coils is usually under 50 ohms. A poor yoke socket or lead can cause an intermittent vertical raster. You might find only one vertical size control in the transistorized chassis.

Tube Chassis. Replace the vertical oscillator and output tube for poor vertical sweep in the tube chassis. Both tube functions can be found in one glass envelope. Check the vertical hold, height, and linearity controls for proper adjustment. If tube replacement and adjustments do not cure the vertical problem, check the vertical yoke circuits (Fig. 12-27).

Suspect a leaky feedback capacitor from plate and the output transformer if you have a positive voltage in the feedback circuits. These capacitors have a tendency to break down under a high peak voltage. Replace these capacitors with ones having 1600 Vdc working voltage. If a lower voltage capacitor is used, the capacitor may very soon short out or break down.

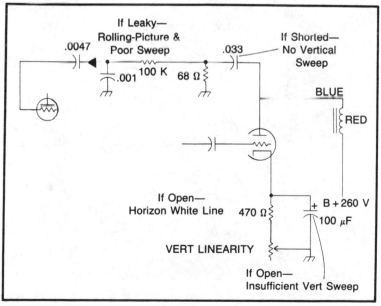

Fig. 12-27. Check the components in this schematic for additional vertical problems in the tube chassis. Resolder the vertical tube socket for poor ac wiring connections.

An open vertical output transformer will inhibit vertical sweep. Check the transformer with the $R \times 1$ scale. The vertical defection yoke works directly into this transformer, so one vertical yoke lead should be removed for a correct resistance reading. While in this circuit, check the resistance of the vertical winding of the deflection yoke. Check for a possibly leaky or open capacitor in the grounded leg of the vertical yoke lead.

ONLY TOP HALF OF PICTURE
SHOWS (TRANSISTOR CHASSIS)

Insufficient vertical height might be caused by the vertical-output circuits. Suspect a leaky vertical-output transistor or IC component (Fig. 12-28). Most small B&W portables have two vertical-output transistors to scan the up and down portion of the TV screen. Usually there is a white line when one of the transistors is open.

Take in-circuit transistor tests with the DMM or a transistor tester. If one of the transistors appears leaky, remove it from the

Fig. 12-28. A faulty vertical-output transistor might limit vertical height. Take a voltage test at the metal tabs or collector terminals to locate the defective component.

circuit for leakage tests. One of these transistors might break down only under working conditions, indicating an intermittent height raster. Measure the voltage at the collector terminals. One transistor might have very low or no collector voltage, while the other equals the power-supply source.

Check the bias diodes and resistors with the vertical-output transistors out of the circuit. Besides the transistors, the large vertical coupling capacitor between the vertical-output circuits and yoke may lose capacity, causing improper height (Fig. 12-29). Very low supply voltage can cause insufficient height problems. Take accurate voltage and resistance measurements on each pin of the vertical oscillator and IC output component to locate an improper vertical height problem.

VERTICAL ROLLING

Transistor Chassis. Vertical rolling can be caused by defective sync circuits. Note if the picture is rolling both horizontally and vertically. If so, the problem is in the sync circuit. Replacement of the sync transistor might solve the problem. Check for improper setting of the vertical size control. Take voltage measurements on the vertical oscillator and amp transistor. Don't overlook a defective filter capacitor for vertical crawling.

Tube Chassis. Replace both sync and vertical tubes. Reset the vertical height and linearity controls. Sometimes over-scanning of these controls will make the vertical sync roll rather easily in some TV chassis. If the raster is adjusted too high, the picture might roll.

Check for leaky or shorted feedback capacitors in the vertical circuits. Remove one end for correct leakage tests. Don't overlook a possibly shorted lead wire on the vertical hold control. Check all three terminal leads of the vertical hold control so that they are not touching one another.

ERRATIC VERTICAL CONTROL (TRANSISTOR CHASSIS)

A dirty or worn vertical size or hold control can cause the raster to either collapse into a white line, produce insufficient vertical height, or erratic rolling. Sometimes these small controls are located on the back of the chassis. They are easily damaged (Fig. 12-30). Slowly rotate the control and note if the raster goes into a white line at a certain point of the rotation. Try to clean up the control with cleaning spray. A worn or broken control should be replaced.

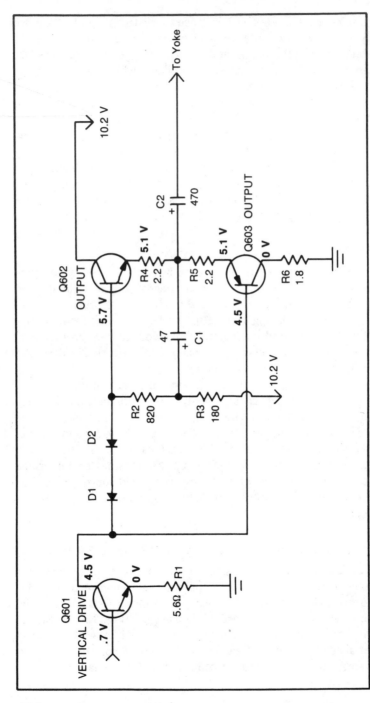

Fig. 12-29. Check Q601, D1, D2, Q602, R3, R4, R5, Q603 and C2.

274

Fig. 12-30. A broken or cracked vertical control may produce intermittent vertical roll, a white line, or improper height. Clean up the control before replacement.

SMOKE FROM THE CHASSIS

Transistor and Tube Chassis. When the chassis of a TV begins to smoke, look for burned power or flyback transformers, bias resistors, sections of burned wiring, and/or tube sockets. First remove the back cover and plug in the TV set and watch for the burned areas. If the set is still smoking, try to locate the burned component.

Don't leave the set on if the smoke is coming from the power transformer. If the transformer is not damaged already, it will be soon. Leaky silicon diodes or rectifiers can cause the power transformer to smoke. The transformer will be quite warm. Remove the secondary leads from the power transformer to determine if the transformer still runs hot. If not, take a voltage measurement of the secondary winding—be careful! Replace the defective component that is causing the power transformer to smoke. If the transformer still smokes and runs hot after all the leads are disconnected, the transformer will need replacement.

A flyback transformer that has arced over will usually show signs of burned areas on the high-voltage windings. Look the transformer over very closely. The fuse might not hold and the horizontal-output transistor is destroyed. In a tube chassis a shorted flyback transformer can make the horizontal output and damper tube run very hot. Replace a burned flyback transformer.

Large wattage voltage-dropping resistors smoke or run very hot when a short or leak is on one end of the circuit. You might find fusible and large heater voltage-dropping resistors running quite warm, which is normal. Use the ohmmeter to locate the leaky component that is causing any resistor to burn or run very hot.

Suspect a leaky or shorted transistor when the bias resistors are burned and charred. The color code might be badly burned so you cannot recognize the value of the burned resistor. These small resistors might have changed value. Look up the burned resistor in the service literature to obtain the burned resistors correct resistance.

Sometimes high voltage or damper circuits can arc over in a bunch of wiring or on the pc board. The connecting wire between several components might be pulled too tight and short against the chassis or other components, causing a shorted area to start burning. Separate the burned wires and insert new wiring between the burned areas. Since higher voltages are found in tube chassis, you will find more burned components in these chassis.

PICTURE TUBE PROBLEMS (TRANSISTOR CHASSIS)

A defective picture tube can cause a black raster, faint picture, overscan lines, very little brightness, very dark picture, no control over the brightness, or an intermittent picture. No picture or brightness could be caused by open heater terminals or improper hv at the anode connection of the CRT. Measure the hv at the anode with a high-voltage probe. Do not use a regular voltmeter to check high voltage. The high voltage in B&W TV chassis might vary from 6 to 18 kilovolts depending on the size of the picture tube.

Sometimes the heater voltage is quite low and cannot be seen at the glass neck of the picture tube. The heater voltage might come from the dc power supply or from a winding on the flyback transformer. Remove the picture tube socket and take a resistance measurement at the heater pins. The heater resistance should be under 20 ohms. If the heater resistance is above 50 ohms, the picture will have very little brightness. The tube should light up with heater continuity.

Look over the schematic to determine where the heater voltage comes from. Measure the dc voltage at the picture tube socket pins if it comes from the low-voltage power source. Check the low-voltage circuits for possible improper dc voltage. Take a low-resistance continuity test if the heater voltage is supplied by the flyback transformer. Note if a low resistance, voltage-dropping resistor is in series with one leg of the flyback winding (Fig. 12-31). A burned or open voltage-dropping resistor might prevent the tube from lighting up.

A very weak picture could be caused by a weak picture tube. Test the picture tube on a CRT checker. A faint picture can be caused by improper boost voltage. Overscan lines with intermittent brightness may result from a shorted B&W picture tube-gun assembly. Turn the brightness up and tap lightly on the rear glass gun assembly and note if the picture comes and goes. Uncontrollable brightness could be a result of a shorted picture tube. Not enough

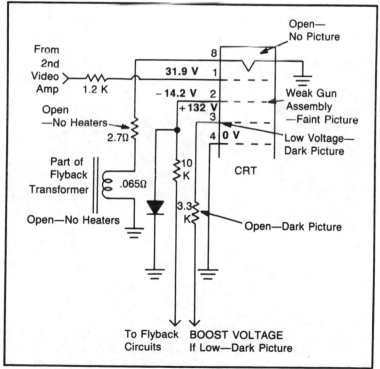

Fig. 12-31. Check these components for a weak, dark or black picture or lines in the picture. When the picture tube heater resistance increases, the picture usually becomes faint or weak.

brightness with a very dark screen can result from insufficient voltage on the grids of the picture tube. Open or improper increase in resistance from the power-source dropping resistor can produce a very dark picture.

ARCING NOISES

Transistor Chassis. Most of the arcing noises occur in the high-voltage (hv) areas (Fig. 12-32). Note if the firing is at the anode terminal of the picture tube. The hv arcing may occur from the anode plug to duct or be caused by liquid spilled on the area.

Unless you have worked around hv and picture tubes, don't try to make repairs. You can receive a terrible shock or be killed if the hv is not discharged properly. Remember the hv can draw an arc over one-quarter of an inch of up to 30 kV in color receivers. Keep your hands away from the hv transformer and hv area. Leave this job to a qualified TV technician.

Tube Chassis. Beside the hv anode lead and flyback transformer, the arcing can occur in the hv rectifier socket. Sometimes only a pin hole is needed to start the hv socket to arc

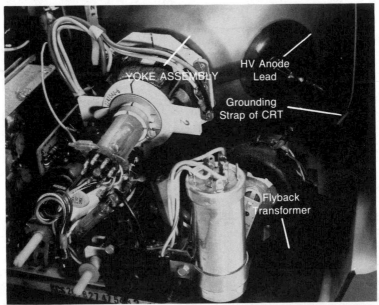

Fig. 12-32. Most arcing noises occur in the high-voltage circuitry. Do not attempt to repair these components unless you know how to properly discharge the picture tube. Leave these more dangerous repair jobs to the qualified TV technician.

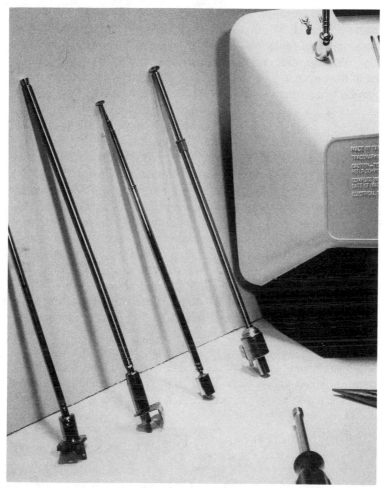

Fig. 12-33. Various dipole antennas found on the rear of the portable B&W TV.

over. These sockets cannot be successfully repaired, so let a TV technician replace them. A small isolation resistor within the hv rectifier socket might be burned through, causing an arcing noise. If you do not know how to ground out the high voltage, do not attempt to make these repairs.

REMOVING THE DIPOLE ANTENNA

Transistor and Tube Chassis. The dipole or ''dog-ear'' antenna must be replaced if it's broken off or even a few sections are missing. Distant stations might be snowy with only one section torn off (Fig. 12-33). You can quickly solve the snowy condition by removing and replacing the dipole antenna.

You might find only one or two dipole antennas on the rear cover of the portable TV. Remove all of the back cover screws and be careful when removing the wire cables that connect to the vhf tuner. Some TV chassis have two sets of screws, one UHF and one VHF set. The dipole antenna is easily removed if the back cover is removed from the TV cabinet. Disconnect all cables and wire leads.

The dipole antenna can be spring mounted or bolted to the plastic cover (Fig. 12-34). First remove the wires from the dipole that connect to or plug into the vhf tuner. Remove the bottom screw or nut to release the dipole. You might find the slotted area worn where it mounts in the plastic cover. Either plug the hole with spray cement or use large mounting washers.

It's possible only the dipole antenna needs replacing (Fig. 12-35). There are some universal dipole rods that slip into the same hole and are held into position with a beveled screw. If the TV is a Japanese make, the universal dipole rod must be exactly the same. American universal rods are usually a little larger than Japanese ones and will not fit inside the ball area.

After the broken dipole assembly has been removed, take the antenna to your local TV shop with the set's make and model number. For instance, if the TV is an RCA, you should try to obtain the original part from your local RCA dealer. The original component

Fig. 12-34. The dipole antenna can be spring mounted or bolted to the back plastic cover.

Fig. 12-35. Before tearing out the old antenna assembly, see if a universal rod can be inserted into the old assembly. It's much cheaper and quicker to just replace the metal.

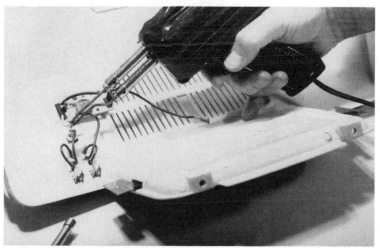

Fig. 12-36. Several hands could be needed to compress the large spring and metal ball so it will fit inside the slotted back area. After it is mounted, solder all lead connections to the dipole antenna.

is much easier to replace. If the dipole is not on hand, they can order it for you. In case the original cannot be obtained, a universal type of dipole antenna can be installed.

INSTALLING THE DIPOLE ANTENNA

Transistor and Tube Chassis. After obtaining the dipole antenna, you will find it's much easier to install than to remove. The original antenna will mount in the same hole. Replace all washers and the retaining nut. Installing a universal-type antenna might require a larger mounting hole. The hole can be enlarged in the plastic back cover with the soldering iron tip. Ream out the hole with the hot iron and cut off the surplus with a knife.

Dipole antennas mounted inside a large compressed spring are sometimes difficult to install. The heavy spring must be compressed tightly against the metal ball before the whole assembly will slip into the plastic slotted area (Fig. 12-36). This might be a little more difficult than it looks. In fact, you could need another hand or two to replace this type of antenna. After replacing the antenna, reconnect and solder all leads before replacing the back cover on the portable TV.

13

Color TV Repairs

Many problems in the color chassis are the same or similar to those in the B&W TV chassis, (Fig. 13-1). The low-voltage power supply symptoms are quite similar, except that in the color chassis the circuits are a little more complicated. Horizontal and high-voltage circuits are repaired in the same manner, except that the hv can exceed 30 kV. The color circuits have been omitted from this chapter because they are quite complicated and require special test equipment. Leave the color circuits to a qualified TV technician.

SET DEAD

The following possibilities should be explored for a no-output condition in your TV set.

Check the Fuse

Transistor Chassis. You might find one or two fuse-protected circuits in the color chassis. Usually the low-voltage power supply is protected with a line voltage fuse, while the horizontal circuits contain a lower amperage fuse. Either fuse could be blown with a dead chassis. With this symptom, you have no sound, no raster, and no picture.

When only the horizontal circuit fuse is blown, there is an overload in the horizontal or high-voltage circuits. Sometimes a transistor or component breaks down or arcs over temporarily

Fig. 13-1. A typical portable color receiver.

knocking out the fuse. Replace the open fuse with one having the same current rating. In many cases the chassis will operate without any further problems. But if the fuse blows at once, suspect problems in the horizontal circuits.

Both the line voltage and horizontal fuse could be open at the same time. This can indicate that an overloaded component in the horizontal circuit has caused both fuses to blow. It's possible that the horizontal-output transistor has become leaky or the drive voltage is missing from the base terminal of the horizontal-output transistor. If only the line voltage fuse is open, you might find problems within the low-voltage power supply or other possibly overloaded circuits.

Locate the open fuse with the R×1 range of VOM. Make sure the power cord is disconnected. If the fuse is removable, check the fuse out of the circuit. In some power supply circuits, the fuse is wired directly to the pc board (Fig. 13-2). These pigtail fuses can be checked with the ohmmeter while they are in the circuit. A normal fuse will have a shorted continuity reading. A defective fuse will be open and have an infinite reading.

Replace all open fuses with ones having the same current rating. Locate the fuse rating, shown on the chassis or on the panel tag. A paper chart might be in the cabinet or in the back of the plastic

284

Fig. 13-2. The fuse can be a plug-in or a pig-tail type, the latter being soldered directly to the pc board. Look closely, as the fuse could be wedged down between other low-voltage power supply components.

cover. If not, check the metal end of the fuse. Place it under a magnifying glass, if necessary, to identify the current rating. Most fuses have both the current and voltage ratings stamped on the metal ends of the fuse.

Tube Chassis. Larger tube chassis might have a power transformer without any line-voltage fuse protection. Sometimes a varistor is in series with one of the black primary ac windings. These grey-black varistors can burn off a terminal or crack and open up the power-line circuitry. Replace the defective varistor with one having the same cold ohm rating (Fig. 13-3).

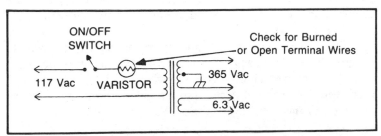

Fig. 13-3. An open varistor might be between the power cord and power transformer. After several years of operation, these varistors have a tendency to burn open.

Look for a fusible wire in the secondary windings of the power transformer. The soft fusible wire can be enclosed inside a spaghetti-type covering. Naturally, the tubes will not light when the fusible heater wire is burned open. Usually either a tube or a dial light assembly has shorted—causing the fusible wire to open. Locating fusible wiring is very difficult, so just take a single strand of wire from a short piece of flexible hook-up wire and solder it in place of the fusible wire.

Check the Switch

Transistor Chassis. An open or worn ON/OFF switch can cause the TV chassis to be dead. Check for a lighted dial light. If the dial light behind the selector knob is on, undoubtedly the ON/OFF switch is normal. A lighted neon dial light can also indicate the low-voltage power supply is functioning. These neon-type bulbs are found in the more recent TV chassis. Because the neon bulb operates from a dc source, you can assume both the switch and low-voltage power supply are functioning.

Sometimes dirty switch contacts will produce an intermittent ON/OFF switch. Spray tuner or contact spray inside the switch area and rapidly turn the switch on and off. If the dial light comes on each time, the switch might operate for a long time without further service. Replace the switch if cleaning doesn't help. A defective switch terminal can be checked with the $R \times 1$ ohm scale with the terminal leads across the switch terminals.

Tube Chassis. The ON/OFF switch might be in combination with an instant-ON or combination radio/record player circuit. The instant ON/OFF circuit could be just another switch contact added to the ON/OFF switch. These can usually be replaced without too much difficulty. But if the ON/OFF switch is incorporated with several different sound and brightness controls like those found in the combination TV and radio/record player, they are very difficult to obtain (Fig. 13-4).

Check the other switch terminals on the combination switch. If they can be cleaned and will function, simply replace the defective ON/OFF switch with another type of switch. Add another push-pull type switch to the front panel; also a temporary toggle switch can be added to the rear cover of the TV.

Circuit Breaker

Transistor Chassis. Simply resetting or pushing in the red

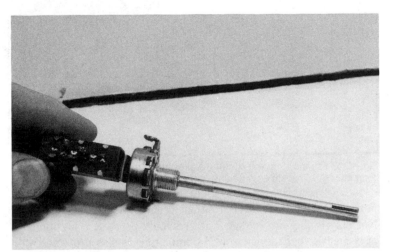

Fig. 13-4. A combination TV console might have a special type of switch that is a little difficult to obtain. These should be ordered directly from the manufacturer.

button of the circuit breaker in the color TV chassis can restore a dead TV set. Power-line surges or a temporary overload condition within the receiver can cause the circuit breaker to open. This is especially true during thunderstorms in your area. So when the TV is dead, look for a small red button on the back of your set and push it in. If the circuit breaker keeps kicking out, suspect an overload condition within the chassis.

After TV repairs, the circuit breaker might not hold or intermittently kicks out. Always replace the circuit breaker with one having the exact current rating. This current rating is usually found stamped on the body of the circuit breaker. If not, locate a schematic diagram for the correct circuit breaker replacement. The defective circuit breaker is located in the ac input circuitry or the dc circuits of the low-voltage power supply (Fig. 13-5).

A defective circuit breaker might not reset when pushed in. This means the circuit is not closed. Check for an open circuit breaker with the R×1 scale of the VOM. Pull the power cord and reset the circuit breaker. Now measure the continuity across the circuit-breaker terminals. No reading indicates the circuit breaker is open. Temporarily shunt a clip lead across the two terminals, and plug in the power cord. Replace the circuit breaker when the chassis is functioning once again.

Tube Chassis. The same tests and methods should be made when a suspected circuit breaker is found in a tube chassis. Some

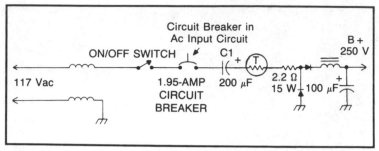

Fig. 13-5. You may find the circuit breaker in the ac input or dc circuit of the color chassis. Check the continuity of the circuit breaker with the R×1 scale.

portable tube chassis have a circuit breaker with three terminals. Not only is the low-voltage power supply protected with one set of terminals, but the horizontal-output tube is also protected with the same circuit breaker (Fig. 13-6). The lower terminals and outside metal body completes the circuit between the cathode terminal and chassis.

A defective circuit breaker might be difficult to remove because the body could be soldered to the metal chassis. You might need a 300-watt soldering gun to loosen the solder around this type of circuit breaker. Don't forget to resolder the metal body of the new replacement to the metal chassis to complete the cathode circuit of the horizontal-output tube. Mark down and check each wire terminal before removing the defective circuit breaker. Remember the terminal that completes the circuit to the metal body goes to the cathode circuit.

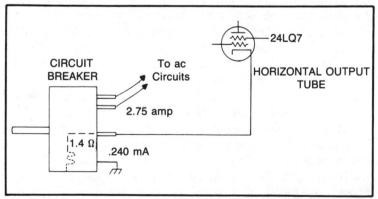

Fig. 13-6. A special circuit breaker might be found in some color TV chassis. This type of circuit breaker protects both the input and horizontal-output tubes when overloaded.

Bad Interlock Cord

Transistor and Tube Chassis. A defective interlock cord could be caused by lightning striking the power line during a thunderstorm. It's best to pull the power cord and disconnect the outside antenna from the TV receiver when a thunderstorm approaches. This also applies to cable TV. Cable TV wires can be struck by lightning and damage your TV set.

When the interlock connections are hit by lightning, you might find one of the pins burned off. Replace it if the ac male pins are damaged at the plug or where they enter the chassis. Sometimes the TV back is not mounted correctly, resulting in a poor interlock fitting. The TV chassis might behave intermittently with this type of problem.

Remove the back cover and check the interlock connections and male plug. Make sure the power cord is pulled from the power line. Take a continuity test of the ac cord with the R × 1 scale of the VOM (Fig. 13-7). Short the ac plug with a test clip. Now push the ohmmeter test leads into the interlock end. Flex the power cord to check for possible breaks. If the meter hand shows a steady shorted reading, you can assume the cheater cord is good.

Check the chassis interlock pins for burned or broken areas. If the pins are only discolored, clean them off with sandpaper. Both pins should be clean to make a good connection with the new cheater cord. Check for broken or burned wires under the TV chassis leading from the interlock socket.

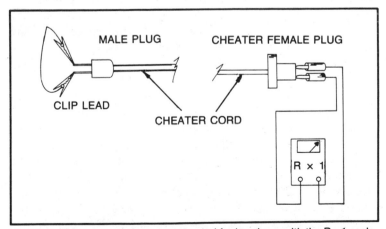

Fig. 13-7. Check the cheater or power cord for breakage with the R × 1 scale. The breaks usually occur at the male and female plugs. If the ac cord is frayed or has breaks in it, replace it.

Silicon Rectifier

Transistor Chassis. When the pilot lights are on, you can assume power is getting to the TV chassis. The ac switch is operating, so check for an open or leaky silicon diode. In some recent TV chassis, the neon pilot light can operate directly from the dc power supply. If this is the case, the low-voltage power supply diodes are normal.

With the power cord pulled, measure the resistance across each silicon diode. For correct tests, remove one end of the diode from the circuit. A good diode will read around 10 ohms and have infinite reading with reversed test leads. A defective diode could be shorted (or show leakage in both directions). Remove and replace the defective diodes. Check for correct polarity. In newer TV chassis, you might find four of these diodes in a bridge circuit.

Tube Chassis. Another method to check for a defective diode is by measuring the ac voltage at the anode terminal. Dc voltage should be measured on the cathode terminal of the diode. Be very careful when taking voltage measurements. Make sure you are away from all metal objects and that the meter is set correctly. You will quickly damage the VOM when taking voltage measurements if the meter is set on the resistance range.

When measuring ac voltage at the anode or negative terminal of the diodes, set the meter to 600 Vac. Plug in the power cord. Measure the ac voltage from chassis or common ground to the anode terminal of the diode. Suspect an open fuse, fusible resistor, or electrolytic capacitor when you have no ac reading. In some tube chassis, you might find an electrolytic capacitor in a voltage-doubling power supply (Fig. 13-8). These electrolytic voltage doubling capacitors are found in early tube and hybrid chassis. This is a very economical method to obtain a higher operating voltage. In these circuits with capacitance input, the doubling circuit will always measure more than twice the power line voltage. Usually the insulated voltage-doubling capacitor is found by itself, because both terminals must be above common ground.

First determine if ac voltage is applied to the negative terminal (body) of the voltage-doubling capacitor. If not, a small fusible or isolation resistor could be open. When ac voltage is found at the negative terminal and not at the positive terminal of the capacitor, suspect a defective capacitor. Pull the power plug and discharge the suspected capacitor terminals with a screwdriver. Now clip another capacitor of the same value across the suspected one. The new capacitor will work okay if it has a larger capacitance and larger work-

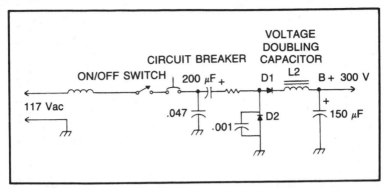

Fig. 13-8. In some tube or hybrid chassis, you might find a defective voltage-doubling capacitor. These capacitors have a tendency to dry up, lowering the dc output voltage source.

ing voltage. Recheck the polarity of the new capacitor. The negative terminals must be clipped together.

Plug in the power cord and the TV chassis should warm up. If not, check for dc voltage at the cathode terminals of the silicon diodes. Improper or no output voltage may be caused by defective filter capacitors or open voltage-dropping resistors.

Voltage Regulator

Transistors and Tube Chassis. No or low-voltage output can be caused by a defective voltage-regulator circuit. Check the dc voltage at the cathode terminal of the silicon diode. If okay, go to the voltage regulator and take dc voltage measurements. When low or no voltage is coming from the collector circuit of the voltage regulator, replace it (Fig. 13-9). Sometimes these regulator transistors will test good but break down under load.

After replacement, if the voltage is still low or there is no voltage output, check all transistors, diodes, and resistors in the regulated circuits. It's best to remove the transistors for accurate tests. Remove one end of each diode for leakage tests. Look for overheated components. Discolored resistors and overheated board connections can point to a defective component.

Leaky Horizontal Output

Transistor Chassis. When the power-supply voltage is much lower than normal and there is no raster, suspect a leaky horizontal-output transistor. Measure the dc voltage at the collector (case) of

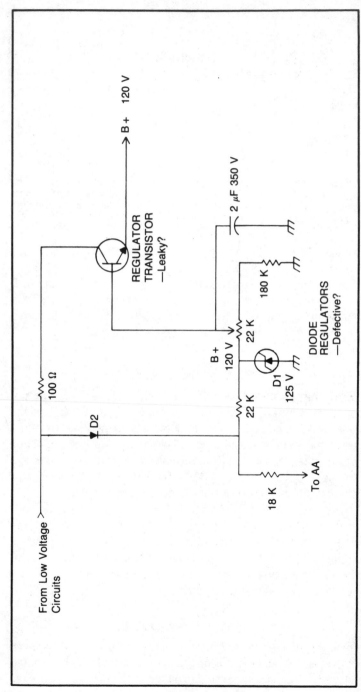

Fig. 13-9. When low or no voltage is at the collector terminal of the voltage-regulator transistor, replace it. This transistor might test okay out of the circuit, but it usually breaks down under load.

the horizontal-output transistor. Place the positive lead to the collector and the negative lead to chassis ground (Fig. 13-10). Replace the horizontal-output transistor when the dc voltage is lower than normal. Compare this voltage reading with the schematic. Usually, the voltage varies between 110 and 160 Vdc.

Most output transistors are mounted with two metal screws. Remove the transistor and take a voltage reading on the collector terminal. Simply push the positive test lead into one of the transistor mounting holes for this measurement. If the voltage is much higher than the normal operating voltage, you can assume the low-voltage power supply is normal.

The raster should return after replacing the horizontal-output transistor. If not, suspect improper drive voltage on the base terminal of the transistor. Because this voltage is very low and the horizontal drive pulse should be checked with a scope, it might be wise here to call a TV technician.

Tube Chassis. Replace the horizontal-output and damper tube when there is voltage at the dc power supply but no raster. Generally, replacement of these two tubes can solve the no-raster problem. If not, note if the plates of either tube run red after a few seconds. Pull the power plug at once or you might quickly ruin the new replacements. Replace the horizontal-oscillator tube if you have improper drive voltage on the output tube.

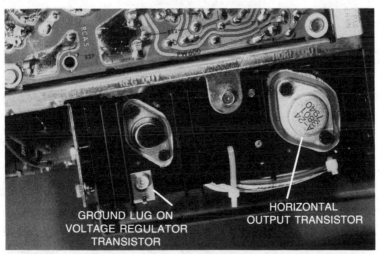

Fig. 13-10. Measure the dc voltage on the collector (case) of the horizontal-output transistor. Place the positive lead to the transistor case and the negative lead to chassis ground like a ground log on another component. Higher-than-normal collector voltage might indicate an open horizontal-output transistor.

A leaky hv rectifier tube can cause both the plates of the horizontal-output and damper tube to glow red. Pull the top cap off the horizontal rectifier tube, if it has one. Now plug in the power cord. The hv cap of the rectifier tube might fire from cap to chassis ground, indicating the presence of high voltage. Replace the hv rectifier. The raster should return. If the tube plates still run red, suspect problems in the flyback circuits. These horizontal and damper tubes run quite warm under normal conditions.

KEEPS BLOWING FUSES

Transistor Chassis. Suspect a leaky horizontal-output transistor, improper bias on the base of the transistor, or a leaky damper diode when the fuse continues to blow. Pull the power plug. Check the resistance between the body of the transistor and chassis ground. A reading below twenty ohms indicates a leaky transistor. In most chassis, the horizontal-output transistor is insulated from chassis ground.

Remove the transistor and check the resistance from the collector to the base and emitter terminals. Replace the horizontal-output transistor when there is a reading below 7 K on the R×1 K range (Fig. 13-11). While the transistor is out of the circuit, check

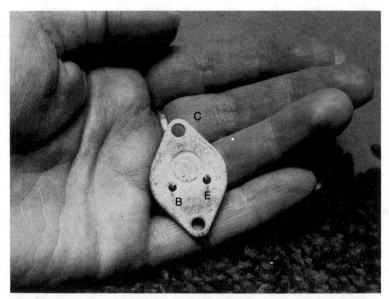

Fig. 13-11. Measure the resistance from collector to the base and emitter terminals. Discard the transistor if the resistance is below 7 KΩ.

294

for a leaky damper diode. This diode is usually found between the collector terminal and chassis ground.

The damper diode resistance should be around 10 ohms with the negative lead on the positive terminal of the diode. Reverse the test leads. No reading should be obtained, even on the $R \times 1$ K scale. A shorted damper diode reads under 10 ohms in both directions. Replace the damper diode with one having a 1200 or 1300 kV peak rating. Do not replace it with an ordinary silicon diode.

Improper bias voltage on the horizontal-output transistor can cause damage to the transistor or cause the fuse to open. Because this voltage is very difficult to measure with the VOM, check the voltage on the horizontal-oscillator circuits. The circuits might be defective when the horizontal-oscillator coil is open.

Don't forget the fuse can blow because of other leaky components within the chassis. To determine if the horizontal-output stages are defective, remove the horizontal-output transistor. Now insert a new fuse. If after you plug in the power cord the fuse does not blow, you know the overload is in the horizontal circuits.

If the fuse still blows, check components in the power supply. If the power supply circuit seems normal, disconnect all wires from the dc output source. Check these circuit wires for a low resistance reading to common ground. Replace the lowest-reading wire to the power source. If the fuse blows, check the outside circuit for leaky components. Replace all other disconnected circuits.

Tube Chassis. Repeatedly blown fuses in the tube chassis can occur with a shorted low-voltage power supply or defective horizontal-output section. Remember, in some tube chassis, the circuit breaker is installed in place of a fuse. The circuit breaker might open at once or after a few seconds of operation.

When the circuit breaker is found in the low-voltage power supply circuit, check this area for leaky components. If the circuit breaker is located within the horizontal section, replace the horizontal output and damper tubes. If the circuit breaker still trips, remove the cap of the horizontal-output tube for a few seconds. If the circuit breaker opens now, suspect problems within the horizontal-output circuit. If the circuit breaker trips only when the horizontal-output tube cap is in place, suspect overload conditions in the flyback and hv circuits.

CHECKING HORIZONTAL-OUTPUT
TRANSISTOR WITH DMM

Because power output transistors short between collector and emitter terminals, a resistance measurement between the horizontal-output collector (case) and ground with the DMM will indicate if the transistor or the damper diode is leaky (Fig. 13-12). Place the black probe on the case of the transistor with the red probe to the chassis. You should have a measurement of 450 to 600 ohms. No measurement indicates the transistor is open. Now reverse the test leads. There should now be an infinite resistance reading.

If a very low measurement is obtained, i.e., under 250 ohms, the transistor is leaky. Most leaky outputs read less than 10 ohms. Take another measurement with reversed test leads. Another low resistance measurement indicates the transistor is definitely leaky. Anytime a transistor shows a low measurement in both directions, the transistor is leaky.

Remove the output transistor from the metal heat sink, if in doubt. Now measure the transistor out of the circuit with the DMM. Because most horizontal-output transistors are npn types, place the positive (red) probe to the base terminal and the negative (black) prod to the collector terminal (case). Take note of this measurement (somewhere between 450 to 750 ohms). Now place the black probe on the emitter terminal. If the transistor is normal, the resistance measurement should be within a few ohms of the first reading.

In case there is no measurement between any two terminals in any direction, the junction to those terminals is open. Always use the positive probe at the base as common terminal. Remember, any time the resistance is low (around .15 Ω) between any two terminals,

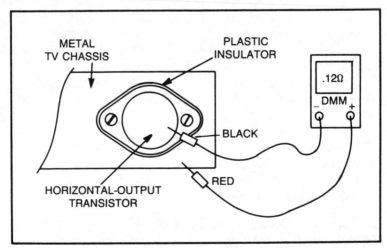

Fig. 13-12. To quickly determine if the transistor is leaky, measure the resistance from the collector (case) to the chassis. Here 12-ohm resistance indicates a leaky horizontal-output transistor.

the junction is shorted. Sometimes all three terminals can have a very low measurement, indicating leakage between all elements.

NO SOUND OR RASTER: HORIZONTAL OUTPUT PROBLEMS

Transistor Chassis. Usually a no-sound and no-raster symptom indicates a defective horizontal-output circuit. In some chassis it's possible to have sound and no raster, but in the more modern transistorized chassis, most of the lower dc voltages are taken from the flyback circuits. Check all components indicated in Fig. 13-13 for additional horizontal raster problems. Do not measure voltages in the flyback or damper circuits with the VOM.

Tube Chassis. In the tube chassis you might have normal sound with no raster. In the hybrid chassis, it's possible to have garbled sound with no raster. Replace all of the tubes in the horizontal and hv circuits. If the no-raster problem still exists, check those components indicated in Fig. 13-14. Do not measure voltage in the damper or flyback transformer circuits with a VOM because you can ruin the meter.

NO SOUND OR RASTER: HORIZONTAL OSCILLATOR PROBLEMS

Transistor Chassis. The horizontal-oscillator transistor provides a drive pulse or voltage for the horizontal-output transistor. When the drive voltage is not present at the transistor, then the output pulse to the flyback transformer will not be produced and there will be no hv applied to the picture tube. In some cases, improper or no drive pulse can damage the horizontal-output transistor. It's best to check the drive pulse with the scope.

You might be able to hear the horizontal oscillator frequency because it operates at 15,575 Hz. If you can hear this high frequency squeal, it indicates the horizontal oscillator is functioning. Of course, it might be off frequency. Try adjusting the horizontal hold control and note the change in the sound.

Measure and compare the voltages on all terminals of the horizontal-oscillator transistor. Improper voltages can indicate a defective transistor. If you suspect the horizontal transistor, remove it and take a resistance measurement. Replace it if the reading is below 10 K. Always replace the transistor if there is a reading in both directions between the collector and any other terminal.

Check the horizontal oscillator coil for broken leads. Measure

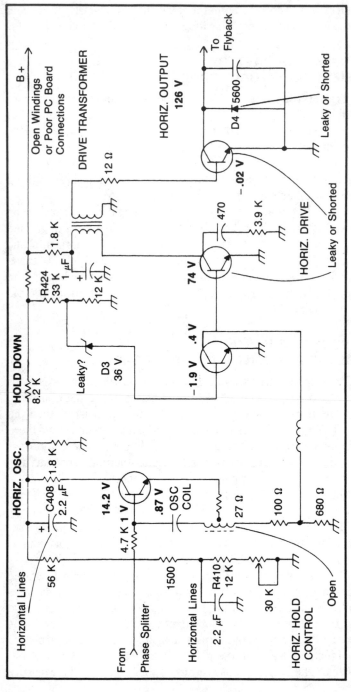

Fig. 13-13. Check these components for additional no-sound/no-raster problems. The sound stages might be dead when the horizontal circuits are defective.

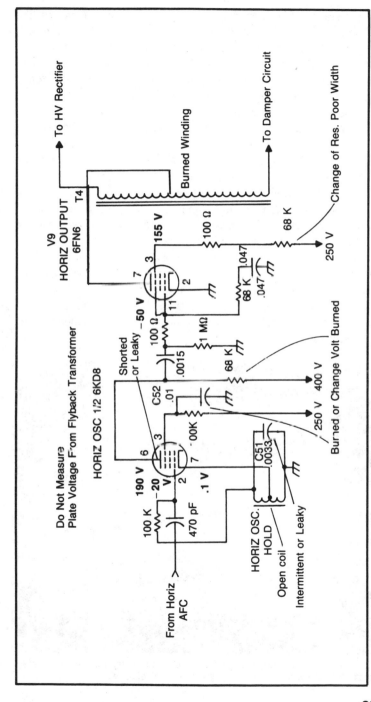

Fig. 13-14. For additional no-raster problems, check these components.

299

the resistance of both windings. Compare these readings with the schematic. The horizontal hold control might have been bumped, breaking off the coil connections. If this is the case, remove the horizontal oscillator coil for repair. After repairing the coil, you might have to readjust the horizontal control to eliminate the horizontal lines. Check other components within the horizontal oscillator circuits for a no sound/no raster problem (Fig. 13-15).

Tube Chassis. In the tube chassis, you may check the horizontal drive voltage on the grid terminal of the horizontal-output tube (Fig. 13-16). This voltage is negative and can vary between − 36 and − 80 volts. The average drive voltage is around − 55 volts. The correct drive voltage can be found on the schematic diagram. When there is no drive voltage applied to the grid terminal of the horizontal-oscillator tube, the horizontal pulse will not be applied to the flyback transformer, resulting in no hv.

Without drive voltage, the plates of the horizontal-output tube will run very hot. Turn the set off so you don't damage the horizontal-output tube. If you find a horizontal output tube with the glass pulled inward because of excessive heat, suspect a defective horizontal-oscillator circuit. Always replace the horizontal-output tube if found operating too long with red plates.

Fig. 13-15. After adjusting the horizontal hold control, try adjusting a separate horizontal-oscillator coil to open up the horizontal lines.

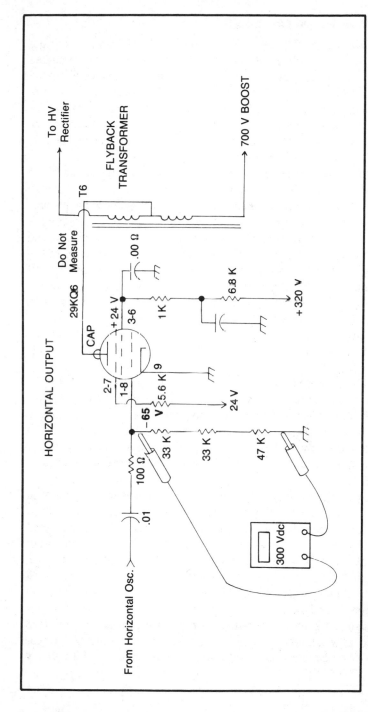

Fig. 13-16. Check the drive voltage on the horizontal-output tube for a negative voltage between −36 and −80 volts. A normal grid drive voltage indicates the horizontal-oscillator circuits are normal. Adjustment of the horizontal hold control should remove the horizontal lines.

ONLY HORIZONTAL LINES

Transistor Chassis. If the horizontal hold control will not remove the large black lines in the raster, search for a fine or coarse horizontal-adjustment control. In some transistorized chassis, the horizontal-oscillator coil is tuned with an iron slug. On the end of the tuning shaft is a knob known as the horizontal hold control. Simply adjusting the horizontal frequency will cause the picture to lock in. In other color chassis, you might find a variable resistance control called the horizontal control.

When the picture has large lines, the horizontal frequency is not locked in. Adjustment of the horizontal hold control, fine or coarse controls, or separate horizontal-oscillator coils might sync the picture. If the horizontal control is a resistance type, look for a horizontal-oscillator coil. Now adjust the slug of the horizontal-oscillator coil until the lines open up and the picture comes in. If you go in the opposite direction, the horizontal lines will get closer together. If the lines are thinner and come closer together, reverse the adjustment procedure. The correct horizontal adjustment is when the horizontal hold control is set in the center of rotation with a locked-in picture. Turn the horizontal hold control to each side and note if the picture goes into horizontal lines at the extreme ends of the control.

When horizontal hold and oscillator adjustments will not lock in the picture, check the main filter capacitors. Shunt a known electrolytic capacitor across each section and note if this changes the horizontal frequency. Usually the defective filter capacitor is the one that feeds the voltage source applied to the horizontal oscillator and output circuits. Also check for a leaky horizontal-oscillator transistor.

Tube Chassis. The horizontal oscillator frequency is adjusted in the same manner as the transistor chassis, except in some chassis, the horizontal hold control (found on the end of the horizontal oscillator coil) might have lock tabs. The metal tab on each end of the rotation will not let the horizontal control be adjusted beyond this limit. Of course, the picture wants to lock in and only needs a turn or two. To adjust, simply pull the horizontal oscillator knob out from the tab area. Now adjust the control until the picture syncs in. Push the knob into position. The picture can now be adjusted horizontally in both directions. Check for a defective electrolytic capacitor in the horizontal circuits when the oscillator is off frequency (Fig. 13-17).

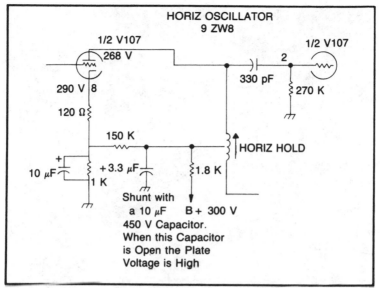

HORIZ OSCILLATOR
9 ZW8

1/2 V107   268 V   1/2 V107

290 V 8
120 Ω   2
                              330 pF   270 K

150 K

+
10 μF   + 3.3 μF   1.8 K   HORIZ HOLD
        1 K
        Shunt with
        a 10 μF   B + 300 V
        450 V Capacitor.
        When this Capacitor
        is Open the Plate
        Voltage is High

Fig. 13-17. Check for a defective filter capacitor in the horizontal circuit of a tube chassis when the horizontal lines won't open up. Shunt a new capacitor across the suspected one.

POOR HORIZONTAL SYNC

Transistor Chassis. The picture might keep rolling sideways or might stand still and then shift for a few minutes due to poor horizontal sync. Note if the picture is locked in vertically. Adjust the vertical control until the picture is vertically still. When the sync locks in vertically but not horizontally, you can assume the sync stages are normal.

One of the most troublesome horizontal sync components is the duodiode found in the base circuit of the horizontal oscillator or afc circuits. You might find two separate diodes in some chassis. These diodes have a tendency to change resistance or become leaky, causing the picture to go out of horizontal sync. Remove the duodiode component (Fig. 13-18). Measure the resistance between the center and each outside terminal. Reverse the test leads and check the resistance. If these readings are quite close, the diodes are good. Don't overlook a leaky horizontal-oscillator transistor for poor horizontal sync.

Tube Chassis. Besides the above adjustments, replace the sync and horizontal-oscillator tube in the tube chassis. Check for a leaky coupling capacitor in the sync circuit. A change in value of plate or bias resistors can produce poor horizontal and vertical sync.

Fig. 13-18. Suspect an afc duodiode when the picture will not sync horizontally. The picture might try to drift either way, or it might sit still for a few seconds and then drift off.

HORIZONTAL PULLING

Transistor Chassis. Excessive horizontal pulling can be caused by a defective low-voltage regulator circuit. The picture might look like it has sync or AGC problems. Check for a too high low voltage source (Fig. 13-19). A leaky active power filter regulator circuit can cause horizontal pulling. Check also for a leaky horizontal-oscillator transistor for horizontal pulling.

Small electrolytic filters in the horizontal-oscillator circuit or those in the power source feeding the oscillator circuit can produce horizontal pulling. Simply shunt each capacitor with one having the same value. Always clip the new capacitor across the old one with the power plug disconnected. Discharge the capacitor before shunting across another one.

Check all soldered connections on the horizontal oscillator and output stages for poor or melted connections. Resolder each connection especially around the small drive transformer terminals. Sometimes a magnifying glass helps to show up cracked connections.

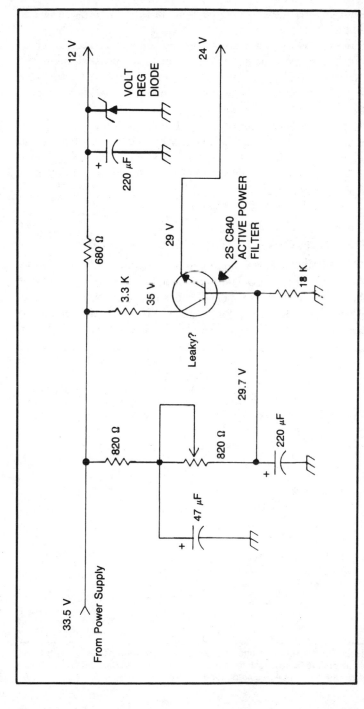

Fig. 13-19. A leaky low-voltage regular diode can produce a higher dc voltage on the horizontal circuits, producing a pulling effect. Measure the voltage from the collector terminal to common ground.

As a last resort, solder all connections in the horizontal oscillator and output sections.

Tube Chassis. If after replacing the horizontal oscillator, sync, and output tube, and the horizontal pulling is still present, shunt the filter capacitor in the horizontal circuit (Fig. 13-20). Also check for a change of resistance in the grid and cathode circuit of the horizontal-oscillator circuit.

Replace the gated amplifier in a tube circuit if it has a gated-pulse amplifier circuit. Check for leaky capacitors and a change in resistance of plate load and cathode resistors (Fig. 13-21). Sometimes you will see horizontal pulling and vertical rolling due to a defective gate pulse amp circuit.

KEEPS DESTROYING THE HORIZONTAL-OUTPUT TRANSISTOR OR TUBE

Transistor Chassis. Improper drive voltage on the horizontal-output transistor can quickly destroy it and kick out a fuse or circuit breaker. After the fuse has opened, check between collector terminal (case) and chassis ground for leakage. In most cases when the horizontal output transistor is destroyed, a leakage exists between

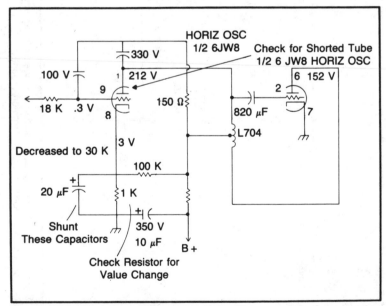

Fig. 13-20. In the tube circuits, shunt all the filter capacitors for excessive horizontal pulling. Also check for a resistance change in the grid and cathode circuit of the horizontal-oscillator tube.

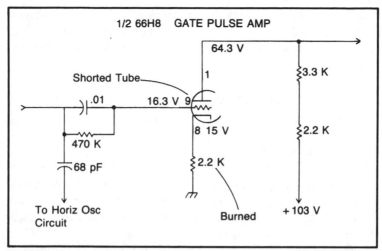

Fig. 13-21. You might have horizontal pulling in the tube chassis which has a separate gated-pulse amplifier stage. First replace the gated-pulse amplifier tube. If horizontal pulling still exists, check for leaky capacitors and a change of valves of resistors in this stage.

collector and emitter terminal. When the voltage is high, either the transistor is open or there is no drive voltage.

The horizontal-output transistor can be destroyed when the hv goes above 32 kV. You will hear some loud cracking and arcing noises around the picture tube. In fact, the picture tube can be damaged if the arcing persists. Check for an open capacitor across the collector and emitter terminals (Fig. 13-22). Sometimes the capacitor is connected between collector and common ground. Replace this capacitor with one having the same capacitance and working voltage. This capacitor can have a voltage rating from 1200 to 2000 kV. Don't replace it with an ordinary bypass capacitor.

Tube Chassis. The horizontal-output tube can be damaged or destroyed if there is no grid drive voltage. The tube might last for a month or two and then no raster. Practically any component in the horizontal-oscillator tube section can cause the problem. You should replace the horizontal oscillator and output tube.

Check all wiring connections in the horizontal stages. Especially resolder all horizontal-oscillator coil terminals. Check for burned or overheated resistors in the horizontal circuits. Make sure the resistance hasn't changed in the cathode bias and plate load resistors of the horizontal oscillator. The horizontal drive voltage can be monitored with the VOM connected to the grid terminal and chassis ground. This negative voltage should range from -36 to -90 volts in most tube chassis. Check the schematic for the correct voltages of your particular TV chassis. Don't overlook a defective hv regulator tube that is causing the hv to go too high and destroy the horizontal-output tube.

HIGH-VOLTAGE SHUTDOWN

In the latest TV chassis, safety circuits have been installed so the high voltage will not, under any type of breakdown, increase enough to endanger the operator. When the high voltage increases over 32 kV, the high-voltage shutdown circuits go into action and shut the chassis down. Besides high-voltage shutdown, a defective component, especially in the horizontal circuits, can shut the chassis down. The electronics technician or serviceman must isolate which problem is causing the chassis to shut down.

Today, with the integrated flyback transformer, many low-voltage circuits are taken directly from the secondary winding of horizontal-output transformer (Fig. 13-23). A defective or leaky component in any one of these low-voltage sources can shut down the chassis. High-voltage shutdown can be caused by an open tuning or hold-down capacitor in the collector side of the horizontal-output transistor, letting the high voltage increase to a dangerous level. The safety circuits then shut down the voltage, and now the chassis is dead. High-voltage shutdown can also be caused by a high power-line voltage (140 Vac). Improper adjustment of the B+ control can cause hv shutdown. If the low-voltage power supply increases, the

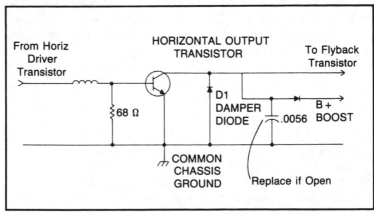

Fig. 13-22. Check for an open bypass capacitor across the collector and common ground terminal of the horizontal-output transistor when the hv begins to crack and arc over.

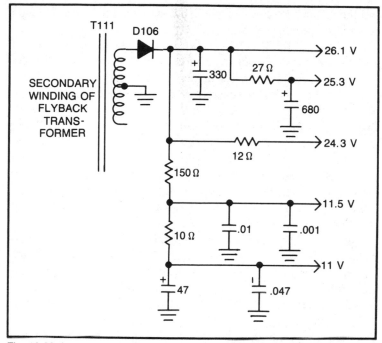

Fig. 13-23. In many of the latest TV chassis, a lot of the low-voltage sources are taken from the secondary side of the horizontal-output transformer. Most are half-wave rectifier circuits with silicon diodes in a resistor/capacitor filtering network.

high B+ voltage might be applied to the horizontal-output transistor, producing excessive high voltage. The following areas can cause high-voltage shutdown:

- Very high power-line voltage.
- A defective low-voltage power supply with increased voltage output.
- Improper adjustment of the low-voltage B+ adjustment.
- An open tuning or hold-down capacitor in the horizontal-output transistor circuits.
- Leaky or shorted high-voltage regulator SCR.
- Defective safety shutdown circuit.

A few tests you can do without a lot of expensive test instruments follow. Note if the high-voltage shutdown occurs after the chassis is on for a few minutes or at once. If it takes the chassis a few minutes to shut down, suspect a defective chassis shutdown symptom. Suspect high-voltage shutdown when the chassis shuts down after the switch is thrown.

First lower the B+ control and note if the chassis stays on. If so, the B+ control is set too high. Check the schematic diagram for a correct B+ setting. If a diagram is not handy, adjust the B+ control so the raster is adequately filled out. Service the low-voltage power supply if the voltage is too high or cannot be turned down. Check the power-line voltage where the TV cord plugs in. Notify the power-line company if the ac line voltage is above 120 volts ac.

Check the horizontal-output transistor for leakage or open conditions. Locate the tuning or hold-down capacitors and check them for accurate capacity. Sometimes these capacitors break the connection inside and produce intermittent hv shutdown. Check the hold-down capacitor for open conditions.

In some of the latest chassis, a metal SCR is used as the high-voltage regulator circuit. Trace the B+ voltage from the collector terminal of the horizontal-output transistor through the primary winding of the flyback and to the voltage source. The B+ voltage comes directly from the low-voltage power supply or high-voltage regulator (SCR).

Remove the SCR from the socket and check it with the ohmmeter. The resistance between gate (G) and cathode (K) should be around 100 ohms in both directions. Replace it if the resistance is below 50 ohms (Fig. 13-24). Most SCRs will measure around 3 megohms from either gate or cathode to the anode (case) in one direction. An infinite measurement should be obtained with reversed test leads. If the measurement is below 1 megohm, replace the SCR regulator. Remember, a shorted or leaky SCR regulator will increase the voltage applied to the collector terminal of the horizontal-output transistor, drastically increasing the high voltage and then producing hv shutdown.

POOR WIDTH

Transistor Chassis. A weak power supply feeding the horizontal-output transistor can produce poor width. Check the voltage between collector (case) and chassis ground. Set the VOM at 300 Vdc. Compare the voltage measured with the schematic. If the voltage is quite low, remove the horizontal-output transistor from the circuit. Measure from the collector screw terminal to chassis ground. This voltage should increase to the supply voltage. If not, check the voltage in the low-voltage power supply.

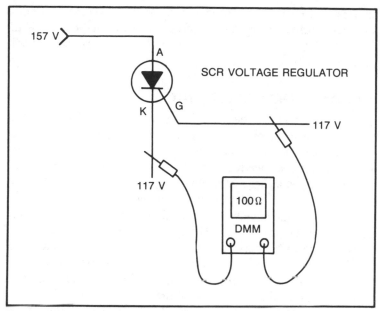

157 V

SCR VOLTAGE REGULATOR

A

K   G

117 V

117 V

100 Ω

DMM

Fig. 13-24. Remove the high-voltage SCR from the circuit for accurate resistance tests. The normal SCR has a resistance measurement between K and G of 100 ohms.

Check the horizontal-output transistor for leaky conditions. Measure the resistance between the collector and the base and emitter terminals. Discard the transistors with a reading below 75 ohms. Sometimes these transistors will break down under load. Simply replace the horizontal-output transistors for poor width conditions.

Look for a width control in some chassis. Adjust this control for proper width. You might find a low-voltage control in the low-voltage power supply. This control adjusts the low voltage to the various circuits. If improperly adjusted, the hv can increase and cause arc over on the anode connection of the CRT. Always set the low-voltage control to the specified voltage found in the service literature.

If the low voltage cannot be adjusted, suspect problems within the voltage regulator circuits. First replace the voltage regulator transistor. These transistors might test good but break down under load. Replace the transistor with one having the same part number or use a universal replacement. A leaky voltage regulator can cause poor width, horizontal pulling, and vertical flipping.

Tube Chassis. Replace the horizontal output, oscillator, damper, and hv rectifier tube for improper width. Look for a width

311

or horizontal linearity control adjustment in the tube chassis. Check for correct drive voltage at the grid of the horizontal-output tube. A change in resistance of the screen grid resistor can cause poor width (Fig. 13-25).

REPLACING THE TRIPLER UNIT

The tripler unit is tied to the output terminal of the flyback transformer and triples the high voltage for the picture tube. This unit internally consists of high-voltage capacitors and fixed diodes (Fig. 13-26). A defective tripler might arc over, firing between plastic case and chassis, and cause the spark gap to arc over intermittently and load down the horizontal-output circuits.

Sometimes the defective tripler unit pops and cracks, indicating arcing inside the plastic case. High arcover marks or a low arcing light might be visible between plastic and metal chassis. Shut down the TV chassis and feel the plastic tripler case. Replace the unit if it is warm, hot, or shows signs of arcover. Do not try to stop the arcover, because this is a waste of time.

A leaky tripler might not arc over but can still cause the circuit breaker or fuse to blow. Suspect a leaky tripler when the chassis has sound without high voltage or a raster. It's possible to measure

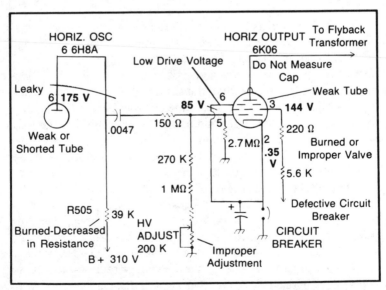

Fig. 13-25. In addition to replacing the horizontal-output oscillator and damper tubes for poor width, check these components. Don't overlook a width or horizontal linearity control for width adjustment.

Fig. 13-26. A spark gap is usually found between the focus and ground terminals of the tripler unit. High voltage arc over can occur between the plastic case and TV chassis, indicating a defective tripler.

1.5 to 5.5 kV volts at the anode connection of the CRT with a leaky tripler unit. When the circuit break kicks out after the chassis has been on for several minutes, suspect a leaky tripler unit.

Simply remove the IN wire terminal from the flyback transformer (Fig. 13-27). This is a heavy, rubber-insulated wire.

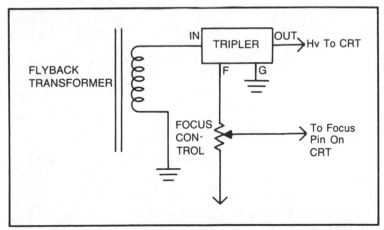

Fig. 13-27. Disconnect the IN terminal of the tripler unit to see if the tripler is loading down the horizontal-output circuits. If the fuse or circuit breaker does not open after removing the terminal wire, suspect a leaky tripler.

Make sure the insulated wire does not touch the metal chassis as it will throw a voltage arc from ¼ to ½ inch. Insulate the bare wire inside a tube carton. If the chassis does not open the fuse or circuit breaker and stays on, suspect a leaky tripler. To make sure, connect the wire again and the circuit breaker should open.

If possible, replace the circuit breaker with the exact part number. All universal tripler replacements work fine. Look up the tripler part number in the many universal semi-conductor transistor replacement manuals for the tripler sections. RCA, General Electric, and Sylvania have direct universal tripler replacements for most color TV chassis.

BEWARE OF HIGH VOLTAGE

Be very careful when working around the TV chassis to prevent shock from the anode terminal of the picture tube. Always keep the anode terminal inside a tube carton or plastic container and not connected to the CRT when working with the chassis on the bench. The high voltage on the TV chassis ranges up to 32 kV.

Although the high voltage shock might not kill you, the shock can cause you to jump or pull away and cause injury to yourself or others. Do not let anyone else stand around while you work unless they are also electronics technicians and know what hv can do. Always treat the high-voltage cable and terminal as a hazard.

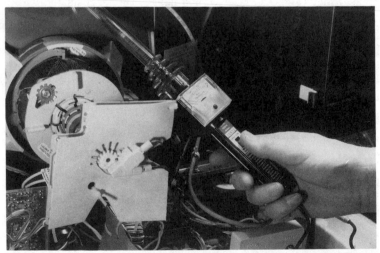

Fig. 13-28. Use a high-voltage probe or meter to measure the high voltage at the anode connection of the picture tube.

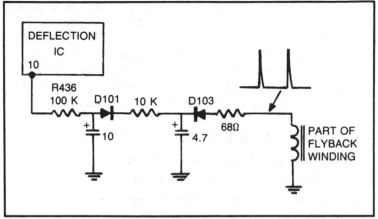

Fig. 13-29. The safety or shunt-down circuits might consist of diodes and capacitors tied to a separate winding on the flyback. Excessively high voltage or a defective shutdown circuit can shut down the chassis.

To measure for correct high voltage at the picture tube anode terminal, use a high-voltage probe or a high-voltage probe with a VTVM (Fig. 13-28). These meters should measure up to 40,000 volts. The high-voltage probe is very valuable in monitoring the high voltage at the picture tube with intermittent hv. *Never try to measure the hv with a VOM or DMM.*

SAFETY CIRCUITS

The hv shutdown or safety circuits can consist of diodes, transistors, SCRs, and electrolytic capacitors. A positive pulse is taken from the separate flyback transformer winding and fed to the safety or hv shutdown circuits and the results applied to the horizontal circuits. In the HEW circuits, the hv shutdown circuits caused the TV chassis to produce horizontal lines with no effect of the horizontal hold control. Today the shutdown circuits ground out the horizontal oscillator or drive pulse and cause the chassis to shut down when excessively high voltage is applied to the CRT.

A typical hv shutdown circuit might only consist of resistors, capacitors, and diodes as in Fig. 13-29. Check the diodes for leaky or open conditions. Test the flyback winding for a broken wire or winding. Remove the wire terminal of R436 from IC 501 to determine if the chassis is in hv shutdown. Do not leave the chassis on for only a few minutes to prevent hv arcover. If the chassis does not shut down at once and play for the three minutes, you can assume excessively high voltage has shut the chassis down.

You might have a transistor or SCR component that switches to the horizontal driver or oscillator transistor in hv shutdown (Fig. 13-30). Disconnect the transistor or SCR terminal that is connected to the horizontal circuits. Now fire up the chassis and if it does not shut down right away, suspect a defective shut-down circuit or excessively high voltage. Check for excessively hv at the CRT. Repair the shutdown/safety circuits if the high voltage is normal.

BRIGHT VERTICAL WHITE LINE

Transistor and Tube Chassis. A bright vertical white line is a sign of no horizontal sweep. The hv can be near normal with

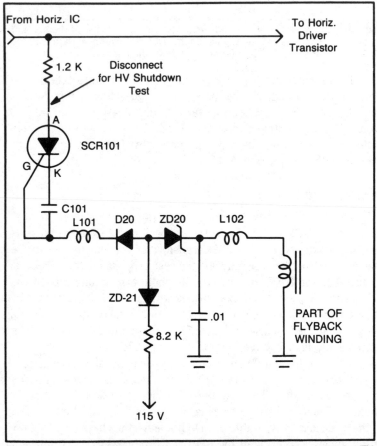

Fig. 13-30. You may determine if the high voltage is shutting down the TV chassis by disconnecting the shutdown circuit. Do not leave the TV set on for only a few minutes in case the high voltage is excessive.

a collapsed horizontal sweep. Check the yoke and all connections leading to the yoke assembly. Suspect a broken wire or poorly soldered connection where the yoke plugs into the TV chassis. Remove the plug and check the horizontal sweep yoke winding with the ohmmeter. Compare these low ohm readings with the schematic. Look for a broken coil wire at the yoke terminals when there is no continuity on the yoke windings. If there is a capacitor on one end of the horizontal yoke winding, shunt a known capacitor across the suspected one. Check for burned resistors in the horizontal yoke windings.

NO SOUND, NO RASTER, AND NO HV

Transistor and Tube Chassis. Usually the no sound/no raster/no hv symptoms are caused by a defective horizontal-output section. Suspect a defective flyback transformer or tripler unit when the horizontal-output section is functioning with no high voltage. A tripler is made up of diodes and a capacitor to triple the voltage supplied by the flyback transformer. Sometimes these tripler units arc over or become leaky internally. It's best not to try and work around the hv section unless you are properly trained. Let a qualified technician service the hv section of the TV receiver.

If the hv comes up with no picture, suspect a defective CRT. Generally, you can hear the yoke expand and by touching the front glass of the CRT you might feel the hv present. Stay away from all high-voltage components, especially the flyback transistors, tripler unit, and anode connections of the picture tube (Fig. 13-31).

Check the CRT for light at the end of the tube. Look at the glass envelope between the socket and conveyance assembly. Sometimes, it's difficult to see the tube light up. If the tube appears dark, pull the power plug. Now check the tube heaters for continuity with the VOM at the R×1 scale. No reading indicates the tube heaters are open and the picture tube must be replaced. If the continuity of the CRT heater is normal, suspect voltage is not getting to the tube socket. The CRT heaters might have a separate winding on the power transformer. Check for proper heater voltage across the transformer heater winding. Check for poor heater connections on the chassis and CRT socket. Usually the CRT heater connecting wires are a heavy twisted pair.

Improper hv to the anode connections of the tube chassis can be caused by a defective hv rectifier tube. This tube is usually inside a shielded cage. Remove and test it out of the circuit. A shorted hv rectifier tube can cause the plates of the horizontal-output tube

Fig. 13-31. Stay away from all high-voltage components. The hv anode lead, flyback transformer, and picture tube sockets have high voltage that can shock or kill.

to glow red. Replace the defective hv rectifier tube, but don't touch any other components within the hv cage unless you are a qualified TV technician. It's better to be safe than sorry. The hv applied to the anode connection of the CRT can be from 25 kV to 31 kV.

HORIZONTAL WHITE LINE

Transistor Chassis. A bright horizontal white line indicates no vertical sweep. Practically any defective component in the vertical section can cause this problem. First check and test the most likely components. Measure the voltage on both vertical-output transistors if there are two in push-pull operation (Fig. 13-32). Improper voltages can indicate a defective transistor. Remove the transistors, test, and replace.

If replacing the output transistors does not fix the vertical sweep, adjust the height or size control. Check for continuity of the vertical yoke windings. An open winding or poor socket connection can result in a horizontal white line. Check all soldered connections on the vertical board assembly. If the transistor chassis has a vertical module, replace it. Check and test each vertical transistor for leaky or open condition.

Tube Chassis. Replace all vertical tubes. You might find one large tube or two separate tubes in the vertical tube section. Make both vertical height and linearity adjustments. Check for correct voltage measurements on the vertical tube terminals and compare them with the schematic. Also check the yoke winding and socket connections for open or broken wires.

INSUFFICIENT VERTICAL SWEEP

Transistor Chassis. When the vertical sweep cannot be adjusted to fill the screen from top to bottom, it is called insufficient vertical sweep (Fig. 13-33). Usually, only one vertical control is found in the transistor chassis. If more than one vertical control is found, adjust the size and linearity control to fill the entire screen.

If the vertical controls will not adjust, suspect problems within the vertical output circuit. Remove, test, and replace the vertical output transistor. Check for defective electrolytic capacitors in the output stages. Check for leaky zener diodes. Resolder the entire vertical board. Double check the vertical output transistor sockets for poor transistor terminal connections. Replace the vertical-output module if one is found in the transistor chassis.

Tube Chassis. First replace the vertical tubes. Next, take voltage measurements. Check all electrolytic capacitors in the vertical-output circuits for open conditions. Shunt each electrolytic capacitor in these circuits. Check the resistance from the cathode terminal

Fig. 13-32. You might find one or two vertical-output transistors in the vertical sweep section. Remove and test each out of the circuit. Check for poor terminal connections.

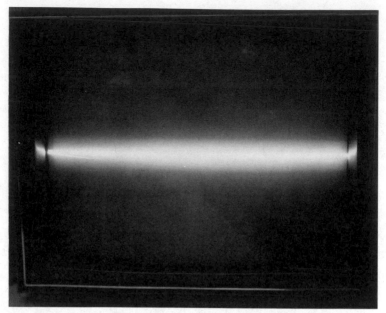

Fig. 13-33. Practically any component in the transistor chassis may cause insufficient vertical sweep. Test and replace each transistor. Shunt all electrolytic capacitors in the vertical circuits.

to common ground. Figure 13-34 shows the various components to check for insufficient height in a tube chassis.

VERTICAL ROLLING

Transistor Chassis. To determine if the vertical rolling is caused by the sync sections, note if the horizontal sync is locked in. If there are no horizontal lines in the picture and it's only rolling up or down, the problem might be where the vertical sync comes from the sync circuits. A leaky coupling capacitor or electrolytic capacitor in the sync circuit may cause vertical rolling (Fig. 13-35).

Take voltage measurements on the vertical oscillator, driver, and output transistor. Compare these readings with the schematic. A leaky oscillator or driver transistor can cause vertical rolling. Check all soldered connections on the pc board. Press up and down on the board and note whether the picture is locked in or begins to roll. You might have to solder the entire vertical board to cure the vertical rolling. Shunt an electrolytic capacitor across the voltage source feeding the vertical stages. Check for leaky bias diodes in vertical-output transistor circuits.

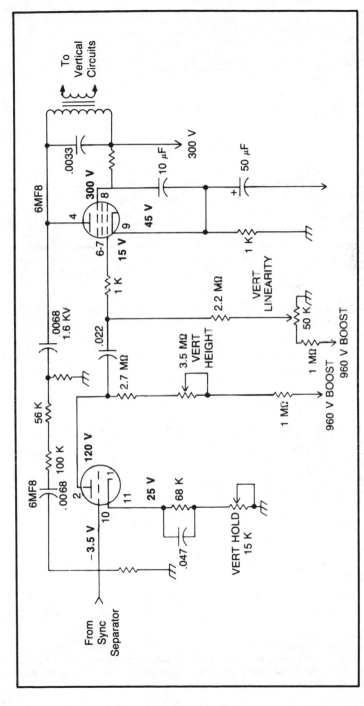

Fig. 13-34. Check the following components in the tube circuits for insufficient vertical sweep. Double check tube socket connections. Resolder the board connections around the vertical tube.

321

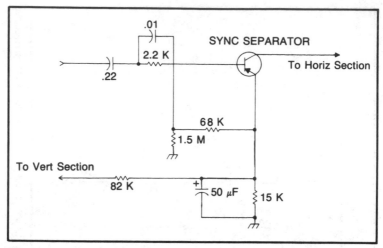

Fig. 13-35. Vertical rolling can be caused by a leaky capacitor in the vertical sync circuits. Check all sync coupling capacitors for open or leaky conditions.

Tube Chassis. Readjust the vertical height and linearity controls. Replace the sync and vertical tubes to cure the vertical rolling. Shunt all electrolytic capacitors in the vertical circuit. Check for a change in resistance or leakage of components in the vertical circuit (Fig. 13-36).

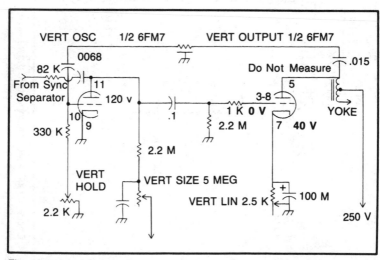

Fig. 13-36. Check these components in the tube chassis for vertical rolling. Defective tubes, leaky capacitors, and a change in resistance cause most vertical problems.

322

VERTICAL FOLDOVER

Transistor Chassis. Vertical foldover usually occurs at the bottom of the raster (Fig. 13-37). Check for poorly soldered connections on the vertical-output transistor terminals. Remove and replace both vertical output transistors. Check for a change of resistance of the bias resistors when the transistors are out of the circuit. Shunt suspected vertical electrolytic capacitors with another capacitor.

Tube Chassis. After replacing the vertical-output tube, check voltages on the tube socket. Vertical foldover problems in the tube chassis can be traced to the vertical-output circuits. Check for a burned resistor or a change in resistance of the cathode resistor. A high grid voltage on pin 5 of most vertical-output tubes indicates a leaky coupling capacitor. Shunt the electrolytic capacitor in the cathode circuit. Check Fig. 13-38 for additional defective components that can produce vertical foldover.

NO SOUND

Transistor Chassis. Check the speaker and output transistor for a no-sound condition. Connect a new speaker across the old

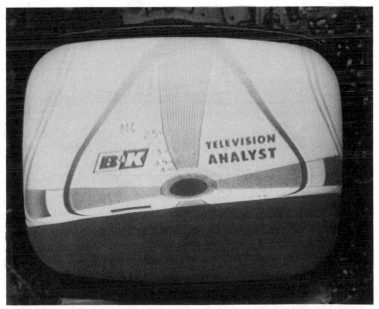

Fig. 13-37. Vertical foldover at the bottom of the raster. Most vertical foldover conditions occur in the vertical-output circuit.

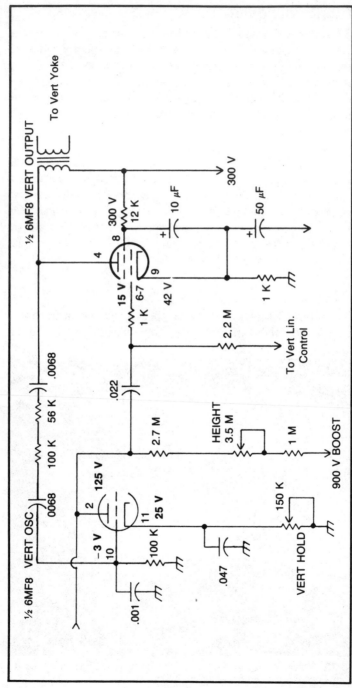

Fig. 13-38. Check the following components for vertical foldover in the tube chassis. Most foldover problems are caused by a defective tube, or leaky electrolytic or coupling capacitors.

speaker terminals. Replace the audio-output transistor, even if it tests good. These audio transistors have a tendency to "pop on" when a tester is connected to them. If there is still no sound, check for an open emitter resistor. Don't overlook a poor connection on the headphone jack.

Next, go to the driver or af amp transistor. Take voltage measurements on these transistors. Improper voltage indicates a defective transistor or other component. Remove each transistor and test it out of the circuit. Replace open or leaky transistors. Check each bias resistor while the transistors are out of the circuit. If the TV chassis has sound modules, replace them. You might find one or more in a module transistor chassis. Shunt a speaker coupling capacitor over the suspected one found in both module and regular audit circuits (Fig. 13-39). Replace the audio-output transistor or IC when there is a popping or frying noise in the speaker.

Tube Chassis. Replace both audio tubes for a no-sound condition in the tube chassis. Take voltage measurements on both tube socket terminals. A very low plate voltage might indicate a leaky grid coupling capacitor or a high-resistance, audio-output transformer winding. No voltage indicates an open winding. Very high plate voltage might indicate an open or burned cathode, bias resistor, or a shorted bypass capacitor across the transformer winding.

WEAK SOUND

Transistor Chassis. Weak sound in a transistor chassis can be caused by a leaky or open diode or transistor. A defective IC in the audio input or output might cause weak sound conditions. Check and shunt each coupling capacitor in the audio stages. Shunt each electrolytic capacitor in the bias circuits. Check for a burned resistor or a change of resistance in the bias and collector stages. Replace the IC output circuit for weak or no-sound problems.

Tube Chassis. Replace the audio-output tubes. Check the cathode resistor for burned or open conditions. Sometimes the audio output becomes shorted and ruins the cathode resistor. Shunt all electrolytic capacitors in the audio circuits. Improper voltages on the sound tubes might indicate an open or an increase in resistance of resistors in the voltage source areas. Check the low-voltage power supply for lower-than-normal voltages.

MUSHY SOUND

Transistor Chassis. A defective speaker with a dropped or

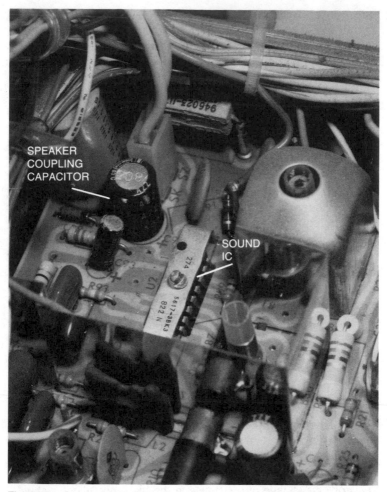

Fig. 13-39. Check these components in a transistor chassis for a no-sound condition. Don't overlook a defective speaker coupling capacitor or open speaker.

warped cone can cause distortion or mushy sound. Remove one speaker lead and clip another speaker across the speaker cable (Fig. 13-40). In push-pull audio circuits you may find one transistor open and the other leaky. Replace the output module for distortion in the modular chassis. Now replace the audio-output transistor.

Check all emitter and base bias resistors for a change of value. Suspect a leaky bias diode in the base circuits. Remove one end for proper resistance measurements. Now go to the audio af or driver transistor. A leaky transistor might produce weak and distorted sound. Remove each transistor and test it out of the circuit.

Tube Chassis. Replace all sound tube for distortion, especially the sound output tube. Check for a positive voltage on the grid terminal. If a positive voltage is found, replace the leaky coupling capacitor. Check for a burned cathode resistor. Sometimes when the audio output tube becomes shorted, the cathode resistor will run too hot and change in value. A leaky bypass capacitor on the plate terminal of the sound output tube can cause distortion (Fig. 13-41).

HEAVY BLACK BARS

Transistor or Tube Chassis. When you find one or more heavy black bars in the raster, suspect poor filtering of the low-voltage power supply. You might notice a crawling raster at the bottom of the picture with the same filter problem. Sometimes, these black bars may float upward through the raster. A loud 60-cycle hum might also be heard in the speaker.

Turn the color chassis off channel to obtain a white raster. Note if there are one or two heavy dark bars in the raster. Locate the main capacitors (Fig. 13-42). Now pull the power cord. Clip a 250 µF capacitor at 450 volts across each capacitor to determine which section of the capacitor is defective. Use two alligator clip leads and observe correct polarity.

Fig. 13-40. A dropped or torn speaker cone can cause distortion in the sound. Clip another good speaker across the speaker connectors to detect a defective speaker.

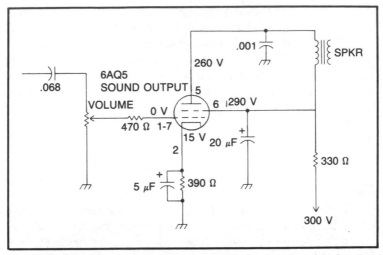

Fig. 13-41. Check the sound-output tube circuits for distortion. A leaky coupling capacitor or burned cathode resistor can produce distortion of the speaker.

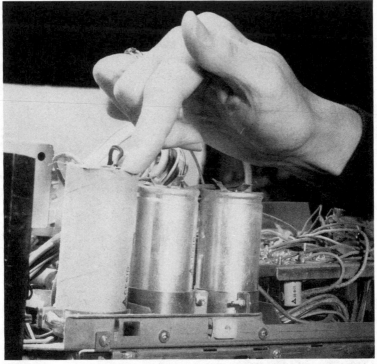

Fig. 13-42. The main filter capacitors are usually clustered together. Clip another filter capacitor across each to determine which capacitor is defective.

Remove the power cord each time the capacitor is clipped across another section. Always discharge the substituting capacitor by touching the clip leads together before clipping to another capacitor. If the capacitor is not discharged, it's possible to ruin components in the circuit. Always observe correct capacitor polarity. The ground or negative terminal (outside metal case) should be clipped to common or chassis ground. When the defective capacitor is shunted, the heavy dark lines will disappear.

A single capacitor can be soldered across the defective one for a temporary repair (Fig.13-43). It's best to replace the entire container of capacitors. Always remember to replace filter capacitors with ones having at least the same working voltage and capacitance. A replacement capacitor with a higher capacitance and working voltage works best if the unit will fit into the chassis.

Don't replace any electrolytic filter capacitors with those having a lower working voltage. The capacitor will run hot and can even

Fig. 13-43. For temporary repair, solder a single electrolytic capacitor across the defective one. Remember you can parallel more than one capacitor to get the correct capacitance to remove the black hum bars.

blow up in your face. If the replacement is lower in capacitance than the defective one, the black hum lines might be even more prominent. It's possible to parallel several single capacitors to acquire the correct capacitance.

GOOD SOUND BUT POOR VIDEO

Transistor Chassis. Insufficient brightness can be caused by a defective video-output stage. First turn up the brightness and contrast controls. Now turn the screen control wide open. If very little brightness is present, look for a brightness limiter control. Adjust these controls for additional brightness. In case none of these adjustments helps solve the brightness problem, go directly to the video-output transistor or IC. Replace the video transistor or IC to cure poor brightness. Poor brightness can also be caused by a weak picture tube or insufficient high voltage. High-voltage problems and picture-tube replacement should be tackled by a professional TV technician.

Tube Chassis. Replace the first and second video-output tubes. If the video-output tube lights up one minute and goes dark the next, check for a poorly soldered heater socket pin. These tubes run quite warm, resulting in potentially poor heater pin terminal connections. Simply wiggle the tube around in the socket. If it begins to light up, replace the tube socket.

Take voltage measurements on the video-output tube socket. Low or improper plate voltage might indicate a change in resistance of the plate load resistor or an open peaking coil. No cathode voltage might indicate an open cathode resistor or contrast control. Check all wiring connections to the brightness and contrast controls. Additional poor video problems may be found in Fig. 13-44.

POOR AGC

Transistor Chassis. When the screen becomes very dark or there is a snowy picture, suspect poor agc action. The picture might go into horizontal lines or flip vertically. The automatic gain control (agc) circuits provide for a constant gain in the incoming TV signal. Locate the agc control at the rear apron or on the TV chassis and adjust for a normal picture.

If the picture cannot be adjusted, check the transistor in the i-f agc delay, agc keying, and rf agc circuits. Remove each transistor and test it out of the circuit. Replacement of either transistor might solve the agc problem. Check all diodes for leakage within these

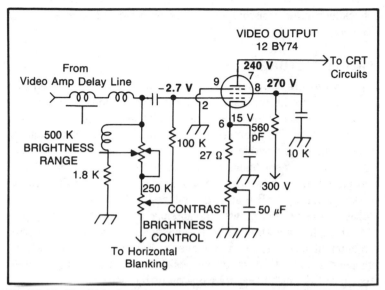

Fig. 13-44. Check the indicated components for video problems in the tube chassis. However, make sure the brightness, contrast, and AGC controls are adjusted before tearing into the TV chassis.

circuits. Shunt the same type of capacitor across all electrolytic capacitors in the agc circuits (Fig. 13-45).

Tube Circuits. Replace the agc tubes for possible agc trouble. Take voltage measurements on each tube socket for improper voltages. Shunt all electrolytic capacitors in tube-type agc circuits.

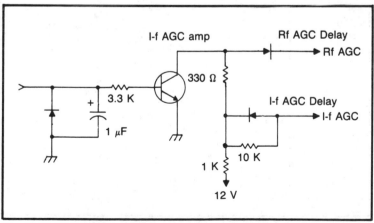

Fig. 13-45. Shunt all electrolytic capacitors in the AGC circuit for poor AGC action. Also, check the diodes.

Check high-value resistors for an open or increased resistance (Fig. 13-46).

SNOWY PICTURE

Transistor Chassis. A snowy picture might be caused by a poor antenna system. If another TV is handy, check it for a snowy picture. Then check the antenna lead and outlet for poor connections. When another TV operates successfully with the same lead-in, suspect problems within the TV chassis.

Most snowy conditions are caused by a defective tuner, i-f stage or agc circuit. A snowy picture can also be caused by a dirty tuner. First, measure the B + and agc voltage on the tuner (Fig. 13-47). Measure the agc voltage with the antenna disconnected and compare it to the schematic. Low or no B + voltage might indicate a shorted component in the tuner or voltage source. If the voltage is low, suspect a burned or increased resistance in the voltage supply resistor. Inspect all resistors on top of the tuner.

The first rf tuner transistor is likely to be the one to cause snow in the picture. Replacement of the transistor might be quite difficult. The transistor is easily replaced if it's sitting on top and at the rear of the tuner or located next to the antenna coils. But if the tun-

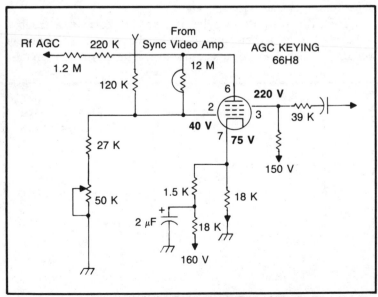

Fig. 13-46. Check these components in the AGC tube circuits for improper AGC control.

Fig. 13-47. Measure the voltage on the TV tuner for snowy conditions. Improper voltages here might indicate trouble in the tuner or voltage source.

er transistors are located inside, you must remove the tuner. Take it to your local TV shop to be repaired.

Tube Chassis. Replace both tubes in the tuner for a snowy picture. If the picture is still snowy, replace the first i-f tube. You might have to tune in each channel after replacing the oscillator tube in the tuner. When the picture will not stay on, suspect a dirty tuner.

After tube replacement, check all B+ and agc voltages on the tuner. Inspect all voltage isolation resistors for burned or broken conditions. When the B+ voltage is low, disconnect the voltage source and again measure the applied voltage. Improperly applied voltage may indicate problems within the power supply. Low agc voltage may be caused by the agc circuits or by the tuner.

CHANGING THE TUNER

Transistor and Tube Chassis. Suspect dirty tuner contacts when the picture becomes erratic but can be cleared up by moving the tuner selector knob. The picture could be snowy until the tuner knob is touched. Most tuner contacts are made of silver and can get dirty and tarnished.

There are many types of tuner cleaning solutions on the market. The most common are sprays with a long tube which applies the solution right on the tuner contacts. A tuner wash not only cleans the contacts but dislodges excessive grease that has been applied to the tuner wafers. You cannot clean a TV tuner by spraying the liquid from the front of the tuner.

It's best to remove all tuner knobs so the tuner can be dropped down for accessibility. Remove the three or four screws around the tuner that hold the tuner in position. Carefully, remove the tuner and pull it out as far as possible. Be careful not to break off any wires that go to the tuner or tuner assembly. Remove the outside metal cover from the tuner assembly (Fig. 13-48). You might find a wafer or a strip-type switching arrangement in the tuner. Spray both sides of the wafer contact points while rotating the tuner knob and shaft.

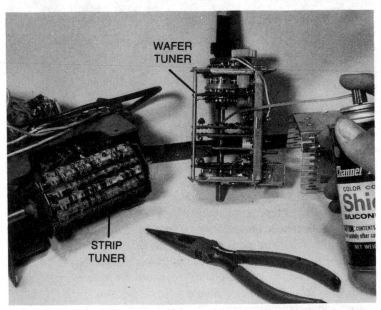

Fig. 13-48. To properly clean the tuner, remove it from the TV cabinet and remove the outside metal cover. Spray each wafer or strip switch section, but keep the spray away from other tuner components.

Get the spray solution on all the wafer switch contacts. Large gobs of grease can be removed with a tuner wash solution. Sometimes the grease will become coated with dirt and dust, preventing good tuner contact.

The strip tuner can be cleaned in the very same manner, except that the strip contacts should be wiped with a cloth. Spray or wipe on the cleaning solution and wipe downward with the metal contacts. If you wipe sideways, the small coils on the strip might be moved and then must be returned for each channel. Spray cleaning solution on the long finger spring contacts as the tuner shaft is rotated. When using tuner wash spray, lay a cloth under the tuner to soak up the dripping liquid. Try to keep the tuner spray away from other interior tuner components. Replace all metal covers. If you don't, you might have to tune each channel separately. The metal shield is placed over the tuner to keep out unwanted stray rf signals. Replace the tuner in the TV cabinet. Now insert the power cord and tune in a local channel. Some channels might have to be retuned with the fine-tuning control. If the tuner is properly cleaned, the stations will not flicker or have any erratic movement when the knob is rotated.

If the tuner contacts cannot be cleaned properly, the tuner must be sent in for a factory cleanup. Factory tuner repair costs only about half as much as a new tuner. Also, a new tuner could be very difficult to obtain for some older color receivers.

REPLACING MODULES

Transistor and Tube Chassis. In a color TV modular chassis, simply replacing the required module can cure 85 percent of the TV problems. In the past 10 years, many of the solid-state TV manufacturers have gone to modular construction (Fig. 13-49). This means any given problem can be solved by replacing the correct module, but be careful as you can spend a lot of money replacing modules. For instance, if you have a horizontal-hold problem and the picture cannot be straightened with the horizontal-hold control, replace the horizontal module. Locate the module chart found on the inside panel or rear chassis. Take the old module to a TV dealer that handles that brand of television. Don't forget to take the model and chassis number along. You usually have to turn in the old module to secure a new one because the dealer must return the module to his distributor.

Some of these modules are very expensive. They can range from $7.50 to $70.00. It's possible in some color or video problems that two separate modules might have to be replaced. If you have any

Fig. 13-49. In this particular chassis, the complete module can be replaced to solve 85 percent of the troubles in the color chassis. Note that you might find more than one defective module causing the same trouble.

doubts about what modules to replace, it might be best to call your local TV technician.

BLACK AND WHITE SETUP

Transistor and Tube Chassis. A black and white setup for any color TV receiver can be found in the service instructions. Many of these adjustments are sometimes lengthy and quite crucial. But anyone can touch up the TV screen with only a few adjustments. Locate the three screen and bias controls, usually found on the rear apron of the TV chassis (Fig. 13-50). Some chassis might have a SERVICE/NORMAL raster switch located on the rear chassis.

The only time the B&W adjustments should be made is when the raster changes to a different color. If any color is predominant, check the raster for a correct B&W raster. Turn down the color gain control. You should have a B&W picture with properly adjusted contrast and brightness controls. For instance, if the B&W picture has a reddish cast, the whole color picture may be bad.

Locate the SERVICE/NORMAL switch and turn it to the SERVICE position. The raster should collapse to a horizontal line. (If you don't have this switch, you must work with a full raster.) Now turn all screen controls down (usually counter-clockwise). Rotate all color bias controls wide open (clockwise position).

With a horizontal line, turn up the red screen control until you can barely see the red line. Adjust the green screen control for a yellow color. Turn the blue screen control for a black and white horizontal line. Flip the raster switch to NORMAL and observe the B&W raster. If the picture highlights are a little too green, reduce the green bias control. Do likewise for any other color highlight in the raster. Make the same B&W adjustment if you don't have the switch. If in doubt, follow the manufacturer's B&W setup procedure.

When one color is weak and will not intensify, suspect a weak picture tube. It's possible to have one or two weak color guns in the picture-tube assembly. If the horizontal line is a white line when switched to the SERVICE position and the raster shifts to another color in NORMAL position, suspect problems within the demodulator circuits of the TV chassis. Try to adjust both screen and bias controls to acquire a black and white raster.

COLOR ADJUSTMENTS

All Chassis. Intermittent or no color conditions are very complex and should be left to a TV technician who has the test equipment to correct these color problems. However, there are a few adjustments you can make before calling a TV technician. First make sure the TV station is tuned in properly and the color control

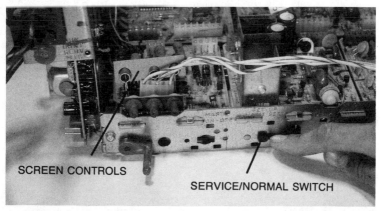

SCREEN CONTROLS

SERVICE/NORMAL SWITCH

Fig. 13-50. Locate the screen and bias control, (usually found on the rear of the chassis) for B&W setup. Locate the normal raster set-up switch before making B&W adjustments.

is fully clockwise. Rotate the fine-tuning control (usually behind the selector knob) until some type of color is tuned into the picture. If you have an automatic fine tuning (aft) or color-processor button on the front panel, make sure it's off. Sometimes the color will be in a burst or color bar pattern, indicating improper adjustment or problems in the color section. Locate and turn the color-killer control clockwise. This control should be located on the back or top side of the chassis. Now check the aft and color-processor button for proper color.

When the color picture comes in, readjust the fine-tuning hue or tint control for the best color picture. The color-killer control might have been set too low or a change in components might prevent the color from appearing in the picture. If only color bars appear in the picture and cannot be locked in with the fine-tuning control, suspect problems in the color section.

In color modular chassis, you might have to replace the color module for improper color. Some color receivers have two separate color modules. In the tube chassis, testing and replacing the tubes in the color section might restore the color picture. Do not make any color coil adjustments without the correct test equipment. Leave the more difficult color and alignment problems to the experienced TV technician.

14

VCR Repairs

There are many VCR repairs the home electronics hobbyist can do. Actually, many repairs on video cassette recorders are related to improper operation and hookup. Also, periodic checkups may save a few service dollars every year. Even a beginner in electronics can recognize mechanical and electronic component breakdown. Although the VCR is a highly technical piece of video equipment, you too can make the simple repairs discussed in the following pages (Fig. 14-1).

Poor recordings can be prevented by practicing regular cleaning and maintenance. Checking out the antenna and cable hookup might reveal why the recordings are intermittent and erratic. Knowing how to spot a defective cassette can prevent damage to the machine and hours of bad recordings. The magnetized tape head can damage the new recording, produce static or poor color, and cause flagging or glitches in the recording.

Inspecting each belt might uncover one with oil spots or cracked areas that cause slow or uneven speeds. Erratic recordings or playback can be the result of dry bearings. Tape unraveling can result from a defective cassette or take-up clutch assembly. In addition to keeping your VCR in shape, you can save yourself expensive repair dollars over the years.

READ THE INSTRUCTION BOOK FIRST

A lot of operational problems in VCRs can be eliminated by knowing just how the machine works. Go over the instruction book

Fig. 14-1. VCRs can be a Beta or VHS machine with optional remote control. Here a Realistic model is controlled by an infrared remote.

from top to bottom. Order a new service manual when you purchase a new video cassette recorder. With these two instruction guides, you can prevent many service problems and save yourself months of waiting for the VCR to be serviced.

The instruction book details important safeguards for your VCR, how to operate the machine, how to keep it clean, and how excessive moisture can damage or prevent the machine from operating. Proper grounding and how to prevent lightning damage are discussed. Keep liquids away from the machine. One spill inside the unit can cause extensive damage and result in hundreds of dollars of repairs.

Although the service schematic may appear huge and confusing, there are broken-down sections of adjustments, partial drawings and block diagrams on how to service the VCR. Most service manuals tell you such things as how to properly hook the machine up to the antenna and TV set, how to disassemble and reassemble the top and bottom covers, how to get at and service the circuit boards, and how to clean the video tape head, transport, and reel-drive systems. Replacement of critical head, belts, and tape-transport motors are also found in the service manual. Moreover, many schematics of the various electronic sections are given in detail.

340

CHECK THE ANTENNA AND CABLE HOOKUP

Poor or broken antenna cable outlet connections can cause intermittent and erratic recordings. Signal drop-out and poor cassette playback can result from a defective or loose cable hookup. First determine if the antenna cable is causing poor reception on the TV set. Flex the antenna input cable for a snowy or erratic picture on the screen. Check the antenna cable for a broken center wire or loose cable connector. Solder all shields to each cable connector so the cable wire will not pull out or produce a poor ground connection.

If the antenna cable is normal, flex the output VCR cable going to the TV set. Poor matching transformer terminal connections might be loose or torn from the VHF and UHF terminals. Make sure the correct flat or round cable is connected to the correct terminal (Fig. 14-2). Remember, the flat cable is 300 ohms, and the round coaxial cable is 75 ohms and must be terminated with matching transformers or on the correct input terminals. A poor or loose antenna and recording cable can result in poor or no recording on the cassette.

TAPE HEAD CLEANUP

To maintain good quality recordings, the video tape head must periodically be cleaned to remove oxide dust from the tape head assembly (Fig. 14-3). Always keep the outside of the VCR clean of dust and moisture. Wipe the surface clean with a damp cloth and a clean dry rag. Keep a dust cover over the machine if it is the top-loading type. Keep outside dust and dirt from falling into the tape transport system.

Remove the top cover of the VCR to get at the tape head and moving guide assemblies. Excess oxide can build up between tape and gap area of the tape head, causing a poor picture. The oxide can build up in this gap area if the tape head is not cleaned every so often. To prevent damage, keep the tape head and components in the transport system clean. The tape head should be cleaned every month, if used extensively.

There are many tape-head cleaning methods and devices on the market. One method is to moisten a clean piece of chamois with a professional head cleaning solution (Fig. 14-4). Hold the chamois to the drum assembly, and rotate the drum clockwise by hand to clean the video heads and tape path.

A spray type video head cleaner may be applied with a plastic tube spray applicator (Fig. 14-5). Hold the spray applicator can approximately four to six inches from the head or part to be cleaned.

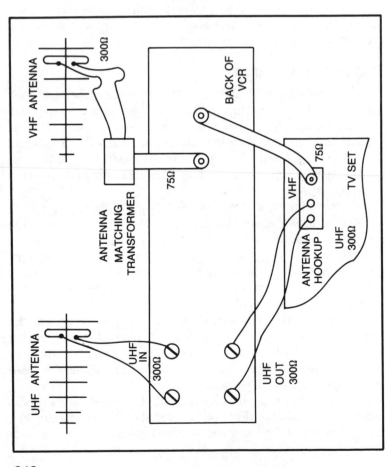

Fig. 14-2. Typical antenna and cable connections for erratic or intermittent program recording. Flex the cables to locate a poor connection.

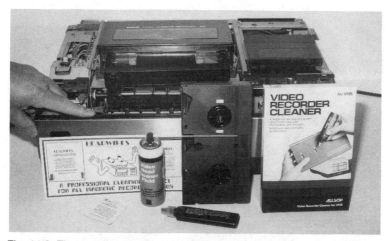

Fig. 14-3. There are many different VCR tape head cleaners on the market, including alcohol-soaked foam swabs, head cleaner spray and the cassette cleaner.

Fig. 14-4. Clean the tape head drum with a chamois soaked in alcohol. Rotate the drum with fingers at the top of the drum assembly.

Fig. 14-5. Oxide dust can be blown from the tape heads and pressure roller assemblies with a can of head-cleaning fluid and a plastic tube applicator.

Spray the head or other parts thoroughly with a wetting spray to flush dust and dirt from the component. The force of the spray should clean away the dirt and excess oxide dust. Be careful to keep the spray away from heat or flame.

The tape head and guide assemblies can be cleaned with a cleaning cassette. Choose a cassette that will remove harmful oxides and residues from the entire tape path (Fig. 14-6). In the early cassette cleaners, only the tape head was cleaned. This nonabrasive wet system cleans the entire tape path. Several drops of cleaning liquid must be applied to the felt pads for good coverage. Insert the cleaning cassette into the VCR as you would a video tape. Push the PLAY or FORWARD key to start the cleaning cycle. After 15 to 20 seconds, press the stop button and eject the cleaner.

Regular cleaning pads and alcohol can be used to clean the head by hand. Always clean horizontally with the drum area. Never clean the drum assembly by moving pad vertically. Do not press down hard against the drum or tape head. Keep your fingers from the surface of the drum area. Rotate the tape head drum from the top and apply the alcohol treated pad as it turns. By cleaning the tape head with a regular routine operation, excess oxide cannot build up on the head surface. There are several packet-type cleaners on the market that can be applied to the tape head and then thrown away (Fig. 14-7).

Fig. 14-6. The felt-type cassette cleaner is first moistened with cleaning fluid and then inserted into the VCR like a tape. Choose a cassette cleaner that will clean all components in the tape path.

TRANSPORT SYSTEM CLEANUP

The transport mechanism should be cleaned after every 400 or 500 hours of use to maintain proper operation. The transport system includes all guide posts, the tension and slant posts, guide roller, pinch roller, and erase and audio control (A/C) heads (Fig. 14-8).

Fig. 14-7. A new type of head cleaning method uses packaged presoaked cleaning pads.

Fig. 14-8. In addition to the main tape-head drum assembly, clean the erase and sound heads, spindle posts, and other transport components.

These tape contact points can be cleaned with a cleaning stick or gauze moistened with alcohol. VCR foam swabs will not separate and leave fibers on the VCR head or components.

Clean all components that the tape touches during the play or record cycle. Remove the dust or packed oxide from the various plastic and metal spindles. If not, the tape might pickup these particles of dust and damage both tape and heads. Be careful not to bend or displace the small guide posts. With a cleaning stick, wipe up the fallen dust on the cassette platform and chassis. Clean up the reel drive and disc brake system with alcohol and cleaning sticks. Allow the cleaned parts to dry before loading the cassette, or you might damage the tape or heads.

DEFECTIVE CASSETTE

The video cassette has an internal supply and take-up reel. The hinged door protects the tape from damage and rough handling. When

346

the cassette is loaded, the machine releases the flap, allowing access to the tape. The VHS cassette is larger than the Beta format. The VHS cassette will play longer than the Beta, up to 6 hours.

Every video cassette comes with an erasure prevention tab. To prevent accidental erasure of a memorable recorded program, the tabs at the rear of the cassette can be broken out. Simply break off this tab with the blade of a pocket knife or screwdriver and the machine will not record or erase on the cassette. If you later want to use the cassette for other recordings, place a piece of vinyl tape over the gap or knocked out area.

Sometimes the VCR can malfunction and spill out tape. If the player continues to operate the tape will get wound around tape heads, guide posts, and pressure-roller assemblies. If the cassette cannot be ejected, the top cover must be removed to get at the excess tape and cassette. Remove the top loading plastic platform to get at the cassette assembly and try to remove the cassette. Be careful not to damage parts and guide assemblies.

Of course you want to try to save the tape. Clean off all components after the tape is removed. Exercise caution because grease and oil from your fingers can get on the tape or tape heads. Some cassettes can be repaired by splicing the tape. Do not repair a broken tape with a piece of adhesive tape as it will damage the tape heads. Nonetheless, repairing a broken video tape is often not worthwhile, even with the best tape-splicing equipment.

DEMAGNETIZE THE TAPE HEAD

A magnetic charge and static buildup on the tape can cause noisy audio, flagging, glitches, or poor color pictures. Intermittent flagging is the pulling or bending of the picture at the top of the screen. Try to remove it with the skew control. Glitches are small thin lines or bars going through the picture (resembling electrical noise on a TV signal at lower channels).

These various charges can be eliminated by demagnetizing the rotating tape head. Use only a VCR head demagnetizer tool. Plug in the demagnetizer away from the VCR. Bring it up to the tape head, but don't let it touch the metal drum. Slowly rotate the drum at the top side. While you are at it, demagnetize the metal tape guides and other tape heads that come in contact with the tape. Slowly pull the demagnetizer away from the VCR and shut it off. Remember to demagnetize the tape head after servicing the VCR or after cleaning.

CLEAN ALL FUNCTION SWITCHES

Erratic or intermittent operation might be caused by dirty function switches. Clean all switches and relays while the top cover of the machine is removed. Do not overlook possibly faulty microswitches—microswitches should be replaced as they are difficult to clean. Push the applicator down into the switch assembly and spray the switch controls. Inspect the switches for broken or jammed mechanisms.

LUBRICATION

The tape transport mechanism is properly lubricated at the factory. Most motors are lubricated for life. Under normal operating conditions, additional lubrication is not required the first years and many components will never need lubrication. Remember to apply only a small amount of lubricant, and only when needed. Do not over-oil.

Clean off the old grease before applying the new. A squeaky bearing might need a squirt of light oil. Although a noisy or frozen capstan motor bearing might respond to lubrication, this should be replaced. Be careful not to let oil or grease drip on the belts or moving components. Clean all oil and grease spots with alcohol and a cleaning stick.

CASSETTE WILL NOT LOAD

If it will not load, make sure the tape is right side up. The plastic take-up and supply-reel assembly of the cassette should be turned down when loading (Fig. 14-9). In top-loading VCRs, insert the cassette all the way and push down on the cassette carriage. In some automatic front-loading machines, a loading motor takes over to pull the tape into the VCR after insertion.

Improper loading of the top-loading machine can result in bent or out-of-line carriages or levers. Make sure the cassette is fully seated. If loading seems difficult, remove the top cover and inspect the loading mechanism. Check for jammed or bent levers or a broken loading assembly.

Erratic or improper front loading might be caused by a defective loading motor or circuits. Locate the loading motor and take a continuity measurement at the motor terminals. Replace the loading motor if the winding is open. Measure the voltage on the loading-motor drive IC (Fig. 14-10). Suspect a leaky IC if the voltage source is low at pins 6 and 7. Suspect a defective mechanism control IC

Fig. 14-9. For proper loading, the plastic take-up and supply reels should be at the bottom side of the cassette.

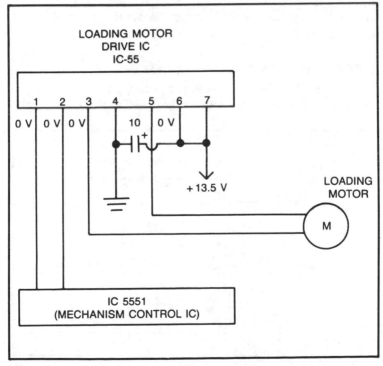

Fig. 14-10. Suspect a defective loading-motor IC if incorrect voltages are found at the motor terminals.

if both the motor and driving IC test normal. If the motor and control IC appear normal, check the loading-motor drive belt (found in some models).

DEAD—NO OPERATION

With no front lights or motor operation, first suspect an open fuse or defective low-voltage power supply. Check all fuses with the ohmmeter and replace with the exact amperage. Make sure the power switch contacts are normal. Check the silicon diodes and corresponding circuits if the fuse doesn't hold (Fig. 14-11). Do not overlook a leaky bridge rectifier circuit. Leaky or shorted transistor regulator circuits can overload the dc supply, causing the fuse to open.

You might find several low-voltage regulator transistors in the low-voltage power supply. Carefully measure the voltage on each transistor terminal and check each against the schematic. In Fig. 14-12, the positive- and negative-regulated 30-volt sources are taken from half-wave diode rectifiers. Improper voltage sources can occur in the regulated circuits or components tied to the different voltage sources.

CHECK FOR BROKEN OR CRACKED BELTS

After cleaning the tape heads and guide posts, take a peek at the different drive belts. Sometimes these belts can be visible after

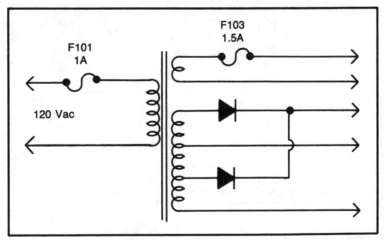

Fig. 14-11. No output condition can result from a defective low-voltage power supply. Test each diode involved for leaky conditions.

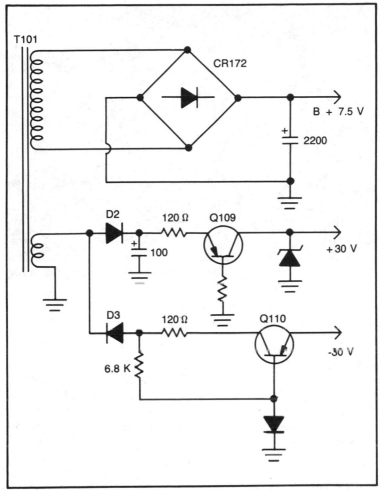

Fig. 14-12. Shorted or leaky voltage-regulator transistors can cause the fuse to open. You might find several low-voltage sources with separate fuses.

removing or pulling up a board section. A broken or cracked belt can cause slow or erratic speeds (Fig. 14-13).

Inspect the belt for cracked or worn areas. Note if the belt is loose or stretched. A slipping belt might be shiny from slipping on the metal motor pulley. Replace any belts or immediately order one if it is stretched or worn. Temporarily apply a coat of liquid rosin to the motor pulley until a new belt is obtained. Check the belts at least once a year for damage. If the belt is put on backwards, it can be thrown off the pulley.

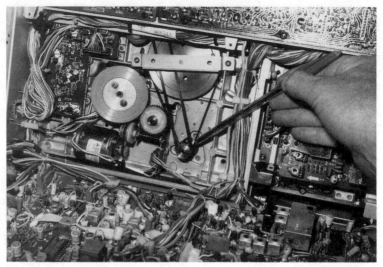

Fig. 14-13. Check the belts for cracked or worn areas. A slipping belt can be identified by a shiny area.

NO REWIND OR FAST FORWARD

If the VCR fails to rewind or fast forward, check for a defective interlock, microswitch and/or relay. Inspect and manually check to see if each switch or solenoid is closing. Measure the resistance of the solenoid for an open winding. Monitor the voltage at the drive motor in REWIND mode. A no-voltage reading can indicate a defective microswitch or relay contacts. Note if the belt is off or slipping in fast-forward mode.

CHECKING TAPE-HEAD RESISTANCE

When no picture or sound is evident with apparently normal mechanical tape movements, check the channel setting of the VCR and TV set. Next measure the dc voltage at the low-voltage sources. A defective video tape head can cause a no-picture, no-sound symptom. Frequently one channel is defective while the other is normal.

An open or defective video tape head can prevent normal record and playback functions. Make sure all oxide deposits are off the tape head gap area. Locate the tape-head wire connections and check each winding (Fig. 14-14). Compare the left and right tape-head windings with the resistance measurements. Suspect video circuit problems if the tape head is normal.

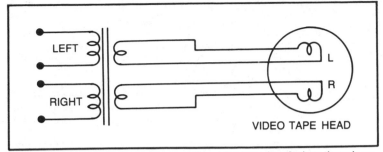

Fig. 14-14. Measure the resistance of the video tape head when there is no record or playback.

CHECKING THE MOTORS

In most VCR recorders today you find drum, capstan, and loading motors. Each motor can be checked with an ohmmeter continuity test. This might not mean the motor is operating correctly, but it does indicate it is not open and therefore should run (Fig. 14-15). Voltage monitored at the motor terminals will indicate other circuits are working and that the motor should rotate.

These motors can have individual ICs to control them (Fig. 14-16). Locate the motor control ICs and take accurate voltage measurements. Most motors are eventually controlled by a large master mechanism-control processor. Leave the master control

Fig. 14-15. Check each motor terminal for continuity if the motor's not working. Measure the voltage at the motor terminals to check for a defective motor.

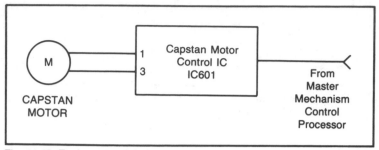

Fig. 14-16. Each motor might have a separate IC controlling motor operation, although they are ultimately controlled by the master mechanism-control processor.

circuit troubleshooting to a VCR specialist after verifying the integrity of the motor control ICs.

CASSETTE WILL NOT RECORD

If one cassette won't record, try another. Does the defective cassette PLAY? Recheck the recording tabs at the rear of the cassette (Fig. 14-17). Many VCRs and cassette players are brought in for repair if one cassette will not record when in actuality the machine is normal and the cassette is at fault. To record, the small tabs at the rear of the cassette must be in place. Always try another cassette when one will not record to determine if the cassette or the recorder is at fault.

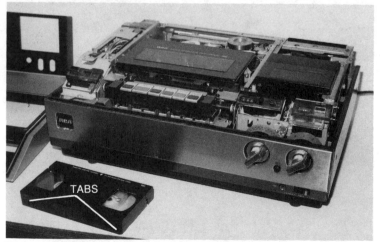

Fig. 14-17. When one cassette will not record but will play, suspect the tab is out at the back of the cassette. Try another cassette.

NO ERASE

Jumbled picture and sound can occur when the recorder does not completely erase the previous recording. First check the channel setting of the TV and VCR. Readjust the tracking control on the front of the VCR. Try another cassette. If all of the above does nothing to improve the picture, remove the top cover of the VCR.

Locate the erase head and clean all oxide from the gap area (Fig. 14-18). Packed oxide on the FE head can prevent the previous recording from being erased. After head cleanup, check the head winding with the ohmmeter. An open head winding or a torn off wire

Fig. 14-18. Locate the erase head (FE) and clean all oxide from the gap area. Double check the head connections and winding when there is a jumbled or messy picture.

connection can also prevent proper erase. A defective FE head must be replaced with the exact part number.

ERRATIC RECORDING

Improper tape speed can result from dry or frozen take-up and supply-reel assemblies (Fig. 14-19). Fluctuating tape speed produces slow and erratic recording and playback. These reels should open freely with the brake band tension released. To check the reels for dry bearings, remove the "C" or lock washer at the top of the reel assembly. Clean off the old grease from the bearing posts with alcohol and cloth. Apply a light coat of grease to bearing post. Make sure all washers are in place before replacing the reel assembly. Clean off the reel disc brake surface with a cleaning stick moistened with alcohol. Make sure both reels are at the same height. If not, one of the play-side washers might be missing.

ERRATIC TAKE-UP

In older VCRs, the tape would sometimes slow down and unravel after a half hour of operation. If the take-up reel slows down or operates erratically, the tape wants to spill out. The clutch assembly at the bottom side of the take-up reel could be slipping. In these models, a plastic ear assembly can be adjusted for greater take-up pressure. This take-up reel adjustment can only be seen from the bottom side of the VCR mechanism (Fig. 14-20).

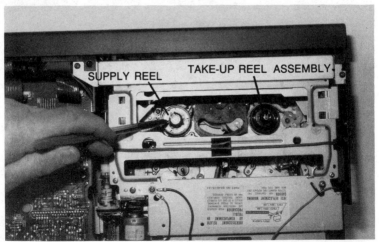

Fig. 14-19. Check the take-up and supply-reel turntables for dry bearings. Replace the entire reel assembly if the clutch is slipping.

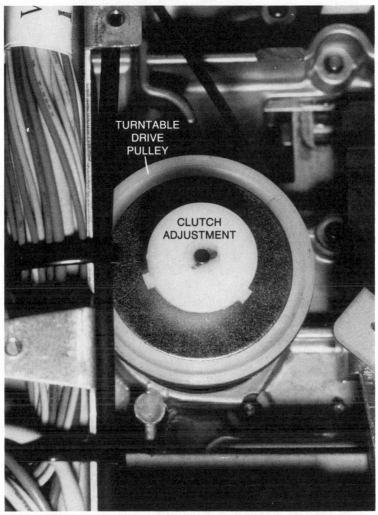

TURNTABLE
DRIVE
PULLEY

CLUTCH
ADJUSTMENT

Fig. 14-20. You might find a clutch tension adjustment at the bottom of the reel turntable drive assembly in older video tape recorders.

First try to tighten the adjustment to correct the clutch slippage. Check the V belt which drives the take-up reel assembly for worn or too loose tension. Replace the belt if cracked or if correct tension cannot be applied. Replace the entire clutch assembly if extra tension and belt replacement does not cure the take-up reel slippage. With the latest VCR reel turntables, the clutch assembly can be a part of the reel assembly; in this case replace the whole reel turntable with a slipping clutch assembly.

BINDING OR BROKEN GEARS

Carefully inspect the plastic or metal cam gears for broken or bent teeth. You might find several cam, main gear, idler, and other worn gears in the VCR mechanism (Fig. 14-21). Clean off the old grease with a cleaning stick and alcohol. Some of these gear assemblies have a light grease applied to the meshing teeth area. For a deformed gear assembly, look it up in the parts layout drawing and check the symbol against the part number in the service manual for replacement. These small gears might be held in position with small U or C washers.

NO SOUND

The no-sound symptom can originate in either the recording or playback mode. Try a test cassette or a known recording to determine if the no-sound symptom is in playback. If no sound is heard at all, suspect improper TV/VCR settings or problems related to the audio circuit. Check the TV/VCR switch on the monitor. If both sound and picture are missing, inspect the connecting cables.

Clean the audio head (A/C) with alcohol and a cleaning stick. Check the audio head winding for open connections with an

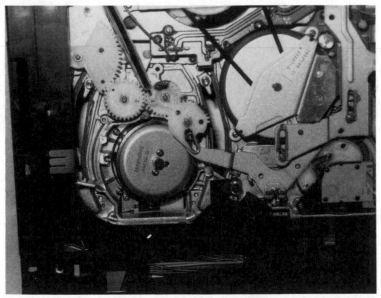

Fig. 14-21. Inspect the idler wheels and gear assemblies for broken or jammed cam components.

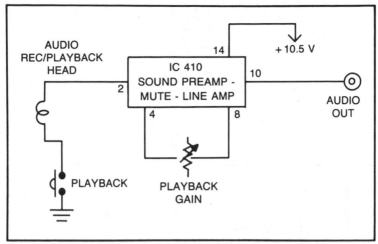

Fig. 14-22. Block diagram of a late model VCR sound circuit.

ohmmeter. Inspect the audio head wiring for a poor or broken connection. Note if the tape is running correctly through the tape guide assemblies and is not out of the tape path. Check and clean the audio switch assembly.

Next check the audio playback circuits. Today most VCR sound circuits consist of one large IC component. In the earlier models, chassis transistors and IC components made up the sound circuits (Fig. 14-22). Locate the large audio IC and take voltage measurements. Check the B+ supply voltage pin. Replace the output audio IC if voltages are considerably off.

DISTORTED SOUND

Weak and distorted sound can be caused by either a dirty audio tape head, bad audio on the tape, a high-level audio setting, or improper agc circuits. Make sure the audio tape heads are clean. Try a test tape or a known recording with good sound. If the sound is weak and distorted, suspect a defective audio circuit.

Go directly to the audio output IC and take accurate voltage tests, because weak and distorted audio are often linked. A leaky audio IC usually causes improper voltage measurements (Fig. 14-23). Take critical resistance measurements on each IC pin to isolate a leaky or open component tied to the audio IC. However, sometimes these voltage and resistance measurements do not indicate that the IC is defective. Because it is the most important audio IC in the circuit, it is best just to replace it.

359

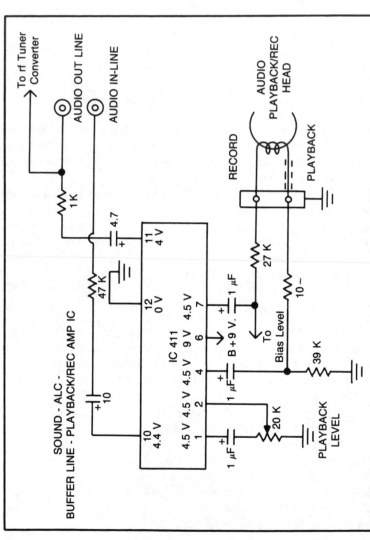

Fig. 14-23. Take accurate voltage and resistance measurements on the audio IC to locate the weak component.

Audio hum is usually caused by poor shields and grounds. Noisy sound can result from a defective tape in the cassette or dirty tape heads. Try another cassette after cleaning the audio tape heads. Check the TV tuning if a low buzz noise is heard in the sound. Readjust the tracking knob on the recorder.

WHAT NOT TO DO

After attempting the most common repairs and the video recorder still does not work right, take it to an electronics technician specializing in VCRs. There might be one right in your home town. If not, the VCR can be taken to a manufacturer's service repair depot. Most manufacturers have VCR service centers throughout the United States.

Do not try to tackle or invade crucial VCR circuits that you know nothing about. Do not try to make tape head, spindle post, and tension post adjustments without the right tools. Do not try to make FM record or color level adjustments without the correct test instruments. Do not adjust or move any adjustment screw or control unless you know what it does, and then do it only with the correct manufacturer's service literature requirements.

Remember, the video cassette recorder is a delicate machine and should be carefully handled when making repairs. When replacing a defective component, write down each part, lead, or terminal so the new one can be replaced easily. Use a low-wattage soldering iron around ICs and transistors. Always obtain a schematic diagram and service literature for a recently purchased VCR for future repairs.

Part 4

Miscellaneous

15

Telephone Answering Machines and Cordless Telephones

There are many different service problems that can develop in telephone-answering machines. Today a phone-answering system can combine a regular telephone with a cassette answering machine, or you can have a separate answering unit. The duo-cassette answering system can provide up to 120 incoming messages with switchable message length (Fig. 15-1). You can get your messages from any phone with a remote control device. The deluxe, IC-controlled answerer can display the time, date, and number of the incoming messages.

A telephone-answering device can contain upwards of twenty transistors, thirty-five diodes, and up to four IC components. Besides the solid-state signal circuits, one or two cassette decks provide mechanical operation. In addition to mechanical and electronic components, solid-state switching of the various diodes and transistors can result in many service problems. When the electronic and mechanical operations are combined together, service problems eventually develop.

NO OPERATION

Go directly to the low-voltage power supply with no tape motion or signal indication. The low-voltage supply might consist of a small power transformer, a bridge rectifier, and a capacitor/resistor filter network (Fig. 15-2). Measure the dc voltage at the filter capacitor.

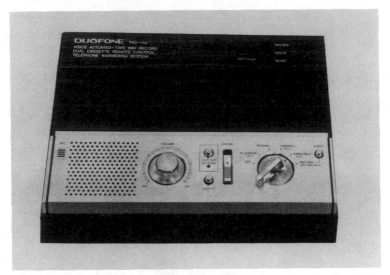

Fig. 15-1. The telephone answering machine can use one or two cassettes to handle incoming and outgoing messages. Some have remote-control operation.

If no dc voltage is detected, check the primary winding of the transformer for open conditions. The power transformer plugs directly into the power line and is on all the time. Test each diode in the bridge rectifier circuit for leakage. If one diode indicates leakage, remove the entire bridge rectifier component from the circuit for accurate leakage tests. Then remove one end of each diode rectifier for shorted or leakage tests.

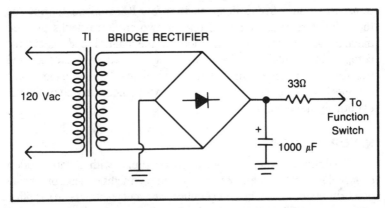

Fig. 15-2. Check the voltage at the low-voltage power supply for a no-operation symptom.

If dc voltage is found at the low-voltage power supply and not at the other circuits, inspect the function switch for dirty contacts or broken wires. The main function switch might route dc voltage to the different circuits. Clean an erratic or intermittent function switch with cleaning spray and an extension tube.

MOTOR DRIVE PROBLEMS

No tape movement can be either a mechanical or electronic problem. Rotate the function switch to the rewind or playback position. If the tape does not move, try the fast-forward button. If nothing happens, check the motor circuits. Take a motor continuity test for open conditions. Measure the motor voltage at the motor terminals. No voltage here indicates a defective motor circuit (Fig. 15-3). Measure the voltage on each transistor. If there's no voltage applied to the motor circuits, suspect a defective function switch.

Try starting the motor by hand. If the motor starts, suspect a defective motor or circuit. If the motor keeps running, check for an open resistor (R27 in Fig. 15-3). When voltage is found on the emitter terminal of Q7 but there's no motor movement, suspect transistors Q7 or Q8. A shorted or burned R32 (in Fig. 15-3) can inhibit the motor.

When the motor is turning but the tape isn't, suspect the mechanical linkages. Look for a broken or missing motor drive belt; replace the motor drive belt if it is off or broken. The motor pulley, flywheels, and drive pulley should always be turning when proper voltage is applied to the motor terminals (Fig. 15-4).

Incorrect Speed. In addition to the motor circuits, check for oil on the motor belt and drive pulleys. Check that the belt isn't too loose or has cracked areas. Wipe off the belt, flywheels, and drive pulley with alcohol and cloth. Note if the motor pulley is black and shiny. Remove the black belt particles with alcohol and a cleaning stick.

Wow and flutter can occur in any mode. After cleaning, if the cassette is turning too slow, look for a motor-adjustment control (Fig. 15-4). Normally, you would turn it in a counter-clockwise direction if the speed is too slow. If the speed is too fast, turn the speed control clockwise.

Suspect a defective motor or circuit when the speed control has no effect on the motor. Replace the motor if it is erratic or intermittent. Replace the motor if it has a flat spot on the armature, requiring it to manually be turned to start. Check Q7 and Q8 when

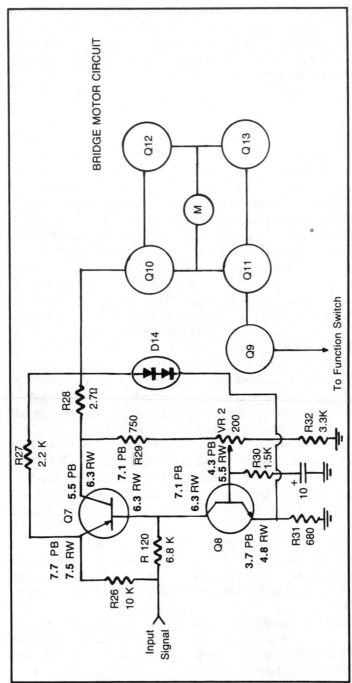

Fig. 15-3. Transistor-bridge, motor-drive circuit. Q7 and Q8 are the motor-control transistors, while Q9 determines the direction the motor turns (PB for Playback and RW for Rewind).

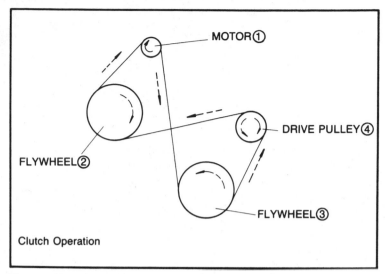

Clutch Operation

Fig. 15-4. The motor, flywheels, and drive pulley should always turn with power applied.

the tape speed cannot be adjusted. Transistors Q7 and Q8 are the motor speed-control transistors. Remove the transistor for leakage tests after suspicion during an in-circuit test.

No PLAY or REWIND Modes. Inspect the mechanical linkage of the flywheels and rewind reels if the motor belt is rotating but you don't have PLAYBACK or REWIND (Fig. 15-5). Next check the main function switch contacts when placed in the rewind mode. Clean all switch contacts with cleaning spray and extender tube. Push the plastic tip down into the switch terminals. Rotate the function switch back and forth as you spray the contacts. A dry or frozen function switch can be loosened up with silicone spray on the shaft bearing area.

Test Q9 for leakage. Transistor Q9 controls the motor's spin direction. Check Q11 or Q12 in the transistor bridge circuit for shorted conditions (Fig. 15-6). Measure R33 (in Fig. 15-6) for correct resistance. Test all four motor output driver transistors if one is found leaky or open. Do not overlook a possibly intermittent drive motor.

Excessive Motor Noise in the Speaker. Noise heard in the speaker is often caused by a defective motor. The motor armature and brushes when dirty produce excessive arcing. Sometimes a $470\text{-}\mu\text{F}$ electrolytic capacitor shunted across the motor terminals can help, but it's best to replace the motor. It may help to reroute the motor leads away from the high-gain tape-head circuits.

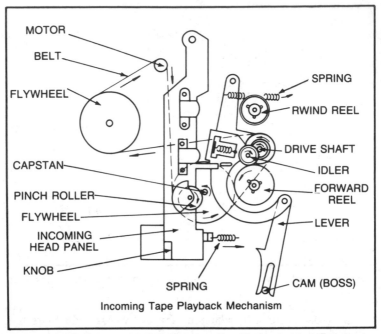

MOTOR
BELT
FLYWHEEL
CAPSTAN
PINCH ROLLER
FLYWHEEL
INCOMING
HEAD PANEL
KNOB
SPRING
RWIND REEL
DRIVE SHAFT
IDLER
FORWARD REEL
LEVER
SPRING
CAM (BOSS)

Incoming Tape Playback Mechanism

Fig. 15-5. Inspect the pinch roller, rewind reel, and forward reel when the motor belt is rotating but there is no playback or rewind.

NO AUDIO PLAYBACK MESSAGE

Locate the audio preamp stages for the record/playback (R/P) heads when both the outgoing message and message playback are inoperative. Measure the voltage on the transistor or IC amps to locate the defective component (Fig. 15-7). Test the suspected transistor amp in-circuit with the diode-transistor test of the DMM. Accurate voltage tests on the terminals of the IC amp frequently indicate a leaky component. Check coupling and bypass capacitors in the preamp circuits. Shunt C24 (of Fig. 15-7) for weak or no audio playback.

NO MESSAGE PLAYBACK

Refer to Fig. 15-8 for the following section. When a weak or no-audio signal occurs during message playback, clip another PM speaker across the speaker terminals. These speakers can have high impedance ratings. The audio circuits can be signal-traced from pin 8 of IC-2B through to the speakers (Fig. 15-8). Test the suspected component when the audio quits. Referring to the figure, take volt-

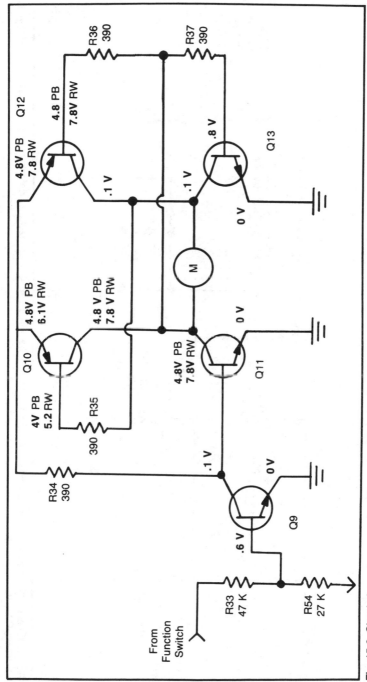

Fig. 15-6. Check these components of the motor-drive circuits when there is no playback or rewind: Q9, Q10, Q11, Q12, the motor, and R33.

371

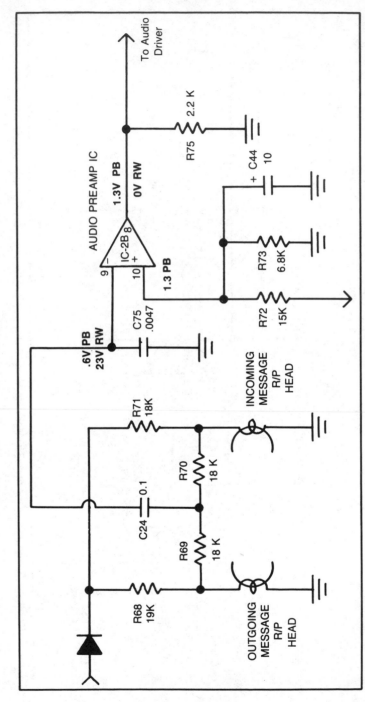

Fig. 15-7. Accurate voltage and resistance measurements on the audio preamp, IC-2B, can isolate a defective IC. Voltages in PB exist during playback; RW—during rewind.

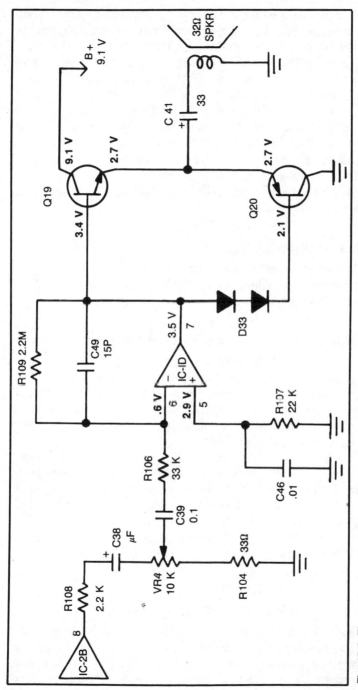

Fig. 15-8. The audio signal in playback messages can be signal-traced with the external audio amp. Accurate voltage measurements might locate a defective IC or output transistor.

age measurements on the driver IC or transistor (IC-1D) to locate a leaky component. Test output transistors Q19 and Q20 with an in-circuit beta tester. Accurate voltage measurements on the output transistors or IC can indicate a leaky or open component. Try to increase the audio with resistor VR4 if the volume is very weak.

Loss of audio in the playback message might be caused by an open R108 (2.2 K) resistor or C38 (1 μF), a coupling capacitor. Shunt a 0.1 μF capacitor across C39 when audio is found on one side but not on the other. An open R106 or VR4 can prevent sound from reaching the driver IC-1D. A leaky bias diode (D33) can cause weak and distorted messages or hum in the circuit. Diode D33 generates a 1.3-volt bias voltage drop between the two base terminals of the audio output transistors.

WON'T RECORD

The telephone unit should record both clear announcements and incoming messages. Difficulties with recording can be treated together or separately.

Records Neither Announcement Nor Incoming Messages

Any defective component between T1 and the recording amp can prevent the message from being recorded. A defective component from the microphone to the recording amp can prevent the announcement from being recorded. If both announcement and message recordings do not record, suspect a leaky or open recording amp IC or transistor (Fig. 15-9).

Referring to Fig. 15-9, check for an open R57 or C17 (a coupling capacitor) in the input circuit of IC-2A. Test the automatic level control (alc) transistor (Q14) for leakage or open conditions. A defective collector load resistor R61 can inhibit both recordings. The alc (Q14) acts as a variable resistor. Critical voltage measurements on terminals of IC-2A and Q14 might indicate if either one is leaky. Test D26 in the circuit for open or leaky conditions with the diode test of the DMM.

Won't Record Announcements

Refer to Fig. 15-10 for the following two sections. Suspect the microphone input circuits when failing to record announcements or messages for incoming callers (Fig. 15-10). Check the microphone connections. Clean the annunciator play/record head. Check this head

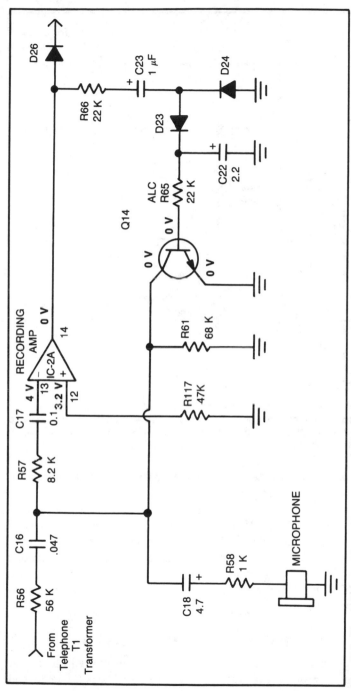

Fig. 15-9. Check the recording amp and input components (such s R57, C17, R61, Q14 and D26) when both the outgoing announcement and incoming messages won't record.

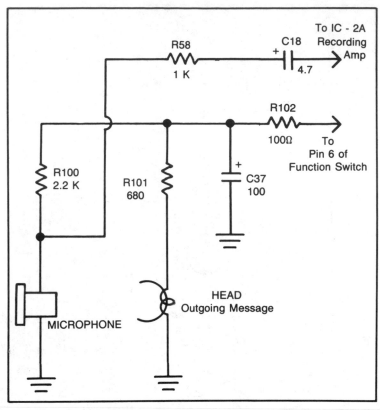

Fig. 15-10. If announcements won't record, suspect a defective microphone or annunciator play/record head. Clean the tape head with alcohol and a cleaning stick.

for continuity with the ohmmeter. Measure the supply voltage at the recording circuits.

Measure the resistance of crucial resistors in the microphone input circuits (R100, R101, and R102). If the incoming message is recorded normally, the defective component must be between the mike and the recording amp. Test all components between microphone and recording IC amp (IC-2A). Measure the resistance of R58 (1 K). Check C18 (4.7 μF) in the circuit with the digital capacitance meter.

Weak or Distorted Announcement

The annunciator play/record head might be covered with oxide, producing a weak or distorted announcement. Check the tape head for a worn area or shorted turns. Do not overlook a defective endless cassette tape. Measure the resistances of R100 and R102. Measure base resistor R68 (18 K) in series with the outgoing message P & R tape head. Test C37 (100 µF) with one lead removed with the digital capacitance meter (refer back to Fig. 15-10). Sub another microphone in the circuit.

Won't Record Incoming Messages

Refer to Fig. 15-11 if the recording of outgoing announcements is okay but there's no recording of incoming messages, test all components from the telephone transformer (T1) to the common junction where both signals meet (point C). Measure the resistance of R56 (56 K). Clip the capacitance meter across C16 (.047) and test for an open condition. Do not overlook the incoming signal P/R tape head. Clean the head with alcohol and cleaning stick. Take a quick continuity test across the recording head winding with an ohmmeter.

Weak and Distorted Incoming Messages

Locate the incoming message play/record head and clean. Check the head for normal resistance, shorted turns, or excessive wear.

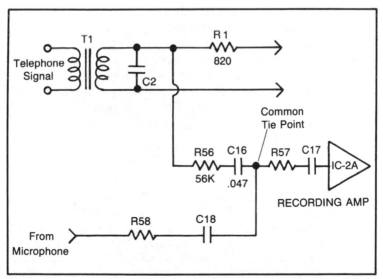

Fig. 15-11. If incoming messages won't record, check from the incoming telephone transformer (T1) to the common tie point of both incoming and outgoing messages (point C).

Inspect the receiving cassette and try another cassette if necessary. Check the resistor in series with the incoming P/R head winding (R71 in Fig. 15-11) for increase in resistance.

AUDIO OUTPUT CIRCUITS

The cassette players in telephone answering machines can be serviced like any other cassette deck—most of the service problems are identical. Although some circuits in the answering machines are different than those in the tape player, the audio output amplifiers are the same. The circuits found in this chapter are quite common to most telephone answering machines. The early answering devices were made up mostly of transistors and diodes, while the latest telephone answering devices contain more IC components (refer to Fig. 15-12.)

In the figure, the volume is controlled by adjusting VR4 (10 K). Here IC-1D is the audio driver with Q19 and Q20 as a push-pull output stage. The 32-ohm PM speaker is capacity-coupled to the audio output transistor with C41 (33 μF).

No Audio Output

A low hum should be audible in the speaker when a screwdriver blade is touched to the center terminal of the volume control. The audio signal can be signal-traced with a recorded message or music in the PLAY position. Check the signal at the input terminal (6) and output terminal (7) with the external audio amp. Proceed to the output transistors and speaker coupling capacitor, C41. Take accurate voltage tests on driver amp IC-1D if no signal is found at output terminal 7. Test Q19 and Q20 in the circuit with the diode/transistor test of the DMM. Do not overlook an open coupling capacitor (C41) or a defective speaker.

Weak and Distorted Audio

First make sure the tape heads are clean. Next check the small PM speaker. Remove one speaker terminal and clip another high-impedance speaker into the circuit. Choose an 8-ohm or higher impedance test speaker. Measure the supply voltage feeding the audio circuits if distorted audio still exists. Try another cassette to determine if it's the recorded message that is distorted or the audio output circuits.

Test Q19 and Q20 for leakage or open conditions if the distortion is located in the audio output stages. Weak and low audio distortion

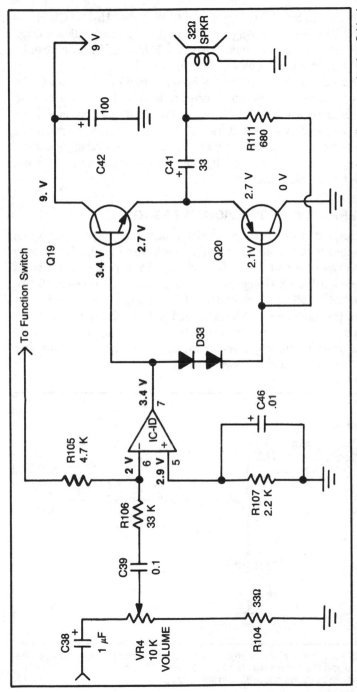

Fig. 15-12. You might find one complete IC component or a combination of IC and output transistors in the audio output circuits. Critical voltage tests and in-circuit transistor tests can quickly locate the defective component.

can be caused by a leaky bias diode, (D33 in Fig. 15-12.) Check capacitor C46 (.01) for leakage at pin 5 of IC-1D. Take critical voltage measurements on the audio driver, IC-1D. The distortion can be signal-traced with the external audio amp.

Also check the input circuits from the audio R/P preamp to the volume control for weak and distorted audio (Fig. 15-13). An increase in resistance of R108 (2.2 K) and R106 (33 K) can produce weak reception. Defective capacitors C39 (0.1) and C38 (1 μF) can cause weak and distorted audio. Check the small audio coupling capacitors, as they have a tendency to dry out and lose capacitance. Do not overlook the alc circuits.

NO ERASURE OF PREVIOUS MESSAGE

Suspect a defective annunciator play/record head for when messages won't erase. You might hear several jumbled messages on the cassette without proper erasing. An increase in resistance or open R101 (680Ω) can prevent erasing of the cassette (Fig. 15-14). Clean and check the continuity of the message play/record head. Check the mounting of the erase head and note if the tape presses against the tape head of the cassette. The tape head might be out of line or have a missing head screw. You should also check for dirty contacts on the selector switch.

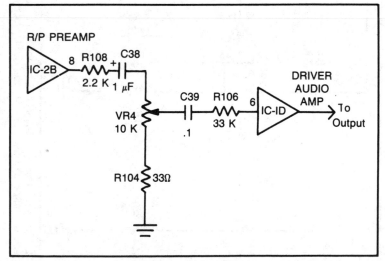

Fig. 15-13. For weak or distorted sound, check the components between the preamp and the driver stage (R108, C38 VR4, C39, and R106). Test the small electrolytic coupling capacitors in the circuit.

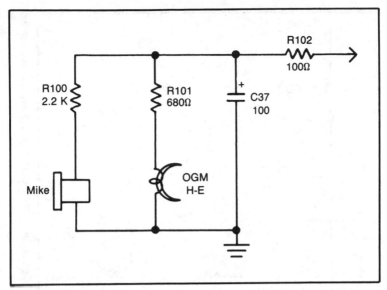

Fig. 15-14. Clean the erase head when it does not erase the previous messages. Also check R101 and make sure the erase head is pressed against the tape.

AMPLIFIER OSCILLATES

Oscillations in the speaker can result from a defective output IC or transistor. Sometimes poor filtering in the power source causes oscillations in the audio circuits. If the amplifier oscillates only in the playback mode, check for a defective diode (D25, D26, or D28 of Fig. 15-15). Diode D25 prevents loading of the input to IC-2B by the output of IC-2A. Diode D26 acts as an additional gate to any leakage signal out of IC-2A when it is shut down and its output pin is at ground. Diode D28 acts as additional gate to a leakage signal out of IC-2B when it is shut down with its output pin at ground potential.

TAPE SPILLOUT

Tape spilling out of the cassette can result from an erratic take-up reel, pinch roller, or dry flywheel and pulley assembly. Clean the capstan shaft and make sure each flywheel spins freely. Inspect the drive pulleys and clean. Check the pinch roller for worn areas. Remove any excess tape between rubber roller and bearing. The tape can wrap tightly around the roller bearing and might be difficult to remove. Replace the rubber pinch roller, drive pulleys, and flywheels when they are worn or have flat areas.

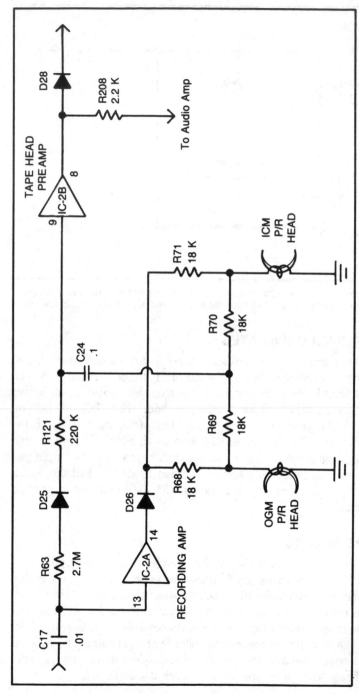

Fig. 15-15. Oscillation in the answering machine amplifier can result from leaky or open diodes in the recording and preamp circuits. In the figure, suspect D25, D26, or D28.

CORDLESS TELEPHONE REPAIR

Although servicing cordless telephones might appear quite complicated, there are many small repairs you can do to keep yours operating (Fig. 15-16). For example, proper battery care and adequate charging of the nickel-cadmium-batteries can save you hours of frustration besides saving money. Setting the digital security code can prevent interference from a neighboring cordless phone or someone riding by. A dead base unit can result from a defective low-voltage power supply. Erratic or noisy reception can be caused by dirty switches or outside interference. The audio circuits can be checked for weak or distorted sound. Knowing how to replace the dipole antenna of the handset when it is dropped accidentally can save you a needless repair charge.

DIGITAL CODING

Many cordless telephones have a digital coding switch to prevent someone from answering or eavesdropping on your conversation. There are a limited number of channels on which cordless telephones transmit, so if one of your neighbors has a telephone that transmits

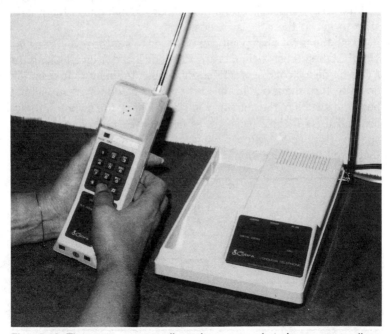

Fig. 15-16. There are many small repairs you can do to keep your cordless telephone operating.

on the same channel as yours, you might have some interference problems. The security code helps prevent other cordless telephones from initiating or answering a call on your phone line. Some cordless phones have three or five separate digital coding switches or a combination of numbers to select to ensure security. The code switch can be a simple three-position slide switch (Fig. 15-17); in other systems, there are five switches that are turned on or off to produce a five-digit code.

Both units must have the same switches in the same position to operate. The security code is an inaudible, transmitted code that identifies your handset to your base and vice versa. Your base unit will accept transmission only from a handset with a matching security code, and the handset will accept transmission only from a base with a matching security code. You can change the security code any time interference occurs from another telephone.

The digital code switches can be located at the rear deck of the base station and inside the battery compartment of the handset. In other cordless telephones, the digital coding is found under plastic strips at the front of each unit. Locate the small hole in the plastic strip and insert a pin or needle. Carefully push the pin to the right and the strip will double up—then pull out the one end of the plastic strip to get at the code switches.

Use the tip of a ball point pen or pencil to set the switches (Fig. 15-18). Often these switches are very small and fragile-looking. In a five-bit digital code system, carefully push them up to turn on, or down to turn them off. In the three-number code system, simply push the switch to the number you want. Check the switch settings on both units if the handset does not answer or call to the base station. Both code switches must be set to the same numbers or there will be no reception.

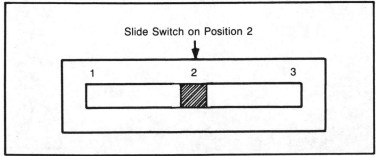

Fig. 15-17. Enlarged view of a three-position slide switch. It selects a digital code to eliminate interference from handset to base units.

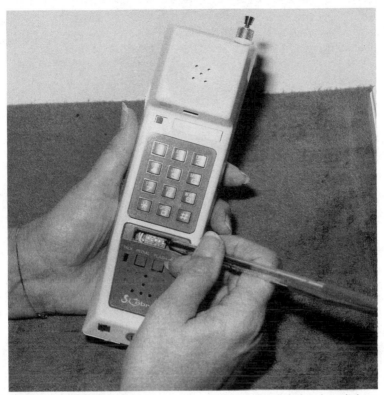

Fig. 15-18. Use a ball-point pen or a pencil to set the digital code switches. Remember, both the handset and base units must be set the same.

CHECK THE BATTERIES

Weak or no transmission can result from poor or dead batteries in the telephone handset. Most cordless telephones have a low-battery light indicator on the handset that tells you when the batteries need charging. Rechargeable nickel-cadmium batteries are used in most handsets. The batteries are charged by the base unit when the handset is in the cradle (Fig. 15-19).

Before using the telephone for the first time, you must charge the batteries for at least 24 hours. Fully charged batteries should last all day long. The batteries should last three years under normal charging conditions. Pick up a new set of batteries at the manufacturer's dealer when they no longer charge up. These batteries are not cheap and can cost from $9.95 to $11.00 per pack.

Remove the battery cover at the back side of the handset. Some of these units have a screw holding the battery lid in position, while

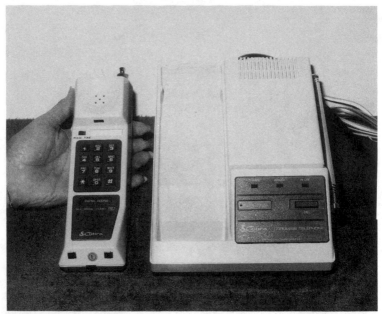

Fig. 15-19. The nickel-cadmium batteries are charged while the handset is in the cradle of the base unit.

others have a slide-type plastic lid (that can be difficult to remove). A plastic ribbon holds the batteries in place. Remove the plastic piece and pull the batteries out (Fig. 15-20). Unplug the battery cable connector. A red and black connecting wire might unplug separately from the small printed circuit board. Reverse the procedure when installing new batteries. Remember, the new batteries must be charged for 24 hours before you can use the handset.

KEEP BATTERIES CHARGED

The battery pack might consist of three nickel-cadmium batteries wired in series. The total pack voltage should be around 3.6 volts dc. Check the batteries on a DMM with the phone power switched on. Clip the voltmeter leads to the battery terminals where they connect to the handset (Fig. 15-21). The battery indicator (BATT LOW) should be lit if the batteries are weak, unless of course the battery-low circuits are not working.

Batteries charging can be hindered if the charging contacts get dirty or tarnished. Wipe off the silver coated contacts with cleaning fluid and cloth. You can occasionally clean them up with a pencil eraser. Keep food or sticky substances away from the charging contacts. These handset contacts rest on the charging contacts in the charging well.

Once the battery pack has been fully charged, you should recharge the handset about two hours for every one hour it is used. Remember, the handset uses a small amount of power even when you are not talking on it. In some units, the charging rate is automatically reduced as the batteries approach full charge. They cannot be harmed by continuous charging.

Let the batteries completely discharge or allow the low battery light to come on before placing the handset into the charging well or base at least once per month to obtain maximum useful life from the batteries. Do not let the handset lie around with the low battery indicator light on for months at a time—they might never again charge up to the required operating voltage.

Fig. 15-20. Remove and check the batteries when the handset is dead or weak in operation. A small screw or plastic slide panel must be removed from the back side of the portable handset.

387

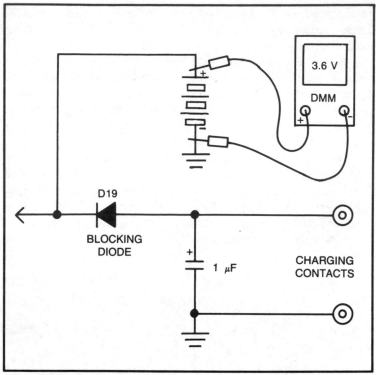

Fig. 15-21. Check the battery pack with the voltmeter at the battery connections inside the portable handset unit.

CHECK THE BATTERY CHARGER

The battery or charger might be defective if the battery will not charge or hold a charge for any length of time. Make sure the contact charging points are clean on both the handset and base unit (Fig. 15-22). Measure the charging voltage at the two shiny pins of the base unit. This dc voltage should be higher than the total battery voltage (3.6 V). In the Cobra Model CP-445S that I tested, the output voltage was + 8.69 volts without the handset in the charging well.

Actually, the battery-charging voltage is taken from the low-voltage power supply (Fig. 15-23). The charging voltage is switched into the circuit when the handset engages the charging switch. An isolation resistor, R2 in Fig. 15-23, is found between the charging switch and the dc power supply. Suspect a defective low-voltage power supply when no lights are lit on the base unit. The charging light will come on with the handset in the cradle. Check coil L208 and R2 (220Ω) with a normal base unit and no charging of the battery.

Clean the switch contacts (SW201A) for intermittent or no battery-charging voltage at the charging pins.

Measure the battery voltage if the LOW BATT light stays on all the time. If (1) the handset operates at a normal distance, (2) the voltage is up, and (3) the low-battery light stays on, suspect a defective low-battery indicator IC or transistor circuit (Fig. 15-24). It's possible the LED won't light up in a defective circuit with the battery down. Check the LED with the diode test of the DMM. Measure the supply voltage feeding the low-battery circuit. Replace IC4 if the supply voltage and LED test normal.

ERRATIC SWITCHING

Intermittent operation of either the base or handset can result from poor switching contacts. Spray the dirty contacts with the plastic extension tube inserted into the side or opening of the switch assembly. Move the switch back and forth to help clean the contacts. Replace the defective switch if it is excessively worn. Check the connecting wires, cable, and sockets for poor connections (Fig. 15-25).

NOISY OPERATION

The handset might make a rushing noise when first turned on. This is normal. Although the cordless telephone uses noise-free FM transmission for the radio communication between handset and base, it is possible for you to occasionally hear cracking noises from the

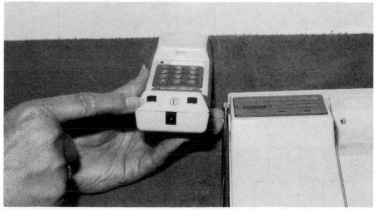

Fig. 15-22. Clean the charging plates or points on the handset and base unit with cleaning fluid or the rubber eraser of a pencil.

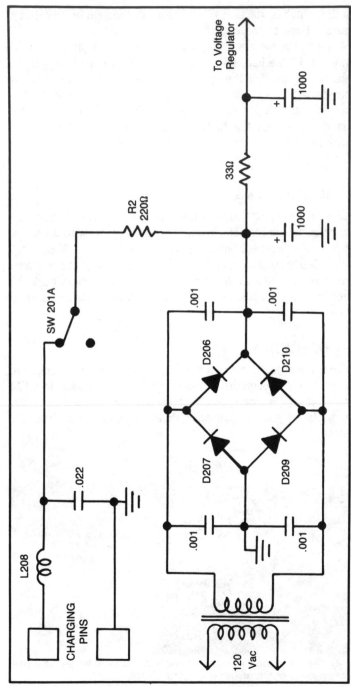

Fig. 15-23. The battery-charging circuit might be taken from the low-voltage power supply. Remember, the dc voltage at the charging pins of the base unit will be higher without a load (the handset in the charging position).

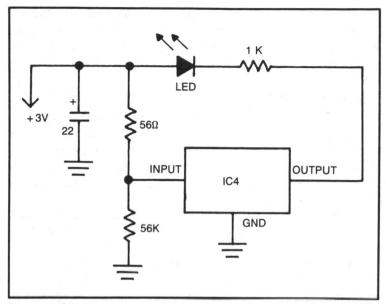

Fig. 15-24. Check the LOW BATT IC or transistor if the light stays on all the time.

base or static-like noises. Humming or buzzing noises might be picked up in the handset. These interfering noises can be caused by electrical video games, fluorescent lights, electrical shavers, appliance motors, or even electrical storms. Check for a noisy appliance nearby if the

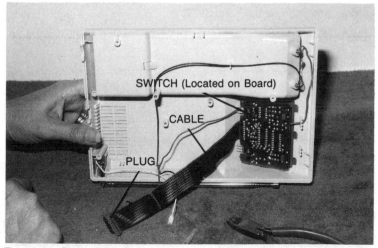

Fig. 15-25. Clean the switch contacts with cleaning spray, and inspect the connecting cable and plugs for erratic or intermittent reception.

noise is always present. Try moving the base unit to another location in the house. Change the digital coding if interference comes from another cordless telephone. Occasionally you'll have a weak and/or noisy call, so just re-dial the call for cleaner reception.

NO BASE OPERATION

Go directly to the low-voltage power supply in the base unit with a no sound/no lights symptom. Lightning or power outtage voltages during stormy weather can disable the unit. Take a resistance measurement of the power-line cord to determine if the transformer is damaged. The ac cable connects directly to the primary winding of the small transformer (Fig. 15-26).

Inspect the transformer and bridge rectifiers for burns or lightning damage. Measure the voltage at the positive terminal of the bridge rectifier circuit. If there is no dc voltage, suspect a defective diode or power transformer. Very low voltage at this point might indicate a leaky IC or transistor regulator circuit. Disconnect the input terminal going to the regulator and note if the voltage rapidly increases.

Low voltage from the power supply circuits might be caused by a leaky regulator or connecting component (Fig. 15-27). Remove the output terminal wire from the regulator. If the voltage increases, a leaky component tied to the regulator might be pulling down the voltage. Check the transistor or IC regulator for leakage if the voltage is still low. A defective filter capacitor can also cause low output voltage and hum in the transmission.

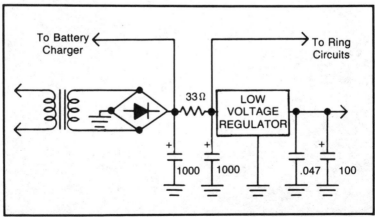

Fig. 15-26. Check for leaky diodes or an open primary winding of the power transformer with no or improper voltage at the low-voltage power supply.

REGULATOR TRANSISTOR ON U-SHAPED HEATSINK

POWER TRANSFORMER

Fig. 15-27. Test the regulator transistor and take accurate voltage measurements for low voltages at the low-voltage power supply.

DISTORTED OR MUSHY SOUND

Distorted audio out of the handset can be caused by the speaker or corresponding sound circuits. Check the output transistor with the diode test of the DMM (Fig. 15-28). Measure the voltage on all terminal pins if the audio-output IC is suspected. Turn up the volume and note any change in volume and distortion.

Although the handset speaker resistance might be quite high, another PM speaker clipped in it's place might indicate if the speaker is defective. Another method is to clip a pair of 32-ohm headphones (like those found in a personal radio or cassette player) in place of the handset speaker. Do not overlook a possibly dried-up filter capacitor in the base unit that is causing modulation distortion in transmission of audio.

WEAK SOUND

Weak signal or sound from the handset can indicate you are out of the range of the base transmitter. Try the handset in the same room as the base unit. Check the batteries for weak signal. If the audio is still weak, check the components in the output circuits of the handset.

BROKEN ANTENNA RODS

No matter how careful the handset or base unit is handled, sooner or later the portable handset will probably be dropped or

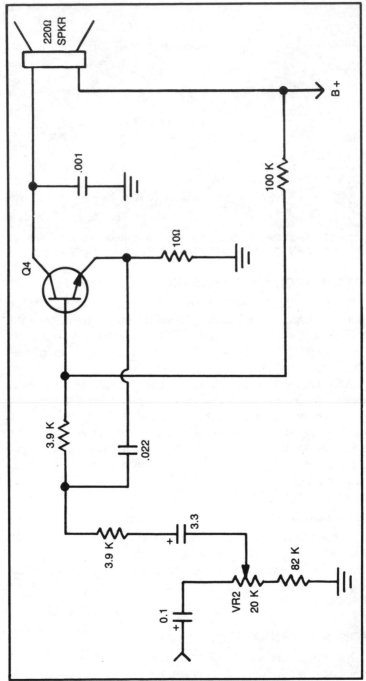

Fig. 15-28. Check the audio output transistor or IC for distorted sound.

Fig. 15-29. The small dipole antenna is very easily broken but can be replaced with the original or a universal antenna.

something could land on the base unit, breaking off or bending the dipole antenna (Fig. 15-29). Replacing the broken dipole antenna is not as difficult as it may seem. These small antenna rods can be replaced with the exact or universal replacements.

The cost of the original telescopic replacement varies from $3 to $5. If the regular antenna is not readily available, use a universal replacement. These telescopic rod antennas are similar to the small, portable FM radio antennas and can be picked up in most electronic parts stores. However, you might have to enlarge or reduce the mounting hole. For an enlarged hole, place a bead of white rubber silicon cement around the antenna for good appearance.

LIGHTNING DAMAGE

It's best to unplug the base unit when leaving for vacation or when a summer storm is brewing to prevent damage to the base and handset. Although lightning might be uncommon in your area, one strike is all that is needed to destroy a wireless telephone system. Lightning can strike nearby or directly on the power lines, causing a powerful surge of voltage that can damage the telephone.

If it is believed the base unit was struck by lightning, remove the bottom cover and survey the damages. Sometimes only a slight charge will damage the power transformer and bridge rectifier circuits. Lightning damage to only a few components may be repaired without too much expense. If either unit is excessively damaged, replace the whole unit. Check with the manufacturer if either unit can be replaced without the other.

WATER DAMAGE

If you accidently leave the handset outside or overnight on the window sill, it could be damaged by rain. Be careful not to spill water or any other liquid inside the portable handset. Any type of soft drink or liquor would be very difficult to remove from the circuit boards.

Remove the back cover and battery compartment lid if liquid is accidently spilled on the handset. Blow hot air from a hair dryer into the wet areas. Since most telephones are operated at very low voltages (3.6 V), component-to-board arcover breakdowns usually do not occur as they would in a high-voltage unit, like a TV. Allow the telephone handset to lay open for a couple of days to dry out before attempting to use it. Also, check the speaker for a warped cone.

NO BEEP OR RING

Usually both the base and handset ring during an incoming call. If the handset does not ring, test it next to the base unit for a signal (see Fig. 15-30). Check the speaker by clipping another one across the speaker terminals. These phones often use a small piezo crystal buzzer or transducer. If the speaker is not at fault, test Q5 with the diode test of a DMM.

OTHER PROBLEMS

Check the ac power and telephone connections to the base unit if it's not working. Is the handset power switch on? Be sure the antennas on both units are fully extended. Is the BATT LOW indicator on? Make sure the handset battery pack is charged. Do the security codes of the base and handset match?

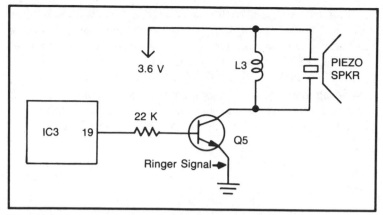

Fig. 15-30. Check the piezo speaker and transistor Q5 when the incoming signal has no beep or ring sound.

If you hear intermittent beep tones when you press TALK, you are out of communication range. Walk closer to the base unit and try again. If you do not receive a signal, you might still be out of range; if the range seems shortened, suspect weak batteries. The distance might be shortened when either the base or handset is close to a metal surface, such as aluminum or steel siding or tinfoil insulation. Relocate the base unit for better reception.

Fig. 15-31. Inspect the board if the base unit has been dropped or something has fallen on it.

Extensive roughing to the base or portable handset can produce a cracked or broken pc board. The telephone may be dead or intermittent. Remove the covers and inspect the board for broken areas (Fig. 15-31). Repair the board wiring with bare hook-up wire across the cracked areas. Check the cracked wiring under a magnifying glass. Set the ohmmeter on the low range (R×1) and recheck the wiring from one soldered point across the cracked area to another connecting component to check for good wiring.

16

Electronic Games, Doorbells, Calculators, Intercoms, and Battery Chargers

This chapter explores how to service five small electronic units used extensively in the home. Although they are small physically, we depend on them. Servicing an electronic game, doorbell, calculator, intercom or battery charger can turn out to be a lot of fun!

CHECKING ELECTRONIC TOYS

Today there are all kinds of electronic toys in the home from a simple baseball game to other very complicated and expensive electronic games (Fig. 16-1). It's very discouraging for a child or anyone else to receive an electronic game as a gift and after a few hours have it stop playing. These games should be able to withstand the wear and rough handling a youngster can give them. Some do and others don't, but here are some ways to check out that electronic toy before giving up and throwing it away.

Batteries

Improper installation of batteries is one of the major causes of problems. Check the arrows shown on the battery holder or look at the instructions to see how the batteries are inserted. Clean the battery contacts with a rough cloth before installation. This helps to keep the battery contacts clean.

Select high-powered alkaline batteries for these games. They will operate much longer under constant playing. When batteries age

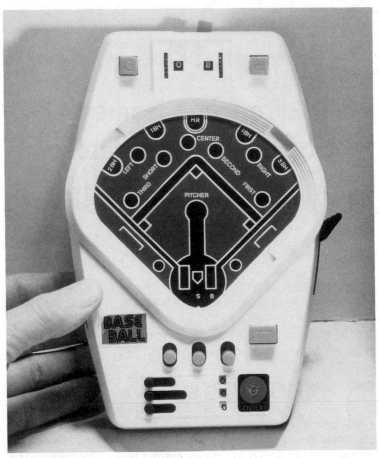

Fig. 16-1. An electronic baseball game made up of simple switches, contacts, and lights.

and begin to leak, they can easily ruin the battery contacts and all components around them. Remove all batteries when the electronic toy will not be used for several months.

If the batteries have leaked and corroded the contacts, scrape off all residue. Use a pocket knife to get at those difficult places. Wipe off the corroded terminals with alcohol and scrape some more. All battery contacts should be bright for good contact.

Visual Checks

After determining which sequence is not functioning, remove the bottom cover. Be careful not to lose any parts. Some of these components anchor to the bottom plate. Visually check the wiring and switches. Check for torn or open wiring. Very fine flexible wire is frequently used around the moving components (Fig. 16-2). The wires might break off where they are soldered to the rotating component.

Check for a broken plastic lever. A broken lever can be repaired with epoxy cement. Remove the two broken pieces and apply cement. Let the cement set overnight. File or grind down the lever so it will work freely. A drop of oil on the lever pivot bearing might help.

Broken rivets can be repaired with bolts or screws. Most moving components are held in position with a metal screw through a plastic bearing. Drill out the defective nut. Install a bolt and nut. Place a drop of solder over the nut area so it will not work free. Add a washer for free movement.

Switches and Lights

You will find a lot of switches, dial lights, and levers in electronic games. A dirty or worn switch might cause an erratic or dead condition. First clean up the suspected switch with cleaning fluid.

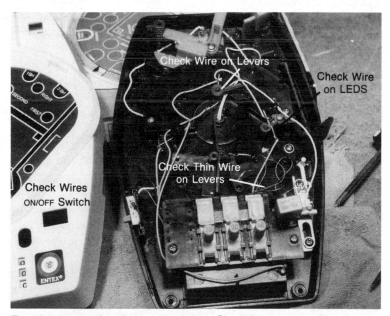

Fig. 16-2. Inspect the wiring and switches. Check for a torn or broken flexible wire coming from the moving levers and switches.

Work the switch back and forth to clean the contacts. Set the VOM to the R×1 scale to check for open switch contacts.

When a given light will not come on, suspect lack of voltage at the light terminals or a defective bulb. Check the bulb continuity with the VOM. Set to R×1 and check right across the dial light terminals. If an LED is used as an indicator, remove one terminal. Then check the LED as with any diode. You should have a low reading one way and no measurement with reversed test leads with a good LED. These LEDs can be obtained from any electronics store.

If the bulb has continuity but still will not light, suspect improper voltage at the terminals. Set the VOM at 15 Vdc scale. Measure the voltage across the dial light. Simply reverse the test leads when the meter hand goes in the wrong direction. Trace the wires to the power supply. They might go through several switches or contacts before connecting to the power source. Use the R×1 scale of the VOM for continuity tests.

The Power Source

Most portable games are powered by batteries. Simply measuring the battery source should indicate a properly applied voltage. Some of the larger games and TV games are powered by an ac adapter. The adapter plugs into the ac line with the dc plug inserted into the electronic game unit. If the unit doesn't turn on, suspect a defective dc source.

Measure the dc voltage at the male plug of the ac adapter. Visually inspect the plug. If the plug is used extensively, the cable can break off at the plug terminals. Good voltage indicates a defective plug, cable, or ac adapter. Check the dc cable and ac power cord for torn wires or breaks.

Check the small power transformer inside the adapter with a resistance measurement across the ac plug terminals; the ac plug should be removed from the power line. Use the R×1 scale and check the cord terminals for continuity. If open, suspect a defective primary transformer winding or cord (Fig. 16-3). Replacement of the transformer is too expensive, so replace the whole ac adapter.

Check both cables for breaks with the VOM set to the R×1 scale. Insert pins into each wire of the cable where the cable enters the body of the ac adapter. Check each wire from pin to male plug for continuity. Infinite reading indicates an open cable. A broken wire inside the cable has a tendency to stretch, so pull each cable wire slightly to find a suspected break. Repair the break by pulling back

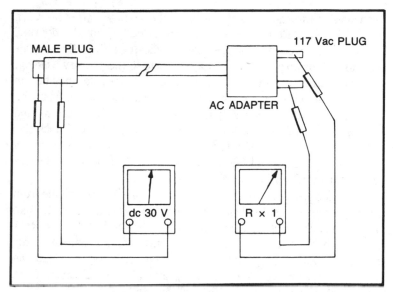

Fig. 16-3. Use the VOM to check the dc voltage source at the male plug. Check for ac cable and transformer continuity with the R×1 scale of the VOM.

the insulation and splicing in a piece of flexible hook-up wire. Solder and tape all connections for safe operation.

CHECKING ELECTRONIC DOORBELLS

The electronic doorbell can be serviced like any other electronic product in your home. Usually the regular or electronic doorbell causes very little trouble. Sometimes lightning or a change in power-line voltage can cripple the unit. Here are some ways to check the defective doorbell or chimes.

Outside Components

A simple doorbell or chimes might consist of a transformer, front and rear buttons, and chimes or a buzzer unit (Fig. 16-4). When both door buttons fail to make the unit ring, suspect defective chimes or faulty transformer. If only one button functions, suspect a defective doorbell button or wiring. Measure the ac voltage at the secondary of the stepdown power transformer. No voltage here indicates a defective transformer or no ac applied to the primary winding.

When the front or rear button will not operate the electronic doorbell, check the outside step-down transformer. Set the VOM to the 60 Vac scale. Measure the ac voltage across the secondary terminals of the transformer. Usually, the voltage varies between 10 and 18 Vac. Remove the transformer leads from the doorbell circuitry. Low or no voltage might indicate a defective power transformer or no power-line voltage applied to the primary winding.

If the unit is on continuously, suspect a shorted doorbell button or cable. Simply remove both front and rear door wires from the doorbell unit. If the unit stops, inspect the doorbell buttons and wiring. See if only one button will activate the doorbell. Check this cable and button for shorted conditions. When the unit is on continuously without either button attached, suspect a defective transistor or IC inside the electronic doorbell.

A defective front doorbell button might prevent the chime from ringing. Remove the doorbell button and all wires to the button. Take a continuity check of the button assembly. Set the VOM to the R×1 scale. Check the resistance across the button terminals. An erratic reading or no reading indicates dirty contacts. Try to clean the contacts with a pencil eraser. Next spray with tuner cleaner. If this doesn't work, install a new doorbell button.

The Power Transformer

A simple method to check the step-down power transformer is to take a small screwdriver and short the secondary terminals. Just touch the two terminals with the screwdriver blade. When the blade touches the terminals, you should see a small arc. Don't leave the blade across the terminals too long. Professional electricians

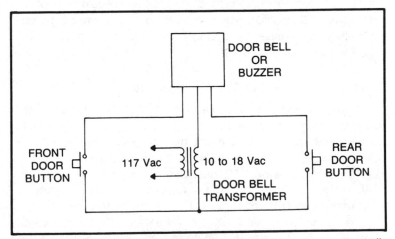

Fig. 16-4. Common wiring hookup for the standard chime or buzzer doorbell unit. Today many units have a chime mechanism.

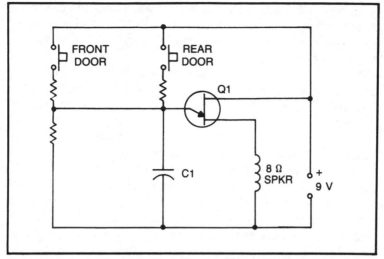

Fig. 16-5. A simple electronic doorbell unit might consist of several resistors, speakers, capacitors, and transistors.

sometimes use this method to check a doorbell transformer, however the best method is to measure the secondary voltage with the 60 Vac scale of the VOM. You should measure from 10 to 18 volts ac if the transformer is normal (Fig. 16-5). No voltage on the secondary might indicate an open secondary winding.

When no ac voltage is found at the secondary terminals of the transformer, suspect ac power is not being applied to the primary windings. To measure the primary voltage, take out the fuse supplying ac to the transformer circuit. These transformers are generally located in the basement. Be careful when measuring any voltages while standing on a cement floor. Stand on a wooden chair to take ac voltage measurements or when connecting and taping up the power transformer leads. Be careful and always shut off the ac power before taking any primary resistance measurements.

If the ac voltage is found at the primary winding, suspect a defective power transformer. Shut off the power and remove the transformer, and measure the primary and secondary windings. A short in the secondary winding usually opens up the primary winding. Replace the stepdown transformer if either the primary or secondary winding is open.

The Power Supply

The electronic doorbell might have its own power transformer or an outside one like any ordinary doorbell. Check the ac voltage at the secondary side at the doorbell unit. If the voltage is between 10 and 18 Vac, suspect problems in the low-voltage power supply.

Measure the dc voltage at the output of the diode rectifier. No voltage here might indicate a leaky or open diode. Visually inspect the diode rectifier. These diodes are the first thing to go when lightning strikes the power line. Remove one end of the diode for correct continuity tests.

Check for an open filter capacitor or defective zener diode. Shunt another electrolytic capacitor across the suspected one. There might be several zener diodes for voltage regulation. Check them the same way as any other diode. A voltage regulator transistor might be used with the zener diode. If a dc voltage is going into the transistor regulator and there is no output voltage, suspect a defective regulator (Fig. 16-6). Measure and compare all voltages to those shown on the schematic.

The Speaker

Most of the electronic doorbells have a speaker instead of chimes or buzzer. Remove the back cover to see the speaker terminals. If the music is distorted, the speaker cone might be warped. No sound can be caused by an open speaker voice coil. Remove one lead from the speaker terminal and set the VOM on the R×1 scale. Check the speaker for continuity. Besides a low reading on the VOM you should hear a click in the speaker when the test leads are connected to the speaker. If not, the speaker voice coil is open. The speaker impedance varies between 8 and 32 ohms. Check the service literature for the correct impedance. Most speakers can be obtained from a local electronics store.

The Amplifier

The electronic doorbell might have an IC or several transistors as amplifiers coupled to the small speaker. Check the amplifier the same way as any other audio unit. If a volume control is found, rotate the control rapidly up and down. Note if any sound is heard in the speaker. Touch the center lug of the volume control with a screwdriver. You should hear a low hum if the amplifier is operating (Fig. 16-7).

Before removing any transistor or IC, take a voltage measurement. Improper or low voltage readings might indicate a defective component. A leaky IC will usually have higher voltage

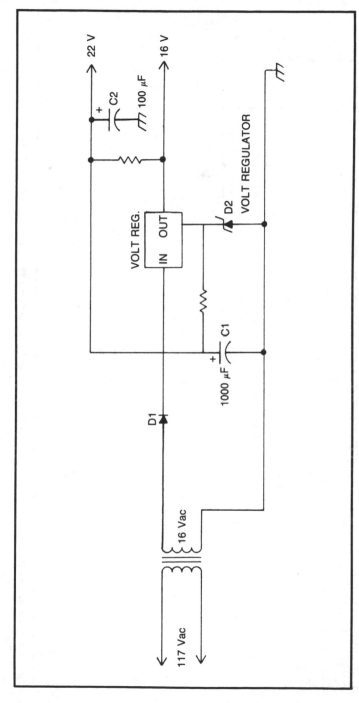

Fig. 16-6. The doorbell power supply might consist of a voltage regulator with zener diodes. A leaky zener diode can cause low-voltage output from the power supply.

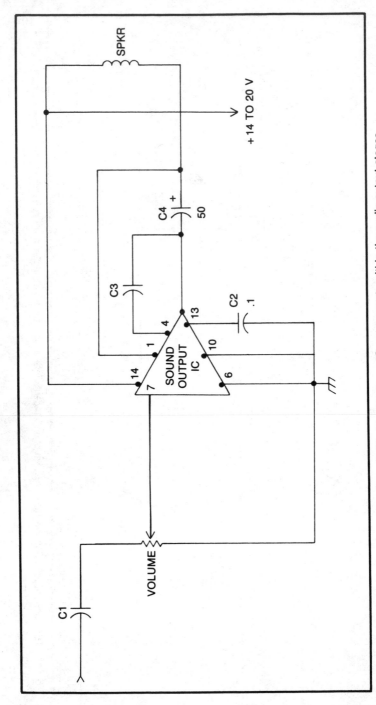

Fig. 16-7. In larger electronic doorbells, you may find transistor or IC components within the audio-output stages.

readings on several terminals. When you have higher voltages and no hum is heard after touching the volume control terminal, replace the defective IC.

The transistor amplifier can be checked by the same method. When improper voltages are found, remove the transistor and test it out of the circuit. In directly coupled circuits, it's possible to have several defective transistors. Remove each one and test it out of the circuit.

Electronic programmable electronic doorbell systems might have several IC and transistor circuits. Follow the manufacturer's troubleshooting procedure for locating a defective circuit in the counter, buffer, or generator circuits. Any defective components can be obtained directly from the manufacturer. If the electronic doorbell becomes extensively damaged by lightning or fire, replacement of the unit could be cheaper than sending it to the factory for repair.

PRACTICAL CALCULATOR REPAIRS

Most of the problems found in a small calculator are really quite simple. However, it seems they break down right when you want to use them. If your calculator is broken, try these practical calculator repairs.

Batteries

When the pocket calculator will not turn on, suspect defective batteries. You might find more than one battery in a pocket calculator. Always remove the batteries when the calculator will not be used for a long period of time. If you don't, the batteries might corrode and leak into the mechanism. Usually, the battery terminals get eaten away, causing poor battery connections. Regardless, it's best to replace the batteries at least once a year (Fig. 16-8).

Because the small calculator draws very little current, the batteries can be safely checked right inside the battery compartment. Measure the voltage across each battery (Fig. 16-9). Then measure the total battery voltage across all of the batteries. For instance, if there are four small AA cells, you should have a total of six volts across them.

Before installing new batteries, clean off the battery contacts and springs. If the contacts are corroded, scrape them off. Clean the contacts with sandpaper. Finish the cleaning process with a cloth soaked in alcohol. Also rub the new battery ends across the cloth for good contact.

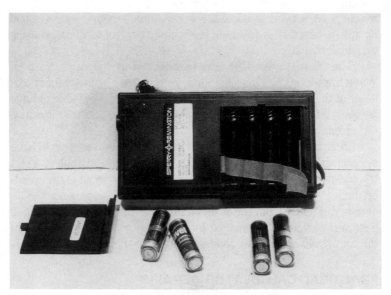

Fig. 16-8. Four AA cells are found this small calculator. Check and clean the battery terminals before installing new ones.

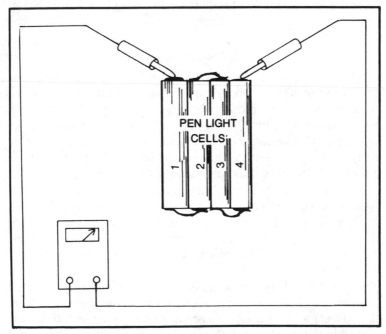

Fig. 16-9. Check the voltage across all batteries with the VOM. Usually the battery voltage doesn't exceed 6 or 9 volts.

Select fresh batteries that are leakproof. These batteries might cost a few cents more, but they are worth it. However, if these batteries are left in the calculator a year or more they could still leak all over the battery compartment.

Sticky Buttons

When plastic buttons work against another plastic surface, they tend to stick. Simply spray all the buttons with a silicon oil-base spray or apply light oil (Fig. 16-10). Let the oil run down around the button area and wipe up all excess with a paper towel. Work the buttons up and down so the oil will work into the sticky areas. Usually only one or two buttons seem to bind, but it's best to clean up all of them while you're at it. If one button still doesn't work, check for correct alignment. Sticky buttons are a nuisance when something important needs to be tallied up.

The Switch

If after the new batteries are installed and the lights still don't come on, suspect a defective ON/OFF switch. Some pocket or larger

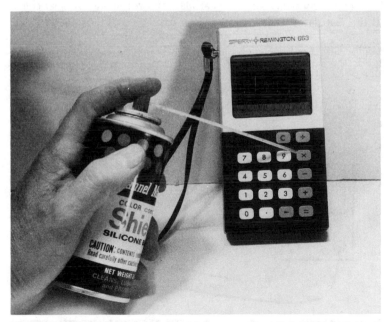

Fig. 16-10. When buttons seem to stick, spray with a silicon base or light oil. Work the button up and down to remove any residue.

calculators have a separate switch to turn the unit on and off. A dirty switch can cause erratic operation. Wiggle the ON/OFF switch while watching the display lights. Spray tuner lube or contact cleaner inside the switch area. Simply apply the spray from the top side. It's possible to clean the switch without removing the cover.

If the switch appears broken or has poor contacts, remove the back cover so you can check switch continuity. Switch the VOM to the R×1 scale and check for continuity across the switch contacts (Fig. 16-11). Be sure to remove the batteries. You should have a dead short across the switch terminals. If not, the defective switch must be replaced.

In some units, the whole keyboard must be replaced with the sealed switch assembly. You might be able to get one at your local electronics store. If the switch is mounted by itself, you can replace it with a small toggle or pushbutton type. Sometimes these small pocket calculators can be sent to the manufacturer for repair for a small service charge. Check the instructions that come with the calculator.

Checking Solar Cells

You might own a small flat calculator powered only by solar cells. If the calculator is dropped you can damage or break these small

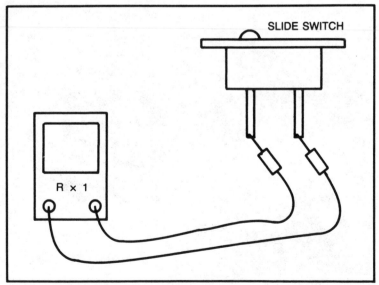

Fig. 16-11. Check for a dirty or open switch with the R×1 scale of the VOM. First remove all batteries.

Fig. 16-12. If no voltage is found at the terminals, a broken solar cell in the small calculator can sometimes be repaired. Simply wire the broken pieces in series if each cell is separate.

solar cells (Fig. 16-12). You can check the output voltage of each or all of the solar cells in series to determine if they are working. Most solar-cell operated calculators have four or six solar cells. Simply multiply the number of the cells by ½ to get the output voltage. With only four solar cells, the voltage should be from 1.85 to 2 volts. Measure the total voltage, as the cells are connected in series.

If the voltage is very low, suspect a broken cell. Locate the defective solar cell by measuring the voltage across each one. The cells can be repaired by soldering the broken cells in series in higher priced calculators. The very small or lower priced units might not be worth repairing.

Broken Connections

The calculator might not function after being dropped. Check for broken connections or a cracked pc board. First check the battery terminals for torn or broken connecting wires. You might find a poor battery spring connection. Make continuity checks with the VOM. Visually inspect the circuit board for cracks or broken areas. If a magnifying glass is handy, use it. Sometimes these fine printed-circuit wiring cracks are hard to locate. Check with the ohmmeter across the cracked wiring. Some pc wiring boards are sprayed with a clear plastic liquid that you will have to carefully scrape off to make resistance measurements.

When the cracked area is found, scrape it lightly with a knife. Clean off any coating on the printed wiring. Repair the broken connections with a piece of solid hookup wire. Tin the wiring with a low-wattage soldering iron, and lay short pieces of bare hook-up wire across each broken connection (Fig. 16-13). If a flexible plastic type board is used, repair each broken wire with flexible hook-up wire.

The Ac Adapter

Some portable and larger desk-type calculators are powered by an outside ac adapter. When the calculator will function on batteries but not on ac operation, suspect a defective ac adapter. Turn the calculator on and flex the connecting adapter cord. Usually a break in the cable occurs at the male plug or where the cable enters the adapter.

Unplug the adapter and check for dc voltage at the dc plug terminal. Set the VOM at 15 Vdc. Plug in the adapter and measure the voltage at the male plug. If the meter reads backward, simply

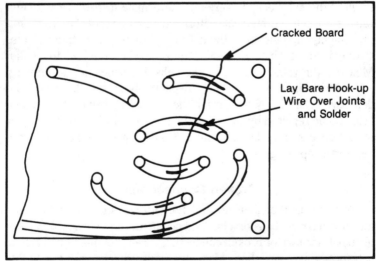

Fig. 16-13. Repair the broken wiring with regular hook-up wire. Scrape off all contacts. Tin the etched wiring, and then solder the piece across the broken area.

414

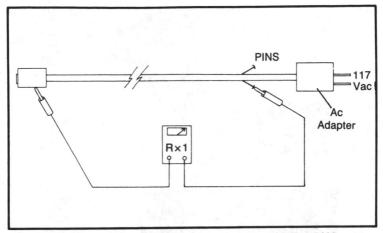

Fig. 16-14. Check the output voltage of the ac adapter with the 15 Vdc range. Stick pins into the cable right next to the ac adapter to measure the voltage.

reverse the test leads. No voltage reading might indicate a defective ac adapter or cable. Check the cable by placing small metal pins into both sides of the cable (Fig. 16-14). Check for voltage right next to where the cable enters the ac adapter by inserting the metal pins in each wire.

If voltage is found at the male plug of the ac adapter, suspect a defective female jack or faulty internal connections within the calculator. Check the female jack for dirty or poor wiring connections. Clean the contacts with alcohol or tuner spray.

A cracked or burned calculator can be repaired with epoxy cement. Repairing a burned cigarette hole or warped case might be a little more difficult. Epoxy cement usually requires mixing the contents of two separate tubes. Holes or large cracks can be repaired by placing masking tape under the hole for support. Broken corners can be repaired with a fiberglass repair kit (Fig. 16-15). After the epoxy cement sets overnight, sand down the rough edges.

REPAIRING YOUR INTERCOM

The home intercom unit can consist of one master unit (radio) with several remote units. Besides having music and communication that can be heard in several rooms, more remotes might be mounted at the front and back doors, or in the basement, the garage, or the den. A very simple intercom might have only one remote with the master unit. But alas, electronic intercoms don't last forever, so here are several different repairs you can make.

415

Fig. 16-15. Repair a burned or broken case with epoxy cement. Use a fiberglass kit for repairing large holes or cracked areas.

The Cable

When only one remote is dead but the others are normal, suspect a broken cable or wired connection. From single remotes, only two wires to master hookups are needed. But for callback, at least three wires are found in the connecting cable.

Simply disconnect the lead to the remote speaker. Mark down each wire terminal on a piece of masking tape. Stick the tape right below the speaker terminal connections and remove the speaker. Now connect or substitute the dead speaker in place of another remote. If only one remote speaker is used, clip the dead speaker directly to the master unit. If the remote is normal, check for a broken cable wire. The cable might have been cut or damaged when moving furniture or when having other electrical or plumbing work done in the house. Check the basement or attic for a broken cable. Visually inspect the most obvious places where the cable might be damaged.

Wrap all the bare wire ends of the speaker cable together at the remote speaker. Now use the VOM as indicator. Use the R×1 ohmmeter range and check for continuity between all cable wires (Fig. 16-16). If you have three wires in the cable, you should read a short between all wires. The wire without any reading is the broken one.

It's possible to have a defective remote without a broken cable. A nail might be driven through the remote cable, shorting out wires, or the wire could be shorted across a sharp furnace duct. To check this condition, remove the wires from both the remote and master units. Keep all bare ends apart. Now check for a shorted reading between any two wires. A low or shorted ohmmeter reading indicates a short between two wires in the remote cable.

Switch Contacts

Dirty or poor switch contacts can cause dead or erratic remote operation. After several years of use, the contacts sometimes become tarnished, causing erratic operation. If the speaker in the remote seems erratic, suspect a dirty switch in the master unit. Likewise, when calling in from the remote speaker, a cutting in and out of a person's voice can be caused by a defective remote call switch.

Remove the back cover of the remote unit. Spray tuner lube or cleaning spray on the switch contacts (Fig. 16-17). Move the

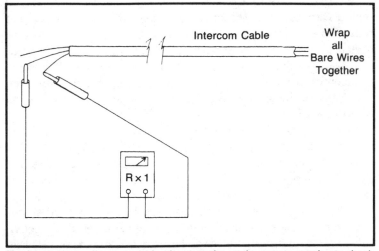

Fig. 16-16. Wrap all remote cable wires together at the remote speaker to check the continuity of the remote cable. Use the R × 1 range of the VOM and check for continuity at the master station. No reading between any two wires indicates a broken wire.

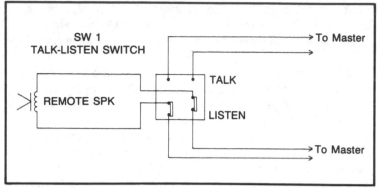

Fig. 16-17. The switch contacts might be dirty. Spray with tuner lube and work the switch back and forth to clean the switch contacts.

switch back and forth to clean the contacts. Replace the switch if worn excessively. While you're at it, clean the switches in both the remote and master units.

The Speakers

When the remote or master speaker becomes distorted or dead, suspect a defective speaker. If only one speaker is defective in a unit with several remotes and a master, check the defective speaker. A defective speaker in the master unit might be the problem if all remotes are distorted. Disconnect a suspected remote speaker and connect it directly to the master unit. With the two units close to one another, you should receive a loud feedback noise. To prevent this, separate the speaker and turn down the volume. If there is no feedback or noise in the remote speaker, suspect an open voice coil. Remove the speaker wires and check the speaker voice coil with the R×1 ohm scale of the VOM (Fig. 16-18).

Replace any speaker having an open voice coil. Be careful as some of these small intercom speakers use a 3.2-, 8-, 16-, or 32-ohm voice coil impedance (Fig. 16-19). Check the physical size and impedance in selecting a new speaker. Most of these PM speakers can be purchased at a local electronics store.

The small speaker might be distorted due to a dropped or frozen voice coil. Simply clip another speaker in place of the defective one—any size or impedance will do here for a distortion test. Usually outside speakers become distorted in a few years because of rain, cold, or hot weather conditions. If both speakers are distorted, suspect a defective amplifier system in the master unit.

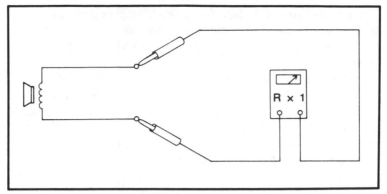

Fig. 16-18. Remove the speaker wires and check with a VOM, set to the R × 1 scale. Check for an open voice coil across the speaker terminals.

Visual Checks

Before tearing into the remote or master amplifier unit, make a few visual checks. Inspect all wiring connections on each unit. When solid bell wire has been used as a speaker cable, the solid wire frequently breaks off right at the mounting screws. Check to see if any wire terminals or connections are shorting out. A broken terminal strip could have pulled off one of the internal cable wires. Determine if either the master unit or only one remote is defective.

Fig. 16-19. The speaker might be only 2½ inches in small units. Replace with one having the correct impedance.

If all remotes are noisy, distorted or dead, suspect a defective master unit. When only one remote is not functioning, check that remote and its cable wiring. Make sure the master unit is plugged into the power line.

After removing the back panel of the master unit, visually inspect the chassis. Look for overheated resistors or transistors. Check for broken or cracked components. A broken connection of the volume control might prevent the amplifier from functioning. If the small intercom unit is powered by a power adapter, check for dc voltage with the 15 Vdc range of the VOM.

The Power Supply

The low-voltage power supply can have a full-wave or bridge rectifier. In smaller units, the master can be powered by an external ac adapter (Fig. 16-20), while in the larger wall unit, the power supply is built right in. Most power supply problems are from incorrect output voltage. The intercom could have been hit by lightning through the ac power line.

Check the output voltage of the power supply. Set the VOM to the 15 Vdc scale. With the ac adapter, measure the dc voltage at the male plug. No voltage might be caused by shorted or leaky diodes. Excessive hum in the speaker can be cured with new filter capacitors.

Remove the power cord and measure the resistance across the two prongs. No reading indicates the primary winding of the transformer is open. Generally, a shorted diode or bridge rectifier loads down the secondary, causing the primary winding to go open. Replace the transformer with a universal 10- to 12-volt ac type.

In the larger built-in wall-type masters, you might find a zener-diode-regulated power system (Fig. 16-21). A leaky zener diode can lower the output voltage. Remove one end of the diode and check

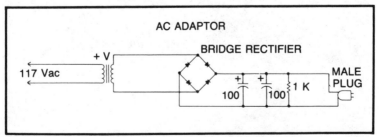

Fig. 16-20. The ac power supply adapter might have a bridge rectifier component. Check the output dc voltage at the male plug.

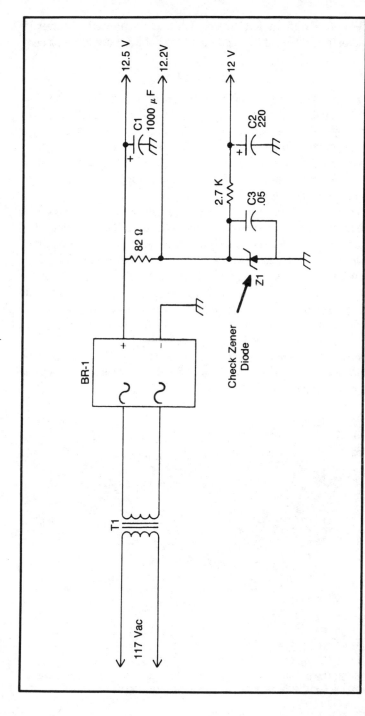

Fig. 16-21. A zener diode can be used for voltage regulation in large radio/intercom combinations. Check the diode for leakage when the output voltage is low.

421

the resistance with the R × 1 scale. Only one resistance measurement should be recorded—if the diode reads in both directions, replace it.

The Amplifier

You might have a combination of transistors and ICs in the small intercom unit. When you hear a loud feedback whistle with the remote speaker connected close to the master, this means that the amplifier section is functioning. Weak voice transmission might be caused by a defective transistor, IC, or coupling capacitor. A dead unit might be the sign of a shorted power supply or transistor in the amplifier section (Fig. 16-22).

To check out the amplifier, remove the back cover. Now plug in the master unit. The remote speaker doesn't have to be connected to check the amplifier section. Rotate the volume control wide open. Touch the center terminal with a small screwdriver blade. You should hear a hum in the speaker. If not, the amplifier is dead from the volume control to the speaker. Now signal-trace the amp with the clicking method. Apply the screwdriver blade to the collector terminal of the transistor or the output terminal of the IC (Fig. 16-23). If a click or hum is not heard, the transistor or IC is defective. Now measure the voltage on the IC or transistor. It's difficult to interpret voltage measurements without a schematic diagram, so check the instruction manual for one.

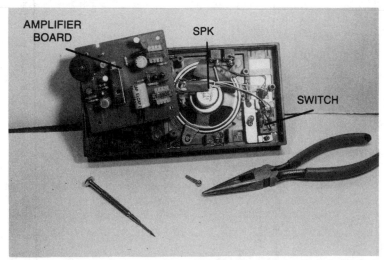

Fig. 16-22. The small amplifier might consist of transistors or IC components. Remove the transistors for ohmmeter tests. A suspected IC should be replaced.

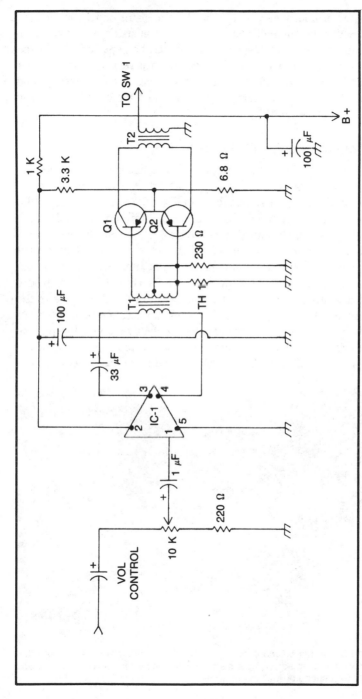

Fig. 16-23. The small amplifier can be signal traced with a screwdriver and click test. Start at the volume control. If a hum is heard here, the trouble is in the preamp section of the amplifier.

423

Low or improper voltages on the transistor or IC can indicate a defective component. Remove each transistor and give it an ohmmeter test. Any suspected IC should be replaced. While the transistors are out of the circuit, check the bias resistors for improper values. Check the continuity of each winding of the interstage and output transformers. Inspect the pc board for cracks or poorly soldered connections.

REPAIRING TUBE INTERCOMS

There are a few tube intercoms still existing in churches, homes, and garages. They never seem to wear out. The tube intercom can have from two to four small tubes. In Fig. 16-24, a 12AT7 and 50L6 GT amp was found in the Macco E-Z talk intercom. A simple slide, push-to-talk switch, and volume control are on the front panel.

Check the small tubes in a tube tester or conduct heater continuity test with the ohmmeter. The ac tube heaters are in series with a large voltage dropping resistor (Fig. 16-25). Measure the continuity across the heater pins with the $R \times 2$ K range of the ohmmeter. A low resistance measurement indicates the heaters are good, and an infinite reading indicates a defective tube. Measure the large dropping voltage resistor's value if the tubes do not light up.

Next measure the dc voltage on the plate and screen grid of

Fig. 16-24. In this Macco intercom, a 12AT7 and 50L6GT tube are wired in series with a voltage-dropping resistor from the ac power line. Check each tube heater for continuity with the ohmmeter.

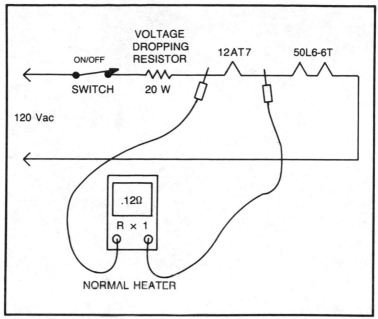

Fig. 16-25. A resistance measurement across the heater terminals of the tube might indicate the tube is open. If the tube heaters appear intermittent, place the ac voltmeter across each of the heater terminals and when the total line voltage appears, you have located the open heater.

the output tube. Suspect an open output transformer or voltage isolation resistor if there is no voltage. If the voltage is very low, check for a shorted output tube. Don't forget to measure the cathode resistor of the output tube if the tube is found leaky. The cathode resistor can be cracked open or burned with a leaky output tube.

Excessive hum with the volume turned down can indicate a dried up filter capacitor. You might have two different electrolytic capacitors in one envelope, rated at 150 volts. Shunt another known capacitor across each filter capacitor to eliminate the hum noise, and replace the filter capacitor when the hum decreases. These filter capacitors can be exchanged with single electrolytic capacitors if the dual units are not available. Spray cleaning fluid down inside the volume control if it is noisy.

FM WIRELESS INTERCOMS

The FM wireless intercom might consist of two or more units that plug directly into the power line. The intercom units are easy to use. Just plug them into ac outlets (Fig. 16-26). The messages

Fig. 16-26. The wireless FM intercom plugs directly into the power line.

are transmitted right through the house wiring. The frequency-modulated system is unaffected by line noise or interference, so each station remains silent until a message is transmitted.

Today wireless intercoms are constructed around several IC circuits plus transistors and diodes. The full-wave low-voltage power supply circuit might consist of two silicon rectifiers and a transistor/zener diode voltage regulator circuit (Fig. 16-27). Measure the output voltage at the emitter terminal of Q2.

The audio output circuits include a regular low-wattage IC circuit (Fig. 16-28). In the figure, resistor VR1 controls the speaker volume with one small IC as the audio amp. Capacitor C28 (47) electrolytic capacitor couples the audio signal to the small 3-inch, 16-ohm PM speaker. For greatest volume efficiency, the defective speaker should be replaced with a 16-ohm impedance speaker. Either a defective speaker, power IC, or speaker coupling capacitor can produce most of the service problems in the audio circuits.

Clean the slide or toggle switches with cleaning fluid or tuner lube to eliminate erratic or intermittent sound. Locate the defective IC or transistor with accurate voltage measurements (Fig. 16-29). Take the voltage measurements of a good intercom, and mark them on the schematic diagram for future reference, because most of these small intercom schematics do not have actual voltage measurements. Locate the leaky or open transistor and diodes in the circuit with the diode test of a DMM.

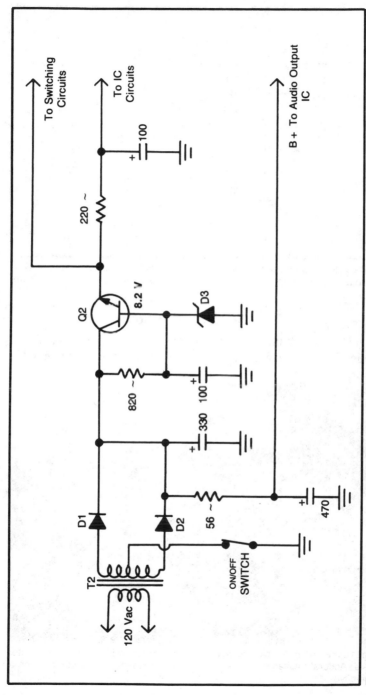

Fig. 16-27. A typical low-voltage power supply consists of a transformer, diodes, filter capacitors, and transistor/zener diode regulator circuit.

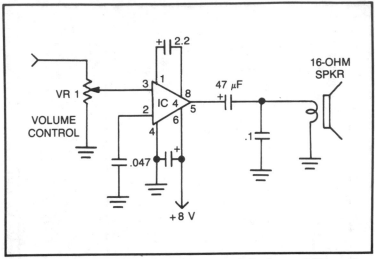

Fig. 16-28. A low-power IC provides adequate audio for the small PM speaker. Here a 16-ohm speaker and microphone are used in this wireless intercom.

The Radio Combo

The wall-mounted master intercom might contain an AM/FM radio. The radio master can be piped to any one of the remotes

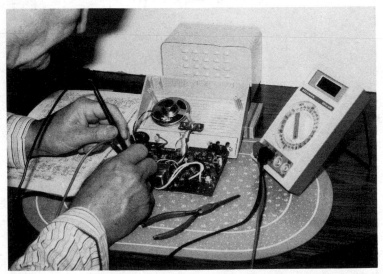

Fig. 16-29. The defective transistors can be located with in-circuit transistor tests. Accurate voltage and resistance measurements can quickly locate a defective IC.

throughout the house. If the music stops but the intercom is normal, suspect a defective radio system within the master unit.

Simply service the radio section as in any AM/FM radio (see Chapter 3). For instance, if the FM section is normal and the AM is dead, go directly to the AM converter or oscillator stages (Fig. 16-30). When the AM is functioning and no FM, go to the FM oscillator and mixer stages. In most of these radios the i-f section is common to both AM and FM stages. If both AM and FM stations are dead, check the i-f section. You might find one complete IC component is the whole i-f section. Improper voltage found on the i-f IC might indicate a leaky component.

CHECKING THE BATTERY CHARGER

One type of battery charger charges up the wet cell batteries, such as the one in your car or the common, small AA, C, D, and rectangular 9-volt cells. The other type charges specially made, rechargeable nickel-cadmium batteries, frequently used in portable radios and cassette players. Some of the small cell battery chargers charge one, two, or a combination of batteries at the same time.

Chargers designed for recharging wet-cell automotive-type batteries usually have a trickle charge rate with minimum risk of overcharge. This same type of battery charger can be used to recharge smaller capacity batteries found in snowmobiles,

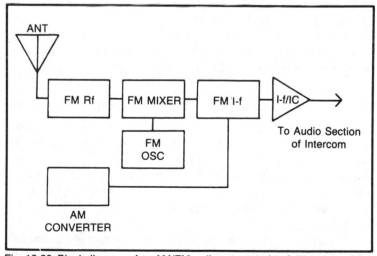

Fig. 16-30. Block diagram of an AM/FM radio connected to the same amplifier section of the master intercom unit. Service the AM/FM section the same as any other radio.

429

Fig. 16-31. The wet-battery trickle charger can offer a dual rate of charging. This charger has a 2- to 6-amp rate for both 6- and 12-volt batteries.

motorcycles, bikes, lawn tractors, and battery-operated lawn-mowers. Today, because there are many different vehicles using the wet battery, the charger might be used extensively and can of course finally break down. Any battery can be overcharged if left unattended for extended periods.

Some wet-cell battery chargers have a combination trickle charge of 2 and 6 amps (Fig. 16-31). Most chargers will recharge 6 and 12-volt batteries. Just flip or slide the switch on the front of the charger. The very low-priced wet-cell chargers might not have a dc ampere charging meter. When servicing, you might be surprised at the few components inside a trickle charger (Fig. 16-32).

Testing the Wet Cell Charger

You can often hear a low transformer hum when the charger is placed on a 6-amp or higher trickle charge. This indicates the transformer is operating. Temporarily brush the positive and negative alligator clips together and note if there is a spark. The dc meter pointer will hit the peg when this occurs and voltage is present. Do not connect the two clips together or you could damage the meter and silicon rectifiers.

Another test is to measure the dc voltage output of the charger. Without a load, the 6-volt charger has a normal 9-volt measurement. The dc voltage is around 15 volts with a 12-volt rate charger when

Fig. 16-32. There may be very few electronic components in a battery charger. This charger contains a power transformer, heavy-duty diodes, thermal cutout, and a current meter.

not connected to the battery. If the normal voltage measurement is very low, suspect leaky or defective silicon diodes.

Suspect a defective transformer, thermal cutout, open meter, defective switches, or leaky diodes without any charging voltages. The typical wiring diagram of a wet battery charger has only a very few components (Fig. 16-33). By switching tap terminals in the primary winding of the power transformer, a 6 and 2 dc amp charge is obtained. Note that the 6-amp tap has less winding resistance than the 2-amp winding.

Basically, the secondary winding of the transformer has heavy number 18 enameled wire (or larger), and the center tap goes to the grounded side. The black negative alligator clip connects directly to the meter, which is in series with a thermal cutout and the center tap of the power transformer. The thermal cutout will open after several seconds if a shorted battery or load is attached to the charger.

Check for burned meter wires or lugs if there is low voltage at the charger terminals. After many hours of operation, these wires and lugs may turn white and grey. Eventually a poor clamp connection can occur at the meter terminals. The damaged or open meter might prevent battery charging. Measure the meter resistance with the low ohm scale of the DMM. The resistance of the meter in Fig. 16-34 was less than .1 ohms. The internal defective meter shunt or winding might increase resistance, thus lowering the output charging voltage.

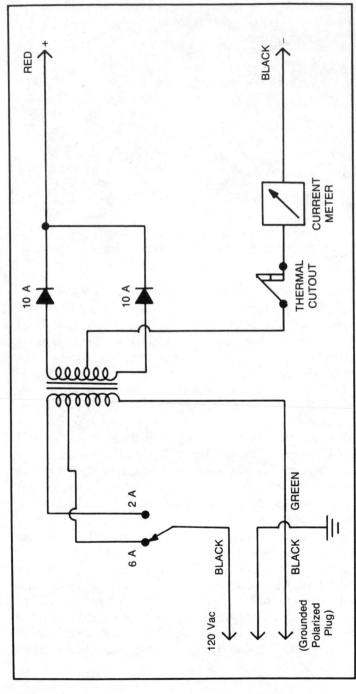

Fig. 16-33. Here is a typical wiring diagram of a wet-battery charger. Different voltage taps of the transformer primary provide the 2- and 6-amp charging rates.

Fig. 16-34. Measure the internal resistance of the chargor motor with the DMM. Here the resistance of the dc ampere meter is less than 1 ohm.

The defective thermal cutout could have open or high resistance points. The contact points might be dirty or burned. Damaged thermal cutout heating material can keep the switch points open and should be replaced. In emergency recharging, both the meter and thermal cutout components can be shunted if defective. However, they should be watched at all times so the diodes and power transformer are not damaged.

Defective Diodes

One of the biggest component failures in the battery charger are the diode rectifiers (Fig. 16-35). Today small silicon high amperage diodes are used, while in the older battery chargers large selenium rectifiers changed the ac voltage to dc. Check the selenium plates for popped off pieces in the old diodes. These selenium rectifiers can be replaced with silicon diodes. The silicon diodes might have overheated connections or become leaky.

Check the silicon diodes within the circuit with the diode test of the DMM. The normal resistance will be high, like the damper diode in a TV, and have a measurement in only one direction (Fig. 16-36). This particular silicon diode had a resistance of 482 ohms. A leaky silicon diode will have a low resistance measurement in both directions.

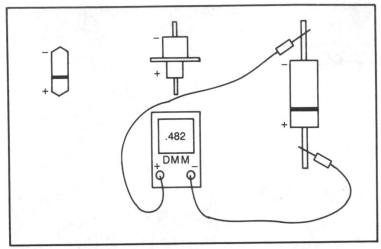

Fig. 16-35. Check the high-amp silicon diodes with the diode test of the DMM. A defective heavy-duty diode can get overheated and leaky.

Replace the defective diodes with the originals, if possible. Heavy-duty amp, stud-mounted diodes can be used if the original diode is not available. Always replace a 6-amp charger diode with a 10-amp diode, and a 10-amp charger with a 15-amp silicon

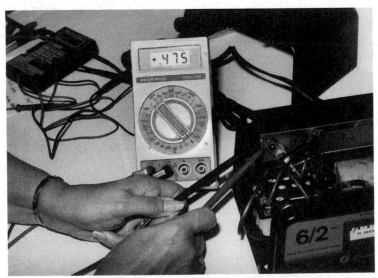

Fig. 16-36. The normal diode has a fairly high measurement, similar to that of the damper diode in a TV chassis. Both of the high-amperage diodes in this charger were over 475 ohms.

replacement. Single, 6-amp, 50 PIV (peak inverse voltage) diodes can be paralleled to acquire the correct amperage in low-amp trickle chargers. One half of a 15- or 25-amp bridge rectifier can be used as diodes in the rectifier circuits (Fig. 16-37). These high-amperage diodes are available at Radio Shack or most electronics supply stores. Bolt or clip the diode contacts together for good current contact.

Other Component Replacement

A defective power transformer should be replaced with the original. Try to get a replacement price for the transformer as it might cost more than a new battery charger. Mark down the color-coded wires before removing it. Cut the transformer leads at the switches and diodes ½ inch too long so they can be easily replaced. Bolt the transformer in place because the original might be riveted to the metal case.

Worn or poor alligator clips can be picked up from the hardware store. Use a heavy-duty power cord in place of the frayed or brittle rubber ac power cable. Replace the defective slide or toggle switches with 1.5-amp types.

Remember, there are a number of hazards involved in charging a wet automobile battery. Make sure the red alligator clip goes to the positive and the black clip to the negative terminal of the battery. The negative terminal is ground in American autos. The battery might charge up in reverse or even blow up if the polarity is reversed. Always follow the manufacturer's safety instructions when charging a wet battery.

Small Battery Chargers

The small units that recharge nickel-cadmium and heavy-duty batteries may be plugged directly into the ac outlet or else connected with an ac cord. Check the battery terminals for corroded or dirty contacts. Make a good contact by bending the battery terminals inward. Measure across the battery terminals for correct charging voltage. A defective diode can lower the charging voltage.

Measure the two male prongs of the ac cord or those found on the body of the charger for continuity (Fig. 16-38). If the transformer winding is normal, the resistance should be under 100 ohms. The transformer is defective if an infinite measurement is obtained. Check the ac cord or where the primary winding connections are soldered to the ac wires. You might have to break the plastic bonded case to get at the small components. Usually it does not pay to repair

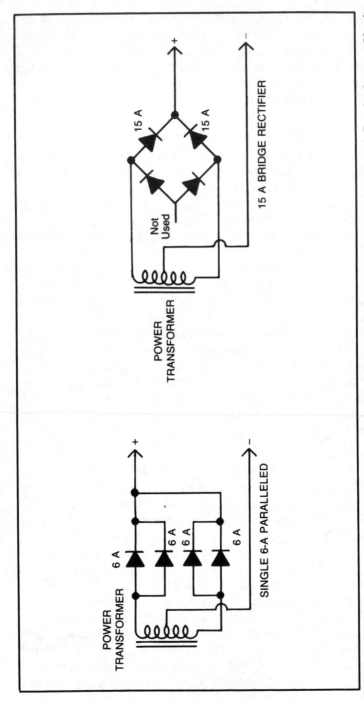

Fig. 16-37. High-amp universal silicon diodes can be used for replacements if the originals cannot be obtained. Regular 6-amp, –50-volt silicon diodes can be paralleled to get the correct amperage.

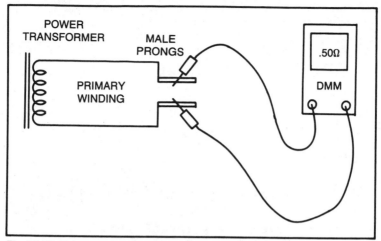

Fig. 16-38. Take a resistance measurement at the ac plug to determine if the primary winding is open. A normal transformer will have a measurement under 100 ohms. Infinite reading indicates an open winding or broken wire connections.

a small charger when it has transformer damage.

Check the small silicon diodes with the diode test of the DMM. If one is found leaky or open, replace with a 2.5-amp silicon diode. Make sure the polarity is correct in soldering the diode into the circuit. Measure the dc voltage at the battery terminals after repairs. Remember, the normal dc voltage will be higher than the battery being tested without a load or battery in the tester.

17

Where and How to Obtain Electronic Parts

After locating the defective component, securing and pricing the correct part might be a little more difficult. You should have no trouble locating components for American-made products, unless the factory has closed down or is out of business. Your biggest problem will probably be with Japanese products, but today even Japanese components are much easier to obtain than they were five years ago.

YOUR LOCAL DEALER

Before attempting to locate a component, get the correct part and model number of the unit. The part number should be listed in the service literature. If no literature came with the unit, take the model number and make of unit to your local radio/TV technician (Fig. 17-1).

The most logical place to obtain a component is from the local dealer who sold you the electronic product. If he doesn't handle parts, he can steer you to the proper channels to secure them. For instance, if your color TV is an RCA or Zenith product, go to an RCA or Zenith dealer. In most cases, exact replacement parts can be obtained from these sources. Exact replacement parts are easily installed and replaced without extra work. If these exact components are difficult to obtain, then other universal parts must be used.

THE MANUFACTURER

Write to the manufacturer if no local dealer handles or will or-

Fig. 17-1. After locating the defective component, take the make, model, and part number to your local radio/TV dealer. If you cannot locate the part number, he might be able to look it up in the various service manuals.

der your replacement component. Usually all American-made manufacturers will give you a list of various distributors in your state or locality. Because some manufacturers sell directly to dealers, they will give you a dealer listing. You might be able to buy directly from some manufacturers. It's always best to go through the correct channels. Try your local dealer or distributor and then go to the manufacturer.

Most Japanese manufacturers have a listing or telephone number of a service organization that secures and supplies components for their units (Fig. 17-2). By writing to them, they might supply various parts depots across the U.S. If your defective unit is not well known, it might be difficult to locate repair parts. You might have to substitute American or Japanese components.

If your local dealer has to order the special part, be prepared to pay for the component in advance. American-made parts can take from one to six weeks to obtain. Japanese components can take from two weeks to three months. Don't be alarmed if these parts don't come for eight weeks. In fact, some Japanese parts may not be obtainable at all. Some of these Japanese electronic units are only on the assembly line a week or two and are then discontinued.

Fig. 17-2. Check the service literature that comes with your unit for various parts depots or repair stations. These listings are sometimes found in the service manual.

LOCAL ELECTRONICS PARTS DEPOT

You might have several local electronics stores in your area. Generally, local electronic wholesalers will only sell to electronic dealers, although there are some that sell to anyone. Today you will find a Radio Shack in many towns. They have a variety of electronics parts from transistors to transformers. If in doubt, check the yellow pages of your phone book.

MAIL-ORDER HOUSES

Electronic replacement components can be ordered through the mail. These large mail order firms might carry your defective component.

All Electronics Corp.
P.O. Box 20406
Los Angeles, CA 90006

Dick Smith Electronics
P.O. Box 8021
Redwood City, CA 94063

ESI Electronics Parts & Accessories
3820 14th. Avenue
Brooklyn, N.Y. 11218

Fordham Radio
260 Motor Parkway
Hauppauge, N.Y. 11788

MCM Electronics
858 E. Congress Park Dr.
Centerville, Ohio 45459-4072

Radio Shack   Main Office
2617 West 7th. Street
Fort Worth, Texas 76107

Besides these you will find other electronics mail-order firms listed in electronics and science magazines. Some firms sell only new products while others sell both used and new components. If you still cannot find the part, try some of the firms shown in the Appendix. You might be able to locate some parts in a readers' exchange column in some electronic magazines.

SPECIFIC COMPONENTS

Some components are harder to find than others. First try to locate them through local electronics stores. Next try the manufacturer. All special components should be obtained through the local dealer or manufacturer. If you're not successful, try the mail-order firms. Common components are listed here in alphabetical order.

Antenna Coils

When a broken antenna coil cannot be repaired, the original should be obtained through the dealer or manufacturer. It's possible to purchase universal ferrite-type antenna coils through mail-order catalogs. Make sure the antenna coil will fit and matches the capacitance of the variable capacitor. You might have to touch up the rf trimmer capacitor for correct tracking of stations.

Capacitors

Let's take the variable capacitor first. This capacitor should be replaced with the original. Try to secure the component through a local dealer or the manufacturer. Since the mounting and size of the variable capacitor is very important, only the original part will do. After replacement, fine tune the oscillator and rf trimmer adjustments.

Most fixed capacitors can be found locally. In fact, they can be obtained just about anywhere. Standard capacitor tolerances are 10 or 20 percent. In older receivers, paper coupling and bypass capacitors are used. These capacitors can be replaced with polystyrene, ceramic, or mylar types. You might find 1 and 5 percent tolerance capacitors in rf and oscillator circuits.

Filter capacitors are aluminum electrolytic, which are polarized. These capacitors are used in power supplies and decoupling circuits. In tube filter circuits, the capacitor might have a range of 50 to 150 μF at 150 volts. In transistorized power supplies, the capacitor can vary from 100 to 2200 μF at up to 50 volts. Large capacitors with high capacitance might be difficult to obtain locally, but most common filter capacitors can be found anywhere.

Surplus or old electrolytic capacitors might not solve your filter supply problems. If the capacitor has dried out or has been on the shelf too long, a poor-filtering hum will be audible in the speaker. Most filter capacitors found locally and obtained from the larger mail-order firms are new. Large surplus capacitors might not fit in the required space, and they may not even have the correct capacitance and working voltage.

Capstan/Flywheel

The original part replacement should be used to replace a defective capstan/flywheel in a cassette or cartridge tape player. Since these capstan/flywheels come in different sizes, only the original can be used for replacement. If the capstan bearing is excessively worn, order both the capstan/flywheel and bearing support (Fig. 17-3).

To obtain the correct flywheel, check for the part number in the schematic or service literature. If the service literature is not handy, take the make and model number to your nearest electronics dealer. Usually the part number can be secured from the service manuals. In case the part number cannot be found, send the make and model number to the manufacturer. Generally, they will locate and send the correct capstan/flywheel. You might have to pay for the component before they ship it.

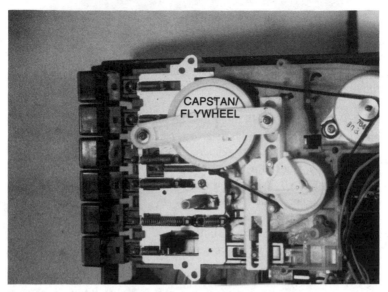

Fig. 17-3. You might find a defective capstan/flywheel assembly in the cassette or 8-track tape player.

Cartridges

Phono cartridges come in crystal and magnetic types. Most crystal units can be obtained locally. Odd or special types can be obtained from the dealer or manufacturer. Some magnetic type cartridges can be found locally, although the expensive units can be obtained only from the manufacturer.

When trying to locate the crystal cartridge locally, remove the cartridge and take it with you. Don't forget the make and model number of your phonograph. Some cartridges have the part number stamped right on the cartridge. Most crystal cartridges can be replaced with universal types. You might find a few magnetic types that cannot be replaced with universal types and must be secured from the dealer or manufacturer.

Coils

Coils come in various sizes and shapes. When a certain coil cannot be repaired, it's wise to get it from the dealer or manufacturer, especially, rf and oscillator coils for the AM and FM bands. This also applies to coils found in the TV chassis. Because these coils come in various shapes, usually only the original will fit. Some universal coils are available for radio receivers.

Diodes

Most power supply silicon diodes can be found locally. These filter rectifiers are common in the 1 and 2.5-amp types. You might find 3-amp or larger diodes could be a little difficult to obtain. Usually, these can be obtained from dealers and manufacturers. Most mail-order firms have a variety of selenium and silicon diodes.

Certain zener diodes might not be found locally, although larger electronics distributors and mail-order firms have them. Be sure to give the correct value of the diode. These zener diodes come in odd voltage sizes. Check for the correct wattage of the defective diode. Usually they are 0.5, 1, or 5-watt types. Do not use surplus diodes for crucial zener diode replacement.

Before suspecting a certain diode, remove one end from the circuit. Check for leakage in both directions. Remember, a signal diode should have a low resistance in one direction, and with reversed test leads, a high reading above 150 kilohms. Signal diodes, such as 1N34, 1N60 etc., are not crucial and can be replaced with universal types. Switching diodes found in the TV chassis should be replaced with exact replacements.

A normal focus diode found in the TV chassis will not read with any ohmmeter tests. If a reading is noted, discard the leaky diode. Most focus diodes are stocked in the average radio/TV shop. Universal types can be used to replace the defective focus diode without any problems.

Be careful when attempting to replace a damper diode. An ordinary diode will not work here. Make certain the replacement has the same or a higher operating voltage. These damper diodes are rated at 1300 and 1500 reverse peak voltages. A good silicon damper diode will have a very low ohmmeter reading in one direction and no reading with reversed test leads. Some of these diodes can be replaced with universal types.

High-voltage stick rectifiers are found in the transistorized black and white TV chassis. You will not have an ohmmeter reading even in the megohm scale when checking these diodes. Use exact replacements when replacing a high-voltage rectifier. If the unit is soldered into the circuit, make securely soldered connections. Cut the diode leads the same as the original. Apply a coat of rubber silicon cement around the various connections.

Dial Lights

Dial lights can be replaced with universal types. Most dial bulbs have the correct replacement number stamped on the shell of the bulb (47, 51, 57, 219, etc.). Bulbs with long leads must be replaced with ones having the correct voltage. Defective stereo light bulbs should be replaced with exact replacements.

Drive Belts

Always take the old motor drive belt and the model number when purchasing a new belt at the local radio/TV or music store. Lay the old belt flat and measure its length. If the belt is broken, fit the ends together, lay it flat and measure its length. Replace the defective belt with a new one having ⅛ inch less length. Remember, these belts can be stretched some without any damage.

Special round or square belts might have to be ordered from the manufacturer. Very thin cassette belts appear quite loose compared to cartridge motor belts. These small belts stretch rather easily. Special belts might have to be ordered from the manufacturer.

Integrated Circuits

Silicon integrated circuits can be replaced with originals or a universal replacement. There are several good replacement guides on the market. RCA, GE, Sylvania, and Motorola each have a replacement guide. *Master Transistor/IC Substitution Handbook,* (Nos. 1416 and 1616 by TAB BOOKS Inc. are good ones.) Simply look up the correct IC number in the replacement guide, then cross-check for the universal replacement (Fig. 17-4).

Some special IC circuits must be ordered from the manufacturer. When replacing Japanese units, either locate a universal replacement or the original. Besides the manufacturer it's possible to locate the correct IC and transistor from regular Japanese suppliers. You can find them listed in electronics magazines or check the Appendix.

Knobs

The channel selector and the ON/OFF knob of the TV set breaks the most because they are used constantly. When the vhf selector knob breaks and cannot be repaired, take the old knob and the make and model number of your TV to your local TV dealer. If the part number is handy, the new knob is easier to locate. There are several thousand different knobs, so a new knob might have to be ordered.

Sometimes the dealer can locate the broken knob by simply looking at the old one. Most uhf selector knobs are stocked items.

Fig. 17-4. Integrated circuits are now found throughout most home electronics products.

It might take several months to locate certain Japanese knobs, but the dealer should be able to locate a used knob for you.

After locating the correct selector knob, make sure all parts of the old knob are taken off the tuning shaft. Usually the small metal clip will stay with the broken piece. When you replace the new knob, the knob may not seat properly. Use a pair of needle nose pliers or a small wire to pull out the remaining pieces.

If you have been using a pair of pliers to rotate the tuner shaft, the shaft might have to be touched up before the new knob will fit. Generally, pliers will tear the flat corners and leave sharp edges, resulting in poor knob seating. Simply take a small file and touch up the round part of the tuning shaft. Then go over the flat side. If the new knob fits rather loosely, check for a missing flat spring. This should be inside the new knob.

Motors

Most cassette and cartridge drive motors should be replaced with exact replacements. There are a few universal ones on the market, but due to mounting space and hookup it's much easier to install the original. Before going to your local dealer or manufacturer, locate the part number and the make and model number of your set. If the part number is not available, check all numbers stamped on the motor belt area. Some motors have the operating voltage listed here (13.2 Vdc). Drive motors must usually be ordered since very few are stocked items (Fig. 17-5).

When trying to locate a phono drive motor for an older phonograph, check on the price. These motors can vary between $17 and $35. Look under the changer base plate for a model number. Usually the phonograph changer is manufactured by another firm. Take the model number of your unit plus the model number of the changer to locate the correct part number.

PC Components

When a pc board breaks or has poor wiring, you should try to replace the damaged board. If a TV is dropped and the board is damaged so badly that it's beyond repair, another board can be ordered from the manufacturer. Use either hookup or bare wire to repair

SMALL CASSETTE
MOTOR

Fig. 17-5. Here a small cassette motor is found in a compact AM-FM-MPX eight-track cassette stereo tape player.

a damaged board. On some poorly dipped boards, you may have to solder each connection. Some of these boards are rather expensive and it takes a lot of time to replace them. The receiver or radio might not be worth the expense involved. On small pc boards you might want to either repair or duplicate the board. There are many pc suppliers on the market. Photographic pc processing can be made from one of the kits offered by various manufacturers. All necessary materials and instructions come in the kit. Most mail-order suppliers carry one or more pc kits.

Picture Tubes

Before attempting to replace a picture tube in the TV chassis, check for price and availability. There are three or four large picture tube manufacturers in the U.S. that supply the bulk of picture tube replacements. You might find some smaller Japanese types that cannot be replaced with American types. These must be ordered directly from the manufacturer.

Take the correct picture tube number to your local dealer. There are several hundred different types, so look for the picture tube number on the bell of the CRT. Sometimes the number is with the tube layout chart on one side of the TV cabinet. If the tube number can't be found, take the make and model of your set to your local TV dealer. He can look up the correct number.

You might have several choices of different picture tubes with the same replacement number. You might find rebuilt picture tubes are less expensive than those with new glass. The rebuilt picture tube uses a new gun with old glass. All new picture tubes are quite expensive.

A new picture tube for a black-and-white portable can vary between $50 and $125. A new tube for a color portable can vary between $100 and $200 dollars. Because the picture tube is the most expensive item, you must determine if the TV is worth repairing. Usually rebuilt CRTs will last as long as new ones.

The warranty of a picture tube varies from 1 to 7 years. The original CRT is warranted for 2 years when you purchase the TV brand new. Most rebuilt picture tubes are guaranteed for 1 year. With some picture tube manufacturers, you can purchase an additional warranty for a few more dollars. Today you might find a manufacturer who will guarantee the picture tube replacement for the life of the TV receiver. Of course, the better the guarantee, the more you must pay for the warranty.

You might have to turn in the old picture tube when purchasing a new one. In many cases, the TV dealer is charged for the old tube. In other words, the old tube must be returned or the new tube will cost more money. To prevent injury, the old picture tube should be replaced and returned in the original tube carton. Always wear goggles when attempting to replace a picture tube.

Relays

You might find a defective relay in an audio or TV chassis. Usually these relays are of a special nature and should be replaced with original ones. Either remove the relay and take it to your local dealer with the correct model number or determine the function of the relay so it can be identified by your dealer. Don't try to use a surplus relay or you may waste a lot of time and money if the new relay will not function in the circuit.

Resistors

Most fixed resistors can be found at any electronics store. Large, low-ohm voltage-dropping resistors might be a little more difficult to locate. Of course, fixed resistors can be wired in series to increase the total resistance and wired in parallel to obtain a lower resistance. To obtain a higher wattage, the resistors can be wired in parallel.

Special fixed resistors should be replaced with originals. Today you might find special heat-retarding resistors in special circuits. A focus voltage-dropping resistor found in the older TV chassis are specially constructed and must be replaced with an original component. Variable Dependent Resistors (VDR) are a special breed and must be replaced with originals. Special high-wattage resistors found in the heater circuits of the hybrid TV chassis should also be replaced with the exact replacements.

Speakers

Today we find audio and TV chassis with many different speaker impedances. Some speakers are a special size and must be replaced with the original. However, most speakers can be replaced with universal types. Make sure the new replacement has the correct impedance and will fit in place of the defective one.

You might find a certain size speaker that only fits inside the car radio. A special car speaker might have to be purchased from the manufacturer. If a universal speaker will not fit, go to your local car dealer and order one or ask where the special speaker can be located. Car radio speakers have impedances of 3.2 to 40 ohms. Most car speakers have an impedance of 3.2 or 8 ohms. In some special transistor radios, the speaker impedance might be from 4 to 10 ohms. In fact, you might obtain a universal speaker with a 10, 20, or 40 ohm voice coil hookup. Most Japanese speakers have an impedance of 8 or 10 ohms.

Speakers located in the console TV can be from 3.2 to 8 ohms, while in the portable, and new TV consoles you might find 8 to 45-ohm speakers. Some of the American TV receivers have a 32-ohm speaker in both console and portable cabinets. Although, the majority of Japanese TVs have an 8-ohm speaker, you might have a 40-ohm, 3½-inch speaker in some small screen receivers.

Large audio tape-player receivers have a combination of speakers in the speaker cabinet. You might want to replace these units with original types. Remember, when replacing a defective speaker always use the correct voice-coil impedance, wattage, and size. Universal speakers can be found at your local electronics dealer or music sound stores.

Sockets

Most tube sockets can be purchased from your local electronics dealer or appliance store. Special focus or damper tube sockets must be replaced with original or universal-type sockets with high-voltage breakdown tolerance. You should never replace a damper or focus tube socket with any other type of tube socket. Picture tube sockets should be replaced with the manufacturer's original CRT harness.

Many of the audio sockets and plugs can be replaced with universal sockets. You might have to change the wiring line-up, but universal sockets and plugs can be used without any difficulty in radio equipment. If the original sockets are of the shielded variety, replace them with shielded sockets. Audio sockets and connections can be found at any local audio or music store.

Solenoids

Most solenoid and relay components are found in the cassette and cartridge-type players. If the solenoid or relay cannot be repaired, order an exact replacement. Usually the solenoid in the auto cassette or cartridge player is jammed in a small space and only the original will fit in this small area. Although some of the channel-changing solenoids found in the cartridge-type players might be manufactured by other firms, it's best to obtain the component from the manufacturer of your unit (Fig. 17-6).

Switches

You shouldn't have any problem locating ON/OFF switches. ON/OFF switches used at the rear of a volume control can be purchased from your local dealer. In some models, you might have enough room to install a universal replacement. Special ON/OFF switches should be replaced with exact replacements. Some manual or automatic channel-changing switches for tape players might be difficult to locate. It's possible to replace most push-type manual tape switches with any universal replacement. But automatic channel switches should be exact replacements because the mounting could be different.

Just about all function switches should be replaced with exact replacements, especially the pushbutton or wafer types. Do not

Fig. 17-6. Power solenoids in a compact tape recorder. One is used to switch on the ac power while the other applies dc voltage to the other circuits.

attempt to replace them with another type. Generally, there are several sets of wafer switches located on one shaft and these cannot be interchanged.

If a defective ON/OFF switch is located on the rear of a function switch, it's possible to keep the rotary wafer switch intact and replace the ON/OFF switch with either a pushbutton or rotary switch. The new switch will of course have to be mounted somewhere on the outside of the cabinet. When one section is defective in a pushbutton switch, usually the whole assembly must be replaced. This is especially true with all switches mounted on one mounting bar. If the switches are individually mounted on a pc board, they can be replaced separately. Order the original when replacing pushbutton switch assemblies.

Tape Heads

Try to replace a defective eight-track stereo tape head with the original one. There are a few universal replacements on the market, but you may encounter mounting problems. Replace only with a universal replacement when the original is not available. Remember, a four channel, eight-track stereo tape head is different from an eight channel. After replacing the eight-track stereo tape head, the head should be aligned for height and azimuth and then demagnetized.

Cassette tape heads come in monaural and stereo. Most small portable cassette players have monaural tape heads. It's possible to interchange and also replace the monaural cassette tape head with other heads. Be very careful when replacing the stereo cassette head with a universal one. Sometimes with these universal replacements, the common terminal is grounded inside the metal case and will not work in ungrounded cassette input circuits. Usually azimuth alignment is only needed when replacing a cassette tape head.

Tone Arms

Practically any piece on the tonearm (or the whole tonearm) must be replaced with an exact replacement. The two plastic end pieces found on most tonearms can be replaced individually, but you might find that the cost of the whole tonearm is cheaper than purchasing each piece.

Since there are only a half-dozen different phonograph manufacturers that supply turntables, it's possible to interchange tonearms if the component is not available from your manufacturing source. In this case, order the defective tone arm from the manufacturer who supplied the turntable.

Transformers

If the original power transformer is available, always use an exact replacement. Not only will you save time in mounting, but the same color-coded wires can be used. It's a lot easier to replace the defective power transformer with the original.

If the manufacturer is out of business or a special transformer cannot be located, then use a universal replacement. Small power transformers found in compact tape player receivers can be replaced with universal types. You might find the size of the universal power transformer is too large. Make sure the secondary voltage is the same with adequate current capacity.

Small power transformers can be substituted from one model to another. Select another model from a well-known manufacturer and compare the voltage and current ratings. Usually the sizes of these transformers are similar (Fig. 17-7).

Power transformers for TV receivers should be replaced with the original. Before ordering the replacement transformer, check the price. These power transformers are not cheap. You might want

Fig. 17-7. A small power transformer steps down the ac voltage for this small tape player.

to trade the TV in if it's very old. When original, large, power transformers are not available, take the make and model number of your set to your local dealer. Let him check for a universal power transformer replacement.

Besides the power transformer, you will find flyback, audio, vertical interstage, and oscillator transformers located in the various electronic units you might have around the house. Before replacing a flyback or horizontal output transformer, check the price of the replacement. Some of these horizontal-output transformers are rather expensive. If an exact replacement is not available, try a universal replacement. You might want to have the high-voltage components replaced by your radio/TV technician.

Transistor interstage and audio-output transformers should be replaced with originals. They might be difficult to find for certain Japanese models. If this is the case, take the unit to your local dealer and see if he can locate one for you. It's rare, but possible, to locate a universal audio transformer for replacement.

Vertical-output transformers found in the TV chassis should be replaced with the originals. Take the make and model number of your set to your local dealer. If the part number is handy, take this along to quickly identify the defective transformer. Because vertical transformers do not usually cause many problems, you might have to wait a few weeks to get the replacement.

Transistors

Today transistors are easily purchased and replaced. Only a few years ago certain Japanese transistors were difficult to locate. The original Japanese transistors can be secured through a mail-order electronics parts house if they cannot be purchased locally. Most American transistors can be located through your local dealer.

When the original transistor cannot be located, try a universal replacement. Most large electronics manufacturers have cross-reference guides, such as RCA, General Electric, Sylvania, Workman, and others. If you do not have any of these transistor reference guides, take the defective transistor part number of the transistor to your local radio/TV dealer and he will look it up for you. In fact, he might have a universal replacement in stock.

Tubes

Radio or TV tubes can usually be found easily. Your local grocery or drugstore might even have a tube tester with a stock of tubes, but if you want your tubes tested under actual conditions, take them to your local radio/TV dealer. Stay away from off-brand tubes. You might save several dollars, but they may not work in a special TV circuit.

Almost any type replacement tube will function in a table radio. Of course, the antique radio tube might be a little more difficult to find. Check locally with your radio/TV dealer if he has been in the business for many years. Some antique radio suppliers are listed in electronics magazines.

Volume Controls

Most radio volume controls can be replaced with universal types. The TV control should be replaced with the original, especially if a certain type ON/OFF switch is found at the rear of the control. When an ON/OFF switch is not located on the back of a volume control in the TV receiver, it's possible to use a universal-type control. These controls may be purchased at most electronics part stores.

Replace the volume controls in the stereo chassis with the originals. Usually the stereo volume control is a dual unit and might also contain special rear-mounted switches. When replacing the volume control in the automotive eight-track stereo player, you might find a control with dual volume, dual tone, and an automatic or manual channel selector switch. In many compact stereo models, the volume and tone controls can be sliding types and should be replaced with the exact replacements.

SUMMARY

To properly locate a defective component, take the part with make, model, and part number to your local radio/TV dealer. If he sold you the unit or sells the same brand, he most likely has the part in stock or can locate it for you. Next check with the manufacturer of your unit. He can tell you where to locate the part and even repair the unit, if needed. When both of these sources are exhausted, try large electronics stores in larger cities and mail-order houses.

Sources of Electronic Components

Mail-Order Electronic Components

ACE Electronics
5400 Mitchelldale
Houston, TX 77092

Active Electronics Sales Corp.
12 Mercer Rd.
Natick, MA 01701

Aldelco
228 E. Babylon Tpk.
Merrick, NY 11566

B&F Enterprises
119 Faster St.
Peabody, MA 01960

Bullet Electronics
P.O. Box 1944
Dallas, TX 75219

Calectro-GC Electronics
Rockford, IL 61101

Chaney Electronics
P.O. Box 3047
Scottsdale, AZ 85257

Digi-Key
P.O. Box 677
Thief River Falls, MN 56701

Electronic Dist., Inc.
4900 N. Elston
Chicago, IL 60630

ETCO Electronic
521 Fifth Ave.
New York, NY 10017

Herback and Roderman
P.O. Box 188
Bridgeport, PA 19405

Integrated Electronics
540 Weddell Dr.
Sunnyvale, CA 94086

John Meshna, Inc.
P.O. Box 62
East Lynn, MA 01904

Olson Electronics
2605 Forge St.
Akron, OH 44327

Poly Paks
P.O. Box 942
South Lynnfield, MA 01904

Radio Hut
P.O. Box 401247
Dallas, TX 75238

Radio Shack
Check your own city

Ramsey Electronics
P.O. Box 4072
Rochester, NY 14610

Surplus Electronics Corp.
7244 NW 54th St.
Miami, FL 33166

Electronic Firms Listed in Various Electronic Magazines

Active Electronic
   Sales Corp.
P.O. Box 1035
Framington, MA 01701

All Electronic Corp.
905 So. Vermont Ave.
Los Angeles, CA 90006

Chaney Electronics
P.O. Box 27038
Denver, CO 80227

Delta Electronics
P.O. Box 2
7 Oakland St.
Amesbury, MA 01913

Dick Smith Electronics
P.O. Box 8021
Redwood City, CA 94063

Digi-Key
P.O. Box 677
Thief River Falls,
   MN 56701

ESI Electronics
3820 14th Ave.
Brooklyn, NY 11788

Fordham
955 Conklin St.
Farmingdale, NY 11735

Formula International, Inc.
12603 Crenshaw Blvd.
Hawthorne, CA 90250

International Electronics Unlimited
225 Broadway
Jackson, CA 95642

Poly-Paks
P.O. Box 942
South Lynnfield, MA 01404

Popular Components
1145 Walt Whitman Road
P.O. Box 866
Melville, NY 11747

Solid-State Sales
P.O. Box 740
Sommerville, MA 02143

Transistors and ICs—American and Japanese

Ancrona Corp.
P.O. Box 2208
Culver City, CA 90230

Circuit Specialists
P.O. Box 3047
Scottsdale, AZ 85257

Digi-Key
P.O. Box 677
Thief River Falls, MN 56701

Frye-Suea Inc.
P.O. Box 40325
Cincinnati, OH 45240

Hanifan Electronics
P.O. Box 188
Bridgeport, PA 19405

International Components Corp.
P.O. Box 1837
Columbia, MO 65205

Jameco Electronics
1021 Howard St.
San Carlos, CA 94070

MCM Audio, Inc.
639 Watervliet Ave.
Dayton, OH 45420

Ora Electronics
7241 Canby Ave.
Reseda, CA 91335

Quest Electronics
P.O. Box 44305
Santa Clara, CA 95054

Solid-State Sales
P.O. Box 74A
Sommerville, MA 02143

Index

Index

Edited by Lisa A. Doyle

Other Bestsellers of Related Interest

HOME WIRING FROM START TO FINISH
—Robert W. Wood

With this do-it-yourselfer's manual on installing and repairing electrical wiring, you can safely and successfully wire an entire residence. More than 421 two-color illustrations and photographs appear throughout the book, making it easy to identify components and follow Wood's step-by-step directions. It's a good introductory text for anyone interested in pursuing an electrician's license. For personal wiring jobs in your own home, this guide will make sure you pass inspection every time. 272 pages, 421 illustrations. Book No. 3262, $17.95 paperback, $26.95 hardcover

TROUBLESHOOTING AND REPAIRING SOLID-STATE TVs
—Homer L. Davidson

Packed with case study examples, photos of solid-state circuits, and circuit diagrams. You'll learn how to troubleshoot and repair all the most recent solid-state TV circuitry used by the major manufacturers of all brands and models of TVs. This workbench reference is filled with tips and practical information that will get you right to the problem! 448 pages, 516 illustrations. Book 2707, $17.95 paperback only

TROUBLESHOOTING AND REPAIRING VCRs
2nd Edition—Gordon McComb

This book has helped more than 80,000 VCR owners keep their machines working at peak performance. With this book and a basic set of tools, you can handle most VCR problems quickly and easily—from simple parts cleaning and lubrication to repairing power supply and circuitry malfunctions. This revised second edition updates the best-selling original volume with the most recent technological advances. 400 pages, 186 illustrations. Book No. 3777, $18.95 paperback, $29.95 hardcover

TROUBLESHOOTING AND REPAIRING CAMCORDERS
—Homer L. Davidson

This superb troubleshooting guide shows you how to repair any brand of VHS, VHS-C, Beta, or 8-millimeter video camera on the market today. Davidson provides clear instructions along with diagrams and service literature from a wide variety of manufacturers, plus hundreds of schematics to speed diagnostics, and repair. Some of the many topics covered include cleaning and lubricating camcorders, system control circuits, audio circuits and microphones, and the various motors in a camcorder. 544 pages, 606 illustrations. Book No. 3337, $22.95 paperback only

ALARMS: 55 Electronic Projects and Circuits
—Charles D. Rakes

Make your home or business a safer place to live and work—for a price you can afford. Almost anything can be monitored by an electronic alarm circuit—from detecting overheating equipment to low fluid levels, from smoke in a room to an intruder at the window. This book shows you the variety of alarms that are available. There are step-by-step instructions, work-in-progress diagrams, troubleshooting tips, and advice for building each project. 178 pages, 150 illustrations. Book No. 2996, $13.95 paperback only

THE TALKING TELEPHONE—and 14 Other Custom Telephone
Projects—Steve Sokolowski

Make an electronic lock that prevents unauthorized phone calls . . . add a music-on-hold adapter . . . make a phone "speak" numbers for the visually impaired . . . even burn a PROM for a character display. These easy and inexpensive projects let you totally customize your telephone. Many of these devices are exclusive to this book—you can't buy a commercially made version anywhere! 352 pages, 316 illustrations. Book No. 3571, $17.95 paperback, $25.95 hardcover

HOW TO DRAW SCHEMATICS AND DESIGN CIRCUIT BOARDS
WITH YOUR IBM PC® —Steve Sokolowski

The author shows how, by using his programs and the directional arrow on the keyboard, you can draw lines, circles, and schematic symbols with your IBM PC. To get you started the author begins with an overview of the designer programs and what to expect from each. Topics covered include loading MS-DOS, designing PCBs, loading Graphic Utility, spacing layout components, etching your own board, and using Designer Options. 188 pages, 93 illustrations. Book No. 3034, $13.95 paperback only

500 ELECTRONIC IC CIRCUITS WITH PRACTICAL
APPLICATIONS—James A. Whitson

More than just an electronics book that provides circuit schematics or step-by-step projects, this complete sourcebook provides both practical electronics circuits AND the additional information you need about specific components. You will be able to use this guide to improve your IC circuit-building skills as well as become more familiar with some of the popular ICs. 336 pages, 600 illustrations. Book No. 2920, $24.95 paperback, $29.95 hardcover

OSCILLATORS SIMPLIFIED, with 61 Projects
—Delton T. Horn

Pulling together information previously available only in bits and pieces from a variety of resources, Horn has organized this book according to the active devices around which the circuits are built. You'll find discussion on dedicated oscillator integrated circuits (ICs), digital waveform synthesis, phase locked loop (PLL), and plenty of practical tips on troubleshooting signal generator circuits. 238 pages, 180 illustrations. Book No. 2875, $11.95 paperback, $17.95 hardcover

TROUBLESHOOTING AND REPAIRING SOLID-STATE TVs
—Homer L. Davidson

Packed with case study examples, photos of solid-state circuits, and circuit diagrams. You'll learn how to troubleshoot and repair all the most recent solid-state TV circuitry used by the major manufacturers of all brands and models of TVs. This workbench reference is filled with tips and practical information that will get you right to the problem! 448 pages, 516 illustrations. Book No. 2707, $17.95 paperback only

Prices Subject to Change Without Notice.

Look for These and Other TAB Books at Your Local Bookstore

To Order Call Toll Free 1-800-822-8158
(in PA, AK, and Canada call 717-794-2191)

or write to TAB BOOKS, Blue Ridge Summit, PA 17294-0840.

Title	Product No.	Quantity	Price

☐ Check or money order made payable to TAB BOOKS

Charge my ☐ VISA ☐ MasterCard ☐ American Express

Acct. No. _____ Exp. _____

Signature: _____

Name: _____

Address: _____

City: _____

State: _____ Zip: _____

TAB BOOKS catalog free with purchase; otherwise
send $1.00 in check or money order and receive
$1.00 credit on your next purchase.

*Orders outside U.S. must pay with international
money order in U.S. dollars.*

**TAB Guarantee: If for any reason you are not
satisfied with the book(s) you order, simply
return it (them) within 15 days and receive a
full refund.**   **BC**

Subtotal $ _____

Postage and Handling
($3.00 in U.S.,
$5.00 outside U.S.) $ _____

Add applicable state
and local sales tax $ _____

TOTAL $ _____